THE EVERYDAY LIVES
OF SOVEREIGNTY

THE EVERYDAY LIVES OF SOVEREIGNTY

Political Imagination beyond the State

Edited by Rebecca Bryant and Madeleine Reeves

CORNELL UNIVERSITY PRESS   ITHACA AND LONDON

First published 2021 by Cornell University Press

Library of Congress Cataloging-in-Publication Data

Names: Bryant, Rebecca (Professor of anthropology), editor. |
    Reeves, Madeleine, editor.
Title: The everyday lives of sovereignty : political imagination beyond the state /
    edited by Rebecca Bryant and Madeleine Reeves.
Description: Ithaca [New York] : Cornell University Press, 2021. |
    Includes bibliographical references and index.
Identifiers: LCCN 2020039285 (print) | LCCN 2020039286 (ebook) |
    ISBN 9781501755736 (hardcover) | ISBN 9781501755743 (paperback) |
    ISBN 9781501755750 (ebook) | ISBN 9781501755767 (pdf)
Subjects: LCSH: Sovereignty.
Classification: LCC JC327 .E98 2021 (print) | LCC JC327 (ebook) |
    DDC 320.1/5—dc23
LC record available at https://lccn.loc.gov/2020039285
LC ebook record available at https://lccn.loc.gov/2020039286

Contents

Illustrations

Acknowledgments

A number of the papers published here were originally presented in October 2015 at the conference "The Everyday Lives of Sovereignty," held in Nicosia, Cyprus, and sponsored by the Norwegian Research Council. Support for the conference was part of the four-year project, "Imagined Sovereignties," directed by Åshild Kolås of the Peace Research Institute Oslo. We thank the NRC for its funding of the conference and this publication, as well as PRIO and its branch office in Cyprus for their support of the project and the long process of bringing this collection into print. Several colleagues commented on earlier versions of the Introduction and generously shared their reflections on the academic lives of sovereignty in the disciplines of IR and political geography. For their astute feedback at different stages of the project we are particularly grateful to Stef Jansen, Penny Harvey, John Heathershaw, Fiona McConnell, Stefanie Ortmann, Ed Schatz, and Chika Watanabe. We are grateful to Roger Haydon at Cornell University Press for his enthusiasm for the project, and to Karen Laun and Jack Rummel for their careful edits of the manuscript.

THE EVERYDAY LIVES
OF SOVEREIGNTY

TOWARD AN ANTHROPOLOGY OF SOVEREIGN AGENCY

Rebecca Bryant and Madeleine Reeves

"Take back control": few slogans capture quite so succinctly a historical moment, a public mood, and promise of political agency. In the febrile spring of 2016, these words became the rallying call for the "Vote Leave" campaign in the UK Brexit referendum. Across the Atlantic, Donald Trump summoned supporters in the US Republican primaries with calls to "Make America Great Again": an old slogan repurposed for an anxious age with promises of border walls and travel bans. Both slogans fused an imperative with an unspecific promise of future change, their rhetorical structure blurring addresser and addressee. Both appealed to a past unity to be recaptured and a waning sovereignty to be reclaimed. Both blurred individual and collective agency such that "taking back control" and "making great again" offered the hope simultaneously of state transformation and the transcendence of personal circumstance.

Political appeals in the name of reclaiming or reasserting state sovereignty are, of course, as old as the nation state itself. Imagined in terms of absolute supremacy within given territorial bounds, nondivisibility, and nontransferability, state sovereignty has always been more fiction than fact. Yet as globalization produces new flows—of goods, of people, of information, of political ideas—so claims to the fragility, the vulnerability, the embattlement of state sovereignty appear ever more widespread and more shrill: in disputes over fiscal policy; in "foreign agent" laws; in new initiatives of border walling; in concerns over foreign meddling in domestic elections or "faceless bureaucrats" overruling democratically elected politicians. Nor are such concerns confined to a political elite, even as they have

1

often served as the rallying cry for political entrepreneurs acting in the name of a disenfranchised "people." Calls to take back control or to bring back order, like claims to make a state great again, are efficacious precisely because they resonate with, and mobilize, hopes and desires that are at once collective and profoundly personal. Who of us does not want more control over our fate, especially in a context where inchoate foreign forces often seem to be undermining the very materials from which a meaningful, future-oriented life can itself be crafted?

This volume seeks to situate sovereign agency at the foreground of anthropological inquiry. We take sovereign agency to denote the variety of practices, strategies, and future-oriented claims that constitute institution and subject in ways that make the latter politically recognizable and capable of agentive action. Sovereign agency, in this sense, is often more aspiration than realization. It is an aspiration for forms of institutional recognition and political legibility that enable efficacious action, or what we call in this volume "state desire." The desire for sovereign agency, in turn, often emerges from a sense of loss—of political voice, of political legibility, of political order—and a yearning to regain it.

As we discuss in this introduction, the concept of sovereign agency has inspired a small body of important work in critical international relations and political theory but has received comparatively little attention in anthropology, despite its ethnographic potential. In this volume, we view the concept as a way to take collective desires and yearnings for agency seriously as objects of ethnographic attention. The concept allows us to step back from questions such as, "*what* is sovereignty?" or who, in a given political configuration, really *is* sovereign—questions of political form and political ontology that have generated rich strands of theoretical debate within anthropology, political science, and international relations—and instead to ask what is being desired when the desire is for a regaining of sovereignty. Who or what is the locus of political imagination in claims to "take back control?" What does sovereignty look like from the ground up?

These questions, we suggest, take our analysis in a rather different direction from much of the extant scholarly literature on sovereignty in anthropology and critical international relations. As we discuss in greater detail below, this literature has generated a rich corpus of debate about how we might properly specify sovereignty, in both analytic and empirical terms. In particular, it has sought to decouple the assumed links between sovereignty, state power, and territory by examining sovereignty as the outcome of situated—and gendered—practices of attribution of legitimate authority (Weber 2014, 2016), as an artifact of the international order (Bartelson 2014), or as a form of "organized hypocrisy" (Krasner 1999) that is constantly being breached by the de facto workings of the international order. This literature has also shed critical light on the relationship between sovereignty and exceptional or constitutive violence: the founding violence of the political order (cf. Benjamin 1996); the violence of the sovereign who stands beyond law; the violence of the camp that stands beyond the protection of the normative order as "nomos of the modern" (Agamben 1998).

Generative as these approaches have been to thinking about the reconfiguring of sovereignty in an age of biometric borders and drone warfare, the ethnographic research that informs this volume, conducted in a variety of settings of partial, compromised, contested, or "failed" state sovereignty, presents us with a rather different set of questions, which situate sovereignty less within a constellation of violence and exceptionalism than within concerns about political agency, political legibility, and political desire. In part, this is a product of the empirical settings and ethnographic methods that have informed our research. Viewed from the perspective of an unrecognized or de facto state such as the Turkish Republic of Northern Cyprus (TRNC), from an administration-in-exile such as Western Sahara, from a *mahalla* in a Tajik-majority exclave of Uzbekistan, or from a local organizing committee of the Catalan independence movement, sovereignty comes into view as an object of vernacular political commentary that is often impassioned, intense, and deliberate. Such settings have made us attentive to the contexts in which sovereignty is spoken of as insufficient or inadequate; where "verticals of power" were felt to be insufficiently transparent; where the experiential uncoupling of state from territory and sovereignty is typically spoken of less as opportunity than as a failure of political order or of political agency.

This has led us to ask a rather different cluster of questions about sovereignty and sovereign agency than that posed in either mainstream US international relations literature or in the so-called English School, both of which share realist assumptions about power and politics in the international system. In particular, this mainstream literature focuses on what makes a state sovereign or not, and how to understand, for instance, the relationship between domestic and international sovereignty. Our concerns, instead, arise from our ethnographic research, where we find the lives and hopes of people we study so often tied to aspirations to "be" sovereign or "have" sovereignty. What, though, does it mean to "have" sovereignty, experientially as well as juridically? How and why do claims to be (prospectively) sovereign have such affective force—the sort of thing that young men and women willingly fight and die for? Moreover, how and when do sovereign desires come to attach to the institutional form of the state, and when to some other source of transcendent political authority? We suggest that, just as very many people appear to delineate their culture best when it seems to be slipping from their grasp, so sovereignty may be best understood as a concept mobilizing as-yet-unfulfilled communal desires. What, we ask, do people recognize being described by the concept of sovereignty, and what do they desire when they believe it is being impeded, eroding, or slipping away?

Our approach to sovereign agency, then, derives from our commitment to ethnography as a tool of theoretical inquiry—and not merely a research "method." Ethnography allows us to defamiliarize categories of political analysis by attending to the variety of ways that particular terms circulate and gain force within social life. Like anthropology's critique of its own central term, *culture*, we move away from searching for a definition ("What is culture?"), which traps us in an ontological loop of identifying what is, or is not, culture or a culture. Rather than trying to ask what state sovereignty is, or to define when and whether a given state meets certain standards of sovereign recognition, we ask instead, "what question is sovereignty intended to answer?" When individuals want to "regain control," "restore sovereignty," or "reclaim the republic," what range of affects, emotions, and political commitments are they evoking and mobilizing?

These questions are both ethnographic, aimed at understanding what people believe sovereignty will do when they desire it, and analytic, querying our own ways of speaking about sovereignty. Critically, this approach allows us to hold as an empirical question how and when desires for sovereign agency become harnessed to the state form, and when not. When we think of examples such as the success of Brexit and the election of Donald Trump, or the rise of religious fundamentalisms, we see that desire for political recognition and legibility does not necessarily map onto a definition of sovereignty from the perspective of the sovereign. Our term *sovereign agency* is intended to capture the desire for a political formation that allows groups to gain a sense of control over their lives. In the chapters that follow we develop this by foregrounding ethnographically three kinds of question:

(1)   What it *means* to be sovereign, experientially and phenomenologically, as well as politically or juridically;

(2)   How and why claims to sovereignty (or nonsovereignty) have such affective force;

(3)   How, when, and why sovereign desires come to be attached to the state form, as opposed to other political forms, and how and why the state has become the primary vehicle for imagining and articulating political futures.

We seek, then, to counter the ontological with the empirical, and to ask not "What is sovereignty?" but "What are people desiring when they desire sovereignty?" As we will see, chapters in this book enable us to think ethnographically about the sort of agency, capacity, and recognizability that people desire when they desire to be sovereign. In the following sections, we lay out this approach in further detail in conversation with literatures in political anthropology and critical international relations.

The Impasse of Sovereignty as "Either/Or"

The slogan, "Taking back control," appears to hinge on nostalgic fantasies about a less interconnected world, one in which borders were impenetrable, sovereignty defined the nation-state, and power was firmly in the hands of that nation's people. It implies a violated sovereignty, playing on the common belief that "real" sovereignty should be clear and indivisible.

Although the world is littered with examples that contradict this Westphalian fantasy of a single state controlling people within a well-defined territory, these are commonly viewed as exceptions. Enclaves, exclaves, protectorates, and autonomous regions are all forms of government that do not fit the Westphalian mold. The UN protectorate of Bosnia-Herzegovina, the autonomous Kurdish government of northern Iraq, the British overseas territory of the Falkland Islands, and tribal sovereignty in the United States all contradict the Westphalian rule. Our list of such sovereign anomalies could be extended: dependencies, stateless nations, and microstates, to name only a few. Indeed, the more closely we examine a map of the world, the more we see that it is covered with exceptions, and there seem to be no states that are not touched by some form of sovereign exceptionality. Moreover, supranational political and legal institutions such as the European Union and the International Criminal Court today reach across borders and compel sovereign states to combat corruption or conform to human rights norms. Yet despite this evidence that authority is never singular and that sovereigns are never supreme, why do we continually revert to viewing this array of actually existing sovereign options as "exceptions" to the Westphalian "rule"?

Chapters in this book examine such sovereign "exceptions" or "anomalies": unrecognized states, governments in exile, contested sovereignties and borders, protectorates, and "failed" states. The international relations literature has tended to view such entities as indicating something about "the rule": for instance, that territory is never uniform or total (Agnew 1994, 2005), or that relations between states are hierarchical rather than equal (Lake 2003, 2008), making the principle of sovereign equality one that is always undermined in practice (Simpson 2004; also, Ashley 1998; James 1992). We argue here that even such critiques trap our discussions of sovereignty in an ontological mode, as though a better, fuller, more accurate definition will help us to know "real" sovereignty when we see it. Exceptions, then, are subjected to an "either/or" scrutiny: their sovereignty is something that exists or does not, while states or other political entities may exist with or without it.

This ontological mode has dominated critiques of sovereignty even at a time when exceptions to the Westphalian "rule" were proliferating. The violent breakup of the USSR and Yugoslavia and the unexpected claims of many groups to self-determination in the post–Cold War period led to a rethinking of sovereignty, as political theorists and international relations specialists have attempted to understand the states and statelike entities that subsequently emerged (e.g., Cornell 2002a, 2002b; Kolstø 2000; Meadwell 1999; Pegg 1998). The proliferation of breakaway states, and their inability to gain recognition for their claims to self-determination, has been used as an example by scholars to question Westphalian sovereignty as a normative framework (Krasner 1999; see also Paul 1999; Strange 1999). Some of the most important critiques have traced the historically contingent emergence of our contemporary notions of sovereignty (Bartelson 1995; Spruyt 1994). Others, building on this work, have observed that understandings of sovereignty have changed over time (Barkin and Cronin 1994; Crawford 2007; Jackson 2007) and cannot be reduced to identifiable standards that apply to all states (Fowler and Bunck 1996; Freeman 1999; James 1986; Østerud 1997; Thomson 1995).

Most important for the purposes of this volume is the literature that has questioned the reification of sovereignty. One critic of the tendency to see sovereignty as a "thing" has instead described it as "a discursive framing of space, time, and identity" (Walker 1996, 16). Indeed, an important literature in political theory has insisted that sovereignty is a "social construct," and that "the modern state system is not based on some timeless principle of sovereignty, but on the production of a normative conception that links authority, territory, population (society, nation), and recognition in a unique way and in a particular place (the state)" (Biersteker and Weber 1996, 3). Historians Douglas Howland and Luise White remark that "sovereignty is a set of practices that are historically contingent—a mix of both national and international processes, including self-determination, international law, and ideas about natural right" (2009, 1). Moreover, they note, "Sovereignty is contested because it is continually negotiated on the ground—over what a state does, to whom, and where" (1–2). In this view, then, the sovereign state arises through discursive claims and practices, both domestic and international, that simultaneously "perform" sovereignty and create it.

The chapters in this book all address examples that encourage us to ask what we may learn about sovereignty when the links that Biersteker and Weber draw between authority, territory, population, and recognition are severed or attenuated. As examples, Alice Wilson's chapter on a government in exile, Sara Friedman and Rebecca Bryant's chapters on unrecognized states, and Louisa

Lombard's contribution about a recognized state that does not control much of its territory all point to the ways in which the links of population, territory, and authority may be weakened or thinned. One assumption of all the chapters is that sovereign anomalies have much to tell us about the working of states as such, especially in terms of what Timothy Mitchell has called the "state-society boundary" (Mitchell 1991). As Mitchell noted two decades ago, "The state needs to be analyzed as . . . a structural effect. That is to say, it should be examined not as an actual structure, but as the powerful, metaphysical effect of practices that make such structures appear to exist" (94). Criticizing the common division between domestic and international, or between internal and external sovereignty, Kevin Dunn has argued that "we need to open up our thinking about the discursive aspect of sovereignty to examine how it constitutes 'stateness' . . . not just within an international community, but within domestic political communities, as well" (Dunn 2009, 224; see also Kapferer 2004; Kapferer and Bertelson 2009).

Such an emphasis on the construction and performance of statehood and sovereignty would seem to call for ethnographic attention to the practice of sovereignty in daily life. Yet interestingly, starting in the 1990s, anthropological attention turned primarily to the "postnational," or to the ways in which transnational processes, including diasporas and mobility of populations, may erode or alter notions of territoriality, governmentality, and citizenship (e.g., Appadurai 1996, 2006; Comaroff and Comaroff 2009). This resulted in a proliferation of ethnographic research on the ways in which neoliberal capital and new transnational mechanisms penetrate, impede, or wear away sovereignty. Studies multiplied that examined the European Union's local penetration (Bellier and Wilson 2000; Shore 2002; Triandafyllidou, Kouki, and Groupas 2013); outsourcing in Mexico (Salzinger 2003) and India (Van der Veer 2005); and the ways in which transnational courts may infringe on and even erode nation-state sovereignty in the name of human rights or international law (Douzinas 2000; Mills 1998; Naidoo 2006; Roht-Arriaza 2006). In these studies, the primary concern was with the state, where sovereignty was assumed to be one of its features.

Sovereignty became an explicit subject of anthropological investigation primarily following the 2001 attacks on the World Trade Center and subsequent US declaration of a "global war on terror," coinciding with the English-language publication of philosopher Giorgio Agamben's works (esp. 1998, 2005). In contrast to the early globalization literature, much of which appeared to posit an Eden of Westphalian sovereignty that had been compromised by globalization, Agamben locates sovereignty not in methods of territorialization and control but in the capacity to define the exception. Building on Carl Schmitt's work on the state of exception, Agamben argues that the sovereign is the one with the right to distinguish "political life" (*bios*) from "mere life" (*zoe*). The latter is the *homo sacer* of his first English-language work's title. Criticizing Foucault for ignoring the law as a critical link between techniques of governance and disciplines of self, Agamben argues that the sovereign's power rests in the capacity to define who is outside the law and therefore may be killed with impunity.

In anthropology, the use of Agamben's work seems largely to have concentrated on the violence of the state, or the state as site of an originary violence. Hansen and Stepputat (2005, 2006), for instance, assert that violence is the crucial realm in which sovereignty is produced. Agamben's observation that in late neoliberalism the state of exception has become the rule, making the paradigmatic figure of the contemporary state the camp, led to an exponential increase in ethnographies of migrant and refugee camps; stateless persons; partial sovereignties; and other sovereign anomalies.

No doubt, the "Agamben effect" in anthropology has allowed for a generative moment in anthropological thinking about sovereigns and sovereignty, particularly when looking at exceptions, or settings of inclusion and exclusion. When viewed from the perspective of the "exceptions" that define this book, however, we see that what constructivist IR and Agambenian anthropological approaches share remain a concern with sovereignty from the view of the sovereign and a wedding of sovereignty to the state. In the classic definition of Westphalian sovereignty, it is clear that a state either *is* sovereign or it *is not*. A state either inspires recognition by other states as the supreme authority over a people and territory, or it does not.

In an oft-cited work that rethinks the anthropology of sovereignty in an era of transnationalism, Jean and John Comaroff find the Agambenian paradigm narrow and remark:

> We take the term "sovereignty" to connote the more or less effective claim on the part of any agent, community, cadre, or collectivity to exercise autonomous, exclusive control over the lives, deaths, and conditions of existence of those who fall within a given purview, and to extend over them the jurisdiction of some kind of law. Sovereignty, *pace* Agamben, is as much a matter of investing a world with regulations as being able to suspend them, as much a matter of establishing the normative as determining states of exception. (Comaroff and Comaroff 2006, 35)

Although the Comaroffs here point to the limits of the Agambenian paradigm, their emphasis on law, and implicitly on the violence that will implement it, still comprehends sovereignty through the state and its legal foundation. It remains, then, a view of sovereignty from the perspective of the sovereign.

Similarly, while poststructuralist IR theory has pointed to the performative nature of claims to sovereignty, that literature has for the most part remained focused on the construction of the sovereign as ultimate agent. One prominent scholar in this movement, Cynthia Weber, notes, "What poststructuralist IR scholars say about sovereignty is that it refers to those practices that attempt to craft an agent in whose name a political community governs by investing that agent with legitimate political authority" (Weber 2016, 3). Although Weber indicates here and elsewhere that sovereignty must be created through practices, she refers to the crafting of an "agent" who is clearly the sovereign. It follows from this formulation of the constructivist approach to sovereignty in IR that: (1) sovereignty, for IR, remains ontologically singular—one either has it or not; (2) that the state is the exclusive agent of sovereignty; and (3) the question of desire *for* or enactment *of* sovereignty (or what we are calling sovereign agency) is analytically redundant. In the quote above, Weber refers to crafting an agent of governance, but she does not ask the prior question: *why?* She does not ask, in other words, what makes that agent agentive, or why we would want to invest any such agent with political authority.

Even in this constructivist view, then, we are returned to a formulation that weds sovereignty to the state. We find that both this and the Comaroffs' formulation above put the cart before the horse—or in this case, the agent before the agency that will drive it. In ethnographic terms, we find that such formulations do not tell us why people might desire sovereignty, or why people might express forms of collective political agency as sovereignty.

We use the idea of sovereign agency to describe what political theorist Patchen Markell (2003) has articulated as an imagined form of effective agency or control in which one will be able to achieve what one wants when one wants it. Markell and others have described this as a desire that is always frustrated. According to Markell, it is a fantasy of achieving full sovereignty that is destined to remain unrealized because it relies on a type of misrecognition: "Not the misrecognition of an identity, either one's own or someone else's, but the misrecognition of one's own fundamental situation or circumstances" (2003, 5; see also Epstein, Lindemann, and Sending 2018). That situation, he argues, is one in which the constraints of social life will always make sovereign agency an impossible ideal or fantasy.

While Markell is writing about struggles for recognition *within* the state, other literature has used Markell's work to argue that "the Hegelian dynamics of misrecognition" that he describes is also relevant to world politics, where it describes "an agency that is driven by ongoing, perpetually unsatisfied desire that international actors harbour to be more agentic than they are" (Epstein, Lindemann, and Sending 2018, 788). In these authors' formulation, agency is not a property of actors but rather "a desire that is always frustrated . . . by the fact that it is dependent on recognition from other actors" (789). Or as Charlotte

Epstein observes, "At the core of all human agency lies an impossible desire to be recognised as the sovereign actor that one never quite is, even when one is a state" (Epstein 2018, 807).

Exploring Sovereign Agency

What, then, does a focus on sovereign agency enable, empirically and analytically? The advantage of examining sovereign agency from the "margins" of Westphalian sovereignty, as the chapters in this volume do, is that it enables us to focus attention on what groups desire when they desire sovereignty, and moments when that desire does or does not turn its focus to the state. This perspective from the margins allows us four main insights into the workings of state desire.

First, as discussed above, it allows us to move beyond thinking of sovereignty as exception and therefore thinking of sovereignty a priori as tied to the state and singular. We contend that it is only by moving beyond sovereignty as exception, and a definitional view of sovereignty from the perspective of the sovereign, that we can introduce communal agency and desire into our analysis—in other words, that we can begin to ask what people want when they want sovereignty.

While as we note above, the Agambenian influence on anthropological thinking about sovereignty has been profound, more recent work has begun to examine the limitations of the Agambenian framework, especially its potential for possible politics. One strand of that critique particularly relevant for the papers here is Ernesto Laclau's trenchant observation that the Agambenian "ban," or the exclusion from the law that nevertheless includes within the law, is a surprisingly narrow concept that reduces all instances of being outside the law to *homo sacer*, or he who may be killed but not sacrificed. This reduction, he observes, excludes the possibility that certain persons may be outside the law of the city because they are *opposed* to that law. Such opposition, Laclau believes, is the beginning for any proper critique or resistance and cannot and should not be reduced simply to "bare life" (see also Płonowska Ziarek 2008). Laclau remarks that "the life of the bandit or the exile can be entirely political" because they are "capable of engaging in antagonistic social practices. They have, in that sense, their own law, and their conflict with the law of the city is a conflict between laws, not between law and bare life" (Laclau 2007, 19; see also Gregory 2006).

As Laclau notes, Agamben focuses on the most extreme cases of being "banned" from the city, especially the death camps of Auschwitz and the figure of the *Musselman*, the one who is reduced to death in life (see also Bernstein

2004; Chare 2006; Deranty 2008; LaCapra 2003). Similarly, in her own analysis of suicide bombers, Diana Enns remarks,

> It seems odd, disturbing even, that Agamben would choose such an abject figure [i.e., the Musselman], devoid of anything we might call political agency, as an exemplary figure. There appears to be no recourse to a politics of resistance here. . . . What's more, there is *no desire*, no longing for liberation, for a dignified, self-determined existence; a desire that saturates every revolutionary or insurrectionary narrative familiar to us (Enns 2004, emphasis in original).

Like Laclau, then, Enns argues that understanding power only through biopolitics results in an incapacity to comprehend "the soul of revolt manifested in its collective voice." This collective voice, she notes, is "the hope of claiming political freedoms, dignity, and self-determination for a people" (ibid.; see also Murray 2006; Luszczynska 2005; Nancy 1991).

This "collective voice" or "soul of revolt" may be understood as the essential precondition for sovereign agency. Enns views the locus of desire as "political freedoms, dignity, and self-determination," but does not specify in what form those would be realized. Recent work in anthropology, however, not only critiques the exclusive attention to sovereign violence but also shows us how and when sovereignty may attach to forms outside the state. Jessica Cattelino, for instance, demonstrates how members of the Seminole community in the United States may seek sovereignty through cultural and other institutions short of the state (Cattelino 2008). Audra Simpson (2014) describes how, in another Native American case, sovereignty may exist across the borders of the sovereign states of the United States and Canada, while in another case from the Americas, Yarimar Bonilla (2012) argues that one may desire political freedom without desiring nation-state sovereignty. Rebecca Bryant and Mete Hatay, building on Ernesto Laclau's observation that abandonment in the Agambenian sense may also be agentive, argue that in cases of rebels and those who seek political freedom, one may "enjoy one's exception" (2011). What this growing body of literature points to is a search for communal agency where the form of the state is not assumed.

As we will see in chapters here, although the locus of that desire has often attached to the state, that form should not be presupposed. Dace Dzenovska, for instance, argues for the importance of the diaspora in creating what she calls "existential sovereignty," a form of sovereign becoming realized in practices such as diaspora politics and language reform that "reiterate the constitutive and ontological link between the self, the cultural nation, and the Latvian state." In her analysis, statecraft and sovereignty are disarticulated, even as existential sovereignty reaffirms the importance of a territorial state. Joyce Dalsheim similarly examines the often ambivalent relationship between popular sovereignty, or the creation of a people who will be the vehicles of nation-state sovereignty, and the ways in which the state disciplines and maintains that "people." Examining the case of Israel, Dalsheim argues that although "the modern state of Israel was founded on Enlightenment ideals to allow Jews to be a free people in a country of their own," the demands of secular statehood "might have made those aspirations impossible for the very ethnos for whom the state was established."

Second, a focus on sovereign agency helps shift our empirical attention from what sovereignty is to what sovereignty does, and how and when and to what ends sovereignty is invoked. Often, the chapters in this volume find sovereignty invoked in perceptions of its absence. Rebecca Bryant's chapter on aerial sovereignty, for instance, uses a now-defunct national airline to show how such institutions may produce a "sovereignty effect" that is profoundly felt in its absence. Bryant argues that if the state may be seen as a vehicle for sovereign agency, the "sovereignty effect" occurs at the moment where the state appears as "ours." A national airline materializes the belongingness of the state in a dual fashion: both as a "homeland in the skies," and also as a way in which the "state" that is "ours" is brought into being. Similarly, in her chapter, Azra Hromadžić examines the "unsovereign state" in Bosnia-Herzegovina, where corruption is rife and disillusionment with the state and its democracy widespread. Hromadžić asks if, in this context, one might find manifestations of that collective voice in what appear to be their opposite: "students' extreme bragging about their cheating savvy, purchasing of exams and use of *veze* [connections]." She asks, then, if and how these may be "indicative and productive of their sovereign agency and, by extension, their (anti-)citizenship in the unsovereign state." In both these instances, a profound sense of loss at the collapse of certain state institutions points to sites and moments where sovereignty may be claimed, materialized, or experienced as absent.

Third, our concern with sovereign agency draws attention to affective dimensions of politics and questions of desire for legibility and recognizability that may or may not be attached to the state. This concern builds on a growing body of anthropological literature that draws us back to the state by examining how desires for "normal life" come to be linked to particular state forms. Stef Jansen (2015) vividly describes the ways that citizens of a post-Dayton Bosnia experience a state that seems less "statelike" than the Bosnia-Herzegovina of the Yugoslav era and hence live in the yearning but not quite expectation of someday having a "real" state. Jansen and others have linked this to a desire for "normal lives," where "normalization" would be a return to a state that "works." Jessica Greenberg, for instance, argues that when Serbians complain that they or their state are "'not normal,' . . . They are trying to make sense of the fact that they no longer feel capable of agentive action or moral interiority in a crisis-ridden Serbian state" (2011, 89). In Greenberg's formulation, desires for the state express a desire for what she calls "agentive action."

As Danilyn Rutherford (2012) notes, if sovereignty is performed, it is performed for an audience. It is an audience, moreover, that must recognize what is being performed as a performance of sovereignty in order for it to become so. "Like social action more generally," she remarks, "the assertion of sovereignty unfolds before the eyes of imagined others" (4). It is in the eyes of those imagined others that one becomes sovereign, but we contend that this recognition by others entails a prior recognizability. Judith Butler, in her important work on the capacity of words to wound, remarks that the act of naming is one that occurs only for those persons and things recognizable as nameable. "One 'exists,'" she remarks, "not only by virtue of being recognized, but, in a prior sense, by being *recognizable*" (Butler 1997, 5). To be recognizable—as a human, a community—is already to acquire existence and thereby agency.

In this volume, Dzenovska and Dalsheim both address the issue of recognizability through those moments of becoming "a people"—and in both those cases, a people that should be recognized as sovereign. Panos Achniotis's chapter demonstrates how the experience of solidarity in the moment of the 2017 Catalan referendum created a moment sensed as sovereign agency and hence a people who could be sovereign. In Madeleine Reeves's chapter, sovereignty becomes literally legible (or not), through mappings that evoke not only territorial integrity or the body of the nation, but also the contested histories of how such borders have been drawn. Her concern is with "how sovereignty appears and disappears from view from the perspective of the thinking, feeling, desiring, mobilizing subject—or the prospective future subject—of a politically sovereign space," and so with sovereignty as it intersects with everyday struggles.

Building on Rutherford's observations of sovereign recognizability, Sara Friedman examines the ways in which the Taiwanese state and civil society attempt to become recognizable to the international community through unilateral implementation of human rights norms. What Friedman calls "aspirational sovereignty" seeks to make Taiwanese recognizable subjects of "sovereign address," even as those efforts remain anxious supplements "to the necessarily incomplete nature of actually existing state rule." In contrast, in Alice Wilson's case, the focus is on institutions and their resources. Looking at the case of the Sahrawi government in exile, Wilson shows, through a careful examination of relations of that government with its exiled people, that "sovereignty can be understood as social relations between governing authorities and governed constituencies played out in relation to resources, not necessarily in territorial form."

Fourth, the concept of sovereign agency allows us to think between and across individual, collective, state, and transnational scales, and simultaneously to focus on how the state acts (and is sovereign, or not), and on how individuals act vis-à-vis claims for or on a prospective state. In this sense, we are interested not only in how the state interpellates, but also how it is *interpellated:* that is, how the state is called into being in the minutiae of daily life. As Torunn Wimpelmann's chapter shows, actors are often very aware of the scales of sovereignty. Using one infamous case of gender violence in Afghanistan, and more generally the interest of foreign governments and international agencies in stemming gender violence in the country, Wimpelmann shows how women's bodies have been interpellated into such scales of sovereignty and have, in turn, become instruments for interpellating the state. Wimpelmann gives an ethnographic reading of one family's public attempts to gain "justice" when a young woman was raped by a politician's son. Reading this at first as the family giving up their own sovereign agency over the young woman's body to the hands of the state, Wimpelmann's surprising conclusion shows us how struggles for control of women's bodies may be differently calibrated in a transnational context.

The interpellation of the state, however, is often expressed through a sense of lost agency, lost sovereignty, and particularly lost "identity," that is, some clear definition of groupness that expresses what makes "us" us, and what makes "ours" ours. It is this loss of state as identity that Bryant, for instance, observes materialized in the loss of a national airline. It is also this sense of loss or "abandonment" that Louisa Lombard's interlocutors in northeastern Central African Republic (CAR) articulated to describe a state whose "absence" they associated with "the decline, dispossession, and disorder that they see as attending to their purgatory position in the world." At the same time, Lombard is interested in the inconsistencies of such state desire, or the ways in which "the desire for stateness coexists with a value of liberty, or freedom from molestation in one's projects." Like Hromadžić and Wimpelmann, Lombard describes a culturally intimate "us" that simultaneously maligns the exceptional state and demonstrates its "we"-ness through ways of "getting by" or "getting around" hampered sovereignty.

Taken together, then, the chapters in this volume all present "exceptional" cases that point us toward ways of thinking about sovereignty ethnographically. These are all cases in which state desire is also entangled with some enjoyment of exceptionality—whether it is students cheating in Bosnia-Herzegovina, Turkish Cypriots getting free tickets on their national airline, poachers looking for passes in CAR, or tribal leaders wrangling in the new political landscape of Afghanistan. As Lombard remarks, these are cases where the state may be both wanted and unwanted, and where "inconsistency can be a constitutive aspect of politics." We believe that such inconsistencies, as well as the desires, hopes, and expectations brought by the state form, are all part of what it means to turn our ethnographic attention from the ontological to the empirical, from the question "What is sovereignty?" to the question of what people desire when they desire it.

References

Agamben, Giorgio. 1998. *Homo Sacer: Sovereign Power and Bare Life.* Translated by Daniel Heller-Roazen. Stanford: Stanford University Press.

Agamben, Giorgio. 2005. *State of Exception.* Translated by Kevin Attell. Chicago: University of Chicago Press.

Agnew, John. 1994. "The Territorial Trap: The Geographical Assumptions of International Relations Theory." *Review of International Political Economy* 1(1): 53–80.

Agnew, John. 2005. "Sovereignty Regimes: Territoriality and State Authority in Contemporary World Politics." *Annals of the Association of American Geographers,* 95(2): 437–461.

Appadurai, Arjun. 1996. *Modernity at Large: Cultural Dimensions of Globalization.* Minneapolis: University of Minnesota Press.

Appadurai, Arjun. 2006. *Fear of Small Numbers: An Essay on the Geography of Anger.* Durham, NC: Duke University Press.

Ashley, Richard K. 1988. "Untying the Sovereign State: A Double Reading of the Anarchy Problematique." *Millennium—Journal of International Studies* 17(2): 227–262.

Barkin, J. Samuel, and Bruce Cronin. 1994. "The State and the Nation: Changing Norms and the Rules of Sovereignty in International Relations." *International Organization* 48(1): 107–130.

Bartelson, Jens. 1995. *A Genealogy of Sovereignty.* Cambridge: Cambridge University Press.

Bartelson, Jens. 2014. *Sovereignty as Symbolic Form.* New York: Routledge.

Bellier, Irene, and Thomas M. Wilson, eds. 2000. *The Anthropology of the European Union: Building, Imagining, and Experiencing the New Europe.* Oxford: Berg.

Benjamin, Walter. 1996. "Critique of Violence." *Selected Writings.* Vol. 1. *1913–1926,* 236–52. Cambridge, MA: Belknap/Harvard.

Bernstein, Jay. 2004. "Bare Life, Bearing Witness: Auschwitz and the Pornography of Horror." *Parallax* 10(1): 2–16.

Biersteker, Thomas J., and Cynthia Weber, ed. 1996. *State Sovereignty as Social Construct.* Cambridge: Cambridge University Press.

Bonilla, Yarimar. 2012. *Non-Sovereign Futures: French Caribbean Politics in the Wake of Disenchantment.* Chicago: University of Chicago Press.

Bryant, Rebecca, and Mete Hatay. 2011. "Guns and Guitars: Simulating Sovereignty in a State of Siege." *American Ethnologist* 38(4): 631–649.

Butler, Judith. 1997. *Excitable Speech: A Politics of the Performative.* New York: Routledge.

Cattelino, Jessica R. 2008. *High Stakes: Florida Seminole Gaming and Sovereignty.* Durham, NC: Duke University Press.

Chaflin, Brenda. 2014. "Public Things, Excremental Politics, and the Infrastructure of Bare Life in Ghana's City of Tema." *American Ethnologist* 41(1): 92–109.

Chare, Nicholas. 2006. "The Gap in Context: Giorgio Agamben's 'Remnants of Auschwitz.'" *Cultural Critique* 64: 40–68.

Comaroff, Jean, and John L. Comaroff. 2006. "Law and Disorder in the Postcolony: An Introduction." In *Law and Disorder in the Postcolony*, edited by Jean and John Comaroff, 1–56. Chicago: University of Chicago Press.

Comaroff, Jean, and John L. Comaroff. 2009. *Ethnicity, Inc.* Chicago: University of Chicago Press.

Cornell, Svante E. 2002a. *Autonomy and Conflict: Extraterritoriality and Separatism in the South Caucasus—Cases in Georgia*. Uppsala, Sweden: Uppsala University Department of Peace and Conflict Research.

Cornell, Svante E. 2002b. "Autonomy as a Source of Conflict: Caucasian Conflicts in Theoretical Perspective." *World Politics* 54(2): 245–276.

Crawford, James R. 2007. *The Creation of States in International Law*. 2nd ed. New York: Oxford University Press.

Deranty, Jean-Philippe. 2008. "Witnessing the Inhuman: Agamben or Merleau-Ponty." *South Atlantic Quarterly* 107(1): 165–186.

Douzinas, Costas. 2000. *The End of Human Rights*. Portland, OR: Hart Publishing.

Dunn, Kevin C. 2009. "Environmental Security, Spatial Preservation, and State Sovereignty in Central Africa." In *The State of Sovereignty: Territories, Laws, Populations*, edited by Douglas Howland and Louise White, 222–242. Bloomington: Indiana University Press.

Enns, Diana. 2004. "Bare Life and the Occupied Body." *Theory and Event* 7(3). http://muse.jhu.edu/login?uri=/journals/theory and event/v007/7.3enns.html. Accessed November 11, 2010.

Epstein, Charlotte. 2018. "The Productive Force of the Negative and the Desire for Recognition: Lessons from Hegel and Lacan." *Review of International Studies* 44(5): 805–828.

Epstein, Charlotte, Thomas Lindemann, and Ole Jacob Sending. 2018. "Frustrated Sovereigns: The Agency that Makes the World Go Around." *Review of International Studies* 44(5): 787–804.

Fowler, Michael Ross, and Julie Maria Bunck. 1996. "What Constitutes the Sovereign State?" *Review of International Studies* 22(4): 381–404.

Freeman, Michael. 1999. "The Right to Self-Determination in International Politics: Six Theories in Search of a Policy." *Review of International Studies* 25(3): 355–370.

Friedman, Sara L. 2015. *Exceptional States: Chinese Immigrants and Taiwanese Sovereignty*. Berkeley: University of California Press.

Greenberg, Jessica. 2011. "On the Road to Normal: Negotiating Agency and State Sovereignty in Postsocialist Serbia." *American Anthropologist* 113(1): 88–100.

Gregory, Derek. 2006. "The Black Flag: Guantanamo Bay and the Space of Exception." *Geografiska Annaler* 88 B(4): 405–427.

Hansen, Thomas Blom, and Finn Stepputat, eds. 2005. *Sovereign Bodies. Citizens, Migrants and States in the Postcolonial World*. Princeton, NJ: Princeton University Press.

Hansen, Thomas Blom, and Finn Stepputat. 2006. "Sovereignty Revisited." *Annual Review of Anthropology* 35: 295–315.

Howland, Douglas, and Luise White. 2009. "Introduction: Sovereignty and the Study of States." In *The State of Sovereignty: Territories, Laws, Populations*, edited by D. Howland and L. White, 1–19. Bloomington: Indiana University Press.

Jackson, Robert. 1990. *Quasi-States: Sovereignty, International Relations, and the Third World*. Cambridge: Cambridge University Press.

Jackson, Robert. 2007. *Sovereignty: Evolution of an Idea*. Cambridge: Polity Press.

James, Alan. 1986. *Sovereign Statehood: The Basis of International Society*. Boston: Unwin Hyman.

James, Alan. 1992. "The Equality of States: Contemporary Manifestations of an Ancient Doctrine." *Review of International Studies* 18(4): 377–391.

Jansen, Stef. 2015. *Yearnings in the Meantime: "Normal Lives" and the State in a Sarajevo Apartment Complex.* Oxford: Berghahn Books.

Kapferer, Bruce, ed. 2004. *State, Sovereignty, War: Civil Violence in Emerging Global Realities.* Oxford: Berghahn Books.

Kapferer, Bruce, and Bjorn Enge Bertelson, eds. 2009. *Crisis of the State: War and Social Upheaval.* Oxford: Berghahn Books.

Kolstø, Pål. 2000. *Political Construction Sites: Nation-Building in Russia and the Post-Soviet States.* Boulder, CO: Westview Press.

Kolstø, Pål. 2006. "The Sustainability and Future of Unrecognized Quasi-States." *Journal of Peace Research* 43(6): 723–740.

Kolstø, Pål, and Helge Blakkisrud. 2008. "Living with Non-Recognition: State- and Nation-building in South Caucasian Quasi-States." *Europe-Asia Studies* 60(3): 483–509.

Krasner, Stephen D. 1999. *Sovereignty: Organized Hypocrisy.* Princeton, NJ: Princeton University Press.

LaCapra, Dominick. 2003. "Approaching Limit Events: Siting Agamben." In *Witnessing the Disaster,* edited by Michael Bernard-Donals and Richard Glejzer, 262–304. Madison: University of Wisconsin Press.

Laclau, Ernesto. 2007. "Bare Life or Social Indeterminacy?" In *Giorgio Agamben: Sovereignty and Life,* edited by Matthew Calarco and Steven DeCaroli, 11–22. Stanford: Stanford University Press.

Lake, David. 2003. "The New Sovereignty in International Relations." *International Studies Review* 5(3): 303–323.

Lake, David. 2008. "The New American Empire?" *International Studies Perspectives* 9(3): 281–289.

Luszczynska, Ana. 2005. "The Opposite of the Concentration Camp: Nancy's Vision of Community." *CR: The New Centennial Review* 5(3): 167–205.

Markell, Patchen. 2003. *Bound by Recognition.* Princeton, NJ: Princeton University Press.

Meadwell, Hudson. 1999. "Secession, States and International Society." *Review of International Studies* 25(3): 371–387.

Mills, Kurt. 1998. *Human Rights in the Emerging Global Order: A New Sovereignty?* New York: Palgrave Macmillan.

Mitchell, Timothy. 1991. "The Limits of the State: Beyond Statist Approaches and Their Critics." *American Political Science Review* 85(1): 77–96.

Murray, Stuart J. 2006. "Thanatopolitics: On the Use of Death for Mobilizing Political Life." *Polygraph* 18: 191–215.

Naidoo, Kumi. 2006. "Claiming Global Power: Transnational Civil Society and Global Governance." In *Transnational Civil Society: An Introduction,* edited by S. Batliwala and D. L. Brown, 51–64. Bloomfield, CT: Kumarian Press.

Nancy, Jean-Luc. 1991. *The Inoperative Community,* edited by Peter Connor and translated by Peter Connor, Lisa Garbus, Michael Holland, and Simona Sawhney. Minneapolis: University of Minnesota Press.

Østerud, Øyvind. 1997. "The Narrow Gate: Entry to the Club of Sovereign States." *Review of International Studies* 23: 167–184.

Paul, Darel. 1999. "Sovereignty, Survival, and the Westphalian Blind Alley in International Relations." *Review of International Studies* 25(2): 217–231.

Pegg, Scott. 1998. *International Society and the De Facto State.* Aldershot: Ashgate.

Płonowska Ziarek, Ewa. 2008. "Bare Life on Strike: Notes on the Politics of Race and Gender." *South Atlantic Quarterly* 107(1): 81–105.

Roht-Arriaza, Naomi. 2006. *The Pinochet Effect: Transnational Justice in the Age of Human Rights*. Philadelphia: University of Pennsylvania Press.

Rutherford, Danilyn. 2012. *Laughing at Leviathan: Sovereignty and Audience in West Papua*. Chicago: Chicago University Press.

Salzinger, Leslie. 2003. *Genders in Production: Making Workers in Mexico's Global Factories*. Berkeley: University of California Press.

Shore, Chris. 2002. *Building Europe: The Cultural Politics of European Integration*. New York: Routledge.

Simpson, Audra. 2014. *Mohawk Interruptus: Political Life across the Borders of Settler States*. Durham, NC: Duke University Press.

Simpson, Gerry. 2004. *Great Powers and Outlaw States: Unequal Sovereigns in the International Legal Order*. Cambridge: Cambridge University Press.

Spruyt, Hendrik. 1994. *The Sovereign State and Its Competitors*. Princeton, NJ: Princeton University Press.

Strange, Susan. 1999. "The Westfailure System." *Review of International Studies* 25(3): 345–354.

Thomson, Janice E. 1995. "State Sovereignty in International Relations: Bridging the Gap Between Theory and Empirical Research." *International Studies Quarterly* 39: 213–33.

Triandafyllidou, Anna, Hara Kouki, and Ruby Gropas. 2013. "Toward an Anthropology of the European Union: Insights from Greece." In *Rethinking the Public Sphere through Transnationalizing Processes: Europe and Beyond*, edited by Armando Salvatore, Oliver Schmidtke, and Hans-Jörg Trenz, 168–186. London: Palgrave MacMillan.

Van der Veer, Peter. 2005. "Virtual India: Indian IT Labor and the Nation State." In *Sovereign Bodies: Citizens, Migrants, and States in the Postcolonial World*, edited by Thomas Blom Hansen and Finn Stepputat, 276–290. Durham, NC: Duke University Press.

Walker, R. B. J. 1996. "Space/Time/Sovereignty." In *Perspectives on Third-World Sovereignty: The Postmodern Paradox*, edited by Mark E. Denham and Mark Owen Lombardi, 13–27. New York: St Martin's Press.

Weber, Cynthia. 2014. "Queer International Relations: From Queer to Queer IR." *International Studies Review* 16: 596–622.

Weber, Cynthia. 2016. *Queer International Relations: Sovereignty, Sexuality, and the Will to Knowledge*. Oxford: Oxford University Press.

SOVEREIGNTY IN THE SKIES

An Anthropology of Everyday Aeropolitics

Rebecca Bryant

In October 2017, the European Aviation Safety Agency announced an increased risk of flight collision over the Mediterranean island of Cyprus (*Cyprus Mail* 2017a). This island of only one million inhabitants has three major international airports serving Europe and the Middle East. On any given day, the main Larnaca Airport serves around fifteen thousand passengers, numbers obviously fluctuating depending on the season. In high seasons, many of those flights come from Russia, even though the flight path from Russian cities is hardly a direct one, taking passengers on a detour around Turkey. Because the Republic of Turkey does not recognize the government of the Republic of Cyprus (RoC), its ports are closed to vessels carrying the RoC flag, and its airspace and waters are also off limit to them. Instead, Turkey recognizes the self-proclaimed Turkish Republic of Northern Cyprus (TRNC), the breakaway state in the island's north that has been condemned by the United Nations and whose own airport, Ercan, is considered by the RoC to be an illegal port of entry to the island.

Only two days after a local newspaper reported this story, and international media picked it up, the same newspaper related that in the previous year, Cyprus had experienced the third largest increase in air traffic in Europe (*Cyprus Mail* 2017b). Of course, the airports being reported on were Larnaca and Paphos, in the internationally recognized southern part of the island. And here, indeed, was the traffic problem, because despite its international isolation, Ercan Airport had experienced a significant increase in traffic over the past decade and was now landing almost twenty thousand planes per year on its one landing strip.[1]

The head of the Mediterranean Flight Safety Foundation—which, despite its name, is a Greek Cypriot institution—gave the newspaper three reasons for the increased risk:

> The main one is that Ankara doesn't recognise the Cyprus government. The second is that the illegal air control at Ercan airport [in the north] is confusing pilots by giving them instructions which are conflicting with the one of the official air traffic control. Also, the Turkish air force gives no notification of its flights putting people in danger. (ibid.)

According to the head of this south Cyprus-based safety foundation, the main problem is Ercan airport's illegality, which puts it outside the range of the "official" air traffic control.

This chapter uses aerial sovereignty as a lens onto the "black holes" in international politics created by unrecognized states. Those black holes are ones of information, but also ones of geopolitics and, as we will see, aeropolitics (Abeyratne 2009). My interest in this chapter is not only in viewing the skies as another space to contest sovereignty, though that is certainly important here. It may be the case that de facto or unrecognized states give us a new lens to think about the governance of the air, and more particularly about what the study of flight, aircraft, and disputes over the air above a territory may tell us about everyday geopolitics.

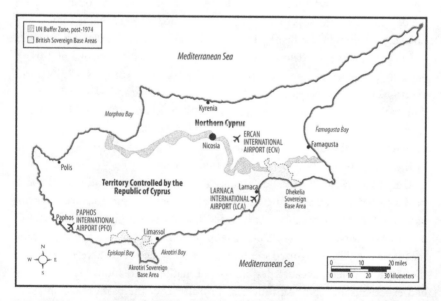

FIGURE 1. Map showing Cyprus's three airports.

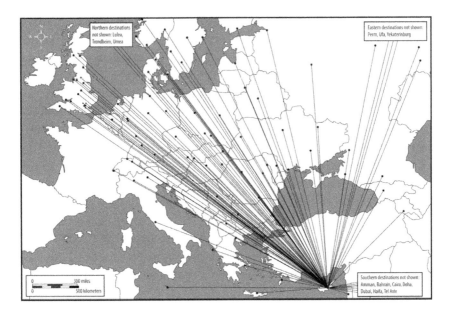

Northern destinations
not shown: Luloa,
Trondheim, Umea

Eastern destinations not shown:
Perm, Ufa, Yekaterinburg

0   300 miles
0   500 kilometers

Southern destinations not shown:
Amman, Bahrain, Cairo, Doha,
Dubai, Haifa, Tel Aviv

FIGURE 2. Map showing some (though not all) of the destinations from
Larnaca Airport.

However, I believe that the anthropological potential of the aeropolitical extends
beyond the aerial space above a territory.

We know, for instance, that national airlines, or "flag carriers," represent forms
of banal nationalism, reifying the nation through their branding and becoming containers of the homeland in the skies (Raguraman 1997). Flight attendant
uniforms, food service, language used, and in-flight magazines are all intended
to reify national airlines as aerial ambassadors of the nation-state (Markessinis
n.d.; Yano 2011). One commentator growing up in Ghana remarked, on the
passing of his own national airline, "To me, a national airline was just another
way a country defined itself, along with its flag, national anthem, and currency.
Ghana Airways . . . was a perfect example, with the red, gold and green colors of
its national flag painted on every plane. They looked proud and elegant, a perfect symbol of statehood" (Lawrence 2012). Moreover, the collapse of more than
two hundred national carriers over the past decades has been resisted by states
(CAPA 2011), while even British Airway's removal of the Union Jack from its
tailfins in the late 1990s produced protests that forced it to put it back (Dinnie
2008, 89). What, then, can the emotional attachment to national airlines, and the
senses of helplessness in the face of globalization produced by their collapse, tell
us about sovereignty and sovereign agency?

In recent years, anthropologists have focused increasingly on the nonspaces (Auge 1995) that so many of us frequent on a regular basis: the liminal spaces of airports (Hylland Eriksen and Doving 1992), with their attendant border and customs regimes (Chalfin 2006, 2008), security controls (Maguire 2014; Moreland 2013), and biometric surveillance (Amoore 2006; Maguire 2009). Interestingly, like studies of land border crossings (e.g., Donnan and Wilson 2010), railways (Bear 2007), and roads (Dalakoglou 2017; Harvey 2005; Harvey and Knox 2012), the social science focus has been primarily on the sedentary space rather than on the vehicle that traverses or moves from or through it (e.g., Hiller 2010; Lloyd 2003).[2] An exception is the ethnographic interest in cars that has explored emotional attachment, affect, and senses of freedom produced by them (e.g., Lutz and Fernandez 2010; Miller 2001). Trains, ships, and airplanes, however, become the space in which other activities are observed—smuggling (e.g., Nordstrom 2007), human trafficking (e.g., Andersson 2014), and tourism (e.g., Dowling and Weeden 2017), for instance. They most often become spaces for controlling mobility (e.g., Peteet 2017; Pickering and Weber 2006) and its dangers (e.g., Budd, Bell, and Brown 2009).

This chapter instead views these moving containers as complexes of meaning that not only link places but also link state, sovereignty, and peoples. National airlines are an infrastructure of mobility, and one of the first in which new states invest. This chapter further develops a recent literature on infrastructures that points to their totemic role in building collectivities. Infrastructures are, after all, "collectively held" (Rodgers and O'Neill 2012, 406) and "hence can become the metonymic sites for wider social discussions of participation and responsibility— that is, can become meaningful for the very definition of a collective" (Coleman 2014, 460). Larkin, for instance, examines how the introduction of media— cinema, radio, television—produced social transformation in colonial and postcolonial Africa, describing these forms of infrastructure as a "totality of both technical and cultural systems that create institutionalized structures whereby goods of all sorts circulate, connecting and binding people into collectivities" (Larkin 2008, 6). Coleman, studying electricity networks in India and Scotland, moves away in his analysis from the strictly materialistic focus of Actor Network Theory to look instead at infrastructures' "very collective crafting in the imagination as emblematic of the state and the political community itself" (2014, 461). Recuperating the political potential of Durkheim's totemism, an idea long out of fashion in anthropology, Coleman shows how the emblem or totem is "the material site where real, but invisible, collective forces gather and are made accessible as representations" (465).

This discussion seems particularly pertinent to a national airline, which I argue here is one of the key sites for totemically representing not simply the collectivity, but the collectivity's manifestation in stateness. Painter (2006), for instance, argues that the "state effect" (Mitchell 1991) manifests itself in the mundane: through regulating our parking, through determining school and shop hours, and so on. And certainly, as I discuss below, national airlines historically have represented the power and technological prowess of the state. But this is not all. Airplanes are also containers that become small pieces of the homeland outside the homeland itself. It is this combination of containment and connectivity, I will argue, that is the key to understanding airplanes' totemic power.

I outline below why national airlines are an important site for materializing the state as something that *belongs* to us, and hence a potential source of sovereign agency. I call that sense of belongingness of the state the "sovereignty effect," a term I use to refer to the ways in which an abstract externality—"the state"—may come to appear as a vehicle for our agency. It is through this totemic power of national airlines, combining both intimacy and potency, both containment and connectivity, that the state—an externality—appears as *ours*.

This chapter uses the rise and fall of one national airline, and the privatization of both the airline and its unrecognized home airport, as a vehicle for exploring both the totemic power of infrastructures and the potential of aeropolitics for anthropology. I argue here that like the recent appropriation of geopolitics for the study of political affect and agency (Jansen 2009, Thrift 2000), aeropolitics offers a lens onto the everyday practices that produce stateness, the effect of sovereignty, and a sense of sovereign agency. Investigating the national airline of an unrecognized state also, I show, gives us a lens onto the role played by national airlines in producing belief in the state—or calling it into question in an era of privatization and globalization. As we will see, the de facto state of the skies is one that tells us much about how we imagine and construct sovereignty today.

Everyday Aeropolitics

On one of the main thoroughfares of north Nicosia, a bland modern building with a fading sign stands empty. The building at one time housed Turkish Cypriots' primary representative of their state in the outside world, the Cyprus Turkish Airlines, or CTA (in Turkish, Kıbrıs Türk Hava Yolları, or KTHY). I still recall the packaged sandwiches with the faint taste of plastic wrapper that they would serve on the short flight to Istanbul, where they would take on other passengers before flying to destinations in Europe, especially the United Kingdom. Like all flights entering or leaving north Cyprus, planes would touch down at various points in Turkey so that aviation authorities could maintain the pretense of allowing no direct flights to the island's north. The touchdown usually occurred in Istanbul, though Izmir and Antalya were also spots for loading and unloading other passengers.

I first arrived in the island in the early 1990s, a period of isolation for the unrecognized TRNC, which experienced trade and other embargoes. At the time, apart from one struggling low-cost carrier, Istanbul Air, CTA was the only airline flying to Ercan. For this reason, the 1990s were the height of CTA's activity, also because at the time the border dividing the island was still closed, making the only routes for exit from the north either ferries to southern Turkey or Ercan Airport. In 2003, as a result of a Europeanization process in the island's south, and subsequent protests in the north, Turkish Cypriot leaders would decide to open the checkpoints. This opening suddenly produced a new social, economic, and political environment in the island, including the opportunity for Turkish Cypriots to fly on direct flights from the Larnaca and Paphos airports.[3]

In the 1990s, however, when CTA more or less monopolized the market, north Cyprus remained a rather difficult destination to get to, one that for tourists was off the beaten track. It was a period when tourist brochures still sold the island's north as an "untouched paradise," and the north's isolation was palpable in the lack of consumer goods, curtailment of trade, and a sui generis administration where kinship and friendship networks held sway (e.g., Bryant and Hatay 2020; Sonan 2014). The latter also gave to the enclosed space of the island's north a sense of intimacy.

That intimacy, moreover, was intensely experienced on Turkish Cypriots' one airline. Flying from those European destinations to the island, I was always struck by the way the atmosphere changed when we took off from Turkey and were on our way to Cyprus. People who had sat patiently for the four-hour journey from London would suddenly be in the aisles, chatting loudly with other passengers. They would joke with the stewardesses, all of whom were Turkish Cypriot. And some people with influence would smoke in the back of the plane, even after smoking had been banned from flights. In the last stretch of the journey, the flight took on the atmosphere of a village bus taking you home.

Indeed, there were many indications that Turkish Cypriots took great pride in seeing this as "their" airline, both an extension of their state as public property, and something that, being public property, was also "their own." Indeed, it being "our own" was the response that we received more than any other when a coauthor and I put the question of what they missed most about the by-then defunct airline in a 2016 Facebook survey, discussed more below. Quite a few respondents simply said, "It being ours," while others expressed it as, "It being an institution that belonged to us," or "Despite all of its negative aspects, it still being ours."

FIGURE 3. Cyprus Turkish Airlines plane taking off from Ercan Airport. Courtesy of Flickr user Pertti Sipilä.

CTA had been born at the same time as Turkish Cypriots' first attempt at statehood, the Turkish Federated State of Cyprus (TFSC). The Turkish Cypriot Legislative Assembly declared the TFSC in February 1975, only a few months after Turkish troops stormed the island in response to a Greek-sponsored coup d'état intended to unite the island with Greece. In the same month as the TFSC's declaration, Ercan Airport opened to civilian traffic, and for thirty-five years the main airline that would fly commercial flights to the north would be CTA, a joint venture of Turkish Airlines—Turkey's national carrier—and the Turkish Cypriot state. Although 50 percent of the airline was owned by Turkish Air, Turkish Cypriots tended to call CTA their "national airline."

The development of national airlines, or flag carriers, is an intrinsic part of the history of aerial sovereignty, which itself reveals interesting parallels with the development of territorial sovereignty over the twentieth century. Prior to World War I, Britain took the lead in demanding controls be put on free movement in the air, primarily because of the "technogeopolitical threat" that its military leaders saw coming from Germany (Butler 2001, 641). At the Paris International Conference of Air Navigation in May 1910, the British position was that "freedom of the air conflicts not at some points only, but at every point with the interest of the State below, because there can be no user of the air which does not to some extent affect the security or the administration of that State" (Richard 1912, 27, quoted in Butler 2001, 640). The 1911 Aerial Navigation Acts introduced aerial sovereignty, denying legal access into other states' airspace without permission and thereby curtailing not only the military but also the economic potential of flight. When Germany nevertheless effectively employed its aerial arsenal in the war, the 1919 Treaty of Versailles sought to prevent further German development of aerial capabilities (655–56).

After the war and into the 1930s, Britain, Belgium, France, and the Netherlands established civil aviation both for economic development and to connect their empires (Raguraman 1997, 240). The national airlines that emerged in this period—Imperial Airways of Britain, KLM, SABENA, and Air France—in a short time developed routes to provincial imperial capitals, thereby serving as a prime symbol of the colonial state's vertical encompassment (Ferguson and Gupta 2002) and technological prowess. It was in the post–World War II period, however, that the principle of air sovereignty was developed in international law. The Convention on Civil Aviation of December 7, 1944 (the Chicago Convention), recognizes, in article 1, "the 'complete and exclusive sovereignty' of states over the airspace above their territory (i.e., both land areas and adjacent territorial waters)" (Talmon n.d.).[4] Moreover, the development of civil aviation has been supported by state military investment (Todd and Simpson 1985).

In the postcolonial period, airlines were used to penetrate hinterlands for purposes of regional development (Raguraman 1997; Todd and Simpson 1985), thereby demonstrating a "state effect" through encompassment and the ability of state officials to "swoop down" (Ferguson and Gupta 2002, 987). They also became a way of demonstrating one's participation in the international community of states—types of ambassadors in the air. Like ambassadors, they could penetrate directly into the capitals of other countries. This was unlike maritime vessels, which primarily dropped anchor at ports on the nation's borders. Like ambassadors, their ability to so penetrate was guaranteed in treaties that also recognized the sovereignty of one's own airspace, while in practice granting sovereign immunity to aircraft of the foreign state (UN Convention 2004). Flag carriers were, as the name suggests, emblazoned with symbols of the nation, while the languages spoken on board, the food served, and flight attendant uniforms all gave a sense of nation-state unity wrapped up in pride in command of modern technology. This pride appeared to exist even in cases like the RoC, where the so-called national airline remained for several decades a subsidiary of the former colonizer's flag carrier.

Indeed, it was through the combination of separateness and connectivity that flag carriers appear to have become mobile containers of the homeland. As Madeleine Reeves notes regarding a two-room airport in a provincial Kyrgyz town, even such a structure that average citizens might never use "materialized connection, mobility, and incorporation into a forward-moving world." Or as one of her informants commented, "From here you can connect to anywhere. You could be in New York in a day" (Reeves 2014, 28). Moreover, this sense of connectivity brought by air travel is not incidental to, but rather central to, the ways in which airlines become totemic representatives of a collectivity. In their influential discussion of the social construction of state sovereignty, Thomas Biersteker and Cynthia Weber had noted, "Sovereignty . . . is an inherently *social* concept. States' claims to sovereignty construct a social environment in which they can interact as an international society of states, while at the same time the mutual recognition of claims to sovereignty is an important element in the construction of states themselves" (Biersteker and Weber 1996, 1–2; see also Weber 1995). State sovereignty is, therefore, not only about the state itself, but also, perhaps primarily, about the system of mutual recognition that supports it.[5] As Sara Friedman remarks in her chapter of this book, "Sovereign recognition becomes conditional on state actors' ability to project governing effects beyond their own borders, to stretch the reach of the state."

Unrecognized states demonstrate the importance of this social and interactive dimension of sovereignty through existence on its margins. We already know much about the desire for separateness demonstrated by, for example, the recent proliferation of walls and walling intended to draw firm boundaries around one's state. Wendy Brown, for instance, argues that the recent desire for walls is motivated by a longing for containment in an increasingly boundaryless world, as well as the "fantasy of impermeability—perhaps even impenetrability" that complements it (Brown 2010, 119). In Brown's description, penetration is the state's (masculine) undoing.

Everyday aeropolitics in unrecognized states, however, demonstrates rather the opposite of Brown's fantasies of containment. Indeed, unrecognized states are already highly contained through various isolating mechanisms, including embargoes and blockades. What such citizens appear to fantasize about is not containment but rather interpenetration—the type of connectivity that both materializes sovereignty and demonstrates statehood through technological prowess. As suggested earlier, despite Brown's assertion of penetration as the state's undoing, the phenomenon of the national airline represents a type of controlled penetration, where a technologically advanced container claiming to represent another homeland/state enters one's airspace to land in the heart of one's capital. To the extent that this is ambassadorial, the result of agreements and treaties, that movement is a confirmation of one's sovereignty—something also confirmed when the violation of airspace is declared an act of war.

This is not to say that containment is not relevant. Indeed, the fact that airplanes *are* containers that are both technologically advanced *and* capable of symbolically transporting the homeland elsewhere appears to make them particularly relevant for materializing sovereignty. In a recent collection of papers discussing the general lack of scholarly attention to containers, archaeologist John Robb observes, "Contents and container are interdependent. Even the simple act of being contained often defines the contents, as when rainwater collects in a cistern and becomes a usable resource" (Robb 2018, 33).[6] He observes that containers transform their contents, giving them different capacities than they would otherwise have. Among the capacities he enumerates are containers' differentiating function; their capacity to transcend time through storage; their mobility, which allows them to transcend space; and their function as categorizers.

In particular, national airlines or flag carriers appear synecdochally to contain the homeland and its people (the passengers) within a container that represents the elements of verticality and encompassment that Ferguson and Gupta (2002) argue are primary ways in which the state effect is manifest. Flying requires putting trust in the captain and crew, who in turn exhibit both hospitality and authority: the friendly, welcoming face of the state. The plane comes synecdochally to stand for the state itself, both giving the abstract concrete form, and appearing to represent qualities of stateness. It is, however, through the combined elements of containment and connectivity that we may particularly see how airplanes materialize sovereignty.

I use the word *materialize* here in two senses. The first of these is the obvious sense in which the airplane gives concise material form to an abstraction: airplanes are able to link people, territory, and abstract stateness in a material sense of wholeness and integrity. They become, in other words, mobile containers of the homeland. The second sense in which I use "materialize," however, refers to its meaning in spiritualism, as a way of causing ghosts to appear in human form. In this sense, we may more directly link it to the previous discussion of totemism, where totems come to represent particular qualities of—or the "spirit" of—a group. We know, for instance, that airplanes give form to the state's aspirational elements—technological advance, modernity, and connectivity, to name a few. As a result, the airplane as homeland not only contains a particular people, as we imagine territory doing, but actually comes to represent that group's qualities through a peculiar form of materialization in which the airplane takes a form that is in some guises anthropomorphic.

Like the homeland, ships—both nautical and aerial—are usually cast as female. Until recent years, male airplane captains and their female crew embodied fantasies of modern male prowess and female sexual availability. Airplanes of national carriers are usually given place names—in the case of CTA, the names of towns and regions in north Cyprus, such as Girne, Lefke, and Karpaz—that again evoke the warmth and familiarity of home. And airplanes of flag carriers become the site both of connectivity through penetration, and through reception—taking onboard foreign passengers who experience culturally coded hospitality as represented through stewardesses who welcome them in one's own language and serve them one's own familiar food.

More than a performance, enactment, or even simple synecdoche, then, national airlines appear as the very materialization of stateness—an abstraction embodied in a metal container that in turn appears to take on a collective human

FIGURE 4. Pilot and stewardesses of Turkish Air, Turkey's flag carrier, in 1974, the year of Cyprus's division.

form. Indeed, it is in this collective human form that it appears to represent both sovereign integrity and agency, and collective aspirations. Much of the sovereignty effect produced depends on these mobile containers of the homeland landing in other states' spaces. And as we will see, for citizens of unrecognized states such airplanes also become the sites for enacting the exceptionality of nonrecognition in transnational spaces—for instance, when a representative of CTA in London accepts one's TRNC passport as a legitimate form of identification. This is why, I will argue, national airlines have been so fiercely protected by states in the era of privatization, and also why the bankruptcy of so many in the past two decades appears to have signaled for many people an erosion of sovereignty.

The De Facto State of the Skies

In 2016, while conducting research for a book project on unrecognized state building, my coauthor and I decided to query his several thousand Turkish Cypriot Facebook friends about what they missed with the loss of Cyprus Turkish Airlines.[7] Although I make no claims to systematic representation in such a survey, the pool of almost five thousand persons represents about 2.5 percent of north Cyprus's citizen population. In addition, the more than two hundred responses that we received in less than two hours were gender balanced and came from a good distribution of age groups, socioeconomic backgrounds, and political affiliations. The simple question that we asked was, "What do you miss the most about CTA?" The reason for asking the question in this way was that I had already noticed a public, emotional attachment to the airline that manifest itself in expressions of loss at the airline's 2010 bankruptcy and closure. CTA was, of course, a significant employer, but even more than that, expressions of anger and demoralization that other airlines had since taken over its routes seemed to point to something that resembled communal trauma.

Ironically, the company's collapse began when it finally became a wholly Turkish Cypriot-owned enterprise. Its bankruptcy had been triggered by the semi-privatization of Turkish Airlines in 2005, when that company's shares in CTA were sold back to the Turkish Cypriot government. This made CTA for the first time an entirely Turkish Cypriot enterprise, a source of great public pride. They then invested in new airplanes, hired more staff, and began scheduled flights to Sweden, Norway, and Finland, with plans to operate flights to other European destinations in Italy, Romania, and Hungary.

By that time, however, there was much competition in the form of new, private airlines flying to north Cyprus—a phenomenon that began with Turkey's neoliberal openings of the mid-1990s but increased considerably in the 2000s. Moreover, as noted above, the 2003 opening of the checkpoints initially led many Turkish Cypriots and foreign tourists to begin using Larnaca Airport, in the island's south, which at the time had cheaper prices and direct flights to Europe. Within five years, CTA was in serious debt, by some reports up to US $100 million, and in order to avoid bankruptcy was sold at auction. The only bidder was Atlasjet, a private Turkish company, which took over the airline's flights to the island and some of its newer planes. Although flights continue to operate at the same, familiar times, the now six airlines flying scheduled or chartered flights into Ercan airport in the island's north are all based in Turkey.

Until the travel disruption caused by the COVID-19 pandemic, Ercan Airport was busy beyond capacity. The expansion of Turkish Airlines over the past decade has turned Istanbul into the hub of a vast international network that connects north Cyprus more closely to the world. Moreover, in the wake of the 2012 financial crisis in the island's south and subsequent bankruptcy of the RoC's state airline, Cyprus Air, Ercan airport in the north began drawing considerable traffic from its "recognized" competitor in the south. Flights left at all hours of the day and night, and on most days and at most times throughout the year those flights were full. At the same time, this appears hardly to be a source of pride or enjoyment for most Turkish Cypriots, who instead express anger and loss, often describing the airline's demise as the fall of their last pretense to have a "state."

CTA had been the most visible and tangible manifestation of that state abroad, landing in London airports even as Turkish Cypriots were unable to open official representation there. It was the airline of the "pirate state" that nevertheless flew twice a day to destinations that linked them to the world. Expressions both of "stateness" and of it being "their own" were particularly prominent in the immediate, emotional responses that we received to our question about the airline's demise.

Indeed, although one might argue that technically the airline was not "theirs" until 2005, in the sense that it was owned in partnership with Turkish Airlines, what seems to have been more important than actual ownership was the affect of ownership. Planes emblazoned with the name of "their own" airline landed in metropolitan capitals in the the United Kingdom and other parts of Europe—of course, after touchdown stops in Turkey. One friend commented that she missed "it being 'Cyprus Turkish Airways' and it landing at Heathrow." Quite a few respondents wrongly remembered that the airline had flown the TRNC flag. "I miss it being the national airline and the flag being flown," commented one. When he was corrected by someone who had worked for the institution, the same friend replied, "It's enough that its name was Cyprus Turkish Air."

The fact that it was "their own" also meant that it was highly accessible to them. CTA employed more than fifteen hundred Turkish Cypriots before its bankruptcy and closure, and this not only made it a significant employer in a "state" with around 180,000 citizens but also gave people many points of access. My mother-in-law, for instance, would make phone calls to certain people every time her granddaughter was coming to visit from Ankara. When the girl was still small, she would make sure that the girl was given particular seats close to the front of the plane and that particular stewardesses attended to her, escorting her on and off the plane and helping her through customs. The airline, then, was both the concrete manifestation and representation of their state in the outside world, giving them pride when they saw it landing in London airports, and a manifestation of community that was "their own."

If the airline had come to stand in some totemic way for the affective aspirations of their statehood, however, this also shows us that the sense of "having" a state, of it "being ours," is not confined to territory but rather depends on manifestations of separateness that appear elsewhere. One Facebook friend remarked, "What I miss the most is the feeling that it [CTA] created of being a bridge to my homeland, something that tied me to my homeland." Still another friend opined, "I would get warm feelings whenever I saw that plane at Heathrow airport, and when I boarded the plane I would feel like I was in my own home." Some cited the hostesses being acquaintances, or their announcements in the Cypriot dialect. Others remembered the sandwiches with hellim, a Cypriot cheese, and Bixi Cola, a Turkish Cypriot imitation of Coca-Cola. Others missed being able to take excess baggage without paying, or buying tickets through connections.

What they missed, in other words, was the cultural intimacy that was created through an institution that materialized their homeland elsewhere. While several former employees of the airline insisted, in replies to other comments, that it became "theirs" in the literal sense of ownership only very late, the response of Turkish Cypriots who had flown the airline and felt a sense of loss at its bankruptcy was, "Still it was ours." As two respondents separately expressed it, "Whatever the TRNC is, that's what CTA was." What was obviously not clear to the former employees was that the sense of belonging created through the airline was not linked to its actual ownership but rather to its materialization of sovereignty, a sense of belongingness in place that was manifest through both separateness (hellim sandwiches, stewardesses' announcements in the dialect, or buying tickets through connections, for instance) and connectivity. One said that she missed,

> the return trip to my homeland on a flight from Istanbul to Nicosia
> or Güzelyurt, the sense of travel and meeting on the plane a friend or

relative I haven't seen in a long time, when I went to the Mecidiyeköy [in Istanbul] office the feeling not that I was buying a ticket but that I was going to drink coffee with a friend, and it [the airplane] being a space that in all of its aspects made me feel that I was an islander, in other words that I was from here.[8]

We see in this response the combination of separateness and connectivity that I have argued was important for the airline to materialize sovereignty.

It was in this sense that the most common answer to the question of what they missed was "everything about it," with several agreeing with one respondent who remarked, "everything about it. . . . Its existence . . . the sense of trust it gave." That sense of trust, moreover, was linked to what one person called, "It being an institution that was ours," where it being "theirs" was reflected in the sense of cultural intimacy that Michael Herzfeld (1997) describes as weaknesses or faults one can only admit to oneself. As one respondent put it, "It [CTA] was badly managed, just like the TRNC. There was cheating, there was stealing, the service was bad, etc." The association of airline and state, then, was in part in the very weaknesses that made its airplanes spaces of cultural intimacy.

It was, then, the personalization and exceptionality of the airline that enabled it to materialize sovereignty precisely through containing a sense of belonging that could be transported elsewhere. Their actual ownership of the airline was clearly less significant than the affect of ownership, or the sense of "it being ours." While the same might be said of any national airline, the materialization of sovereignty was particularly effective here insofar as it also overcame many of the political impediments to realizing that sovereignty. After all, one of the things that we expect our own state to do for us is to help us navigate the wider world through, for instance, issuing passports and other documents and establishing embassy representation. While Turkish Cypriots' overseas representations were unrecognized and ineffective and their passports largely unacceptable outside Turkey, "their" airline could help them navigate the connectivities from which their state was excluded. As we will see, this important role in materializing sovereignty has become most obvious in its recent absence.

Black Holes of Sovereignty

In early 2013, a Turkish firm took over the management of Ercan Airport, which had been privatized as part of a packet of austerity measures that the Turkish government imposed on its aid to the island's north.[9] Since the 1960s, when the intercommunal conflict had pushed Turkish Cypriots into enclaves (see Bryant and Hatay 2011), the Turkish government has financially and militarily aided this minority community. After the Turkish military intervention of 1974 and subsequent division of the island, Turkey became the isolated state's main financier. Today, the Republic of Turkey gives more than $600 million every year to keep the unrecognized state afloat, and much of this funding goes to its bloated bureaucracy. Although unions and leftist political parties protested privatization and other austerity measures, the right-wing government then in office succumbed to Turkish government pressure in order to continue financing a political system in which votes are often gained through the distribution of public service jobs.

One of the Turkish firm's primary responsibilities was to build a new airport next to the old one to accommodate the rise in traffic. In the more immediate term, however, the firm began to raise capital by reorganizing the airport parking space and selling advertising. Today, Ercan Airport is plastered both inside and outside with advertising for airlines, hotels, casinos, and private universities. The firm has also sold prime parking space to hotels, casinos, and tour operators to park buses and limousines close to the main exit. The airport that was once considered state infrastructure has become for many people a symbol of the state succumbing to what many leftists call "wild" or "rampant" capitalism (*vahşi kapitalizm*). Moreover, because much of this capitalism is coming to the island via Turkey, left-wing critics have begun to call this a new form of colonialism that has taken away what they refer to as their "political will" (*siyasi irade*).[10]

The past fifteen years have seen the increasing integration of the island's north into the global economy, primarily because of the growth of Turkey's economy and the links that north Cyprus has to it. In addition, when the RoC became an EU member state in 2004, the EU officially admitted all of the island, although the *acquis communautaire*—the EU's body of law—is suspended in the island's north. This new status has meant, however, that Turkish Cypriots now interact more freely with representatives of the EU and other transnational bodies, tying the space in the north more closely to the rest of the world. However, as I discuss elsewhere (Bryant 2021), this has been accompanied by an increasing lack of belief in their own state and its sovereignty.

Reasons for this may be seen in the demise of their airline, and in the way that the exceptionality discussed earlier as a source of intimacy instead has come to reflect the north's status as a black hole of sovereignty. As a recognized state bound by international protocols and treaties, Turkey's recognition of the TRNC has its limits. Turkish Cypriots often cite the fact that Turkish Cypriot football teams cannot play matches with teams in Turkish leagues, as those are "recognized" teams who play with "recognized" states. This even includes the RoC, such that Greek Cypriot teams have gone to play in Turkey and vice versa, but Turkish Cypriot teams are not able to do the same. Such examples could be multiplied. Of course, these are structural problems of the international system of states and the responsibilities produced by recognition—in this case, not Turkey's recognition of the RoC government, but recognition of the RoC by the rest of the world, hence placing it in football leagues with Turkish teams. Turkish government officials, on all formal occasions, are careful to reiterate their support for the independence and sovereignty of the TRNC. But as one union leader expressed it to me, "On paper Turkey is the only country that recognizes us, although in practice it's not that way."

One recent example concerns Turkish Airlines' policy regarding the entry of passport information for online ticket sales and check-in. Many Turkish Cypriots are the possessors of three passports: one from the TRNC, valid for travel to Turkey and, in the past, to the United States and United Kingdom; one from Turkey, which gives them to Turkish Cypriots as laissez-passer travel documents without citizenship; and one from the RoC, which claims Turkish Cypriots as its citizens. The last of these is now the most valuable, as the RoC is an EU member state. Juggling this set of documents is in any case a complicated endeavor, but it was made more so by the loss of their national airline. Today, it is possible to purchase tickets to Ercan through the websites of Turkish Air, Pegasus, Atlasjet, and Correndon, among others. It is also possible to send express packages to north Cyprus through DHL and FedEx, and these will be marked with Ercan as their destination. Even more ironically, after the private Greek carrier Aegean Airlines bought Greece's failing national carrier, Olympic, Greece's main carrier became a code share and miles partner with Turkish Air. This means, then, that a Turkish Cypriot carrying a Turkish Air frequent flyer card can gain miles for flying from Larnaca Airport and can even use the Aegean Airlines lounge there. Or, she can fly into Ercan via Istanbul and later use the miles collected to fly on Aegean from Larnaca to Amsterdam.

Despite all of these forms of tacit recognition (McConnell 2009), figuring out how to reflect Turkish Cypriots' complicated passport situation in online check-in has proven more than an internationally recognized carrier can handle. Whenever one wants to check in for a flight on the Turkish Air website, it is necessary first to enter passport information, as the responsibility for checking that passengers have valid travel documents has in recent years fallen more and more to airlines. There is a space to add visa information, though the system does not demand it; it is possible, for instance, to enter one's Turkish passport number without demonstrating a visa for Europe and still be able to check in. Things are a bit different for Turkish Cypriots, however. For a number of years, the drop-down box from which passengers had to check the country of their passport and residence did not list the TRNC, north Cyprus, or even simply Cyprus. Instead, the choices for Turkish Cypriots were either Turkey or Southern Cyprus (Güney Kıbrıs). Because some younger Turkish Cypriots who were born or came of age after the 2003 opening of the checkpoints do not possess Turkish passports, this means that even if they were traveling to Turkey and would present their TRNC identity documents at the border, they needed to enter their RoC passport information in order to check in online.

However, in late 2017 this system suddenly changed. Without warning, Southern Cyprus disappeared from the options in the drop-down box, and Turkish Republic of Northern Cyprus appeared there as an option. This presented an even more serious dilemma, because it meant that Turkish Cypriots traveling to anywhere besides Turkey were unable to enter valid passport information, as they would be traveling on their RoC passport. As a result of this change, long queues began forming at Ercan, when passengers were unable to get their boarding passes online.

This passport dilemma is also a materialization, but in this case it materializes the black hole of sovereignty represented by an unrecognized state. There is literally no way for an internationally recognized airline to represent Turkish Cypriots' passports in their online check-in system: either the passport is entirely erased and replaced by that of the RoC, or the passport is included while at the same time making check-in impossible. This becomes, then, the quotidian materialization of the same black hole of sovereignty discussed in the introduction, an anomaly in the otherwise functioning system of aerial sovereignty by which airplane captains, control towers, and ICAO planners coordinate with each other. The problem, as described there, is not the failure to engage with controllers at Ercan Airport, but rather Turkey's failure to recognize the government of the RoC—thereby sidestepping the issue of Turkish Cypriot control over their own airspace. In the past, it was the very exceptionality of such a sovereign black hole that an airline had transformed into cultural intimacy, materializing sovereignty through its forms of separateness and connectivity, that created belonging to a homeland. In the absence of that vehicle for sovereign agency, however, exceptionality becomes disempowering, a lack of agency materialized in a global but impersonal check-in system that forces them into queues they now have no way to jump.

In this chapter I have argued that national airlines have played a significant role in materializing sovereignty, both as mobile containers of the homeland and as aerial ambassadors that symbolize connectivity and technological prowess. I have used the word *materialize* to suggest that this is not only or primarily about the airplane's materiality—one emphasis of a recent literature on similar infrastructures (esp. Harvey 2005). Neither, however, do airlines simply symbolize the nation in an ideological way—even though aircraft are inevitably bearers of the emblems of the nation. As we see from the responses to my simple question, what people missed about Turkish Cypriots' airline was not the symbolism or name per se, but rather, "it being 'Cyprus Turkish Airways' and it landing at Heathrow." If infrastructures are one of the ways in which an idea of an "external state" emerges (e.g., 136), that state's connectivity with others may be encapsulated in the ability of such a flying container of the homeland to travel elsewhere.

However, if, as we have argued in this volume's introduction, the state may be seen as a vehicle for sovereign agency, the "sovereignty effect" must surely occur at the moment where the state appears as "ours." Like other chapters in this volume that examine aspirations to stateness as desires for communal agency, here, too, we find through the emotional attachment to a defunct national airline expressions of the dual nature of that belongingness. I have used the word *materializing* sovereignty to express this dual aspect, where it is not only that "the state" seems to appear in material form, but also that something else—in this instance, the "state" that is "ours"—is brought into being. If boarding a national airline's plane from Heathrow or Schiphol evokes the experience of a village bus taking one home, or if it can be described as a "bridge to my homeland," this is also a space where sovereignty is materialized and where the aircraft totemically creates "the people" to whom it belongs.

For citizens of an unrecognized state, part of this effect has depended on transforming what is otherwise an international "black hole" of sovereignty into a site of intimate agency. A recent literature on desires for "normality" in the former Yugoslav states explores this in part in relationship to loss of mobility, in contrast to the former socialist Yugoslavia, where citizens carried a passport that enabled them to travel. As Jessica Greenberg remarks, "Yugoslavia was a state whose sovereignty was most apparent when its citizens were mobile." The loss of that mobility also signaled for them the loss of a "normal" state, while desires for "normality" expressed "a desire to be subject to disciplinary regimes of power—a state that works" (Greenberg 2011, 90).

Today, Turkish Cypriots are more mobile than ever—young people study in Spain and the Netherlands, professionals go to workshops in Italy and the United States, and people take vacations to Cuba and the Maldives. However, to do so they use RoC passports and fly on airlines that are not their own. Carrying the RoC passport is an ambivalent act, because while many Turkish Cypriots argue that they were founding partners in the RoC and so have a right to them, showing the passport and not that of the TRNC is simultaneously an acknowledgment of the latter's failures. Similarly, while they can now travel cheaply and easily to Thailand or Brazil with Turkish Air, it means traveling on an airline that is not "their own" and doing so with the passport of a state that denies their own claims to statehood.

In the post-Yugoslav context, Stef Jansen has argued that the red passport had given citizens of the socialist state a "place in the world" (2009, 14) that was lost in the crisis-ridden states that succeeded it. We might say that in the absence of such a passport that they could fully claim as "their own," CTA gave them such a "place in the world," landing at Heathrow and Schiphol and welcoming foreign passengers with their hellim sandwiches and announcements in the dialect. In this case, however, that "place in the world" was always already a "black hole," but one that could be almost "normalized" through this mobility, which instead transformed it into the intimacy of discounted tickets and baggage allowance waivers.

What became clear after CTA's demise is that this exceptionality is a double-edged sword, on the one hand creating a sense of intimate belongingness in the state—a sense that "it is ours"—and on the other hand a sense of being outside the "normal" order of things. For instance, one respondent to our survey remarked, "If CTA was shut down because of these negatives . . . then it's long past time to shut the doors on the TRNC shop. Because the illegality and bad management of the TRNC is maybe ten times worse than CTA was." Indeed, if respondents saw the CTA as standing for the TRNC, it was in no small part because of the implicit comparison between the poor management of CTA and the corrupt administration of the TRNC. The idea that it is "time to shut the doors on the TRNC shop" indicates the double-edged nature of exceptionality, or being outside the "normal" order, where intimacy can accompany failure.

It is here, then, that we see the role of the sovereignty effect in transforming a space and system outside the "normal" order from a "black hole" of sovereignty into the intimacy of a homeland. Insofar as a national airline materialized sovereignty, it did so by landing ships with names like Girne and Karpaz in Heathrow and by offering hellim sandwiches to British tourists. While black holes have a gravitational pull that draws all into itself, I have argued here that one of the most important aspects of national airlines in their materialization of sovereignty is their capacity to transport the dreams and aspirations that constitute sovereign agency outside the borders of such an exceptional space.

Notes

1. According to Wikipedia's Ercan Airport article, this number is 1,646 per month, with more than 200,000 passengers per month (https://en.wikipedia.org/wiki/Ercan_Inter national_Airport). While the source that Wikipedia cites for this is not open to public scrutiny, the Ercan online flight board shows that on an average winter day thirty-one planes land at the airport, or 11,315 per year. Taking into account the much larger number of flights during the high season, Wikipedia's number of 19,752 aircraft per year is not unreasonable.

2. See, e.g., Salter 2008, a collection of papers that focuses on airports as "national spaces that connect to international spaces, frontiers that are not at the territorial limit, and grounded sites that embody mobility" (ix), but does not have a single one concentrating on airplanes or airlines.

3. This is a period that has been extensively documented. See in particular Bryant 2010; Hatay and Bryant 2008.

4. Interestingly, the extent of vertical sovereignty remains under dispute, while debates over the boundary between state sovereignty and outer space have emerged in an era of high-altitude military aircraft (Reinhardt 2007).

5. Jens Bartelson takes this argument a step further when he remarks, "Perhaps the main ideological foundation of the concept of sovereignty is not primarily to legitimize particular claims to political authority, but rather to legitimize the international system within which those claims can be understood as meaningful" (Bartelson 2014, 63). As should be clear from the argument advanced in this chapter, it appears that Bartelson here has swung too far to the other side of the pendulum, and a more balanced view would take into account the interaction between tacit forms of sovereignty and the reproduction of the state system.

6. The conclusions of these papers also point to the possibility that airplanes as containers may be one of the primary factors in their having been overlooked as objects of study themselves. Authors in the recent collection observe that curiously, despite their ubiquity and necessity, it is normally the thing contained (food, water, gunpowder, etc.) that has been the object of study, while the thing containing has disappeared from view (see Robb 2018; Shryock and Smail 2018).

7. The book project itself entailed ethnographic and archival research over about six years on the emergence of a space that came to be known as "north Cyprus" after the island's 1974 division. That research serves as background for observations made here.

8. Güzelyurt (in Greek, Morphou) is a large town in Cyprus's west that at one time had a small airport where certain CTA flights would land.

9. "KKTC'nin dünyaya açılan kapısı: Ercan Havalimanı," *Airporthaber*, March 4, 2014, http://www.airporthaber.com/ercan-havalimani-haberleri/kktcnin-dunyaya-acilan-kapisi-ercan-havalimani.html.

10. "Political will" is a term often used in leftist public discourse in the island. For more on this in relation to Turkey, see Bryant and Yakinthou 2012.

References

Abeyratne, Ruwantissa. 2009. *Aeropolitics*. New York: Nova Science Publishers.
Amoore, Louise. 2006. "Biometric Borders: Governing Mobilities in the War on Terror." *Political Geography* 25: 336–351.
Andersson, Ruben. 2014. *Illegality, Inc.: Clandestine Migration and the Business of Bordering Europe*. Berkeley: University of California Press.

Auge, Marc. 1995. *Non-Places: Introduction to the Anthropology of Supermodernity.* Translated by J. Howe. London: Verso.

Bartelson, Jens. 2014. *Sovereignty as Symbolic Form.* London: Routledge.

Bear, Laura. 2007. *Lines of the Nation: Indian Railway Workers, Bureaucracy, and the Intimate Historical Self.* New York: Columbia University Press.

Biersteker, Thomas J., and Cynthia Weber. 1996. "The Social Construction of State Sovereignty." In *State Sovereignty as Social Construct,* edited by T. J. Biersteker and C. Weber, 1–21. Cambridge: Cambridge University Press.

Brown, Wendy. 2010. *Walled States, Waning Sovereignty.* Brooklyn: Zone Books.

Bryant, Rebecca. 2010. *The Past in Pieces: Belonging in the New Cyprus.* Philadelphia: University of Pennsylvania Press.

Bryant, Rebecca. Forthcoming 2021. "Sovereignty in Drag: On Fakes, Foreclosure, and Unbecoming States." *Cultural Anthropology* 36(1): 52–83.

Bryant, Rebecca, and Mete Hatay. 2011. "Guns and Guitars: Simulating Sovereignty in a State of Siege." *American Ethnologist* 38(4): 631–649.

Bryant, Rebecca, and Mete Hatay. 2020. *Sovereignty Suspended: Building the So-Called State.* Philadelphia: University of Pennsylvania Press.

Bryant, Rebecca, and Christalla Yakinthou. 2012. *Cypriot Perceptions of Turkey.* Istanbul: Turkish Economic and Social Studies Foundation.

Budd, Lucy, Morag Bell, and Tim Brown. 2009. "Of Plagues, Planes and Politics: Controlling the Global Spread of Infectious Diseases by Air." *Political Geography* 28: 426–435.

Butler, David L. 2001. "Technogeopolitics and the Struggle for Control of World Air Routes, 1910–1928." *Political Geography* 20: 635–658.

CAPA (Center for Aviation). 2011. "American Airlines Goes Broke: Can a 'National' Airline Be Allowed to Fail?" https://centreforaviation.com/insights/analysis/american-airlines-goes-broke-can-a-national-airline-be-allowed-to-fail-63802.

Chalfin, Brenda. 2006. "Global Customs Regimes and the Traffic in Sovereignty: Enlarging the Anthropology of the State." *Current Anthropology* 47(2): 243–276.

Chalfin, Brenda. 2008. "Sovereigns and Citizens in Close Encounter: Airport Anthropology and Customs Regimes in Neoliberal Ghana." *American Ethnologist* 35(4): 519–538.

Coleman, Leo. 2014. "Infrastructure and Interpretation: Meters, Dams, and State Imagination in Scotland and India." *American Ethnologist* 41(3): 457–472.

Cyprus Mail. 2017a. "Risk of Flight Collisions in Nicosia Airspace." October 9. http://cyprus-mail.com/2017/10/09/risk flight collisions nicosia airspace.

Cyprus Mail. 2017b. "Cyprus Records Third Highest Increase for Airline Passengers in EU for 2016." October 11. http://cyprus-mail.com/2017/10/11/cyprus-records-third-highest-increase-airline-passengers-eu-2016.

Dalakoglou, Dimitris. 2017. *The Road: An Ethnography of (Im)mobility, Space, and Cross-Border Infrastructures in the Balkans.* Manchester: Manchester University Press.

Dinnie, Keith. 2008. *Nation Branding: Concepts, Issues, Practice.* Oxford: Elsevier.

Donnan, Hastings, and Thomas M. Wilson, eds. 2010. *Borderlands: Ethnographic Approaches to Security, Power, and Identity.* Lanham, MD: University Press of America.

Dowling, Ross K., and Clare Weeden, eds. 2017. *Cruise Ship Tourism,* 2nd ed. Oxfordshire, UK: CABI.

The Economist. 2014. "State-Controlled Airlines: Flags of Inconvenience." https://www.economist.com/news/business/21612190-why-governments-are-so-keen-keep-their-loss-making-airlines-aloft-flags-inconvenience.

Ferguson, James, and Akhil Gupta. 2002. "Spatializing States: Toward an Ethnography of Neoliberal Governmentality." *American Ethnologist* 29(4): 981–1002.

Greenberg, Jessica. 2011. "On the Road to Normal: Negotiating Agency and State Sovereignty in Postsocialist Serbia." *American Anthropologist* 113: 88–100.

Harvey, Penelope. 2005. The Materiality of State-Effects: An Ethnography of a Road in the Peruvian Andes. In *State Formation: Anthropological Perspectives*, edited by C. Krohn-Hansen and K. G. Nustad, 123–141. London: Pluto.

Harvey, Penelope, and Hannah Knox. 2012. "The Enchantments of Infrastructure." *Mobilities* 7(4): 521–536.

Hatay, Mete, and Rebecca Bryant. 2008. "The Jasmine Scent of Nicosia: On Returns, Revolutions, and the Longing for Forbidden Pasts." *Journal of Modern Greek Studies* 26(2): 423–449.

Herzfeld, Michael. 1997. *Cultural Intimacy: Social Poetics in the Nation-State.* New York: Routledge.

Hiller, Harry H. 2010. "Airports as Borderlands: American Preclearance and Transitional Spaces in Canada." *Journal of Borderlands Studies* 25(3–4): 19–30.

Hylland Eriksen, Thomas, and Runar Doving. 1992. "In Limbo: Notes on the Culture of Airports." Available at http://hyllanderiksen.net/Airports.html.

Jansen, Stef. 2009. "After the Red Passport: Towards an Anthropology of the Everyday Geopolitics of Entrapment in the EU's 'Immediate Outside.'" *Journal of the Royal Anthropological Institute* 15(4): 815–832.

Jansen, Stef. 2014. "Hope For/Against the State: Gridding in a Besieged Sarajevo Suburb." *Ethnos* 79(2): 238–260.

Jansen, Stef. 2015. *Yearnings in the Meantime: "Normal Lives" and the State in a Sarajevo Apartment Complex.* Oxford: Berghahn Books.

Jauregui, Beatrice. 2014. "Provisional Agency in India: *Jugaad* and Legitimation of Corruption." *American Ethnologist* 41(1): 76–91.

Larkin, Brian. 2008. *Signal and Noise: Media, Infrastructure, and Urban Culture in Nigeria.* Charlotte, NC: Duke University Press.

Lawrence, David. 2012. "Some Lessons from Privatizing National Airlines." *The World Bank Blog: Private Sector Development,* July 26. http://blogs.worldbank.org/psd/some-lessons-from-privatizing-national-airlines.

Lloyd, Justine. 2003. "Dwelltime: Airport Technology, Travel, and Consumption." *Space and Culture* 6(20): 93–109.

Lutz, Catherine, and Anne Lutz Fernandez. 2010. *Carjacked: The Culture of the Automobile and Its Effect on Our Lives.* New York: St. Martin's Press.

Maguire, Mark. 2009. "The Birth of Biometric Security." *Anthropology Today* 25(2): 9–14.

Maguire, Mark. 2014. "Counter-Terrorism in European Airports." In *The Anthropology of Security: Perspectives from the Frontline of Policing, Counter-Terrorism and Border*, edited by M. Maguire, C. Frois, and N. Zurawski, 118–138. London: Pluto Press.

Markessinis, Andreas. n.d. "Airline Companies as Nation Branding Ambassadors." Nation-branding Whitepapers Series, http://andreasmarkessinis.com/nation-branding/whitepapers/airline-companies-nation-brand-ambassadors.pdf.

McConnell, Fiona. 2009. "De Facto, Displaced, Tacit: The Sovereign Articulations of the Tibetan Government-in-Exile." *Political Geography* 28: 343–352.

McConnell, Fiona. 2016. *Rehearsing the State: The Political Practices of the Tibetan Government-in-Exile.* West Sussex, UK: John Wiley and Sons.

Miller, Daniel, ed. 2001. *Car Cultures.* London: Berg Publishers.

Mitchell, Timothy. 1991. "The Limits of the State: Beyond Statist Approaches and Their Critics." *The American Political Science Review* 85(1): 77–96.

Moreland, Jeanette. 2013. "The Anthropology of Airports: Security and the Apparatuses of State Borders." Ph.D. diss., State University of New York at Binghamton.

Nordstrom, Carolyn. 2007. *Global Outlaws: Crime, Money, and Power in the Contemporary World.* Berkeley: University of California Press.

Painter, Joe. 2006. "Prosaic Geographies of Stateness." *Political Geography* 25: 752–774.

Peteet, Julie. 2017. *Space and Mobility in Palestine.* Bloomington: Indiana University Press.

Pickering, Sharon, and Leanne Weber, eds. 2006. *Borders, Mobility, and Technologies of Control.* Dordrecht: Springer.

Shotter, J., and Billig, M. 1998. "A Bakhtinian Psychology: From Out of the Heads of Individuals and into the Dialogues between Them." In *Bakhtin and the Human Sciences: No Last Words,* edited by M. M. Bell and M. Gardiner, 13–29. London: Sage.

Raguraman, K. 1997. "Airlines as Instruments for Nation Building and National Identity: Case Study of Malaysia and Singapore." *Journal of Transport Geography* 5(4): 239–256.

Reeves, Madeleine. 2014. *Border Work: Spatial Lives of the State in Rural Central Asia.* Ithaca: Cornell University Press.

Reinhardt, Dean N. 2007. "The Vertical Limit of State Sovereignty." *Journal of Air Law and Commerce* 72: 65–137.

Robb, John. 2018. "Contained within History." *History and Anthropology* 29(1): 32–36.

Rodgers, Dennis, and Bruce O'Neill. 2012. "Infrastructural Violence: Introduction to the Special Issue." *Ethnography* 13(4): 401–412.

Salter, Mark B., ed. 2008. *Politics at the Airport.* Minneapolis: University of Minnesota Press.

Sampson, Anthony. 1984. *Empires of the Sky.* London: Hodder and Stoughton

Shryock, Andrew, and Daniel Lord Smail. 2018. "On Containers: A Forum. Introduction." *History and Anthropology* 29(1): 1–6.

Sonan, Sertaç. 2014. "In the Grip of Political Clientelism: The Post-1974 Turkish Cypriot Politics and the Politico-Economic Foundations of Pro-*Taksim* Consensus." Ph.D. diss., University of Duisburg Essen.

Talmon, Stefan. n.d. "Air Traffic with Non-Recognised States: The Case of Northern Cyprus." Available at http://users.ox.ac.uk/~sann2029/FCO_Paper%20by%20Dr%20Stefan%20Talmon.pdf. Accessed November 23, 2017.

Thrift, Nigel. 2000. "It's the Little Things." In *Geopolitical Traditions: A Century of Geopolitical Thought,* edited by K. Dodds and D. Atkinson, 380–387. London: Routledge.

Todd, Daniel, and Jamie Simpson. 1985. "Aerospace, the State, and the Regions: A Canadian Perspective." *Political Geography Quarterly* 4(2): 111–130.

Torpey, John. 1998. "Coming and Going: On the State Monopolization of the Legitimate 'Means of Movement.'" *Sociological Theory* 16(3): 239–259.

United Nations Convention on Jurisdictional Immunities of States and Their Property. 2004. Available at https://treaties.un.org/doc/source/recenttexts/english_3_13.pdf.

Weber, Cynthia. 1995. *Simulating Sovereignty: Intervention, the State, and Symbolic Exchange.* Cambridge: Cambridge University Press.

Williams, Alison J. 2011. "Enabling Persistent Presence? Performing the Embodied Geopolitics of the Unmanned Aerial Vehicle Assemblage." *Political Geography* 30: 381–390.

Yano, Christine R. 2011. *Airborne Dreams: "Nisei" Stewardesses and Pan American World Airways.* Durham, NC: Duke University Press.

SOVEREIGNTY AS GENERATOR OF INCONSISTENT STATE DESIRE IN NORTHEASTERN CENTRAL AFRICAN REPUBLIC

Louisa Lombard

One of the classic texts in political anthropology is the edited volume *African Political Systems* (Fortes and Evans-Pritchard 1940). The book consists of cases intended to chart a typology of ways of doing politics, with the main differentiator being whether the society had a central organization (a state) or not (was stateless). The book's contributors sought to avoid normative thinking about politics. That is, they argued for not taking for granted what content the category of politics might have in particular places. Political philosophy had long explored the questions of what politics ought to look like (implied: for everyone). The Fortes and Evans-Pritchard volume would do something different and focus on "observed behavior": what specific people actually do (4). The contributors assumed that for the most part people have a stable social milieu and that they do as it dictates that they ought.

In this chapter, I return to a largely "stateless" remote African terrain in order to take up a contemporary version of Fortes and Evans-Pritchard's project. They, like the contributors to this volume, noticed that sovereignty and state were not one and the same. But, working as they did during the colonial period, they did not extensively pursue what kinds of desires people might have for recognizability and control—for, as the editors of this volume have termed it, sovereign agency. Thinking with sovereign agency in this context shows that the old differentiation Fortes and Evans-Pritchard made between normative philosophy and behavior/practice does not hold, and underscores instead the prevalence of political inconsistency and the role of sovereign agency in fostering it.

Inconsistency is perhaps particularly pronounced in "contested state spaces" (Dunn 2009) like the northeastern Central African Republic (CAR), where the formal legal realm of political institutions—which is very far from a global-normative conception of statehood—is far from realized. The gap between the ideal and the actual is so large that all sorts of other justifications can be reasonably marshaled to explain away inconsistencies. But by adding people in northeastern CAR to this volume's discussion of sovereign agency and its relation to stateness my intention is not to suggest that Central Africans are particularly insincere (quite the opposite!), disordered, or unruly. Indeed there are strong resonances between dynamics in northeastern CAR and, for instance, the simultaneous "hope *for* and hope *against* the state" that Stef Jansen (2014, 254; emphasis in original) identified in Sarajevo. Rather, I do so to provoke: to encourage reflection as to whether inconsistency might in fact be more the norm in politics than the exception. Consistency cannot be assumed; it is a project, and one that people undertake with varying degrees of vigor (Laidlaw 2013), even people who state their convictions or desires fervently. It is moreover embedded in other kinds of interests and projects, like the factional politics Wimpelmann discusses in her chapter in this book.

Northeastern CAR occupies a limbo position: formally part of a state, but effectively mostly ignored by centralized administration. The three northeast-ernmost prefectures of the CAR make up nearly a third of the country's territory but are home to less than 4 percent of its human population.[1] I have elsewhere referred to it as an "autonomous zone" (Lombard 2015), a riff on the more active constructions of autonomous zones as the products of desires and actions taken to resist state power (Bey 2003; Graeber 2007). Instead, I use the term to show that such spaces can also be the product of largely indifferent abandonment by centralized regimes. Northeastern CAR might, at first glance, seem to also be a space of nonsovereignty—or at least to be a space of nonrelevance to understanding sovereignty, given how far it strays from ideal-typical conceptions of sovereignty (Bartelson 1995; Anghie 2005). But in the same way that Michael Taussig (1992, 132) argued that perhaps fantasies regarding the center, rather than the state's ideologies, are more important for understanding the state idea, perhaps also persons and groups at the margins of the state can show us something about sovereignty, and about politics more broadly.

In northeastern CAR, as I will discuss further below, people express a strong desire for an end to their "abandonment" by the state—for infrastructure and other largesse they see as properly the work of the state—and an associated desire for a Leviathan-like power that can regulate and evict threats. At the same time, when state officials or others acting in the name of the state attempt to control and regulate the actions of people in the area, those targeted often protest vigorously. The desire for stateness coexists with a value of liberty, or freedom from molestation in one's projects, which is a local manifestation of a project for sovereign agency. In other words: when we pull the quintessential ethnographic move of considering both what people say and what they do, we find that what people say ought to be the case and what people do (and also, depending on context, say) are not always consistent. What do people desire when they desire sovereignty, this book asks? They might desire quite contradictory things, such as to be under the control and consistent regulation of another (a desire for stateness, for the simplicity of life lived in a working state) as well as to have liberty, to be free from others' regulation (to enact one's will without impediment).

A call to appreciate ideational and behavioral inconsistency in the regulatory realm, which spans across the interlinked but not entirely overlapping elements of sovereign agency and stateness, is this chapter's first conclusion. But there is more to learn from inconsistency than simply to note that it is important. Attention to sovereign agency provides an angle for doing so. "The 'sovereignty effect' must surely occur at the moment when the state appears to be 'ours,'" observes Bryant (chapter 1, this volume). Another way of saying "ours" is "not yours," and while the importance of exclusivity to political communities of course varies, this operation of differentiation always takes place. The enactment of "ours" requires that "we" be treated differently from "you" or "them." When national belonging is fairly settled, the inconsistencies in this process become less visible. "We" are citizens, while "you" are not; this distinction determines who should properly enjoy the ownership and exception that inhere in the claim "ours"—who gets to enjoy a proprietary feeling when it comes to political dynamics. But in northeastern CAR, and perhaps in contested state spaces more generally, the categories of "us" and "ours" do not have stable, broadly agreed-on content. The persons who are "not us" and against whom egregious regulatory authority gets wielded, and those persons who will be shielded from it, are contested rather than settled categories. This is particularly clear in the case of the area's history of armed conservation. A desire for a state that will control and regulate and do statelike things coexists with an opposing value of liberty, and an important mechanism through which these values compete is the sovereign effect of delineating "ours" (or at least, "not yours"), that is, proprietary feeling, which is my shorthand for the status of enjoying exception from the regulation due those who do not own/belong. The second conclusion of this chapter is therefore that sovereign agency can *generate* or *exacerbate* states of inconsistency.

State Desire

People in northeastern CAR experience their position as one of abandonment by the state. French speakers lament, "L'état nous a abandonné," or just "Nous sommes abandonnés."[2] It's an interesting word choice, in that it implies that at some previous time people were included in some meaningful way, and now they are not. Looking at historical documents suggests that any inclusion was only ever limited. During much of the period of French colonialism (from the turn of the twentieth century to independence in 1960), northeastern CAR was designated a *district autonome* (autonomous district), because it was too far from the capital to be expected to keep up with the circulars and other directives about governing practice. The people of the region were moreover seen as semiforeign, in the sense that the French understood them to have arrived only as a result of the nineteenth century's raiding polities, which, though centered further north, had by the late nineteenth century spread substantially into what is now CAR (Cordell 1985). Reports by the lone colonial officials posted to the area in the 1930s and 1940s describe the extremely limited means at their disposal to undertake governing projects, such as getting people to cultivate cash crops (this could be achieved only with force [Brégeon 1998]), writing reports (some reports include plaintive requests for such basic materials as a typewriter [Lignier 1936]), or keeping prisoners locked up (there was a perennial lack of effective chains [Lignier 1936; Mollion 1992]).

The situation did not change much with independence. The only truly nationalistic president the country has had, Jean-Bédel Bokassa (in power 1966–79; self-proclaimed emperor from 1977–79), most notably used the Northeast for two things.[3] One was safari hunting. After a falling out with the country's most prominent hunting guide, Bokassa created the "presidential park" of Avakaba. In the early 1970s, the lights from his lodge there were visible from the town of Ndele, tens of kilometers away.[4] The other was as a site for "exile"—note this was not qualified as "internal exile"—for undesirables (Gallo 1996).

The disregard apparent in using the region as a site for exile is not central to how Bokassa is remembered in the region today, however. When I visited in 2008, residents of Birao, CAR's northeasternmost town, told me that when Bokassa was in power, if there was a problem or any kind of insecurity in their area Bokassa would quickly alight from his plane and resolve things himself. People described Bokassa—approvingly—as inspiring the fear of a true Leviathan, while also building modernizing infrastructure. At a volleyball match in Ndele in 2009, I watched from the sidelines with two young men from town as a player known as Bokassa jumped and yelled at his teammates with the irascibility of the Tasmanian Devil. He claimed a family connection to the former emperor but the name (or nickname) also fit because he shared his namesake's infamous temper. My interlocutors then began to speak of the greatness of the first Bokassa, explaining that all the buildings we saw around us were the product of his putting an infrastructural vision into action. In fact, many were holdovers from the colonial era. As it was still early in my fieldwork, I was a bit surprised at how favorably they presented Bokassa, who is known outside of CAR mostly for his costly self-importance, and I noted that Bokassa could be very tough too, even brutal.[5] "All presidents kill people," one of the young men replied. "Bokassa killed the right people."

In elevating Bokassa to an ideal, people often forget that not just Bokassa the person was different from their current leaders; also, the relational position of the country was quite different. Their nostalgia for that period is also nostalgia for a period when CAR did not have the levels of violent conflict—the rebel groups and the international interventions—that it has had since the turn of the twenty-first century. These conflicts and the new social forms they have entailed have contributed to the sense, widespread among Central Africans, that a previous period of calm and control has given way to a disorder that dispossesses them and that they cannot contain (Ceriana Mayneri 2014).

Another source of state desire (lamentation over abandonment by the state and its associated desire for a different, ideal state that will control and care for) is the accounts people collect of how states other than their own work. One older man among whose occupations was rebel spokesperson described how if a French citizen is taken hostage in Darfur (a common practice around this time, 2009–10), the whole French government would mobilize to get this person back. They would send planes, money, special forces, whatever it took. Looking around where we were sitting beside a home in Tiringoulou, a small town between Ndele and Birao (as the crow flies, not as the road leads—as the Yankee expression has it, "You can't get there from here"), he saw no material traces of the state. No buildings, no proper roads. The way the Central African state operates—functionaries' apparent apathy about residents' material deprivation—is "not normal," many people told me. They were making a normative, moral, statement: this is not how it should be. The state, through these normative registers, was a "common object of yearning" that was "opaque" to Central Africans, and yet its "categories were ever present," as Jansen has described for people in Sarajevo (2015, 6).

One way that those normative categories become part of people's lives and experiences are the various global country rankings that have proliferated in the last twenty years. Central Africans note that their country is "behind" or "last" in the world according to any kind of material measure. As per the current rankings, they are correct: after a decade being among the last handful of countries on the

UN Development Program's Human Development Index, as of 2017 the CAR fell to the final spot, ranked 188 out of 188. Rankings like this are born of the post–Cold War division of the world into allegedly equal and unattached nation-states, in which the maintenance of the state system is the highest goal (Ghosh 1994). They make it possible to "compare newly like sovereign states—suddenly Senegal was 'just like' France and could be compared as such. Rather than demonstrating the disastrous relational effects of colonialism, these tools [for measuring national economies] were employed to demonstrate global poverty in ostensibly discrete nation-states and to intervene, now in the name of economic growth" (Appel 2017, 298). But while one can deplore the distortions inherent in ignoring those relational effects, these models both reflect and shape Central Africans' experience of their position in the world. Their state was never "normal" in the ways they imagine (probably no states are), but they once could boast some firsts: the first university in Central Africa, as well as the first television station. Now, they are first only in the number of peacekeeping missions their country has hosted (twelve) (Olin 2015; Lombard 2016c), and number two in the world in maternal mortality.

During a conversation with some members of a rebel group in Tiringoulou in October 2009, a recurrent theme was these men's desire for someone to come and exploit the oil that prospective studies argued exists not far from there, near the town of Boromata. They spoke of oil exploitation as a kind of fountain-like wealth that would splash over everyone, which is decidedly not the way that people in CAR's oil-exploiting neighbors Chad and Sudan (now South Sudan) have experienced things. I tried to suggest that the benefits of oil wealth are frequently not equally or fairly shared. One of the men turned to me with an exasperated look. "Maybe, but at least we would have a *road*. Anything would help us. We are destitute."[6] Another man mentioned that he had spoken with a foreigner once who advised him that the oil was not likely to ever be exploited because of the "bad governance" of the country's leaders. Those kinds of statements, too, contribute to the sense among Central Africans—including in the furthest reaches of the country like the Northeast—that their state is not as states should be, in turn producing the desire for a change.

In the last ten years, humanitarian aid has arrived in limited form in northeastern CAR. A few international NGOs provide tarps and buckets and food to people who have had to flee their homes due to an attack, and they operate health clinics. This does little to change people's perception that their position is one of abandonment. If anything, it underscores it. As one rebel officer put it, "Me, too, I am discouraged, like the population. NGOs come here and do distributions, but they are just small things. They are mocking us."[7] People should not have to be in the position of needing humanitarian assistance. This is as clear to Central

Africans as it is to those advocating for such aid, and this is true even though the humanitarian assistance is a kind of material largesse people in the area have never before received from statelike actors.

One marker both of the disorder and of a desire for order is the roadblocks that have proliferated in recent years (Schouten and Kalessopo 2017). These are barriers—sometimes a tree trunk or pole, other times whatever sharp debris people have on hand—that are positioned at key spots (usually the edges of towns or villages), such that those wishing to travel by the road (pedestrians might be able to take other routes) must be subjected to some kind of questioning and/or search, and often forced to pay to continue on their journey. Roadblocks may be operated by government forces (soldiers, gendarmes, or police), by rebels, or by entrepreneurial village committees. Northeasterners argue that as they attempt to travel south toward the capital they are subjected to increasing discrimination and extortion at these roadblocks, because the operators see them as dangerous foreigners, not fellow Central Africans. A roadblock is one of the first manifestations of a rebel group, because it provides them with money and a material edifice evocative of a kind of control and presence they wish to project. Roadblocks are, in other words, part of a political repertoire that has meaning for people in the area. People place them both in the political "ought to be" and in the political "as people do." Most agree that the roadblock phenomenon has gotten a bit out of hand, and that traversing them can be stressful and even humiliating (Lombard 2013). But many, if not most, simultaneously argue that roadblocks are absolutely a necessary element of governance, because, if they were well-operated, they would permit a *necessary* control of who and what was circulating in the country.

People thus had almost-contradictory convictions about roadblocks. They were both sites for extortion, and a necessary element of a proper mode of governance. These sentiments were not contradictory, however, because people appealed to the ideal type: roadblocks as they existed were not as they should be, but roadblocks in theory were essential. The ideal roadblock was often described in ways that could be summed up as a kind of professionalism (that is, the separation of personal from public interests, and following rules consistently). But in terms of roadblocks as they exist, the most contested domain is *who* they should regulate, and who should be excepted from regulation. The roadblock becomes "ours"—or at least, *not* "not ours"—for those who are not harassed at it.

When people in northeastern CAR lament their abandonment by the state and express their desires for what a state should be, and what they think their own state should do, they invoke how they have experienced their history and the decline, dispossession, and disorder that they see as attending to their limbo position in the world. I see no reason to evaluate their statements as anything other than sincere, as convictions. And yet when faced with someone trying to control or regulate them, whether that person is a government employee or someone else acting in the name of regulation in a statelike mode, many Central Africans either evade or denounce such efforts. Particularly illustrative in this respect is the case of armed conservation, the largest regulatory initiative in the region from the colonial period onward, the stated goal of the largest aid projects the region has hosted (particularly from the mid-1980s to the mid-2000s, but still today in reduced form), and an agenda that explicitly foments the language and practice of state and sovereignty.

I turn next to these experiences of armed conservation. They show that the desires and values associated with sovereignty can be both held with conviction and, strictly speaking, inconsistent. Pragmatism partly explains this state of affairs. The ideal is so far off that people develop other ways of living, without therefore renouncing the ideal. Another reason is that regulatory practices create moments when the state appears ours, or wrongly not ours. They are moments when, in addition to the practice of aspects of statehood, claims are made about ownership and belonging—claims, that is, about the emotional and affective sides of politics that the concept of sovereign agency gets at. In northeastern CAR, who has the proprietary position of owning/belonging (and thereby enjoys a measure of exception from regulation) and who is disowned/foreign (and thereby subject to egregious regulation) are less settled than elsewhere.

A Brief History of Armed Conservation

Both during the colonial period and after, state officials and their aid donor tutors have identified wildlife as northeastern CAR's primary source of value. Today, fully 31 percent of CAR's territory is designated a "zone of hunting interest" (Binot et al. 2006), and most of that is in the east. Government directives have thus long established strict rules about human entry into protected areas and exploitation of animals. Due to the geographical-relational and human characteristics of the space, and the lack of extension of administrative bureaucracy to the zone, these rules have always been very difficult to enforce. Nevertheless, there have been attempts, and there have been more attempts to enforce rules in the domain of conservation than in other regulatory domains.

In the late 1950s French administrators worried that their territory was being "invaded" by Sudanese hunters and herders and decided to operate patrols with the objective of arresting unwelcome interlopers from the east. The reports sub-mitted upon completion of these "actions de présence" listed not a single arrest. As the colonel leading the patrol mission acknowledged, "It is likely that Suda-nese hunters and herders who might have been met by the detachment slipped away as it approached" (Alain 1960). Nevertheless, another officer argued, the patrols "permitted us to mark the vitality of our sovereignty in the face of Sudan" (Bertin 1958). Colonial reports about northeastern CAR intermittently made use of this Bodinian language of "marking" sovereignty. The officer made marking sovereignty sound like an accomplishment, and perhaps, in its own way, it was. But plenty of other users of the space took little notice, laughed, or otherwise went on using their greater knowledge of the terrain to continue doing as they saw fit. Indeed, the limited extent of anyone's capacity to police such a vast and little-peopled zone has long been a draw for people such as certain foreign hunt-ers who wanted to hunt as they deemed most profitable (Rushby 1965; Le Noël 1999; Roulet 2004).

Until the 1970s, northeastern CAR was a sleepy wilderness beloved by big game hunters (Roulet 2004). But beginning in the 1970s another kind of hunter, those interested in making a profit from selling ivory and other wild goods, started capturing the area's resources. At the same time, the area became increas-ingly attractive to cattle herders, who were already facing pressure in the form of drought in their usual grazing lands to the north. An assortment of people involved in aid to CAR mobilized to combat these unlawful users of the space. In other places where armed conservation has been pursued, conservation has been decidedly a nation-state project (e.g., Kenya [Leakey 2001] or Tanzania [Neumann 1998, 2001]). In contrast, in CAR the people involved in armed con-servation have largely seen "the state" as absent while acting in the name of the state, on its behalf. A wide variety of people (safari hunting guides and their employees; an extrastatal militia organized through a European Union grant; French soldiers; mercenaries funded by a private association that is in turn funded by safari hunters) have been involved in enforcing state dictates.

Nevertheless, the main players in this conservation enforcement scene have been notably stable and persistent, and they have statelike qualities even if they see themselves as not fully part of any state. These are those associated with the European Union–funded conservation projects that began in the mid-1980s and continued, with one gap in funding (2004–7) until the present. In their first two decades, these projects brought massive infrastructure development, primarily in the form of bases (which quickly became villages, if not towns), equipment, and *pistes* (small roads).[8] Since then, due in part to repeated looting and a gen-eral lack of maintenance, the material-construction dimensions of these projects have been more minimal.

Throughout, the projects have been formally attached to the Ministry of Water and Forests but operate substantially autonomously since they have a separate budget and split hierarchy (in theory, they answer to both the ministry and the European Union; in practice, they answer in only partial ways to each). During the fat years, the project had about one hundred tracker-guards working to patrol the parklands. During leaner years, such as the period of my most intensive research in the area, in 2009–10, there were about seventy, and they ranged across an area the size of Portugal. The projects' stated goal of thorough, consistent policing was thus utopian, to put it mildly. But they effectively encouraged people to think of these lands and the life in them as properly under Central African stewardship. It's just that that national category is quite a bit more striated than it might at first appear. As in Sara L. Friedman's discussion of Taiwan in this volume, who counts as national (who belongs, who enjoys privilege) is a key node of contest through which sovereign agency works.

For instance, some foreign herder/hunters pay grazing/hunting taxes to nearby heads of villages for the rights to use the open spaces; others pay similar fees to the personal agents of the area's mayors. They do so with the understanding that these are the proper regulatory agents. Perhaps more important than enforcing national exclusivity in resource use, then, is the attractiveness of how the state can appear "ours" at the moment when its rules no longer apply to "us"—that is, when one can claim exception from regulatory rules. The "treat everyone the same" dictate of bureaucratized regulation runs counter to the allure of the kind of ownership that comes from being exceptional, from being beyond regulation. The importance of this kind of sovereign agency, a variety of liberty, does not negate the parallel allure of being subjected to state control, in the normative senses discussed earlier. The two work together, and even seem to exacerbate each other.

For instance, one morning in Ndele in early 2010 I sat on the verandah of the local office of the Water and Forests Ministry with the idling employees while they talked about the news in Sango, CAR's main language.[9] One of the guards, who I will call Sam, was leading a discussion of a much-talked-about recent incident. Sam stood out among the guards. He dressed better than the others, such as in freshly laundered, name-brand track suits (not the kind of faded or Chinese-knockoff apparel available in Ndele), and he had greater facility with cosmopolitan life (checkbooks, the French language, etc.). He was comfortable in Ndele but also projected the air of someone who knew it was a way station during a career that would move only to more important places.

The incident under discussion concerned a man named Clovis, a fellow Water and Forests employee posted even further north and east than Ndele. Clovis had a leave to go to Bangui, and he hitched a ride on the back of one of the Sudanese commercial trucks that serve as the only transit in the area. Everyone traveling from the Northeast to the capital must gather as much foodstuffs as she can along the road, and especially meat—ideally smoked game meat, because it lasts a long time and has a rich flavor that satisfies. These foodstuffs will be given as gifts to family and friends. Food of all kinds is much more expensive in the capital, and there are beloved "wild" flavors that are therefore hard to obtain. Neglect to bring any food, and you might as well not go at all, because your family will turn you away, people say. Smoked game meat from the Northeast is almost all illegal, however, because the areas around the roads are almost all protected, no-commercial-hunting zones, and because the stack of regulations and permits required to hunt legally (even in open areas) is so onerous and expensive that none but the wealthy foreign safari hunters can afford to obtain or abide by them.

Among his belongings on the truck that day, Clovis carried a sack with smoked meat. The vehicle was stopped by antipoaching guards employed by the conservation project. They demanded to go through the belongings of everyone on board. Clovis was dressed in plain clothes. If he had worn his camouflage work uniform, perhaps he would have appeared "one of us" (that is, not someone to be bothered) to the antipoaching guards. But he did not, and so his things were searched like everyone else. The guards took his sack of meat, even though he carried a laissez-passer document from the Water and Forests chief at Ndele saying he should be allowed to pass unchecked. (Such papers are a service some *kota azo* [big people] provide in order to smooth what can be an arduous journey through roadblocks to the capital; they are an attempt to transfer the deference accorded the person issuing the paper to its bearer [see Lombard 2013, 2020].)

As the story was being told, various participants interjected how angry they would have been if they had been in Clovis's place. Sam said with fervor, "If it were me in Clovis's place, the whole town would know what had happened. I would not let them get away with it [that is, he would use violence against them if necessary]." The secretary noted that she frequently bought meat from the antipoaching guards, a statement she offered as proof of their hypocrisy. She added, "And the paper Clovis got from the head of office here—doesn't that have any value for them? And if tomorrow they were the ones to show up here in front of our authorities [who would, she implied, treat them with the same lack of privilege], how would they feel? It's not right."

Later that morning, I chatted with Sam (in French now) about the conservation strictures for the area. They seemed impossibly harsh to me. How would people get enough to eat if they couldn't hunt? Sam disagreed. The laws were not just fair but served the greater good, he argued. He began an explanation that could have been used for one of the conservation project's reports, so clear and unequivocal was its defense of hunting regulations. He illustrated his points by explaining how much more money people stood to gain by refraining from hunting (that is, from ceding such rights to tourists who would pay vast sums in trophy fees, most of which was devolved to localized councils to allocate for village projects), as opposed to hunting for themselves. I said I was skeptical. He continued to disagree, arguing that what appeared to me draconian prohibitions are a good system for Central Africans, and that such work is an important function for the state to take on.

How should one put together the two sets of equally convincing statements Sam made that morning? He had, first, said he would enact violence against anyone who tried to usurp his ability to hunt and/or transport meat as he saw fit, and then avowed that no Central Africans should be allowed to do such things. One possible interpretation would be to say that the latter comments were the reflection of what he expected I, a foreigner of presumed humanitarian/conservation sympathies, would want to hear—that is, that he averred the stance that would be more likely to bring more aid to CAR. And there was likely an element of that. The tendency to aver a rule or principle while making exceptions for oneself is arguably universal, but it is particularly pronounced in relation to elements of stateness in CAR. State employees in CAR see the rules as important but expect their status—that of state employee—provides exemption from them. Interestingly, according to the hunting laws, the opposite is the case: state employees caught in breach of the law are supposed to be subjected to double the penalties imposed on regular folks. This further supports my contention that the chasm between the normative/formal/legal ideals and the actual fosters the inconsistencies described in this chapter, and that the mechanism at work is sovereign agency. What is desired is to enjoy the proprietary feeling, which consists of a combination of owning/belonging and being excepted from egregious regulation.

Elsewhere (Lombard 2016a), I have argued that Sam's remarks should be understood as a practice of camouflaging: "Camouflage shifts the focus off questions of sincerity (i.e., the idea that one statement was his true sentiment, and the other a put-on, like a mask) and places it on how people productively manage contradictions, blending in with a range of landscapes/surroundings by showing different facets in different settings" (8). Camouflage is a skill that people cultivate, and in doing so they become able to collaborate across a wider range of actors and entities than would otherwise be the case. Camouflage is not a status or position that people get slotted into by powerful state actors keen to elide any discrepancies between the ways they "see" (Scott 1985) their realm and its actual messiness. In northeastern CAR, everyone involved in making things happen and collaborating across long distances—aid officials and roadblock staffers alike—actively find ways to use camouflage because doing so allows them to participate in the landscapes they wish to access. Nor is camouflage necessarily a synonym or analogy for the disorder that attends to statecraft, in the manner of arguments positing that law and disorder are mutually constitutive (Comaroff and Comaroff 2006). Jusionyte, describing practices of camouflaging by the state on the Argentine side of the Tri-Border region, has argued, "In the two scenarios examined here—wearing the mask of law to cover up crime and engaging in crime from a position authorized by law—investigating how state authority supplies the cover for its own deception has proved a constructive way of understanding the state's processual and performative nature" (2015, 132). But that argument does not parse the actors' own understanding of ethics.

Camouflage, as I developed it, allows for the inconsistencies apparent in Sam's various comments that morning without ascribing them to bad faith or trickery. They instead emerge as a version of "contested gridding practices" (Jansen 2014, 243)—that is, contested, or inconsistent, participation in establishing what shall count as normal, ordered routine. But from the perspective of political desires that "may or may not be attached to the state" (as the Introduction to this volume directs us to explore), camouflage displaces a bit the "should"—the moral-aspirational. In so doing it flattens the two opposing values that are at play in Sam's comments. In advocating for the application and enforcement of rigorous state regulation regarding hunting, Sam was echoing the comments cited earlier in this chapter by people who decried state abandonment and asserted that "normal" states care for and protect their citizens while also controlling movement and preventing national dispossession. In protesting that hunting and meat transport should not be policed, Sam was instead arguing for liberty, conceived in the "negative" (Berlin 1969) sense of freedom from molestation in one's projects. The importance of liberty becomes clear in looking at incidents when people in northeastern CAR have stepped away from practices of camouflage to instead denounce what they see as egregious regulatory overreach (Lombard 2018). And the positive side of negative liberty is that it can be a vehicle for the desire for the realm of the political to feel like it is "ours," a variety of sovereign agency.

Liberty Desire

Isaiah Berlin (1969) distinguished between what he called positive liberty, which is freedom to pursue one's vision of the good life, and negative liberty, which is freedom from molestation by others as one goes about one's projects. It is this latter meaning that is most readily apparent among actors in northeastern CAR. People accord liberty importance in discourse, and its importance is also discernible in people's actions. One can locate hints that there might be ethnoregional roots to the value of liberty in contentions such as Graeber's about the divine kings the region has historically been known for: "What most Africans ask of their sacred kings is what most Europeans demand of their welfare states: health, prosperity, a certain level of life security, protection from natural disasters.... However, most do not feel it necessary or desirable to grant them police powers in order to accomplish this. The question of governance, then, is not the same as the question of sovereignty" (Graeber 2011, 6–7). But certainly more important has been the area's purgatory position in relation to statehood. Formally part of a state but effectively largely outside administrative control, any would-be centralizing or policing projects have been far more coercive and brutal than they are in places where regulatory authority is less materially impoverished and/or less contested, and it therefore makes sense that people would resist.

From the colonial era onward, two main traits have defined a person's relationship to state coercion and control. One is whether the person draws a state salary and thereby has a material entitlement from the state (Lombard 2016b). The other is whether one can claim exception from regulation. The state in Equatorial Africa has always been privatized. During the colonial period most of the region's territory was leased to private companies to exploit (and, effectively, regulate) for their own profit (Coquéry-Vidrovitch 1972). Or think of Bokassa's "presidential park," a playground for his exclusive enjoyment. In a sense, then, for those who are "in," there is an excess of the sovereign agency of feeling like the state is "ours," and a deficit for everyone else. The sense that CAR is falling behind encourages people to think that their state is not as it should be, and encourages the related desire for a controlling, regulating state that does not make exceptions and that is not so privatized. But the desire, or even need, to belong among those enjoying liberty remains. An example from the days of more-intensive antipoaching and conservation efforts shows how desire for statelike programs coexists with a desire for liberty. Claiming liberty is a process of declaring an exception for those who participate in making the claim, and it can contain an effervescent "ours."

Idongo was the conservation projects' model village.[10] It was a model both because residents were so enthusiastic about implementing the conservation project's terms and because it lay near the most profitable safari hunting concessions, which meant they stood to gain more revenue from safari hunting taxes. These factors combined to make the scheme seem more viable in Idongo than elsewhere, and conservation project staff hoped that its success would inspire others. Early accounts were positive and made it as far as the French press. One article in 2003 noted that conservation had brought modern forms of state largesse to Idongo: "The elderly have the right to a small pension" (AFP 2003).

Later in 2003, antipoaching guards caught several people from Idongo hunting in a protected area. The guards seized the men's guns. The next night, the guards caught Idongo's conservation committee president's son, as well as a few others, in the act of hunting. The guards jailed all of the men. The following morning a crowd of Idongo residents, joined by people from neighboring villages, rushed onto the conservation project base.[11] They attempted to take the guards' weapons. They succeeded in destroying the radio post. Some shot their own guns. No one was seriously injured, but at least one guard had his clothes torn.

Not every incident of regulation by the antipoaching guards was denounced in this manner. In the archives covering these armed conservation projects, I came across many legal statements and other accounts of dispossession and even killing by antipoaching guards that were followed by no outcry. The mobilization in this case probably owed at least in part to the fact that it was a person with extensive social relations—the local president's son—who had been targeted. Those relations could be entreated to stand up. After some negotiations, the conservation project staff released the Idongans they had arrested. A mostly unspoken entente was at work. (It was unspoken in the sense of being a "known unknown" [Geissler 2013] that was indecorous, but not taboo, to mention.) The entente's content was essentially that everyone should try to give each other space to pursue their projects. As the Sango expression puts it, "I look but I don't see" (*Mbi bâ, mais mbi bâ pépé*) (Lombard 2016a). Put otherwise, they were in the same space and could not avoid looking around, but they would nevertheless neglect to draw conclusions about what became apprehensible as a result of that looking around. In that way, they would not have to be consistent in the application of principle, whether those of the legal-formal realm or any other that might compete with "live and let live."

But let us return briefly to the Idongans' actions. They communicated that they—the people participating—could not be treated like that, could not be subjected to such regulatory overreach. In rejecting what had been done to them they gained a measure of the proprietary feeling. They gained a sense, perhaps fleeting, of being part of a "we" and of having ownership of it. Acts like theirs commonly get glossed as vengeance. And that is likely a factor. But it is not the only one. Because in addition to any "eye-for-an-eye" desires to punish, Idongans also sought to demonstrate that they could not be subjected to the kind of treatment the conservation project staff was attempting to put in place.

That treatment, from another perspective, is a good example of the kinds of statelike practices of control and regulation that people in the region see as proper, and in relation to which people see themselves as abandoned. To be fair, one should not be too quick to pack all statelike things into one category of stateness. Central Africans might appreciate certain statelike capacities while refusing others. And Central Africans would likely explain away the apparent inconsistencies through reference to the disparity between statelike capacities as they *should be implemented* and statelike capacities as they *are implemented* in their midst. They would be correct to draw this distinction, for the people who claim to be their leaders and civil servants depart massively from the ideals they themselves espouse, and from the laws they themselves pass. However, Central Africans' explanations have a tendency to underplay their own roles in maintaining these disparities. I do not recount their stories in order to apportion blame for what Central Africans see as the suboptimal politics of their country. I do so to allow us to pause and consider that a person might desire two (or more) different political values at once, with similar or equal fervor, and the related obligation to connect discourse and practice without turning such a project into a "gotcha" operation. In doing so, one finds that what is desired when sovereign agency is desired—such as liberty—can undermine state effects—such as consistent control and regulation—in the process generating both greater inconsistency and solidarity (though often of a fleeting nature) among those who participate in the quest for sovereign agency.

When presented with contradictory convictions or practice, a common response among those seeking to understand and explain has been to dissolve "one pole of the paradox": "Their response to finding two apparently contradictory phenomena in the world is to insist that one of them cannot be true" (Steinberg 2013, 499, 501). That is, it has been to say that one side of the issue has been insincerely presented, or else is a mask for something else, or simply does not exist in the way people talk about it. People in northeastern CAR present us with perhaps especially contradictory, or paradoxical, understandings of everyday sovereignty. I argue, following Steinberg, that it is not enough to dissolve one side of their ideas and practices about sovereignty—either the desire for state welfare and security, or the desire for liberty. But if CAR is a particularly striking case, it is so not because it is different, but because it reveals something at work elsewhere but generally not recognized.

Many accounts of peasant politics instead dissolve one pole of the paradox, such as by presenting their interlocutors as at best tolerant of state authority, and as *really* deploying "weapons of the weak" (Scott 1985) or otherwise finding ways to resist, despite having to pretend to want the state in public settings. David Graeber is prototypical in his approach:

> Let me make a broad generalization. Confronted with someone bent on imposing unwanted authority, a typical Malagasy response will be to agree heartily with whatever demands that person makes, and then, as soon as they are gone, to try to go on living one's life as if the incident had never happened. . . . Something along these lines is often considered a typically "peasant" strategy: it is an obvious course to take when one is in no way economically dependent on those trying to tell one what to do. But there are many other routes to take, all sorts of possible combinations of confrontation, negotiation, subversion, acquiescence (Graeber 2007, 167).

Notably, on this extensive list, nothing on the spectrum of participation or welcome or excitement is included as part of the mix, in part because the "state authority" has been defined as "unwanted." But what if it is *both* wanted and unwanted? Central Africans are not insincere or simply self-serving in the desires and actions they express and undertake in relation to political projects. Here as elsewhere, inconsistency can be a constitutive aspect of politics. Of course, there may be times when Central Africans, again just like people everywhere, are insincere or self-serving. But a position of analytical moral superiority is never enough of an answer, since it relies on assigning a prior lack of truth to one's interlocutors' statements while preserving one's own.

In northeastern CAR, and arguably in contested state spaces more broadly, the gap between the formal/legal realm of statehood (what is "on the books") and the experience of statehood (the people and programs attempting to augment state-like capacities) is experienced as cavernous. Moreover, it has become increasingly difficult to ignore the conceptions of statehood ideally incarnated in the normative visions of things like the Human Development rankings.[12] Faced with these dynamics, the realm of deontological ethics, of ethics-through-consistency, becomes both drained and strained. But this does not mean that people never feel the state to be (however fleetingly) theirs, or unfairly not theirs. What is particularly pronounced in northeastern CAR is the changeable nature of "ours," which is not neatly aligned with formal citizenship but instead moves according to who can claim exception and liberty. Statehood-limbo makes it impossible to *either* reject or enjoy—whether in conviction or in practice—the utopian vision provided by normative conceptions of statehood. People get caught in between, and so are desires for legibility and recognition beyond this space, at the same time as their position is not wholly unfree. The old observation that sovereignty and state should not be conflated (Radcliffe-Brown 1940), and that both are essential to politics, remains true. Indeed, a future direction might be to explore the ways that sovereign agency and state capacity (for control, order, coercion) can run counter to each other, such as in the case when belonging is in flux and state authority is contested.

Notes

1. According to the 2003 census, Vakaga, the northeasternmost prefecture, had a population of 37,595 and an area of 46,500 square kilometers; in Bamingui-Bangoran, that ratio is 38,437/58,200, and in Haut-Kotto it is 69,514/86,650.

2. Sango-speakers say "Ala tourné peko na i"—you/they turned your/their backs on us, which gives the same sense of a move taken away from a position of some regard.

3. "Truly nationalistic" in the sense of launching national projects like a youth corps and otherwise cultivating nationalistic sentiment.

4. It has been unused since, but no one would take me there since it is legally only for the president (which does not mean Central Africans cannot use the area, only that bringing a foreigner there would draw unwanted notice).

5. As depicted, for instance, in Werner Herzog's 1990 film *Echoes from a Sombre Empire*.

6. He spoke in French, and the word he used, several times, was "la misère," which has an insistent plaintiveness that the aid-speak "pauvrété" lacks.

7. Of course, statements like his must be understood in context: in addition to describing his own feelings, he most likely saw this conversation as an opportunity to advocate on behalf of people in his region, since I in different ways (through my publications, as well as informal conversations) transmit messages to aid donors.

8. This is a relative descriptor, of course. The inputs were massive in the context of "abandonment," but would have been less remarkable in most other places.

9. I also discuss Sam's storytelling in Lombard 2016a, 2020.

10. I also recount these events in Lombard 2018, 2020.

11. Eyewitness accounts I collected ranged from eighty to three hundred; counting and estimating people in a crowd is not something people in this area frequently do, so the estimates are likely not very precise. The key fact they all wished to impart was that there were many people, and that they were a match for the antipoaching guards.

12. In reflecting on a heated conversation with an imam in rural Egypt, Amitav Ghosh presented a different side of the dilemmas faced by formerly colonized peoples in relating to each other and the world:

> Instead, to make ourselves understood, we had both resorted, I, a student of the "humane" sciences, and he, an old-fashioned village Imam, to the very terms that world leaders and statesmen use at great, global conferences, the universal, irresistible metaphysic of modern meaning; he had said to me, in effect: "You ought not to do what you do, because otherwise you will not have guns and tanks and bombs." It was the only language we had been able to discover in common. (Ghosh 1993)

References

AFP (Agence France-Presse). 2003. "A Idongo, les anciens ont même droit à une petite pension." Bangui: AFP.

Alain, Colonel. 1960. Letter: "A Monsieur le Général de Corps d'Armée, Commandant Supérieur de la Zone d'Outre-mer No 2; Etat-Major 3eme bureau. Objet: Campagne de Birao 1960." Brazzaville. No. 210/CSC.3/SC. Vincennes, Service historique de l'armée de la terre. Carton 6H 47.

Anghie, Antony. 2005. *Imperialism, Sovereignty, and the Making of International Law*. Cambridge: Cambridge University Press.

Appel, Hannah. 2017. "Toward an Ethnography of the National Economy." *Cultural Anthropology* 32(2): 294–322.

Bartelson, Jens. 1995. *A Genealogy of Sovereignty*. Cambridge: Cambridge University Press.

Bayart, Jean-François. 2000. "Africa in the World: A History of Extraversion." *African Affairs* 99(395): 217–267.

Berlin, Isaiah. 1969. *Four Essays on Liberty*. Oxford: Oxford University Press.

Bertin, Colonel. 1958. Note de Service # 806/3/S. Objet: Campagne de Birao. December 31. Service Historique de l'Armée de la Terre (SHAT) 6H 47.

Bey, Hakim. 2003 (1985). *T.A.Z.: The Temporary Autonomous Zone, Ontological Anarchy, Poetic Terrorism*. New York: Autonomedia.

Binot, Aurélie, Vincent Castel, and Alexandre Caron. 2006. "L'interface faune-bétail en Afrique Subsaharienne." *Science et changements planétaires/Sécheresse* 17(1): 349–361.

Bordier. 1959. Note: A l'attention de Monsieur le Chef du District Autonome de BIRAO. De: Haut Commissariat après de la République Centrafricaine. Cabinet Militaire. No. 208/CM.BE Bangui, February 5. SHAT, 6 H 47.

Brégeon, Jean-Joël. 1998. *Un Rêve d'Afrique: Administrateurs En Oubangui-Chari: La Cendrillon de l'Empire*. Paris: Denoël.

Cattelino, Jessica. 2008. *High Stakes: Florida Seminole Gaming and Sovereignty*. Durham, NC: Duke University Press.

Ceriana Mayneri, Andrea. 2014. *Sorcellerie et prophétisme en Centrafrique: l'imaginaire de la dépossession en pays banda*. Paris: Karthala.

Collins, Robert O. 1960. "The Transfer of the Lado Enclave to the Anglo-Egyptian Sudan, 1910." *Zaïre: Révue Congolaise* 14(2–3): 193–210.

Comaroff, Jean, and John L. Comaroff. 2006. "Law and Disorder in the Postcolony: An Introduction." In *Law and Disorder in the Postcolony*, edited by Jean Comaroff and John L. Comaroff, 1–56. Chicago: University of Chicago Press.

Cordell, Dennis D. 1985. *Dar Al-Kuti and the Last Years of the Trans-Saharan Slave Trade*. Madison: University of Wisconsin Press.

Coquéry-Vidrovitch, Catherine. 1972. *Le Congo au temps des grandes compagnies concessionnaires, 1898–1930*. Paris: Mouton.

Dunn, Kevin C. 2009. "Environmental Security, Spatial Preservation, and State Sovereignty in Central Africa." In *The State of Sovereignty: Territories, Laws, Populations*, edited by Douglas Howland and Luise White, 222–242. Bloomington: Indiana University Press.

Fortes, Meyer, and E. E. Evans-Pritchard. 1940. "Introduction." In *African Political Systems*, edited by E. E. Evans-Pritchard and Meyer Fortes, 1–23. Oxford: Clarendon.

Gallo, Thierry. 1996. *Les oisifs de Birao: S'évader ou périr*. Paris: L'Harmattan.

Geissler, Paul Wenzel. 2013. "Public Secrets in Public Health: Knowing Not to Know While Making Scientific Knowledge." *American Ethnologist* 40(1): 13–34.

Ghosh, Amitav. 1993. *In An Antique Land: History in the Guise of a Traveler's Tale*. New York: Vintage.

Ghosh, Amitav. 1994. "The Global Reservation: Notes Toward an Ethnography of International Peacekeeping." *Cultural Anthropology* 9(3): 412–422.

Graeber, David. 2007. *Possibilities: Essays on Hierarchy, Rebellion, and Desire.* Chico, CA: AK Press.

Graeber, David. 2011. "The Divine Kingship of the Shilluk: On Violence, Utopia, and the Human Condition, Or, Elements for an Archaeology of Sovereignty." *HAU: Journal of Ethnographic Theory* 1(1): 1–62.

Jansen, Stef. 2014. "Hope for/Against the State: Gridding in a Besieged Sarajevo Suburb." *Ethnos* 79(2): 238–260.

Jansen, Stef. 2015. *Yearnings in the Meantime: "Normal Lives" and the State in a Sarajevo Apartment Complex.* New York: Berghahn.

Jusionyte, Ieva. 2015. "States of Camouflage." *Cultural Anthropology* 30(1): 113–138.

Laidlaw, James. 2013. *The Subject of Virtue: An Anthropology of Ethics and Freedom.* Cambridge: Cambridge University Press.

Leakey, Richard, and Virginia Morell. 2001. *Wildlife Wars: My Fight to Save Africa's Natural Treasures.* New York: Macmillan.

Le Noël, Christian. 1999. *On Target: History and Hunting in Central Africa.* Agoura Hills, CA: Trophy Room Books.

Lignier. 1936. Rapport du 3e trimestre 1936. Ndele, le 30 septembre 1936. ANOM, AEF, GGAEF, D/4(3)/48.

Lombard, Louisa. 2013. "Navigational Tools for Central African Roadblocks." *PoLAR: Political and Legal Anthropology Review* 36(1): 157–173.

Lombard, Louisa. 2015. "The Autonomous Zone Conundrum." In *Making Sense of the Central African Republic,* edited by Tatiana Carayannis and Louisa Lombard, 142–165. London: Zed.

Lombard, Louisa. 2016a. "Camouflage: The Hunting Origins of Worlding in Africa." *Journal of Contemporary African Studies* 34(1): 147–164.

Lombard, Louisa. 2016b. "The Threat of Rebellion: Claiming Entitled Personhood in Central Africa." *Journal of the Royal Anthropological Institute* 22(3): 552–569.

Lombard, Louisa. 2016c. *State of Rebellion: Violence and Intervention in the Central African Republic.* London: Zed.

Lombard, Louisa. 2018. "Denouncing Sovereignty: Claims to Liberty in Northeastern Central African Republic." *Comparative Studies in Society and History* 60(4): 1066–1095.

Lombard, Louisa. 2020. *Hunting Game: Raiding Politics in the Central African Republic.* Cambridge: Cambridge University Press.

Mollion, Pierre. 1992. *Sur Les Pistes de l'Oubangui-Chari Au Tchad, 1890–1930: Le Drame Du Portage En Afrique Centrale.* Paris: L'Harmattan Edition.

Neumann, Roderick P. 1998. *Imposing Wilderness: Struggles over Livelihood and Nature Preservation in Africa.* Berkeley: University of California Press.

Neumann, Roderick P. 2004. "Moral and Discursive Geographies in the War for Biodiversity in Africa." *Political Geography* 23(7): 813–837.

Olin, Nathaniel. 2015. "Pathologies of Peacekeeping and Peacebuilding in CAR." *Making Sense of the Central African Republic,* edited by Tatiana Carayannis and Louisa Lombard, 194–218. London: Zed.

Radcliffe-Brown, A. R. 1940. "Preface." In *African Political Systems,* edited by E. E. Evans-Pritchard and Meyer Fortes, xi–xxiii. Oxford: Clarendon.

Roulet, Pierre-Armand. 2004. "Chasseur Blanc, Coeur Noir"? La Chasse Sportive En Afrique Centrale. Une Analyse de Son Rôle Dans La Conservation de La Faune Sauvage et Le Développement Rural Au Travers Des Programmes de Gestion

Communautaire. Les Cas Du Nord RCA et Du Sud-Est Cameroun." Ph.D. diss., Université d'Orléans.

Rushby, George. 1965. *No More the Tusker*. London: W. H. Allen.

Schouten, Peer, and Soleil Kalessopo. 2017. *The Politics of Pillage: The Political Economy of Roadblocks in the Central African Republic*. Antwerp: IPIS.

Scott, James C. 1985. *Weapons of the Weak: Everyday Forms of Peasant Resistance*. New Haven: Yale University Press.

Steinberg, Jonny. 2013. "Working Through a Paradox About Sexual Culture in South Africa: Tough Sex in the Twenty-First Century." *Journal of Southern African Studies* 39(3): 497–509.

Taussig, Michael. 1992. *The Nervous System*. New York: Routledge.

"BECAUSE I HAVE A HOOKUP"

Cheating Citizens and the Unbearable State in Post-Dayton Bosnia-Herzegovina

Azra Hromadžić

On a sunny afternoon in October 2005, I visited Davor in his Mostar apartment.[1] We were soon joined by several other students from the Mostar Gymnasium where I was doing research at the time. In the middle of our hanging out, Davor's mother came into the room where we were sitting and reminded Davor that he had to study for the exam. Davor smiled, gestured toward his cell phone and said: "I am all ready." Everyone laughed, including Davor's mother, who, her voice serious, but her lips disclosing a glimpse of a smile, said: "It would be better if you actually learned something . . ." I sensed that there was a (hi)story that made this joke possible, so I asked Davor to explain it to me. He said that last year, at the end of the third grade (US eleventh grade, seventeen years old), he failed in German. He had one more opportunity to pass the grade at the end of summer by taking an oral exam. So, he grew his curly and thick hair long in order to cover a *buba* (bug)—the wireless headphone attached to his cell phone—and he passed the oral exam by secretly calling a friend, repeating the question to her, and having her slowly read the text that he then clumsily pronounced after her.

While I was initially surprised by Davor's mother's reaction and the fact that the teacher appeared not to detect this almost overt cheating performance,[2] what astonished me even more was Davor's extensive bragging about his cheating savvy.[3] I sensed that these discursively exaggerated and widely accepted practices and articulations of what my informants referred to as *prepisivanje* (cheating, copying) were telling a complicated story about Bosnia's postwar predicament,[4] a story that is at the heart of this chapter.[5]

Cheating, I argue here, provides a window onto citizens' responses to the unbearable, externally made, and internationally supervised—thus only formally sovereign—Bosnian state that emerged from the 1992–1995 war and socialism. Bosnia is one of the most bureaucratically layered, fragmented, expensive, and politically complicated states in the world. Paradoxically, it is both massive in terms of bureaucracy prone to corruption, and "empty" in terms of sovereignty and citizen identification (see Hromadžić 2015a). As a result, this unbearable state generates massive disillusionment among its citizens, especially youth (Hromadžić 2015a; Greenberg 2014), a great number of whom left the country, or plan to leave it, for places—real or imagined—where the future is ostensibly more certain (Hromadžić 2018b).

In what follows I use complex and seemingly contradictory cheating discourses and practices as a lens through which to approach youth's enactments and performances of sovereign agency and (anti-)citizenship in the unbearable state in Bosnia-Herzegovina.

More specifically, I argue that cheating practices and discourses should be interpreted as two-fold. They constitute a powerful critique of and distancing from what I refer to below as the Bosnian "democratic predicament," a democracy gone wrong. At the same time, they are a historically and socially situated desire for incorporation (what Jansen [2015] calls "gridding") into the corrupt state. As will become clear below, Bosnian student cheaters often described their cheating savvy, purchasing of exams, and use of *veze* (connections) as a way to be "sovereign," by which I mean recognized, visible, and incorporated within the contours of the broken state. This is a context saturated with disillusionment, mistrust, corruption, and discontent. As a result, the focus on cheating as sovereign agency shows how the state, however "empty," becomes operative in part through the affective registers of students' duplicitousness—yearning, anger, desire, and despair, all at once (Introduction, this volume).

Contours of the Unbearable State

Over the past decades, the anthropology of the state has turned from a focus only on the state's cultural construction, the ways in which it appears as coherent and singular (Gupta 1995), to also looking at how citizens construct relations with the state in everyday life (Sharma and Gupta 2006, 11). On the one hand, corruption may provide a means to maneuver the state, but on the other hand it may provide an important discourse for critiquing the state. Akhil Gupta (1995), for instance, argues that corruption works as a powerful grammar through which people communicate their worries, anxieties, hopes, and ideas, as well as develop strategies to face and maneuver the world around them. Nowhere are these multilayered and contradictory processes and experiences of the (corrupt) state possibly more visible than in simultaneously postwar and postsocialist Bosnia-Herzegovina and its *democratic predicament*.

I understand Bosnia's democratic predicament as a complex set of feelings and beliefs, born out of practice, disillusionment, and imagination that portray and understand Bosnian democracy as "gone wrong," a democracy that is fundamentally undemocratic. These seemingly contradictory critiques of and desires for incorporation into the corrupt state illuminate student-citizens' prolonged disappointment and disillusionment with democracy as a predicament and, to some extent, with themselves.

This sentiment of an undemocratic democracy is informed by two interrelated sets of processes; one "political" and the other "economic." Politically, there are irreconcilable tensions at the heart of the Dayton Peace Agreement which, after three and a half years of war, brought peace and international supervision to Bosnia-Herzegovina in 1995.[6] First, the agreement put sovereign power in the hands of the "international community," not Bosnian citizens.[7] This means that Bosnia-Herzegovina has been subject to transnational governmentality (Ferguson and Gupta 2002), a mode of governmentality, arising from the Dayton Agreement, that places the postwar Bosnian state in the political and legal hands of an international diplomatic, military, and economic elite (Chandler 1999). For example, the principal international actor coordinating civilian aspects of the Bosnian transition and recovery has been the Office of High Representative, an ad hoc international institution set up to implement the Dayton peace plan. The High Representative is the highest civilian authority in the country and is also the European Union's Special Envoy. The office is therefore invested with the ultimate power of decision making,[8] including dismissal of noncooperative but democratically elected local politicians.[9]

Second, the agreement favored the idea of one unified Bosnia, but it inserted a consociational model of power-sharing democracy that legitimized and institutionalized war-produced ethnic fragmentation. The ethnicization of the postwar state, which has been widely critiqued, when coupled with transnational governmentality, contributes to the experience that the Bosnian state and its people are not sovereign but that their destinies are determined by *stranci* (foreigners).[10] The state is thus paradoxical—both emptied of its real citizens (who are reduced to ethnic collectivities) and omnipresent, since it is bureaucratically massive.

In addition, installing this extremely complicated, malfunctioning, and expensive bureaucratic machinery provided a fertile context for excessive corruption by the ethnonational elites.[11] Most of these elites are individuals who gained power during the war through unlawful means, while advocating the ethnic cause

(Hromadžić 2015a; Kurtović and Hromadžić 2017; Mujanović 2018). They successfully manipulated the existing ethnonational sentiments to mask their corruption, leading many Bosnians to cynically observe that their postwar democracy is a pretense, covering its essentially undemocratic, corrupt, elite-favoring nature.

In vernacular discourses, this is sometimes explained as the country being run by *lopovi* (thieves), mafia, and *tajkuni* (tycoons), who are the only ones who are "truly sovereign" in practice and who manipulate people's fear of ethnic others for their own economic benefit. In that way the state institutions and illegal groups often form "unruly coalitions" where these illicit groups project control and exist as legitimate protectors and representatives of territories and people. In addition, they simultaneously help, protect, and abuse people in their areas of influence, while at the same time representing the state and the law (Verdery 1996). One good example of this is Hamdo "Tigar," a current representative in Bihać, a city located in the northwestern pocket of the country. This celebrated war hero tirelessly defended the city during the war and frequently shared food with people, while simultaneously engaging in prolific black market smuggling and constant terrorizing of the population though excessive violence, fear, and threat.

Many people compare the new, chaotic situation to socialist times, by saying, "The communists were thieves, but not like these guys." This attitude is nicely captured in the following comment posted on the Internet forum *reci.ba*: "The communist pilfered but gave us some as well, the ones [elites] today give us nothing."[12] This person points at the ambiguous and contextual nature of morality: there is (former socialist) corruption that is acceptable, and there is the present-day corruption (in democracy) that is wrong. The rules of what is acceptable change over time. For example, historically, obligations to kin and friends have been rooted in a moral economy that often privileges these relationships over duties to the state (see chapter 1, this volume). The issue with the new economies of morality is that they violate these long-standing social obligations because the new elites use their connections and networks solely for self-advancement, unscrupulously and insatiably. In other words, the new elites do not share with those they are "supposed to" help.[13] Therefore, one of the aspects of people's frustrations with the new forms of corruption in democracy is not only that they are immoral but that they disrespect the old, accepted forms of corrupt but ethically acceptable behavior, leaving *narod* (people, common folk) disoriented and disenchanted, without a "pattern" to follow. Josip, a jobless, middle-aged informant of mine, tellingly captured this sense of disorientation and disappointment, when, in response to my question about his job search, he said: "Ma pusti, Azra, razočarao sam se u ljude" (Let go, Azra, I am disappointed in people).

In addition to expressing frustration and anguish, Josip's comment illustrates how the postwar and postsocialist disenchantment is not limited to "the political" (ethnic group politics, elites, etc.); rather, it seeps into the "ordinary" lives, one's most intimate beliefs and self-orientations, signaling the limitation of the social world as one knows it. Under these conditions, many Bosnians lament, being a "just" person becomes almost impossible. As Samir, a youth from Mostar, bluntly put it, "Ako si pošten, najebao si" (if you are honest, you are fucked). I heard numerous Bosnians complain about being compelled, attracted, and resigned to participate in corruption and, at the same time, feeling frustrated, disappointed, and betrayed by their own actions, thus fostering a belief that "they are no longer normal agents capable of moral action in the world" (Greenberg 2011, 89). This causes much cynicism and related distancing of Bosnian citizens, especially youth, from their corrupt state and its democratic predicament. At the same time, by dislocating agency to context, these students were able to claim innocence and lack of power, while engaging in masterful and conspicuous cheating practices.

Furthermore, what puzzled me most about Josip's and Samir's remarks is a perceived paradox at the heart of the complaint: that the war-generated "immoralities" not only stretched into the postwar "democratic" times, but that they were amplified, becoming the basis for new intimacies, subjectivities, and political agency. Intrigued by the negativity of vernacular connotations of peace, democratization, and late capitalism, I asked Enver, a sixty-year-old acquaintance of mine, who had a reputation as being an honest *komunjara* (derogative for a communist), for an explanation. He told me that most people, when talking about injustices that make up their everyday life, somewhat cynically say: "Well, that is capitalism!" often followed by: "You wanted democracy, here you have it!" People's stories thus indicate that in general "things got worse" since the war ended. Enver, semi-jokingly and semiprophetically concluded: "They say that we are trotting behind Europe. We skipped Europe and its democracy!" He paused and said, while laughing: "I otišli u helać!" (And went straight to hell/chaos). This comment evaluates the current Bosnian situation in relation to a particular (post)democratic imaginary that already puts Bosnia-Herzegovina spatially/temporally "beyond" democracy.[14] One reaction to the perceived increase in disorder and injustice that ordinary people link to their postwar and postsocialist democracy is the widespread, humorous, and ironic call for the return of *Titin pendrek* (Tito's baton)—the powerful symbol of Tito's police state and dictatorial control—to take care of contemporary tycoons and other "corrupt leaders." In this way, Bosnians are critiquing their democratic (dis)order by pointing to the need for a greater, Titoesque mode of sovereign discipline and order making, even if they do not want socialism per se to return (Velikonja 2009). These "nostalgic" and seemingly humorous invocations of Tito's rule are not oriented toward the past, however, but rather serve as powerful critiques of the present experiences of democratic, capitalist, and moral complexities and predicaments, characterized by the *lack of a system.*

The Vanishing System

Numerous Bosnians explain and evaluate the profound ideological, political, economic, and social changes that shape their corrupt state and democratic predicament by pointing at the collapse of the system—during the Yugoslav times, they explain, there was a system of values, rules, and practices that was enforced, lived, and embodied. In Bosnia, the war and the end of socialism all but destroyed this order, creating massive social, economic, and moral ruptures that resulted in what felt like an existential crisis, "forcing good people to behave unethically" (Greenberg 2011, 89). As a result, I was told, while Bosnians remain generally hospitable and straightforward people, Bosnian youth, who came of age without the system, are morally "rotten," and the logic continues, refugees are "thieves," ex-communists are "hypocritical and naïve," villagers are "backwards" (see Hromadžić 2018a), and politicians only care about themselves. "In conclusion," said one teacher at the Mostar Gymnasium where I conducted much of my research (see Hromadžić 2015a), "Narod je jadan i pokvaren do srži" (People are wretched and rotten to the core).

This lived disappointment with the Bosnian state and its democracy is often contrasted to a democratic *ideal*, which, according to my informants, is just in principle, where there is *uređena država* (an organized state with the rule of law) that recognizes the sovereignty of the narod (people, common folk), and where everyone respects the rule of law. Without these components, Bosnia-Herzegovina, some of my informants argued, could not become a *real* democracy and, the logic goes, they could not become real democratic citizens. For example, Enver explained to me why he felt their democracy was not *prava* (right):

> Stranci [foreigners or internationals] have a final say about our lives. Sometimes this seems necessary to me because we have those lopovi [thieves; local political elites] [in charge]. They only manipulate people's fears of another war. But, remember, it is Dayton [Peace Agreement] that allows for this manipulation. So, the whole thing is wrong . . . we have *lažnu demokratiju* [fake democracy].

Enver is not alone in this sentiment; Igor, a sport policymaker in his mid-thirties, added another dimension to this disillusionment with democracy:

> If someone does something wrong to me, I have nowhere to turn to. I can go to the police . . . but if the person who did me wrong has good connections, my case will disappear. As if I do not exist. I will see the guy next day walking around, *pun sebe* [full of himself]. *Gdje to ima?*

[Where else does this exist?]. . . . And that is what is different about you and me. In *Amerika* [the United States] where you live, people feel a sense of entitlement and you believe, fundamentally, in your system. You believe that you can write to your congressman or your senator. Try sending a letter to one of our politicians—people would call you a fool, say that you lost your mind, that you are wasting paper.

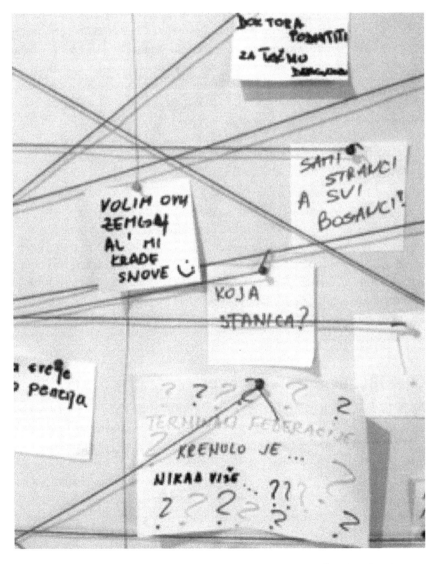

FIGURE 5.   "I love my country, but it is stealing my dreams ☺" Mapping the Crisis Exhibit. Bihać, August 2014. Photo by Azra Hromadžić.

These comments by Enver and Igor resonate with multiple other characterizations of the democratic present that I observed in the field and that hint at the tension: the contradiction between what is experienced as the unbearable, corrupt state that generates a democratic predicament without a proper system (rule of law), and some better, system-supported democracy elsewhere, maybe nowhere (in Enver's case, the United States where the rule of law is allegedly in place). This profound disillusionment with the unbearable state produces a form of political imagination that sharply distinguishes between *here* and *now* (i.e., a corrupt and undemocratic state in Bosnia) and *there* and *then* (an imagined and real "West"), where *država je uređena* (the state is ordered), where economic security is reachable and where "proper democratic citizenship" is practicable (see Hromadžić 2015a).[15] This disillusionment that feeds the desire and expectation to leave or want to leave the current state was beautifully encapsulated by Sanja, a student at the University of Bihać, who said: "Professor, I want to *try* to stay, but I do not know how," indicating the difficulty of staying within the country that, as another student wrote, "You love but that steals your dreams."[16]

This disillusionment with the state also provides a background against which the youth I befriended could simultaneously critique and engage in an active maneuvering and perpetuation of the current system. By invoking multiple temporalities and geographies of citizenship, youth were able to claim innocence and lack of agency ("the context makes us do this . . .") where their prolific cheating becomes a *performance*—reaction to the state "here and now." This discursive strategy allows youth to position themselves as moral and truly sovereign citizens in the future, elsewhere, while engaging in elaborate cheating in the lived present.

Cheating as Sovereign Agency

While there is much contemporary discussion about cheating in media and in the economics literature, scholarly treatment of cheating, especially in anthropology, is still relatively scarce. Some of these works attempt to bring clarity to the notions and definitions of cheating. For example, in his article "Cheating," Stuart Green (2004) defines the concept of cheating, while also exploring its rules and mechanics, the links between various forms of cheating, and the relationship between cheating and other "morally wrongful" acts, such as "stealing, promise-breaking, deceiving, disobedience, and disloyalty" (Green 2004, 137).[17] Furthermore, in his alarmingly titled article "An Epidemic of Cheating?" Chisholm (1992) focuses on the "who and why" of cheating and provides some ideas about how to treat, discourage, and punish different forms of academic dishonesty—actions that he finds necessary and morally obligatory in order to honor those students who do not cheat.

Unlike these relatively abstract, normative, and acontextual studies of cheating, the emerging anthropological and philosophical studies that focus on these practices demonstrate the need to link cheating practices to their wider political, social, and economic environments (see especially Blum 2009). For example, in their work "Cheating the Academy as Solidarity," philosophers Colombo and Vlasak (2010) contrast the "traditional model" of academia where education is understood as "good-in-itself," to the currently prevalent model of "instrumental rationality," where education becomes a "means to an end" (i.e., getting a job). The authors argue that the recent trends in US education are moving toward the latter direction, leading them to ask: "Might cheating then be seen as a form of solidarity among students as they collectively navigate and actively resist this oppressive institution [academia]?" (Colombo and Vlasak 2011, 1). Colombo and Vlasak thus examine an important and shifting relationship between solidarity, morality, cheating, and the future that is extremely relevant to the Bosnian context.

In Bosnia, two main discourses developed: one focusing on cheating in relation to the (imagined) socialist past, and the other reflecting on cheating as the postwar democratic predicament. School used to be at the center of moral instruction and social upbringing throughout Yugoslav socialism. During the time of massive socialist growth and modernization in the 1950s and 1960s, teachers had an especially strong influence on their students; while many of the students' families were constrained by traditional, religious, and conservative value systems that they frequently and secretly attempted to transmit to their children, the teachers' role was to "liberate" youth from the limitations of tradition and family, and to educate them in a way suitable for the modern age of state socialism. Therefore, the role of teachers was of great importance for the socialist regime, which charged teachers/education with the project to limit and contain the sources of traditionalism, religious practice, ethnonationalism, and other related forms that the regime named as "backward" or threatening to its socialist ideology.

The massive transformation of education in the early years of socialism points to the socialist regime's great investment in schooling, and to the related authority of teachers, who were generally better educated than the rest of the population. As a result of socialist education policies, which included mandatory elementary school education for all children, illiteracy in the former Yugoslavia shrank rapidly. For example, the illiteracy rate dropped from 44.6 percent in 1931 (the Kingdom of Yugoslavia) to 9.5 percent in 1981 (Latifić 1996, 99–100).

The position of schools and schooling, however, changed drastically during the recent times of "war and peace" in the Balkans, which brought monumental political and social upheavals leading to war-produced adjustments and experiments in teaching, including the staircase schools or the improvised schools in the hallways/basements of apartment buildings (Jansen 2014, 244–47). The larger social, economic, and political transformations also exaggerated social injustices, amplified forms of conspicuous corruption, and increased disillusionment, political withdrawal and "hibernation" in the general population. The uncomfortable marriage between the two "transitions"—to capitalism and democracy—generated the crumbling of socialist services, and a strong desire for a fast road to material success, which often excluded traditional education. As a result, schooling became the site of semiabandonment and enormous critique; an arena where greater frustrations about the absence of the system were being articulated via processes of massive cheating, purchasing of exams/diplomas, and devaluation of types of knowledge that were difficult to transfer into (immediate) economic capital. School was therefore dislocated from the center of the socialist project to the margins of the postwar undemocratic democracy. The investment in public education also shrank quickly, and when coupled with tremendously complicated bureaucracy, ethnicization of curricula, fragmented education infrastructure, inadequate facilities, dramatic reduction in teachers' salaries, and low spirits in the profession, teaching and studying became exceptionally morale sapping (Farrell 2001, 18).

The respect and authority of traditional (socialist) schooling was significantly diminished, I was told, by the infiltration of prolific corruption and connections into education. This created a great amount of frustration, dissatisfaction, and feelings of helplessness in the face of larger transformations, which were experienced as endemic to modernity, democracy, and capitalism. University students all over Bosnia-Herzegovina told stories about injustice in education, where, according to these accounts, (some) professors randomly decided who should pass exams. For example, one student, Irena, told me of a professor who, without reading any exams, used a divider and stabbed a stack of students' papers—the students whose papers stuck to the divider were the ones who passed. Another student, Dado, told me of a professor who, during his official office hours, locked his office so that students could not come in and "bother him." I was also told, on numerous occasions, of students who never attended university but who received a degree because they had powerful connections.

These pervasive complaints about and frustration with professors' corruption, and corruption in education at large, were frequently articulated via humor: once in May 2015, I was traveling in a small van with a group of student activists from a northwestern Bosnian town to a town in Republika Srpska. As we were driving through a little village, one of the students, Lamija, exclaimed: "Open the windows everyone, maybe a Masters' diploma will fly in." Everyone laughed, including the ethnographer, at Lamija's joke. I soon learned that one could, according to the bus rumors, buy a university diploma very cheaply at the bus station in this village. Lamija turned to me to tell me another, related joke: "You know, one of the new Ministers in the Cantonal government once said: 'If I knew that getting a Ph.D. diploma was so easy, I would have finished high school!'"—indicating that he purchased his Ph.D. and that he never completed high school.

These bitter jokes and commentaries are a powerful critique of the corrupt state and its unqualified and dishonest elites who use education as their playground. The practice of buying exams and diplomas is so widespread among Bosnian politicians that in 2018 Kenan Vehabović, a secretary of the Joint Service of the Parliamentary Assembly of Bosnia and Herzegovina, asked for the verification of all the diplomas of the parliamentarians. His request was denied. Commenting on this situation, Aida, a student at the University of Bihać, told me: "Unfortunately, this is not surprising at all. Most of them [politicians] have purchased diplomas, everyone knows that. If the highly positioned politicians, even the key leaders in our Parliament, are proven cheaters, how can they tell us not to do that? So we cheat as well. That is how it is around here." Aida's cynicism and demoralized tone is similar to Emina's comment when she said, "I just copy things from the Wikipedia because that is what my teachers do." Aida and Emina point at the double nature of cheating, which is experienced as "simultaneously a wise thing to do and self-devaluing" (Rajković 2017, 49). This morally compromised context generates youths' massive disillusionment in the educational system and the state that generates it, where youth feel somewhat "safe and comfortable within its embrace, while being increasingly demoralized by it" (Rajković 2017, 49).

When I mentioned to some students' parents that I was researching cheating they told me that during the socialist times cheating was different: it was curbed by the functional system, and it was seen as an act of collective solidarity. Socialist cheating practices required a certain intimacy and a sense of groupness and identification with a segment of a student body, which was organically achieved since the educational structure put the same thirty or so students in one classroom for the first eight years of their elementary school education. Some of them continued to study together for an additional four years of secondary education. As one informant, Esma, told me: "We were like family. All forty of us." I was told that these students, "the family," would spontaneously, over the years of coming together and studying together, unify against the authority (teacher/school), in order to help a fellow classmate succeed and better the overall class ranking, and thus their collective status, at the school. In this sense, cheating under socialism was constructed as prohibited but not necessarily immoral—it was expected from classmates to help each other pass exams and share knowledge, by whispering answers during oral examinations, for example. Thus, even those who did not cheat for their own benefit would still be expected to help their classmates.

At the same time, there was a system in place, I was told, composed of multiple written and unwritten mechanisms that imposed limits on how much one could achieve by cheating—a complex web of oral and written exams that could reveal, separate, and award those who "really knew" from those who cheated or got lucky. This allowed for a historically specific form of cheating to emerge that relied on the expectation of a socialist system-delivered justice and socialist subject production. This is in sharp contrast with the present order of things "without a system," where the students I befriended felt that relying on hard work and honesty was not rewarded at all, as Ivo explains: "How can I study when I have straight As and no means to continue education and my classmate Ivona, you know her, she has all Ds and we all know that she will get into Zagreb University because you know who her dad is, don't you? They are *tajkuni*, they have those seventeen trucks . . . how can I keep on studying, trying, and hoping knowing that? Cheating [even though I do not do it myself] makes more sense!" Therefore, the sense I was getting from Ivo and other students is that a textbook citizen-participant marks one as foolish and naïve.[18] In this context, the logic goes, *their* cheating should not be treated as *any* cheating, but more as a historically specific, morally invested response to these larger social inequalities and moral worlds in flux, which appear to be out of students' control, and where their response is directed at minimizing larger corruption and inequalities that inform their democratic predicament.

Meanwhile, while waiting to leave the country or for a better future to arrive in Bosnia, many youth engage in two main tactics: "political hibernation"—active and agentive withdrawal from the *official* politics (see Hromadžić 2014)—and cheating, tactics of sociopolitical maneuvering and self-maintenance within the unbearable state. In other words, cheating is one of the possible techniques that youth in Bosnia use in order to navigate their existence in the Bosnian state while "transport[ing] the[ir] dreams and aspirations that constitute sovereign agency outside the borders of such an exceptional space" (chapter 1, this volume). Therefore, students' approach to cheating as an appropriate response to and critique of the current state paints practices of buying exams or appropriating works of others as acceptable and efficacious *reactions* to a context which, as some youth stated, evokes "illicit" and "immoral" action. At the same time, while complaining about the unbearable state that "makes them cheat," youth skill-fully maneuver this corrupt and cheating-prone political and social field, thus constituting themselves as both the primary victims and active contributors to this (dis)order. This youth agency is therefore two-fold: both located in the indi-vidual actor—the cheater—and in the cheating-friendly context. Consequently, these student cheaters feel themselves to be complicit in their failing political system, where cheating becomes an ongoing, performative activity of mocking oneself and the values one holds (Rajković 2017, 49). As a result, students found their own behavior both "understandable and risible, laughable and shameful" (Rajković 2017, 56).

This two-fold, humorous yet reprehensible, experience of cheating became especially apparent during my fieldwork in Mostar in 2005–6 (see Hromadžić 2015a). On a cold February day in 2006, during the teachers' strike, a heated discussion took place during a geography class when only eight of thirty stu-dents were present, so that the teacher decided not to start a new lesson.[19] In the cold and mostly empty classroom, the students and the teacher energetically and informally chatted about education, corruption, the strike, youth, and their future. Here is an excerpt from this conversation.

> HARUN: Our society is made in a way that everyone tries to finish some school, to get a diploma, and not to gain any knowledge. The goal is just to get into university.
>
> HALID: This country should disappear from the face of the Earth!
>
> TEACHER: You will get out of here, [you will] go to university, you can change something. Students change the world, so why do not you take things into your own hands?
>
> DAVOR: Why do not you change the situation, professor?
>
> TEACHER: We also agree that things need to change, that reform is needed. How many times did we go on strike? We do not get anything, but we start working again because of you. . . . Here, I have a student who has straight As, his parents have no money, and he will probably stay in Mostar, probably will not be able to continue his education, and the one he shares his desk with has all Ds but he will go to Zagreb to the University because he is *pun para* [full of money].
>
> DALIBORKA: That is why we are all unmotivated and demoralized.
>
> AIDA (WHISPERING TO ME): *I zato ja ne učim nego prepisujem* [And that is why I do not study but cheat].
>
> HARUN: We talked to the teacher Vedrana the other day about this—how can you start this school full of energy and leave feeling apathetic?

TEACHER: What can I say to a student who spends five hours every day studying at home, has all As and then someone who never studies, who just sits at home, comes here and passes into the next grade?

HARUN: Well, teacher, that is because there are new rules now, you know. It goes like this: "I can, I want, and I have connections!"

We all laugh.

This dialogue captures youth's approaches to their state, corruption, education, morality, and future. Students describe themselves as "demoralized and unmotivated," and they see no exit from the situation but to either use their connections and cheating to achieve their goals or to withdraw from political life altogether in order to preserve their sense of (political) self for better times, while hoping they will eventually leave the country. The teacher agrees with the students, but she also challenges them to do something about the situation, because they are young and "should take things into their hands." Students are tired of being called on to change the situation, and they call on the older generations "to clean up the mess they made," the attitude embedded in the student's response "why don't you change the situation, teacher?"

This exchange also suggests that there is something in the changing postwar culture emerging at the intersection between international practices, transnational forces, and local politics that is twisted, immoral, stale, and hard to change. This view makes many ordinary Bosnians assume their fellow citizens are prone to corruption and immorality, since it is in their "postwar culture." This creates an ironic situation in which even those who most openly criticize corruption end up being prone to it; many students admit that they would use connections to get where they want to be if their connections were strong enough, since that is the only approach that the unbearable state knows and values. In this way, youth who see themselves as the main critics of corruption become potential and skilled agents in it.

The transformation of the popular slogan "I want, I can, I will!" into Harun's "I want, I can, and I have connections!" is also very telling. The first version, popular during Tito's regime, was used above all to motivate and describe Tito's socialist youth. It suggests individual agency, progress, and one's determination to achieve success by relying on one's own hard labor and willpower. The new, twisted version of this phrase, ironically uttered by Harun and followed by our collective laughter, suggests something different, however: the possessive verb "to have [connections]" shows ownership as well as displacement of individual agency to the web of connections, which are never under control of an individual agent.[20] In other words, youth recognize that "their ability to be moral [is] irreparably and structurally compromised" (Rajković 2017, 47).

Furthermore, our laughing together and students' making fun at their own sense of moral failure is a hallmark of a long-standing sense of lack of agency (51–52). Students (and ethnographer) laughing together is thus symbolic of affective contradictions—signaling our discomfort, demoralization, abandonment, and sense of nonchalance in the face of failure (48) on the one side, and a problematic dependence on the state and the "practical embeddedness in social structure" (55–55) of cheating on the other.

Regardless of being active performers in the process, youth often discursively dislocated their sovereign agency to the context—the act which allowed them to claim innocence, moral superiority, and "reactive agency." This became especially clear to me in spring 2017, when I was teaching on a Fulbright Scholarship at the University of Bihać. During one of our many discussions about the Bosnian state and students' futures, I mentioned my interest in prolific cheating practices. One student, Emina, immediately and unhesitatingly responded: "Look. If my professor orders us to by a bulk-pack for his class and all there is inside are pages printed out from Wikipedia . . . yes, from Wikipedia. . . . I get so angry and sad, at once. What can I learn from him? So, I do not read for that class, I do not put any effort in it, I just copy things from Wikipedia and memorize some information from it." Sanjin added, "It is not just this professor. The whole University is like that. Half of our professors purchased their diplomas." At the point, Tanja shouted from the back row: "Kakva *država*, takvi mi" (Like the state, like us), capturing and summarizing accumulated disillusionment where youth gave up on the state and where people feel themselves not fully to be "normal" but rather compromised agents (see the Introduction, this volume; also see Greenberg 2011; Jansen 2015). Furthermore, in this context of material and ethical entrapment, Tanja's comment shows how students both "ridicule and mimic" (Rajković 2017, 59–63) the state.

Many students openly told me that they were cheating, sharing with me their amazing knowledge about new technologies of cheating, including the "invisible" pen, cell phone, recorders, wireless headphones, "invisible" headphones, camera pens, and cheating watches. Sometimes they even used me as a tool for cheating. For example, in Bosanski Petrovac I was asked to pass *puškice*, or "little rifles" among students. Puškice were small pieces of paper on which students would write as much information as possible and hide them somewhere visible only to them to use during the exam.[21] In addition, I witnessed students use "bugs," write on their hands, desks, chairs and classroom walls, swap exams, whisper answers to each other during oral exams, frequently copy large amounts of context from Wikipedia on their essays, and use phones to support their cheating practices.

In our conversations, students gave me multiple explanations for why they were cheating. For example, Igor mentioned that there were some good things

FIGURE 6. Production of *puškice* during recess, October 2006. Photo by Azra Hromadžić.

FIGURE 7. Production of *puškice* during recess, October 2006. Photo by Azra Hromadžić.

about the former, socialist educational practices—such as oral examinations and an emphasis on classical education—which they believed their school system still somewhat resembled. He complained, however, that there was no value in memorizing how many cows Denmark has, thus echoing many students' (and parents') frequent critiques of teachers who "torture" students with unnecessary information. This focus on memorization in the former system was seen as a relic of the socialist past when, according to the narratives of some parents and teachers, socialist education was maybe better in some respects, but it was not geared toward developing students' critical thinking; rather students were expected to memorize large amounts of unnecessary data (also see Larson 2013), including the number of cows in Denmark. Therefore, numerous students did not want to "waste" their time studying; cheating seemed more agentive and, in a sense, "moral." What was *truly* immoral was that their teachers (and, by extension their state) required that students memorize what they saw as unnecessary, useless information that was anyhow available on the Internet and thus easy to access.

In addition, students also frequently bragged about their connections, which allowed them to get into universities without taking an entrance test, or about receiving a passing grade at an oral exam at which they never appeared. One morning as I was rushing to class using the now-familiar Mostar shortcuts, I met Nermin, one of the students from my class, a troublemaking young man who already had several police arrests for different misdoings, and who was among the least achieving in a class of excellent students. I liked talking to Nermin because he was straightforward and intelligent. He also had a great sense of humor, and he entertained the class. As we were walking past Mostar's ghostly ruins—leftovers from the recent war—I hesitantly asked him what he planned to do in the future. He responded quickly and assertively: "I think I will study law." I could not resist asking: "How will you get into that department when you have bad grades?" He looked at me and without hesitation replied: "Jer ja imam štelu" (Because I have a hookup). The following November, I went back to Mostar to visit friends and found out that Nermin had indeed enrolled in the university and was studying law, side by side with those students who studied hard throughout high school because they had no connections. A couple of years later, I again returned to the field and asked about Nermin. Sandra, one of the students from "my" class, told me that Nermin was still "studying," that he was a junior now, but that no one ever saw him at the university. Sandra concluded: "Sve je moguće u Bosni!" (Everything is possible in Bosnia).

Sandra's cynicism reveals how for many of the youth I encountered during my fieldwork, Bosnia emerged as a site of exception: a place where the rules of moral action are different from other places. By being able to separate their "cheating actions" *here and now*, from how they will act *there and then*, students were able to negotiate morally self-diminishing consequences of their cheating actions. This allows for some preservation of self-worth and ethical stance that one feels one is unable to fulfill in the current state (Rajković 2017, 65). This dialectic of closeness and openness, and hereness and thereness that imaginative horizons generate, allows students to navigate affective and moral contradictions, and it powerfully shapes students' strategic maneuvering in the context of the unbearable state. The actual political present and political participation are evaluated and experienced in relation to the eventual—a more egalitarian democratic future (or its opposite, a Titoesque type of solid dictatorship) that has not and might never arrive, but that provides an "imaginative possibility—to hope, to the optative, to moods, like the subjunctive, born by our grammar" (Crapanzano 2004, 14). This means that young people imagine and experience themselves as plural subjects who cheat in the present while concurrently inhabiting "democratic time" in an either geographically or temporarily evacuated future, the eventual. In this context where systemlike, patterned qualities of statehood, sociality, and conduct all but vanished, cheating is one of the methods used to get by and to get on. In this way cheating becomes simultaneously an act of sovereign agency and self-empowerment, and a performance of mocking oneself and the values one holds (Rajković 2017, 29).

Student cheating in Bosnia-Herzegovina has a dual social force: first, these cheating practices are an expression of youth's agency fueled by the cheating-prone context and contemporary disillusionment with the unbearable state in Bosnia. At the same time, however, these students are working efficaciously within that broken system, causing its perpetuation. Consequently, cheating emerges as both a site of ideological critique ("see what these bad people and broken rules made me do") and smart, prudent deployment of the "broken rules" to advance one's life project, here or elsewhere.[22]

Students' cheating does not necessarily signal their solidarity in the sense of contingent *groupness* as it did during the (imagined) Yugoslav times, but it suggests new political and educational youth agency and subjectivity—anxious, economically driven, postwar, and postsocialist youth citizens who increasingly saw cheating as a useful tool to maneuver their "here-and-now" predicament. Therefore, saying "no" via practices such as cheating, use of veze, and "buying" exams are, among other things, examples of youth sovereign agency. These everyday tactics are used to contest what Enver called "the Bosnian democracy as masquerade." When combined with saying "no" to memorizing how many cows Denmark has, these strategies are productive of evaluating, contesting, questioning, and desiring the (proper) state.

This ambivalence between actions and desires "here and now" and "there and then" also reveals how the state is still something to be engaged with, even if via cheating as a form of critique.[23] Bosnian youth's view of clientelism, nepotism, and cheating is intimately linked to contemporary techniques of the state. Employment cheating, veze and štele do not hinder the "system" but rather allow young Bosnians to get "incorporated" into the state, manage ambiguity, make relations, reproduce social personhood, and reestablish power relations (see Brković 2017) in Bosnia's sociopolitical *meantime* (see Jansen 2015).

In another chapter, Rebecca Bryant shows how an airline comes to stand for the state in part because of its corrupt management. In a similar fashion, I see cheating as the way for some Bosnian students to articulate their complex and seemingly contradictory desires for a form of legibility, visibility to the state, recognizability of the state, and incorporation into the state, while simultaneously and mercilessly distancing themselves and critiquing the state that encourages cheating as a form of political becoming.

Cheating is frequently explained by students as a necessary and effective practice which allows contemporary, unfinished, and partial forms of sovereign agency to unfold, enabling youth to maneuver the contours of democracy and capitalism. In other words, cheating emerges as a site of youth's political and economic "maintenance" (Berlant 2007). These combined, historically informed processes are making Bosnian-Herzegovinian youth into complicated agents suitable for their double—postwar and postsocialist—transformation. Their ingenuity makes me uncomfortable to label them—as is often done—as lost, sacrificed, morally compromised, or as one teacher remarked, morally "rotten" youth (also see Greenberg 2011, 95). Instead, I see them as active, spatially and geographically plural agents who try to maneuver, more or less successfully, their space and their participation in the constantly shifting, (un)democratic context created by the recent war, the end of socialism, and related larger global restructuring.

Notes

1. All names have been changed to protect informants' identities.

2. After I spent more time in the field, this reaction became much clearer to me. I spoke to numerous students' parents, who, troubled by their children's behavior and irritated by teachers' accusations (see the next endnote), blamed the teachers for unnecessarily torturing their children with useless knowledge and for their ill-suited training inappropriate for the "new times." Sometimes, they even physically threatened and assaulted teachers (by coming to school, yelling at teachers, or even beating them)—a practice that was unheard of during socialism, where teachers were protected by the system and thus demanded and received respect.

3. I remember hearing teachers comment that sometimes they knew that their students were cheating, but that they intentionally turned their backs on the practice, since they felt it was *morally necessary* to let certain students pass the class, especially those

who were sportsmen, or came from poor families, or whose families the teachers, or their friends and family, knew. Once, I overheard a teacher comment, while talking to a relative and a parent of a child who got "a Two" (in the United States, a "D") on an exam in a math class: "Pa mogla je, brate dragi, zažmiriti, pustiti ga da malo prepiše, da se djete džaba ne pati." (Well, she [the teacher] could blink, turn away . . . let him cheat a little bit, so that the child does not have to suffer for nothing.)

4. In this book I mostly use Bosnia-Herzegovina when referring to the state. Where stylistically more appropriate, however, I use the shorter construction, Bosnia.

5. Of course, there were those students who never cheated and who had a very strong moral stance against cheating. They were, however, in the minority, and they are not the focus of this chapter.

6. Bosnia-Herzegovina became an independent state on April 6, 1992. On the same day that Bosnia-Herzegovina was officially recognized, Serbian paramilitary units and Yugoslav People's Army attacked Bosnia's capital, Sarajevo, and initiated a war in Bosnia-Herzegovina. The army of the self-proclaimed Serbian Republic of Bosnia and Herzegovina (Republika Srpska or RS) within Bosnia-Herzegovina, with the help of men and weapons from Serbia, succeeded in ethnically cleansing, thus brutally unmixing, intertwined communities and lives (Hayden 1996), and conquering close to 70 percent of the country's territory by the end of 1993.

7. Regardless of the tendency in most academic and policy accounts to unify and reify the international community and refer to it as an abstract, unformed, and static "it" (Coles 2007, 54), this entity is a dynamic, complicated, overlapping, uncoordinated, and conflicting bundle of simultaneously converging and diverging people, projects, interests, agendas, and practices.

8. The exercise of power by the High Representative and other international organizations has significantly diminished since 2006. During the time of my research, in 2005 and 2006, this power was very palpable, however.

9. There have been seven High Representatives: Carl Bildt, Carlos Westernport, Wolfgang Petritsch, Paddy Ashdown, Christian Schwarts-Schilling, Miroslav Lajčák, and the current High Representative, Valentin Inzko.

10. See, among others, Ćurak 2004; Gagnon 2004; Gilbert 2008; Hromadžić 2015; Jansen 2007; Mujkić 2007, 2008; Sarajlić 2011.

11. Some reports suggest that Bosnia-Herzegovina is the most corrupt country in Europe (Blagovčanin 2012, 2014).

12. http://www.reci.ba/usr/106/scr/mojglas.php?voxpopuli_id=463. Accessed July 31, 2008.

13. The person who wrote the above comment suggests that this is not how communism operated. During the communist times, the elites were corrupt but shared some of their takings with *narod*, which partially legitimized their corrupt behavior. This notion is very similar to Lomintz's study of rural Mexico where "corruption is accepted if some of the benefits of this appropriation spill over to the rest of population—that is, by patrons who demonstrate generosity and solidarity with their people and who finance local fiestas" (Lomintz quoted in Haller and Shore 2005, 13).

14. Interestingly, it also suggests that that there might be a form of "European democracy" that is possibly good, and that the problems observed in Bosnia are maybe not inherent to democracy but rather linked to its specific Bosnian manifestation. I am grateful to Nick Long for this comment.

15. This sentiment and belief in the rule of law in the West has been changing since the recent crisis of democracy and the state in the United States and Western Europe.

16. In early August 2014, a unique exhibit was organized at Bihać's main art gallery. The exhibit, prepared by a New York City-based Bosnian artist, filmmaker, and media

scholar Amir Husak, was titled "Ništa više nije isto: Kultura krize i društvene promjene u Bosni i Hercegovini" ("Nothing Is the Same Anymore: The Culture of Crisis and Social Changes in Bosnia-Herzegovina"). This four-day-long event included video recordings of the Bosnian Spring protests; photographic exhibits featuring protests in several Bosnian towns; a wall dedicated to the memorabilia and photographs from the socialism-built, war-devastated and privatization-decapitated Bihać textile factory "Kombiteks"; an interactive "map of crisis" in Bihać; and an expert panel.

17. Green's paradigmatic account of cheating involves two elements: "First, the cheater must violate a prescriptive (rather than descriptive), mandatory (rather than optional), regulative (rather than practice-defining), and conduct-governing (as opposed to decision-governing) rule. Second, the rule must be fair and enforced even-handedly, and must be violated with an intent to obtain advantage over some party with whom the rule-breaker is in a cooperative, rule-governed relationship" (Green 2004, 137).

18. This sentiment is nicely captured in an interview with a student in Serbia who exclaimed "Kažu mi da sam luda, jer temeljno učim!" ("They tell me that I am crazy for being so studious") (S Media 2012).

19. Teachers' strikes became a regular phenomenon in postwar Bosnia-Herzegovina, mostly for economic reasons such as not being paid or because salaries were low in comparison to those of other government employees. This time, the main reason for the strike was the request of the teachers' unions of primary and secondary schools to receive the same base salary as those employed in the city and cantonal administrations (see Hromadžić 2015b).

20. I am grateful to Jessica Greenberg for this insight.

21. *Puškice* are today considered to be a cheating mechanism of an older generation. However, in more rural and poor regions of the country where many youth do not have access to new technologies, *puškice* continue to inform cheating practices.

22. I am grateful to John Burdick for these ideas.

23. I am grateful to Nick Long for this insight.

References

Appadurai, Arjun. 1996. *Modernity at Large: Cultural Dimensions of Globalization.* Minneapolis: University of Minnesota Press.

Aretxaga, Begoña. 2003. "Maddening States." *Annual Review of Anthropology* 32: 393–410.

Berlant, Lauren. 2007. "Slow Death (Sovereignty, Obesity, Lateral Agency)." *Critical Inquiry* 3(4): 754–780.

Blagovčanin, Srđan. 2012. "Bosnia and Herzegovina: Captured State," in *Unfinished Business: The Western Balkans and the International Community*, edited by Džihić Vedran and Daniel Hamilton. Center for Transatlantic Relations, Johns Hopkins University. http://transatlantic.sais-jhu.edu/publications/books/Unfinished%20Business%20Pdf/ch00_frontmatter.pdf.

Blagovčanin, Srđan. 2014. "Kratka istorija korupcije u BiH." http://balkans.aljazeera.net/vijesti/kratka-historija-korupcije-u-bih. Accessed on February 28, 2014.

Blum, Susan. 2009. *My Word! Plagiarism and College Culture*. Ithaca: Cornell University Press.

Bringa, Tone. 2003. "The Peaceful Death of Tito and the Violent End of Yugoslavia," in *The Death of the Father: An Anthropology of the End in Political Authority*, edited by John Borneman, 63–103. New York: Berghahn Books.

Brković, Čarna. 2017. *Managing Ambiguity: How Clientelism, Citizenship, and Power Shape Personhood in Bosnia and Herzegovina*. Berghahn Books.

Chandler, David. 1999. *Bosnia: Faking Democracy after Dayton*. London: Pluto Press.
Coles, Kimberly. 2007. *Democratic Designs: International Intervention and Electoral Practices in Post-War Bosnia-Herzegovina*. Ann Arbor: University of Michigan Press.
Colombo, Louis, and Aaron Vlasak. 2010. "Cheating the Academy as Solidarity." In *The Public Life of Ethics*, edited by Louis Colombo and Aaron Vlasak. Inter-Disciplinary.Net. http://www.inter-disciplinary.net/publishing/id-press/ebooks/the-public-life-of-ethics/.
Crapanzano, Vincent. 2004. *Imaginative Horizons: An Essay in Literary-Philosophical Anthropology*. Chicago: University of Chicago Press.
Ćurak, Nerzuk. 2004. *Dejtonski Nacionalizam: Ogledi o Političkom*. Sarajevo: Buybook.
Desruisseaux, Paul. 1999. "Cheating Is Reaching Epidemic Proportions Worldwide, Researchers Say." *Chronicle of Higher Education*. https://www.chronicle.com/article/Cheating-Is-Reaching-Epidemic/5854. Accessed on April 28, 2019.
Farrell, Séamus. 2001. "An Investigation into the Experimental School Strategy in the Promotion of School Improvement and of Social Cohesion Through Education, in Bosnia and Herzegovina." Master's thesis, University of Ulster.
Ferguson, James, and Akhil Gupta. 2002. "Spatializing States: Toward an Ethnography of Neoliberal Governmentality." *American Ethnologist* 29(4): 981–1002.
Gagnon, V. P., Jr. 2004. *The Myth of Ethnic War: Serbia and Croatia in the 1990s*. Ithaca, NY: Cornell University Press.
Gilbert, Andrew. 2006. "The Past in Parenthesis. (Non)post-Socialism in Post-War Bosnia-Herzegovina" *Anthropology Today* 22(4): 14–18.
Green, Stewart. 2004. "Cheating." *Law and Philosophy* 23(2): 137–185.
Greenberg, Jessica. 2010. "There's Nothing Anyone Can Do About It": Participation, Apathy, and 'Successful' Democratic Transition in Postsocialist Serbia." *Slavic Review* 69(1): 41–64.
Greenberg, Jessica. 2011. "On the Road to Normal: Negotiating Agency and State Sovereignty in Postsocialist Serbia." *American Anthropologist* 113(1): 88–100.
Greenberg, Jessica. 2014. *After the Revolution: Youth, Democracy, and the Politics of Disappointment in Serbia*. Palo Alto, CA: Stanford University Press.
Gupta, Akhil. 1995. "Blurred Boundaries: The Discourse of Corruption, the Culture of Politics, and the Imagined *State*." *American Ethnologist* 22(2): 375–402.
Haller, Dieter, and Cris Shore, eds. 2005. *Corruption: Anthropological Perspectives*. London: Pluto.
Herzfeld, Michael. 2005. *Cultural Intimacy: Social Poetics in the Nation-State*. 2nd ed. New York: Routledge.
Higgott, Richard A., Geoffrey R. D. Underhill, and Andreas Bieler, eds. 2000. *Non-State Actors and Authority in the Global System*. London: Routledge.
Hromadžić, Azra. 2014. "'Only When the Spider Web Becomes Too Heavy': Youth, Unemployment, and the Social Life of Waiting in Postwar and Postsocialist Bosnia-Herzegovina." *Journal of Social Policy (Revija za Socijalna Politika)* 11: 45–87.
Hromadžić, Azra. 2015a. *Citizens of an Empty Nation: Youth and State-making in Postwar Bosnia and Herzegovina*. Philadelphia: University of Pennsylvania Press.
Hromadžić, Azra. 2015b. "Dissatisfied Citizens: Ethnonational Governance, Teachers' Strike and Politics of Professional Solidarity in Postwar Mostar, Bosnia-Herzegovina." *European Politics and Society* 16(3): 429–446.
Hromadžić, Azra. 2018a. "Streets, Scum, and People: Discourses of (In)Civility in Postwar *Bihać*, Bosnia and Herzegovina." *Anthropological Theory* 18 (2–3): 326–356.
Hromadžić, Azra. 2018b. "Dissolusioned with Dayton in Bosnia-Herzegovina." *Current History* 117(797): 102–108.

Jansen, Stef. 2005. "National Numbers in Context: Maps and Stats in Representations of the Post-Yugoslav Wars." *Identities: Global Studies in Culture and Power* 12(1): 45–68.

Jansen, Stef. 2007. "The Privatisation of Home and Hope: Return, Reforms and the Foreign Intervention in Bosnia-Herzegovina." *Dialectical Anthropology* 30 (3–4): 177–199.

Jansen, Stef. 2014. "Hope for/against the State: Gridding in a Besieged Sarajevo Suburb." *Ethnos: Journal of Anthropology* 9(2): 238–260.

Jansen, Stef. 2015. *Yearnings in the Meantime: "Normal Lives" and the State in a Sarajevo Apartment Complex.* Oxford: Berghahn Books.

Kasapović, Mirjana. 2005. "Bosnia and Herzegovina: Consociational or Liberal Democracy?" *Politička Misao* 42(5): 3–30.

Kurtović, Larisa. n.d. "Limits of In/Action: Everyday Politics of Dis/Engagement in Postwar Bosnia-Herzegovina." Unpublished paper.

Kurtović, Larisa, and Azra Hromadžić. 2017. "Cannibal States, Empty Bellies: Protest, History and Political Imagination in Bosnia." *Critique of Anthropology* 37(3): 262–296.

Larson, Jonathan. 2013. *Critical Thinking in Slovakia after Socialism.* Rochester, NY: University of Rochester Press.

Latifić, Ibrahim. 1996. *Jugoslavia 1945–1990 (razvoj privrede i društvenih djelatnosti).* http://www.znaci.net/00001/120_7.pdf.

Mujanović, Jasmin. 2018. *Hunger and Fury: The Crisis of Democracy in the Balkans.* Oxford University Press.

Mujkić, Asim. 2007. "We, the Citizens of *Ethnopolis.*" *Constellations* 14(1): 112–28.

Mujkić, Asim. 2008. "Ideološki problemi konsocijacijske demokratije u Bosni i Hercegovini." *Status: Magazin za Političku Kulturu i Društvena Pitanja,* 122–132.

Ohmae, Kenichi. 1996. *The End of the Nation State: The Rise of Regional Economies.* New York: Free Press.

Rajković, Ivan. 2017. "For an Anthropology of the Demoralized: State Pay, Mock-Labour, and Unfreedom in a Serbian firm." *Journal of the Royal Anthropological Institute* (24)1: 47–70.

Sampson, Steven. 2002. "Weak States, Uncivil Societies, and Thousands of NGOs: Western Democracy Export as Benevolent Colonialism in the Balkans." In *Cultural Boundaries of the Balkans,* edited by S. Rečić. Lund University Press. http://www.anthrobase.org/Txt/S/Sampson_S_01.htm. Accessed August 13, 2008.

Sarajlić, Elder. 2011. "The Convenient Consociation: Bosnia and Herzegovina, Ethnopolitics and the EU." *Transitions 51 (1–2): 61–80.*

Sassen, Saskia. 1998. *Globulization and Its Discontents.* New York: New Press.

Schechner, Richard. 1985. *Between Theater and Anthropology.* Philadelphia: University of Pennsylvania Press.

Scott, James C. 1998. *Seeing Like a State: How Certain Schemes to Improve the Human Condition Have Failed.* New Haven, CT: Yale University Press.

Sharma, Ardhana, and Akhil Gupta. 2006. *The Anthropology of the State: A Reader.* Hoboken, NJ: Wiley-Blackwell.

S Media. 2012. "Za sve koji su u ispitnom roku: Kako snalažljivi studenti polažu ispite!" December 26. http://www.smedia.rs/vesti/vest/95306/Varanje-na-ispitima-Studenti-Obrazovanje-Polaganje-ispita-Za-sve-koji-su-u-ispitnom-roku-Kako-snalazljivi-studenti-polazu-ispite-FOTO-VIDEO.html. Accessed March 28, 2013.

Solioz, Christophe. 2003. "The Complexity of [In]formal Networks in Bosnia and Herzegovina." *Muabet: Local Dimensions of Democracy Building in Southeast*

Europe. http://www.watsoninstitute.org/muabet/docs/christophe_solioz.doc. Accessed September 9, 2008.

Taylor, Diana. 1997. *Disappearing Acts: Spectacles of Gender and Nationalism in Argentina's "Dirty War."* Durham, NC: Duke University Press.

Torsello, Davide. 2011. "The Ethnography of Corruption: Research Themes in Political Anthropology." *QoG Working Paper Series* 2.

Trouillot, Michel-Rolph. 2003. "The Anthropology of the State in the Age of Globalization: Close Encounters of the Deceptive Kind." In *Global Transformations: Anthropology and the Modern World*, 79–96. New York: Palgrave Macmillan.

Verdery, Katherine. 1996. *What Was Socialism, and What Comes Next?* Princeton, NJ: Princeton University Press.

ASPIRATIONAL SOVEREIGNTY AND HUMAN RIGHTS ADVOCACY

Audience, Recognition, and the Reach
of the Taiwan State

Sara L. Friedman

On December 3, 2016, I departed Chicago for Beijing to spend two weeks in the People's Republic of China (PRC) as a scholar escort for a delegation of congressional staff people.[1] The date would have been of no particular significance were it not for the congratulatory phone call that US president-elect Donald Trump had accepted from Taiwan's president Tsai Ing-wen a mere day before my departure. Viewed as a serious breach of protocol, the phone call sent shock waves through diplomatic, government, and policymaking circles on both sides of the Pacific. It was the first time a US president or president-elect had spoken directly with the president of the Republic of China on Taiwan since 1979.

Why all the fuss over a phone call? Diplomatic protocol concerns aside, the phone call signified President-elect Trump's potential recalibration of the critical US-PRC relationship by engaging Taiwan's leader using the "state-to-state" model soundly rejected by the PRC regime. Much of the hand-wringing focused on the call's consequences for the United States' long-standing, yet precarious, balancing act of supporting the democratic government on Taiwan without upsetting the PRC's leadership by officially recognizing Taiwan as a sovereign state. Equally important, therefore, was what the exchange intimated about Taiwan's status as an independent nation-state and the key role of US recognition in producing a fragile Taiwanese sovereignty.

But the phone call did something else as well. Through the medium of a transpacific call, it simultaneously projected Taiwanese sovereignty beyond the borders of the island nation and across physical and discursive space. The flow of words between President Tsai and President-elect Trump created a shared space of sovereign recognition through the medium of a congratulatory phone call. The behind-the-scenes work of advisors on both sides to engineer the phone call, President-elect Trump's decision to accept the call, and the reverberating effects of the two leaders' verbal interaction—all of these signifying acts reaffirmed "recognition" as a core component of sovereign address. Instead of assuming that sovereignty existed as the backdrop to Tsai and Trump's exchange, the phone call produced sovereign recognition as an admittedly uncertain possibility.[2] In other words, without jumping to grandiose conclusions about the efficaciousness of a phone call, we nonetheless can see in this exchange President Tsai's desire to produce a space of sovereign recognition through President-elect Trump's tacit acknowledgment of her status as a state leader and to contemplate the possibilities provoked by the phone call's sovereign potential.[3]

This chapter uses the concept of "aspirational sovereignty" to explore how the Taiwanese state enacts and projects sovereignty claims through everyday governing practices. Taiwan occupies an anomalous place in the contemporary global configuration of recognized nation-states, unrecognized states, and partially recognized states. As a vibrant democracy that enjoys formal diplomatic recognition from a shrinking number of states and informal recognition from many others, it operates in a contested international domain where any act that suggests official sovereign standing is quickly challenged or blocked by the PRC government, which continues to claim Taiwan as a renegade province.[4] The chapter examines how different political logics and governing practices generate recognizable and recognized sovereignty for Taiwan, with a particular focus on governmental and civil society responses to cross-border migration flows. It assesses sovereign efficacy by analyzing the spatial reach of state effects, the specific audiences addressed by governing practices, and the potential forms of recognition offered by those audiences. Although the chapter takes cross-border migration as its point of departure, it focuses not on immigrants themselves (whose views and experiences I address in depth elsewhere [Friedman 2015a]), but instead on specific groups, individuals, and institutions that form around immigrants: the bureaucrats and officials charged with managing migration flows and activists and other public figures who organize and speak publicly in support of human rights, especially immigrant rights. In different ways, these groups enact and demand a particular kind of Taiwanese state, one that they argue best serves a specific vision of an international community that includes a sovereign Taiwan in its midst.

The various actions taken by these groups raise the question of how to locate efficacious state effects and how to understand overlapping scales of sovereign address (see also chapter 5, this volume). Some might see the decisions made by state actors at the border as an enactment of effective sovereignty, but those very same actors might view their location at the border as a sign of weakness and constraint. To be efficacious, in their eyes, one should be located elsewhere, outside the borders of the state and specifically on foreign soil. Sovereign recognition becomes conditional on state actors' ability to project governing effects beyond their own borders, to stretch the reach of the state through materializing stateness and sovereignty elsewhere, as Bryant (chapter 1, this volume) argues in her analysis of national airlines. But when sovereignty is understood as the power to cultivate a healthy, productive national population, then those very same practices, situated at the border, project sovereignty effects inward by promoting specific gendered and familial roles in the name of producing ideal national families.

The chapter evaluates the governing practices that take place at Taiwan's borders as biopolitical modes of sovereign assertion. Biopolitical techniques regulate cross-border flows and evaluate family reunification claims that provide rights to entry, residency, and naturalized citizenship. These governing practices (such as border interviews and postentry bureaucratic evaluations) assess the goals and future contributions of permanent immigrants as part of investigating the authenticity of a cross-border marriage as a relationship that bestows on immigrant spouses the right to residency and ultimately citizenship in Taiwan. Border evaluations position Taiwan as an active member of an international community of nation-states invested in sovereign acts that discipline as they produce: they control cross-border flows and shape the composition of nations and families.

Human rights advocacy, on the other hand, enacts sovereignty in a very different mode through the claims it makes on state actors and governing practices. It seeks to will into existence international recognition of Taiwanese sovereignty by openly advocating Taiwan's support for international human rights norms, including the government's decision to unilaterally ratify United Nations' human rights covenants and make those covenants the basis for domestic law (Chen 2018). By asserting its juridical adherence to international human rights norms and regimes, the Taiwan government enacts its desired status as a UN member state (despite the PRC's repeated efforts to block its admission), projecting outward its participation in transnational sovereign spaces. This projection represents a different dimension of the "transnational aspects to statehood" found in sites of military and diplomatic intervention such as Afghanistan and Bosnia (see the chapters by Wimpelmann and Hromadžić): in Taiwan's case, human rights advocacy operates as a hinge, so to speak, linking sovereign projects with diverse visions of what the state is or should be. For example, support for human rights also emboldens some state actors and local activists to argue for extending human rights protections to all within the country's borders, regardless of nationality or citizenship status. In these instances, human rights advocacy introduces alternative political futures for Taiwan that may not be rooted in a Westphalian model of state sovereignty or juridical citizenship.

By exploring alternative visions for Taiwan's political future, the chapter contributes to a growing body of ethnographic literature that takes seriously non-Westphalian political possibilities, including "would-be sovereigns" (Rutherford 2012), "make-believe" sovereignty (Navaro-Yashin 2012), and "non-sovereign futures" (Bonilla 2015). In so doing, it queries the stable distinction between de jure and de facto sovereignty by asking what makes a state sovereign, what acts are required to produce recognition, and how the performance of sovereignty requires both specific audiences and specific audience responses (Bobick 2017). Migration is critical to this process of producing sovereignty precisely because, as Abarca and Coutin (2018, 8) argue, the sovereign state "comes into being" in significant ways through its relationship to noncitizens. Put another way, sovereignty requires noncitizens as much as citizens, for it rests precariously on the recognition of others. It is precisely in these relational spaces, I suggest, that unrecognized or exceptional states may find resources for imagining governance and sovereign recognition differently. Faced with repeated experiences of containment and isolation, such states express aspirations for sovereign recognition through tropes of mobility (see also chapter 1, this volume). In Taiwan's case, these desires include both the state's ability to regulate cross-border migratory flows and the imagined mobility protections offered by transnational human rights principles to citizens and noncitizens alike.

My discussion to follow draws on an admittedly eclectic archive. It builds from the vexed domain of engagement among Chinese marital immigrants to Taiwan, their citizen spouses, and Taiwanese state actors but expands outward from these encounters to examine broader public debates about migration, human rights, and sovereignty claims. The chapter is inspired by a decade of ethnographic research on post-1987 marital immigration from the PRC to Taiwan and the immigration policies and governing institutions developed by the Taiwan government to regulate this highly contentious population, the largest group of permanent immigrants to the country. As exceptional immigrants, categorized neither as natives nor as foreigners, the Chinese spouses of Taiwanese citizens embody the contradictions faced by the Taiwanese polity. The modes of sovereign assertion adopted by state and societal actors in response to the entry of Chinese spouses link the fate of this contested immigrant group to the fate of the Taiwan nation-state as a whole (Friedman 2015a).[5] By attending to the diverse audiences addressed by state actors and public activists, the chapter explores how migration creates different opportunities and obstacles as these groups imagine alternative political futures.

Aspirational Sovereignty

Taiwan's status in the international community is unusual precisely because it functions as an independent state with a democratically elected government, independent military, and its own flag and currency, but it is formally recognized by only the Vatican and fourteen small states in Africa, Oceania, and Latin America.[6] It is denied admission to almost all international bodies, including the United Nations and its subsidiary organizations. Taiwan's anomalous sovereign standing derives from China's mid-twentieth century civil war, which ended in defeat for the then-ruling Republic of China (ROC) government under the leadership of Chiang Kaishek and his Nationalist Party. With Communist victory looming in 1949, Chiang's government fled across the Taiwan Strait where they reestablished the Republic of China on Taiwan. The Cold War politics that dominated the post–World War II era meant that many nations, including the United States, initially recognized the ROC on Taiwan as the legitimate government of all of China, destined ultimately to retake the mainland and depose Mao Zedong's Communist regime (the People's Republic of China). But this recognition became harder to sustain as the cross-strait stalemate continued over decades. In 1971, the ROC lost its United Nations seat to the People's Republic of China on the mainland, followed in 1979 by the US government's decision to switch its diplomatic recognition from the ROC to the PRC. This trend left the ROC on Taiwan stranded in a no-man's land of not quite sovereignty; it became what Mengin (2008), following Foucault, terms a heterotopia of Westphalian society, an other space that exposes both the norms of the international order and their inherent failures.

Beginning in the late 1980s and 1990s, Taiwan underwent a rapid process of democratization that inspired a flowering of support for Taiwanese independence across many sectors of society. The PRC government, however, has refused to revise its stance that Taiwan is a renegade province destined to reunite with the mainland, and it threatens military action in response to any official assertions of Taiwan's independence. The PRC actively blocks all formal efforts by the Taiwan government to secure sovereign recognition from the international community, such as applying for membership in the United Nations and other international bodies or participating in international fora such as the Olympics under the name Taiwan or even the ROC. The constant threat of PRC retaliation and the ever-deepening economic ties across the Taiwan Strait require Taiwanese state actors to negotiate a fraught terrain of sovereign action, ever alert to possible ripple effects in cross-strait relations as they struggle to carve out a space for sovereign recognition in the international community.

Faced with these conditions of contested sovereignty, Taiwan's bureaucrats and officials utilize a diverse array of governing strategies to assert sovereign standing. In place of grand pronouncements of statehood or the flexing of military muscle, they enact sovereignty through the repetition of everyday bureaucratic practices, such as those that call into being a state's power to manage cross-border mobility and police access to residency and citizenship rights. Acts such as producing documents, stamping papers, monitoring border flows, and investigating the familial relationships that make foreigners eligible for immigration are not merely the mundane work of border and population management; they also proclaim sovereignty in the face of international denial or indifference (Bobick 2017; Navaro-Yashin 2012). Their repetition offers the promise that by acting as a sovereign, a contested state may, over time, be recognized as such by the international community.

Biopolitical Sovereignty or Migration Regimes Redux

Taiwanese state actors are highly attuned to the potential sovereignty effects produced through biopolitical modes of border regulation and the governing infrastructures that support these regulatory practices. On numerous occasions, immigration officials and bureaucrats emphasized to me how important it was for them to create immigration institutions and engage in modes of border control that articulated the country's sovereign aspirations, ever cognizant of the impact these actions might have on the PRC and other members of the international community. For many, the most powerful sign of state sovereignty was the consolidation of Taiwan's existing immigration policing units into the National Immigration Agency (NIA), officially established under the Ministry of the Interior on January 2, 2007. A senior border officer who worked at Taiwan's main international airport expressed this sentiment explicitly as we chatted one March evening in 2008 during a lull in the arrival of travelers from China: "Only with the establishment of the NIA could we proclaim that Taiwan is a sovereign, independent nation-state [*zhuquan duli de guojia*]," he argued, emphasizing how bureaucratic normalization created a recognizably sovereign status for Taiwan (interview, March 20, 2008). For this official, robust governing institutions supported the work that he and his colleagues carried out at the border; in so doing, they generated an efficacious state apparatus and communicated that effectiveness to audiences at home and abroad. Acutely aware of their status as administrators of a largely unrecognized state, border officers engaged in internationally shared governing practices to affirm juridical power and regulatory capacities taken for granted by recognized sovereigns (Navaro-Yashin 2012).

Not all bureaucratic practices contributed equally to generating sovereign recognition, however, as this very same official reminded me. Continuing our conversation in the airport control zone, he added, "Only when the Entry/Exit Immigration Police Department [the NIA's predecessor unit] was upgraded to the level of an agency could [we] effectively manage our duties with respect to mainland Chinese" (interview, March 20, 2008). Ostensibly addressed to the superior hierarchical ranking of agencies as compared to departments, the officer's statement underscored how cross-strait migration invested certain kinds of governing practices with a productive power that exceeded their intended scope. From his perspective, it was not just any kind of immigrant who was more effectively managed by the NIA, but specifically those from the PRC. His emphasis on state efficacy affirmed the importance of the border as a site for producing the territorial integrity of the nation-state and as a space where sovereign claims could be projected internally, to diverse groups of citizens and immigrants in the country, and externally, to audiences of would-be immigrants and other states—especially the PRC. The spectral presence of these various audiences infused the space of the border with sovereign potential (Rutherford 2012), holding forth the possibility that the governing practices conducted there would effectively generate recognition of Taiwan's sovereign power.

I have discussed these border governing practices in greater detail elsewhere, focusing specifically on the interviews that NIA officers conduct at the border with mainland Chinese spouses arriving in Taiwan for the first time (Friedman 2010, 2015a). When the Taiwan government established the immigration interview system in the early years of the new millennium, it sought guidance and training from local consular representatives from the United States, Canada, and Australia. These requests and the governmental-level interactions that followed positioned Taiwan as an active participant in state-led border control initiatives, in effect proclaiming its shared status as a sovereign body despite the ambiguous, not quite state-to-state nature of these interactions. Fully aware that a state that did not enact such material practices invited the impression of failed or inactive sovereignty, Taiwanese state actors actively contributed to what they perceived as a shared sovereign project of border regulation. At the same time, they acknowledged the potentially limited effects of these state practices, not only because the government's claims to sovereignty were contested by some members of that international community but also because they were forced to interview Chinese immigrants in the liminal space of the border.

Precisely because the PRC does not recognize Taiwan as a sovereign state, it does not permit Taiwanese authorities to establish official government offices in the mainland where state actors might conduct predeparture interviews with immigrant spouses (nor does the PRC have formal government offices in Taiwan).[7] As a result, Taiwanese immigration officers must wait until Chinese spouses arrive at their first port of entry before officers are able to assess the authenticity of the marriage and to decide whether or not to grant the Chinese spouse admission to the country. Elsewhere I have analyzed how the charge of evaluating the authenticity of a cross-strait marriage is itself fraught with contradictions about the very nature of "truth" and "intention" (Friedman 2015b). Here I temporarily put this issue aside to focus on the potential sovereignty effects produced by the border interview as a governing practice.

Border interviews enact Taiwan's sovereign statehood in several ways. As a senior immigration official proclaimed to me in June 2009, "The border interview is an open declaration of sovereignty." But that assertion of sovereignty takes different forms and addresses different audiences. On the one hand, border interviews are the first face-to-face encounter that a Chinese immigrant has with a representative of the Taiwan government, a border officer who literally embodies the state and its power to decide whom to allow into the country and who will embark on a path to future residency and citizenship in Taiwan. In this interaction, the audience for sovereign address is an immigrant, specifically from the PRC, seeking entry to Taiwan as the legal spouse of a Taiwanese citizen.

This disciplinary mode of sovereign power is also paired with an educational-therapeutic mode of governance, whereby the border officer uses the interview to educate both Chinese and citizen spouses about the roles expected of them as members of Taiwanese families and to counsel them about care responsibilities and difficult family circumstances they might face. This productive dimension of sovereign power fosters what bureaucrats define as healthy couples and families, willing into being a robust national population able to serve as the foundation for sovereign claims despite widespread anxieties about the impact of marital immigration on the quality of the Taiwanese body politic. Below I discuss an interview I observed at Taiwan's main international airport in June 2009 that combined these two biopolitical modes in a single encounter.

June 22, 2009, Taoyuan International Airport, Taiwan: When I entered the small, featureless interview room at Taoyuan airport's Terminal One on a weekday evening, the border officer had already started the interview. A middle-aged man well into his career as a former immigration police officer now turned bureaucrat, Mr. Pei was intently questioning an attractive young woman in her twenties.[8] Her hair was dyed a reddish hue and her eyes were tinted blue from colored contacts; she had wrapped a scarf around her bare shoulders to ward off the air-conditioned chill of the airport. As I listened to Mr. Pei's questions and the woman's responses, I soon realized that she was entering Taiwan for the second time after remarrying her husband. Their first marriage had ended in divorce due to conflicts with her in-laws and her husband's general absence from their daily life as he focused on setting up a new business. Mr. Pei combined investigative questions that probed their past marital history with therapeutic commentary that urged the wife to take the marriage more seriously this time. Throughout the interview, he adopted a counseling role that emphasized the value of harmonious spousal relations and intergenerational family ties, while repeatedly reminding the young woman that her ability to enter Taiwan and acquire legal residency was contingent on the success of this second marriage.[9]

Mr. Pei conveyed these dual messages even more explicitly in the interview that followed with the young Taiwanese husband.[10] Here Mr. Pei immediately launched into questions about the couple's conflictual marital history, prompting the husband to admit that he had ignored his wife after they first married, his energies directed elsewhere as he struggled to establish his own business venture. Although Mr. Pei acknowledged the importance of the husband's provider role, he simultaneously reminded the young man that it was precisely under such conditions that his marriage and family life would suffer. "You must cherish your marriage," Mr. Pei admonished the husband, and then immediately cautioned him about future obstacles were their marriage to fail again. "This is your second time [to marry the same woman]. I've seen couples who marry three times. We will block you at the border and not admit [your wife] again if you don't take marriage seriously." Mr. Pei concluded the interview by reminding the husband that a cross-strait marriage was not as simple as a domestic union: not only were the procedures required to formalize the marriage more time-consuming and complicated, but as was clear from the interview process itself, marrying across the strait invited state actors into the intimate details of couples' everyday lives and relationship dynamics. The "we" in Mr. Pei's cautionary warning—"we will block you at the border"—invoked an effective state apparatus vested with the sovereign power to "not admit" the young man's wife into the country should he refuse to take his marriage seriously. By urging the husband to spend more time with his wife so that they could care for and develop feelings for one another, Mr. Pei affirmed his role as the face of a Taiwanese state whose sovereign efficacy was enacted not only through banning entry but also through cultivating marital and familial relationships identified as "healthy" for the nation as a whole.

In this interview, Mr. Pei combined the disciplinary face of sovereign power with the productive power to foster life by counseling a young couple on the value of marriage and harmonious intergenerational relations. The combination of these two modes of border control enabled Mr. Pei to represent a robust state that engaged in sovereign practices widely adopted by other members of the international community, countries that were similarly committed to cultivating a "healthy" national population through immigration regulation and the promotion of specific family ideals (Neveu Kringelbach 2013). As a representative of an anomalous state, however, Mr. Pei was well aware that mundane bureaucratic acts such as the border interview produced potential effects that extended well beyond the immediate charge to evaluate the authenticity of a particular couple's marriage. They were also bids for sovereign recognition that positioned Taiwan among other states engaged in similar practices that enacted sovereign control over territory, people, and mobility.

The immediate audience for Mr. Pei's sovereign address, however, was much closer at hand: an immigrant spouse and her citizen husband. In this regard, we might view the interview exchange as Mr. Pei's attempt to forge a contract between himself and the couple in which the latter consented to the effective governing power of the Taiwanese state to evaluate, observe, and decide on their marriage. This consent, as Audra Simpson (2016, 330) astutely notes, "is bound with recognition and its refusal," the recognition of the state's sovereign power and the ever-present possibility that this power will be refused, whether by citizens themselves or by audiences of immigrants, would-be immigrants, and other states.

The Limits of Biopolitical Sovereignty

Although interviewers remained committed to their charge to identify which immigrants had a legitimate right to enter Taiwan through a bona fide marriage to a citizen, they expressed increasingly serious doubts about their ability to realize this goal through the border interview. When I returned to Taiwan in the summer of 2009 to observe additional airport interviews, a senior airport border official bemoaned to me the pressure interviewers faced precisely because of their liminal position at the border: "No other country requires its border officers to make a decision so quickly!" Simultaneously asserting Taiwan's membership in a community of other states whose border officers ostensibly had more time and resources to make sovereign decisions, this official and others with whom I spoke that summer frequently complained about the ineffectiveness of their interview procedures given their location at the border. But I also noticed other concerns surfacing in their complaints about diminished effectiveness: many argued that they could no longer do their jobs well because they faced growing restrictions on what they could ask during interviews given pressure from Taiwanese NGOs to respect the human rights of immigrants and citizens.[11] An older male interviewer asserted that this growing emphasis on human rights forced interviewers to be too lenient in their questioning. He advocated eliminating the border interview altogether and replacing it with a three-month visa and an in-country interview that could investigate the couple's relationship in greater depth.

What does it mean to claim that a commitment to human rights erodes the power of a biopolitical mode of sovereign assertion? Might espousing and pro-tecting human rights also enact sovereignty, but in a different mode, and if so, how do we assess its effects in comparison with biopolitical governance focused on border control and population management? If biopolitical governance works through disciplinary techniques premised on a hierarchical relationship between state actor and supplicant, then it demands that citizens and immigrants acknowledge the fundamental terms of a sovereign contract: an effective state recognized as legitimately controlling people, resources, and mobility across a defined territory. The discourse and practice of human rights, however, poten-tially refuse this sovereign contract by imagining political efficacy differently. Taiwanese public discourse on the role of human rights in projecting effective sovereignty reveals both the desire to uphold a Westphalian sovereign contract and recognition of the impossibility of such a contract given Taiwan's anomalous political status. These public debates introduce ways of thinking the political "otherwise," thereby introducing alternative futures that might resolve Taiwan's current political predicament.

The possibility of framing Taiwan's political future in terms of human rights only emerged in the aftermath of nearly forty years of martial law and the pro-cess of democratization and civil society building that followed (Chen 2018). The 2000 presidential election saw the unprecedented victory of an opposition candidate, Chen Shui-bian, who represented the pro-Taiwan independence Democratic Progressive Party (DPP). Under President Chen's leadership, the government promoted the slogan, "a country established on the foundation of human rights" (renquan liguo), as part of its ultimately unsuccessful campaign to secure Taiwan's admission to the United Nations as a sovereign nation-state. By foregrounding the country's commitment to human rights, the DPP government sought to establish Taiwan as an integral member of a like-minded community of sovereign states dedicated to eradicating rights abuses—a position that also distinguished Taiwan's democracy from the PRC's more authoritarian regime. Immigration rights activists, by contrast, appealed to human rights to demand government accountability to its own "human rights-as-sovereignty" claim, and they did so by requiring that the government uphold United Nations covenants that protected the rights of migrants and immigrants. In short, the discourse of human rights served two purposes. On the one hand, the state's espoused commitment to human rights undergirded its sovereignty claims (exemplified by campaigns to join the UN), projecting sovereign aspirations outward beyond national borders. On the other hand, local NGOs and human rights supporters appealed to an international discourse of human rights in calling on the government to formulate more humane (im)migration policies, reorienting human rights claims to promote egalitarian state effects at home. Both positions underscore the intense work that human rights discourse is expected to do both to distinguish the Taiwanese polity from that of the PRC and to create a new place for that polity in a (potentially reimagined) international community of states and nongovernmental institutions.

Who Deserves Human Rights?

By the twenty-first century, immigrant rights NGOs in Taiwan had begun to advocate for human rights protections as part of campaigns to improve the treatment of all marital immigrants to Taiwan, both "foreign" spouses (primarily from Southeast Asian countries) and mainland Chinese spouses. As I have discussed elsewhere, these campaigns encountered significant difficulties as they struggled to integrate both groups under a shared rights agenda (Friedman 2015a, ch.3). Chinese spouses faced a different, and in many cases more onerous, set of policy restrictions precisely because they were regulated under a separate legal regime designed to manage contentious political relations across the strait by categorizing PRC citizens not as foreigners but as "residents of the mainland area." Fears of an unofficial "invasion" from China through cross-strait marriages led lawmakers to craft more restrictive policies for Chinese spouses than those faced by other marital immigrants: for example, a longer wait time to citizenship, more complex and restrictive immigration stages, and controls on legal work rights and eligibility for certain kinds of employment (see Friedman 2015a). As a consequence of these separate regulatory regimes, Chinese spouses' concerns about unequal treatment did not always match those of foreign spouses, differences that were sometimes erased under collective campaign strategies.

When advocating for Chinese spouses, activists also faced additional challenges because Chinese immigrants tended to be seen by bureaucrats and the Taiwanese public as less deserving of human rights protections than their foreign counterparts. Stereotyped as crafty operators who manipulated rights and legal protections to serve their own advantage, Chinese spouses were less readily assimilated into the popular imagination as sympathetic victims who suffered from racism and class oppression. The combination of separate law and policy regimes with negative stereotypes of Chinese spouses' marital motives meant that the obstacles Chinese spouses faced as marriage migrants were more difficult to challenge through activist campaigns that advocated human rights protections for all immigrants.

The fraught question of Chinese spouses' human rights reemerged on the national stage in 2012 following the reelection of Nationalist Party president Ma Ying-jeou, who announced that his administration would revise existing regulations governing Chinese spouses in Taiwan to equalize their status with all other marital immigrants (Chai, Chen, and Kao 2013). His announcement put cross-strait immigration and citizenship policies back in the limelight of public debate after a hiatus following reforms in 2009. Some parties retained a discriminatory stance toward Chinese immigrants, with groups such as the Taiwan Solidarity Union advocating denying political rights to mainland Chinese spouses even after they became Taiwanese citizens, espousing a form of "disaggregated citizenship" for this group alone.[12] Other parties, however, shifted their position to align with President Ma's. The Mainland Affairs Council (MAC), the governmental body responsible for cross-strait policymaking, abandoned its prior support for the differential treatment of Chinese spouses and proposed that the laws should be revised to equalize Chinese spouses' wait time to citizenship with that of other foreign spouses (Chai and Wang 2013).[13] Mainland Affairs Minister Wang Yu-chi argued that if Taiwan were to continue pressuring the PRC to improve its human rights record, then the government had to practice what it preached by treating Chinese spouses in Taiwan equally with other immigrants (Chai and Wang 2013).[14]

Jumping into this debate, Nationalist Party legislator Lu Hsiu-yan made an even stronger argument for the transnational portability of human rights: "Human rights do not discriminate by nationality, race, [or] place of origin. We must have a uniform approach. By penalizing spouses from a particular country, we violate the true meaning of democracy and human rights" (Zhang 2013). Both Minister Wang and Legislator Lu, therefore, called on Taiwan's government to uphold universal human rights by applying them to the country's most contentious group of newcomers and future citizens: the Chinese spouses of Taiwanese citizens.

Certainly, public deployment of a discourse of human rights was not new in Taiwan in 2012, as I discussed above. When prominent political actors such as Wang and Lu identified equalizing the treatment of Chinese spouses with support for human rights, however, they were making bids for sovereign recognition that addressed audiences both near and far: Taiwanese citizens with diverse political affiliations and agendas, PRC government representatives who ada-mantly claimed Taiwan as a part of China, and a community of recognized states and international observers closely attuned to the sovereign assertions enacted through such speech acts. These bids for recognition reverberate across diverse scales of sovereign address and attest to the need, in not quite sovereign states especially, to speak effectively to audiences that span local, national, and trans-national domains.

Faustian Bargains

Political figures are not the only contributors to these vociferous debates about the human rights of Chinese spouses and their connection to Taiwan's sover-eignty claims. Well-known Taiwanese artist Chen Chieh-jen publicly tackled this very topic in his 2008–9 video art production, *Empire's Borders I*, which he included in exhibitions mounted both in Taiwan and internationally. This work takes the US and Taiwan governments to task for violating the human right to cross-border mobility in the name of sovereign control over people and terri-tory. Created in response to Chen's own humiliating treatment by an American visa processing officer when he applied for a visa to attend the post-Katrina New Orleans Biennial, *Empire's Borders I* integrates marriage and sovereignty in a sin-gle representational frame as it contrasts the fate of young, unmarried Taiwanese women denied visas to the United States (ostensibly for fear that their unmarried status will encourage them to emigrate) with the experiences of Chinese immi-grant wives who encounter discrimination and suspicion when they seek to enter Taiwan or establish residency and citizenship through their marriage to a citizen. Filmed in black and white using a stripped down, documentary style, *Empire's Borders I* features sixteen women who impassively narrate painful encounters with bureaucratic representatives of sovereign power: for Taiwanese women, the American Institute in Taiwan (AIT), the unofficial consular office of the United States, and for Chinese immigrant wives, Taiwan's National Immigration Agency (NIA).[15] Their accounts starkly depict the arbitrary nature of border control and citizenship decisions that enact sovereignty through evaluating applicants' motives for cross-border mobility. Chen's choice to pair Taiwanese with Chinese border-crossers and AIT with the NIA situates Taiwan and its sovereignty claims at the borders of both the United States and the PRC.

July 25, 2011. A Second-Floor Studio Located on a Narrow Alley in Taipei City: A thin wisp of smoke trails from the lit cigarette that artist Chen Chieh-jen holds casually out the window of his studio, and it dissipates slowly in the slight breeze that has sprung up in the wake of a sudden rainstorm. Chen pauses to draw deeply on his cigarette and then continues explaining to me what he sees as five different overlapping forms of sovereignty in Taiwan. Ultimately pessimistic about the future resolution of Taiwan's international status, he concludes, "I feel that Taiwan . . . is at once the border of America and the border of mainland China."

Chen's commentary during our meeting that day reflected his familiarity with Western theories of state power and sovereignty, and our discussion ranged widely from Foucauldian biopower and Agamben's state of exception to Hardt and Negri's multitude. In his assessment of the overlapping domains of sovereign power in Taiwan, Chen reiterated a point he had made at the end of *Empire's Borders I*. The video concludes with shots of two texts presented in both English and Chinese. The first details an August 26, 2008, news release from Taiwan's Ministry of Foreign Affairs that claims Taiwan may become eligible for US visa-exempt status in the next two years if it meets key "antiterrorism" requirements, including introducing microchip-embedded passports and sharing antiterrorism intelligence. The inclusion of this news release underscores the video's critique of ever more stringent border controls, as if such technological "improvements" might diminish the violence that underlies every border decision. The possibility that Taiwanese might be liberated from the arbitrary power of AIT interviewers is presented as a Faustian bargain that weighs the lure of sovereign recognition against the disciplinary power of a global security apparatus.[16]

Chen pairs this text with a description of proposed revisions to the policies regulating Chinese spouses in Taiwan, thereby reaffirming the linkages between Taiwan's aspirations for sovereign recognition and the material practices used by the government to manage Chinese marital immigrants. Although the actual policy reforms implemented later in 2009 would prove some of the details incorrect, the text itself and its juxtaposition with news of eased restrictions on future Taiwanese travel to the United States affirmed the key role of cross-strait marital regulation in the Taiwan government's sovereign aspirations. By pairing the two, Chen critiqued the assumption that expanded international recognition of Taiwan as a sovereign state rested on the government's intense regulation of Chinese spouses, irrespective of whether those regulations conformed to existing legal standards for other foreign spouses or to universal principles of human rights.

Closely attuned to the costs of this Faustian bargain, Chen Chieh-jen argued forcefully when we met in 2011 that under a Westphalian system, Taiwan would never have the power to induce other states to recognize its national sovereignty. As a consequence, he advocated an altogether different approach to the dilemma of sovereign recognition: given that Taiwan could never compete politically or economically with the PRC or the United States, its only option was to build the best form of democracy possible, to become the place where anyone, regardless of citizenship status, could receive equal treatment. Pausing to ask rhetorically why Taiwanese should be concerned about the fate of Chinese spouses in Taiwan, Chen replied, "Once you treat others unequally, how can you then complain that others treat you unfairly?" Shifting to the second-person "you" to distance himself from this stance, Chen contended that Taiwan's only viable path out of its sovereignty impasse was to enact laws and governing practices that made it a global beacon of equality and human rights protection. If Taiwan treated all who entered its borders fairly, Chen argued, it would become a new model of democracy freed from the constraints of national sovereignty. Put simply, Chen's model of aspirational sovereignty erased the citizen/noncitizen distinction as the ostensible foundation of sovereign claims.

Chen's solution shared key features with the argument made by Legislator Lu above that Taiwan could not simply espouse a commitment to human rights without enacting them fairly at home. But Chen also acknowledged that, were Taiwan to continue to play by the rules of sovereignty that governed a Westphalian system of nation-states, it was certain to lose. As he astutely noted, that system was based on power and force (*liliang*), and on those counts Taiwan could never compete with the PRC or effectively challenge its stance that Taiwan was merely a renegade province. Decoupling territoriality from sovereignty, Chen argued that Taiwan's best chance of acquiring recognized standing in the international community was to deploy moral suasion against so-called hard power, transforming the nature of power itself by fully enacting the government's commitment to the equal protection of all, regardless of citizenship status. As an example of the "separate lives" of sovereignty and territoriality (Appadurai 2003, 347), Chen's vision also distinguished the nation and its territory from the state by opening up the borders of the nation and identifying as worthy of protection all who found themselves, even temporarily, on national soil.

Chen's idealism resonates with a strand of argument in migration studies advocated most clearly by legal scholar David Jacobson. Examining how undocumented immigration flows have altered North American and Western European nation-states, Jacobson argues that "international human rights codes, rooted as they are in the documents establishing nation-states, are becoming the vehicle that is transforming the nation-state system" (1996, 2).[17] Human rights protections do not bespeak an end to states altogether, but underscore a shift in the mission of the nation-state from sovereign control and national self-determination to responsibility for "persons *qua* persons" regardless of national affiliation, precisely the argument espoused by Chen Chieh-jen and Legislator Lu (1996, 8–9).[18]

Jacobson's recasting of the state has significant consequences for nationality and the promise of belonging it affirms. If states no longer espouse a particular investment in their own citizens, the value of citizenship itself is weakened, and distinctions between citizens and noncitizens break down. As a result, Jacobson argues, "the premise that an individual or group of people has to 'belong' to a territorially bounded nation in order to enjoy rights is superseded or at least diluted" (1996, 106). The qualifier "at least" tempers Jacobson's optimism, although it does not prevent him from envisioning a radically altered role for the state and its bureaucracy with respect to both ethno-cultural communities and an international order organized around universal human rights.

By defining this new international human rights order as implemented and protected by states, however, Jacobson overlooks a key question that preoccupies a diverse array of actors in Taiwan: what might this new order offer states still struggling to claim sovereign recognition and affirm the value of national citizenship? By appealing to Taiwan's obligation to promote universal human rights, how are these actors advocating sovereignty in a different register, and how does this register coexist with modes of biopolitical governance, such as border interviews, that are understood by the state actors who enact them as necessary assertions of Taiwanese sovereignty premised on a distinction between citizens and noncitizens?

Orders of Causality

The precise role of human rights governance in advancing different visions of Taiwan's sovereignty was debated openly in responses to a highly contentious case that attracted public attention beginning in November 2011. Following a long investigation, the FBI arrested Liu Hsien-hsien, director of the Taiwan Economic and Cultural Office in Kansas City (Taiwan's de facto consular office in the US), on charges of foreign labor fraud for abuses she committed against two Filipina housekeepers who had worked in her Kansas home.[19] In the end, Liu pleaded guilty to one count of fraud under a plea agreement, served three months in jail, and paid eighty thousand US dollars in restitution to the two women (Sudekum 2012). She was deported back to Taiwan in February 2012, where she escaped criminal prosecution but faced sanction and possible disciplinary action from the Control Yuan, the branch of government responsible for monitoring the conduct of civil servants (Morris 2012).

Liu's case brought the vexed status of Taiwanese sovereignty into the media spotlight both at home and in the United States, where the question of immunity for Taiwanese diplomats sparked intense discussion of whether the US recognized Taiwan as a sovereign nation and whether the Taiwanese government effectively protected its diplomats abroad.[20] The case also initiated a heated debate about the role of human rights discourse and policy in mitigating sovereign uncertainty. A mere week after Liu was arrested in Kansas City, Taiwan's *Apple Daily* ran an opinion piece titled, "How To Defend Sovereignty Without Discussing Human Rights?" (Yang and Shi 2011a). Coauthored by Yang Zong-li and Shi Yi-hsiang, both members of the NGO Covenants Watch, the piece described the government's concern with diplomatic immunity qua sovereign recognition as a "false issue."[21] At stake in Liu's case, the authors argued, was her abuse of human rights, a sign that even Taiwanese civil servants had not been adequately educated in the protections enshrined in the United Nations' International Covenant on Economic, Social, and Cultural Rights and International Covenant on Civil and Political Rights, both of which the Taiwan government had ratified unilaterally in 2009 and committed to implement fully within two years (Chen 2018). The government's emphasis on sovereign recognition in response to Liu's arrest was putting the cart before the horse, so the authors contended. "Only by first achieving international human rights standards," they concluded, "will [Taiwan] be able to defend national sovereignty."

Yang and Shi's article received a response the following day from political scientist Yang Yong-nian, who reversed Yang and Shi's order of causality by arguing that without sovereign recognition, Taiwan was in no position to protect the human rights of its citizens abroad (Yang 2011). Were Liu's diplomatic immunity to be recognized and she returned home, Professor Yang asserted, then Taiwan could discipline her itself, clearly demonstrating to the rest of the world the value the government placed on human rights. In their final rebuttal published two days later, Yang and Shi accused Professor Yang of missing the point entirely. They argued that by ratifying the UN covenants, the Taiwanese government had done two things: it had committed itself to protecting the human rights enshrined in the covenants, and it had symbolically positioned itself as a signatory state on equal footing with other states that similarly obligated themselves to protecting human rights. Moreover, Yang and Shi contended, the covenants guaranteed human rights protections for all people, regardless of nationality, a relevant domestic issue in Taiwan where accounts of abuses against migrants were not uncommon. Therefore, the authors chastised Professor Yang for assuming that the Taiwan government's respect for and protection of human rights applied only to the stakeholders in Liu's case and to Taiwanese citizens abroad. "Human rights are the only weapon available to the weak," Yang and Shi concluded. "The clear demonstration of basic human rights and respect constitutes the greatest common factor able to limit state authority across national borders" (Yang and Shi 2011b).

The debates that swirled around Liu's arrest put sovereignty and human rights on equal footing as core principles that would determine Taiwan's standing in the international community. And yet, contests over which one preceded the other invoked radically different visions of the nation-state, the role of the state in producing effective sovereignty, and the very value of sovereignty itself. Would Taiwan become a beacon of human rights and democracy that offered equal protection to all regardless of nationality, the vision to which Yang and Shi aspired (together with Chen Chieh-jen and Legislator Lu), or would it become a recognized sovereign power emboldened to protect its citizens abroad and appropriately discipline its own government representatives even for abuses committed outside the country, as Professor Yang proposed? Whereas immigrants to Taiwan and the disenfranchised of the world featured prominently in the first vision, citizens and state actors occupied center stage in the second. As a consequence, the two visions also espoused different strategies for Taiwan to assert its own sovereignty and define the very form of international belonging to which it aspired.

A certain idealism about human rights clearly pervades some sectors in Taiwan, as seen in the position that realizing the government's commitment to protecting the human rights of all constitutes the foundation for a successful sovereignty strategy. For those who advocate this stance, biopolitical techniques of sovereign assertion actually undermine Taiwan's chances of acquiring a more secure standing in the world, despite their conformity to standards of border control adopted by established states such as the United States. Recognizing that the current international system does not create an even playing field for anomalous states such as Taiwan, those who espouse protecting human rights as a mode of claiming sovereignty envision a path to recognition that diverges in significant ways from those available to established sovereigns.

These arguments supporting the human rights of all, regardless of nationality, do something more as well: they advocate a different vision of an international system and the role of nation-states within it. Human rights provide a platform for imagining a world in which borders do not divide populations or distribute rights unequally across and within them. Instead, precisely because of their transnational portability, human rights enable diverse actors to envision the political differently. Whether this alternative vision wholly rejects sovereignty as a basis for organizing political collectivities is a separate issue, however, returning us to the question introduced above of how human rights advocacy itself acts as a mode of sovereign assertion.

Lest we assume too quickly that these different visions of sovereignty have faded in recent years with deepening cross-strait tensions, I conclude with a 2017 statement issued by the ROC's Office of the President. This statement protested the PRC's refusal to allow Taiwan to attend the 2017 meeting of the World Health Assembly even in its previous status as an observer party. The statement opens with a bold statement of sovereignty: "The Republic of China is a sovereign state.

Taiwan is not a province under the rule of the People's Republic of China" (Office of the President 2017). It goes on to declare the illegitimacy of PRC efforts to exclude Taiwan's 23 million people from the international health system. Up to this point, the statement reads very much like an assertion of Westphalian sovereignty (whether under the name ROC or Taiwan) and a challenge to another state's infringement of that sovereign right. The next paragraph, however, shifts radically in discursive register by beginning with the statement: "Health is a universal human right." It continues with the claim that because neither health nor disease are confined within national borders, the World Health Organization must represent and serve the health needs of all people and not advance the political objectives of any particular country. The statement asserts Taiwan's inclusion in the international community and argues that, as a consequence, "its people are entitled to enjoy the same rights to good health as everyone else in the world."

The government's statement does not end with the stance that the people of Taiwan deserve equal rights and treatment. Instead, the final two sentences effectively blend sovereignty claims with human rights protections, espousing the Taiwan government's determination "to participate in and contribute to the international community" and "to ensure the rights of our people to good health." What is not articulated in this statement is as significant as what it claims. The statement does not specify how or through what political model the government will participate in the international community nor does it articulate a precise vision for how it will cooperate with "the proper authorities in other nations" to guarantee its own people's rights to good health. Moreover, both the English- and Chinese-language versions of the statement retain some ambiguity as to who is included in the category, the people of Taiwan. The English-language statement uses "people" throughout: "the people of Taiwan," "its people," "our people." The wording leaves open the possibility that both citizens and noncitizens are included in these necessary rights protections. The Chinese-language statement, however, ultimately narrows its scope of inclusion. Until the very end, the statement declares its object of protection to be the "people" of Taiwan (*ren* or *renmin*), a usage that retains some vagueness about political inclusiveness (Zhonghua Minguo Zongtongfu 2017). But in its final sentence, the statement asserts the government's commitment to ensuring the rights of its people to good health. Here, generic people are replaced with nationals (*guoren*), explicitly narrowing the scope of protection to those with a recognized political claim to inclusion and belonging. This narrowing, ironically, works against the more expansive definition of human rights as spanning national borders that appears earlier in the paragraph.

The tension between expansive and narrow definitions of who is worthy of human rights protections reflects different positions on Taiwan's aspirations for sovereign recognition and the means through which the government might most effectively seek inclusion in a desired international community. Like President Tsai's 2016 phone call with President-elect Trump, these aspirations do not simply refer to an existing political reality into which Taiwan inserts itself as a recognized sovereign; instead, they seek to call into being certain spaces of interaction, modes of power, and audiences necessary to recognize desired terms of belonging and inclusion. The seductiveness of "voicing an utterance that creates its own truth" (Rutherford 2012, 21), as in the opening line of the presidential statement, "The Republic of China is a sovereign state," lies precisely in the appeal of calling into being conditions of possibility that do not yet exist and thinking otherwise about sovereignty, state power, and the basis of international community. Perhaps it is these alternatives that constitute the future promise of the Tsai-Trump phone call.

Notes

1. This chapter is based on more than two years of nonconsecutive ethnographic research conducted in Taiwan and China between 2003 and 2013 with support from the National Science Foundation (BCS-0612679), the Wenner-Gren Foundation for Anthropological Research, and the Chiang Ching-kuo Foundation for International Scholarly Exchange. I am deeply grateful to the many cross-strait couples who generously shared their lives and thoughts with me, to Chen Chieh-jen for introducing me to his work, and to the Taiwanese bureaucrats and officials who provided invaluable insights into the workings of immigration regulation. An earlier version of this chapter was presented at the conference, The Everyday Lives of Sovereignty, held in Nicosia, Cyprus in 2015. I thank Rebecca Bryant, Madeleine Reeves, and the other participants for inspiring conversations about sovereignty from below. A 2018 keynote address to the Annual Conference of the Taiwan Association for Philosophy of Law and Social Philosophy provided a valuable opportunity to clarify my analysis. I am grateful to Chao-ju Chen and the conference organizers for making this opportunity possible and to Margaret Lewis and Gardner Bovingdon for insightful comments on the final draft. I remain responsible for any errors or inadequacies.

2. This formulation is indebted to Gregson and Rose's critique of assumptions that "heterosexual space simply exists, always already there, vulnerable only to incursion" (2000, 437).

3. The phone call was covered extensively in the press in the United States, Taiwan, and the PRC. Media attention returned to the phone call in the days leading up to Chinese president Xi Jinping's state visit to the United States in April 2017 as pundits speculated whether Taiwan would be discussed during the meetings between President Trump and President Xi.

4. In recent years the PRC government has stepped up its efforts to block all signs of Taiwan's standing as a nation-state, regardless of whether these signs emanate from Taiwan or elsewhere. No longer confined to acts such as public displays of the ROC flag, PRC efforts to symbolically erase Taiwan's independent existence now extend to drop-down boxes on the websites of international airlines, hotels, and clothing retailers, to name just a few recent examples.

5. Although Agamben (1998, 2005) alerts us to the significant role of exceptionalism in sovereignty's constitution, he does little to help us understand the lived experiences of

the exceptional subjects who are so vital to his vision of sovereignty. Scholars studying immigration and citizenship in various parts of the world have challenged Agamben's portrayal of a universal subject of exception, arguing instead that contextual specificities matter deeply when analyzing how inclusion and exclusion are forged through particular bodies and their relationships to different states (Partridge 2012; Ticktin 2006; Willen 2010). Precisely because otherness is not generic, the practices and discourses that mobilize otherness in the service of sovereign claims will differ significantly in accordance with specific histories (see also Fernando 2013; Surkis 2010).

6. That number has shrunk from twenty-one states plus the Vatican in 2015, a consequence of the PRC's successful campaign to isolate Taiwan through providing incentives for countries to switch their diplomatic recognition in accordance with the PRC's "one China" policy.

7. The only other group required to undergo immigration interviews are foreign spouses from Southeast Asia, but these immigrants are interviewed prior to departure at Taiwan's de facto consular offices in their home countries.

8. Mr. Pei is a pseudonym.

9. This was not the only case I encountered in my research of a cross-strait couple that had divorced and then married each other again. See Friedman 2015b.

10. Both the citizen and Chinese spouse are interviewed at the border, although separately. The interviews take place in the control zone of the airport if the couple has flown to Taiwan together. If the citizen spouse is already in Taiwan, he or she is interviewed outside of immigration control.

11. Policy reforms that were to take effect for Chinese spouses in August 2009 made border officers even more pessimistic about the value of their interviews, since now Chinese spouses would receive legal work rights shortly after first entry (eliminating the need to determine whether the Taiwanese spouse would be able to support his partner until she could work legally in Taiwan).

12. Benhabib (2002) coins the term *disaggregated citizenship* to describe a situation in which immigrants are granted some citizenship rights (for instance, social and economic rights) but are denied (perhaps permanently) access to other key rights, such as voting.

13. The MAC proposed reducing the total time to citizenship from six years to four, the time frame applied to foreign spouses. To date, this reform has not been implemented and Chinese spouses still face a six-year wait time to citizenship.

14. On the potential role of human rights in the crafting of official cross-strait agreements, see Chen 2015.

15. The women in the first part of the video are actresses from a local theater troupe who recite narratives culled from public responses to a blog that Chen established in the aftermath of his humiliating experience at AIT. The second section features Chinese wives narrating their own experiences. Portrayed standing in the control zone of Taiwan's main international airport, facing away from immigration with their luggage carts in front of them (as if they are being deported), the Chinese women read aloud from notes jotted on the back of official forms.

16. Taiwanese were only granted visa-exempt status by the United States in November 2012.

17. For an earlier version of this argument, see Soysal 1998.

18. Sally Engle Merry argues that participation in the international human rights regime—for instance, by ratifying human rights treaties—also "allows countries to claim civilized status in the present international order" (2006, 79).

19. Liu was charged with taking away the employee's passport, preventing her from leaving the house without permission, forcing her to work sixteen to eighteen hour days, paying her a quarter of the wages specified in her contract, monitoring her with video

surveillance cameras, and harassing her with verbal abuse and threats. Liu was alleged to have abused a previous Filipina housekeeper as well (Oberman 2011).

20. Taiwan's Ministry of Foreign Affairs demanded that Liu be released immediately on the grounds that she enjoyed diplomatic immunity, but the US State Department claimed that Liu was only a consular officer and, therefore, enjoyed immunity only when carrying out official duties (Chang 2011; Chou and Wu 2011).

21. Yang and Shi were also, respectively, assistant secretary of the Taiwan branch of Amnesty International and member of the human rights section of the Taiwan-Philippines Friendship Association.

References

Abarca, Gray Albert, and Susan Bibler Coutin. 2018. "Sovereign Intimacies: The Lives of Documents within US State-Noncitizen Relationships." *American Ethnologist* 45(1): 7–19.

Agamben, Giorgio. 1998. *Homo Sacer: Sovereign Power and Bare Life*. Translated by Daniel Heller-Roazen. Stanford, CA: Stanford University Press.

Agamben, Giorgio. 2005. *State of Exception*. Translated by Kevin Attell. Chicago: University of Chicago Press.

Appadurai, Arjun. 2003. "Sovereignty without Territoriality: Notes for a Postnational Geography." In *The Anthropology of Space and Place: Locating Culture*, edited by Setha M. Low and Denise Lawrence-Zúñiga, 337–349. Malden, MA: Blackwell.

Benhabib, Seyla. 2002. "Transformations of Citizenship: The Case of Contemporary Europe." *Government and Opposition* 37(4): 439–465.

Bobick, Michael. 2017. "Sovereignty and the Vicissitudes of Recognition: Peoplehood and Performance in a De Facto State." *PoLAR: Political and Legal Anthropology Review* 40(1): 158–170.

Bonilla, Yarimar. 2015. *Non-Sovereign Futures: French Caribbean Politics in the Wake of Disenchantment*. Chicago: University of Chicago Press.

Chai, Scarlett, Hung-chin Chen, and Y. L. Kao. 2013. "Taiwan to Loosen Rules on Chinese Spouses Obtaining ID Cards." Central News Agency, Focus Taiwan, April 10.

Chai, Scarlett, and Jamie Wang. 2013. "Taiwan Should Improve Human Rights for Chinese Spouses: MAC." Central News Agency, Focus Taiwan, May 9.

Chang, S. C. 2011. "Talk of the Day: Taiwan-U.S. Ties Tested by Diplomat's Arrest." Central News Agency, November 13.

Chen, Yu-Jie. 2015. "Human Rights in China-Taiwan Relations: How Taiwan Can Engage China." *Hong Kong Law Journal* 45(Part 2): 565–89.

Chen, Yu-Jie. 2018. "Isolated but Not Oblivious: Taiwan's Acceptance of Two Major Human Rights Covenants." In *Taiwan and International Human Rights: A Story of Transformation*, edited by Jerome A. Cohen, William P. Alford, and Chang-fa Lo, 207–225. New York: Springer.

Chou, Jay, and Lilian Wu. 2011. "Taiwan to Seek Full Diplomatic Immunity for Diplomats in U.S." Central News Agency, Focus Taiwan, December 24.

Fernando, Mayanthi L. 2013. "Save the Muslim Woman, Save the Republic, Ni Putes Ni Soumises and the Ruse of Neoliberal Sovereignty." *Modern and Contemporary France* 21(2): 147–165.

Friedman, Sara L. 2010. "Determining 'Truth' at the Border: Immigration Interviews, Chinese Marital Migrants, and Taiwan's Sovereignty Dilemmas." *Citizenship Studies* 14(2): 167–183.

Friedman, Sara L. 2015a. *Exceptional States: Chinese Immigrants and Taiwanese Sovereignty*. Berkeley: University of California Press.

Friedman, Sara L. 2015b. "Regulating Cross-Border Intimacy: Authenticity Paradigms and the Specter of Illegality Among Chinese Marital Immigrants to Taiwan." In *Migrant Encounters: Intimate Labor, the State, and Mobility Across Asia*, edited by Sara L. Friedman and Pardis Mahdavi, 206–229. Philadelphia: University of Pennsylvania Press.

Gregson, Nicky, and Gillian Rose. 2000. "Taking Butler Elsewhere: Performativities, Spatialities, and Subjectivities." *Environment and Planning D: Society and Space* 18: 433–52.

Jacobson, David. 1996. *Rights Across Borders: Immigration and the Decline of Citizenship*. Baltimore, MD: Johns Hopkins University Press.

Mengin, Françoise. 2008. "Taiwan as the Westphalian Society's Foucaldian Heterotopia." *Sociétés Politiques Comparées* 7: 1–21.

Merry, Sally Engle. 2006. *Human Rights and Gender Violence: Translating International Law into Local Justice*. Chicago: University of Chicago Press.

Morris, Mark. 2012. "Home Isn't So Welcoming for Deported Taiwanese Envoy." *Kansas City Star*, June 18.

Navaro-Yashin, Yael. 2012. *The Make-Believe Space: Affective Geography in a Postwar Polity*. Durham, NC: Duke University Press.

Neveu Kringelbach, Helene. 2013. "'Mixed Marriage,' Citizenship and the Policing of Intimacy in Contemporary France." International Migration Institute Working Papers Series Paper 77. http://www.imi.ox.ac.uk/pdfs/wp/2013-WP2077.pdf.

Oberman, Mira. 2011. "No Diplomatic Immunity for Taiwan Official: US." Agence France-Presse, November 14.

Office of the President, Republic of China (Taiwan). 2017. "ROC Government's Position on Mainland Chinese Authorities to Interference with Taiwan's Participation in WHA." May 22. http://english.president.gov.tw/Default.aspx?tabid=491&itemid=39239&rmid=2355.

Partridge, Damani J. 2012. *Hypersexuality and Headscarves: Race, Sex, and Citizenship in the New Germany*. Bloomington: Indiana University Press.

Rutherford, Danilyn. 2012. *Laughing at Leviathan: Sovereignty and Audience in West Papua*. Chicago: University of Chicago Press.

Simpson, Audra. 2016. "Consent's Revenge." *Cultural Anthropology* 31(3): 326–333.

Soysal, Yasemin Nuhoğlu. 1998. "Toward a Postnational Model of Membership." In *The Citizenship Debates: A Reader*, edited by Gershon Shafir, 189–220. Minneapolis: University of Minnesota Press.

Sudekum, Maria. 2012. "Taiwan Official Deported, Sentenced to Time Served." *Associated Press*, January 27.

Surkis, Judith. 2010. "Hymenal Politics: Marriage, Secularism, and French Sovereignty." *Public Culture* 22(3): 531–556.

Ticktin, Miriam. 2006. "Where Ethics and Politics Meet: The Violence of Humanitarianism in France." *American Ethnologist* 33(1): 33–49.

Willen, Sarah S. 2010. "Citizens, 'Real' Others, and 'Other' Others: Governmentality, Biopolitics, and the Deportation of Undocumented Migrants from Tel Aviv." In *The Deportation Regime: Sovereignty, Space, and the Freedom of Movement*, edited by Nicholas P. De Genova and Nathalie Peutz, 262–294. Durham, NC: Duke University Press.

Yang, Yong-nian. 2011. "Meiyou zhuquan he lai renquan?" (Without Sovereignty, Where Will Human Rights Come From?). *Pingguo Ribao* (Apple Daily), November 15.

Yang, Zong-li, and Yi-hsiang Shi. 2011a. "Bu tan renquan ruhe hanwei zhuquan?" (How to Defend Sovereignty without Discussing Human Rights?). *Pingguo Ribao* (Apple Daily), November 14.

Yang, Zong-li, and Yi-hsiang Shi. 2011b. "Renlei zunyan chaoyue guojie" (Respect for Humanity Crosses National Borders). *Pingguo Ribao* (Apple Daily), November 17.

Zhang, Yongtai. 2013. "Tai zhengfu fangkuan lupei qude shenfenzheng, zai ye dang piping ci ju shi xuanju kaoliang" (Taiwan Government to Relax [Restrictions] on Mainland Spouses Acquiring Citizenship, Opposition Party Criticizes Act as Election Ploy). *Voice of America*, April 10.

Zhonghua Minguo Zongtongfu. 2017. "Zhendui Zhongguo Dalu Dangju Zhi Han Ganrao Wo Guo Canyu WHA: Zhonghua Minguo Zhengfu Lichang." May 22. http://www.president.gov.tw/Default.aspx?tabid=131&itemid=39237&rmid=514.

GENDER, VIOLENCE, AND COMPETING SOVEREIGN CLAIMS IN AFGHANISTAN

Torunn Wimpelmann

In the summer of 2008, a series of unprecedented TV broadcasts took place in Afghanistan. Several families from the province of Sarepul appeared on national TV to demand that the government bring men who had raped their daughters and nieces to justice.[1] The culmination of these broadcasts was a disturbing TV clip showing twelve-year-old Anisa weeping as she described how five armed men entered the house at midnight, beat her family members, and sexually assaulted her. Anisa's parents, also in tears, appealed to President Karzai for justice, declaring their intention to commit mass suicide if the government continued to ignore their case. Her uncle then explained that attempts to report the rape in their home area of Sarepul had only resulted in threats and abuse at the hands of the local police, and he accused the police chief of having links to the rapists. The broadcast followed on from a number of TV appearances by Sayed Noorullah, uncle of another rape victim from Sarepul and the first to go public with his pursuit of justice. Like Anisa's uncle, Noorullah had been subjected to threats and abuse when trying to report the rape of his thirteen-year-old niece by two men, one of them the son of a powerful former commander-cum-MP in the province. But rather than being cowed, Sayed Noorullah had resorted to the media, a novel outlet for public grievances against government misconduct in Afghanistan. His increasingly angry descriptions of government inaction on various national TV channels finally saw him launch into a brazen attack on President Karzai himself; "May God's curse be upon you and your entire tribe." Shortly after, Anisa's family had also come forward to speak of their ordeal, and the government was at last shamed into action. Senior police officials in Sarepul were fired, and Noorul-lah, who by then had appeared on TV half a dozen times, was summoned for a personal audience with President Karzai. In the months that followed, a number of men, including the son of MP Payenda, were sentenced to life imprisonment for the assault on Noorullah's niece.

The Sarepul rape cases generated attention across Afghanistan. Some thought the families' public appeals for justice unsettling and inappropriate. By speaking openly about the rapes, the families from Sarepul had violated social norms about keeping such violations a matter of private shame. Calling for government intervention was a double admission of weakness and impotency; not only had the families disclosed what had happened, they had demonstrated their inability to seek redress on their own. But for others, the TV appearances represented hopeful signs of change for the country's women. The fact that, rather than to treat the incidents as matters of private shame, the families chose to seek justice for the young girls, suggested "an important change in how Afghans view the abuse of women" (Kargar 2008) and that the post-2001 activism against violence toward women was yielding results.

As these different views suggest, whether and how the Afghan government should intervene in cases of gender violence emerged as a highly contested issue in the country in the years following the 2001 overthrow of the Taliban government. At stake were, for one, the kind of gender relations that should receive public sanction. As long pointed out by feminist analysis, the construction of a private sphere in which violence against women is exempt from legal and political scrutiny masks the subordination of women to their fathers and husbands (Schneider 1991). Ultimately, this gendered subordination can be understood in terms of sovereignty, in the sense that Comaroff and Comaroff (2006) understand it: "We take the word sovereignty to connote the more or less effective claims on the part of any agent, community, cadre or collectivity to exercise autonomous, exclusive control over the lives, deaths, and conditions of existence of those who fall within a given purview, and to extend over them the jurisdiction of some kind of law" (35). The ability of husbands, fathers, or others to inflict violence to the point of death on female family members without outside intervention can be said to constitute a sovereign power. In turn, feminist struggles to make such violence against women a punishable crime represent a potential transfer of sovereignty over women from household leaders to the government. Similarly, the framing of rape as an offense against women—rather than against their husbands or other guardians—represents a potentially radical shift in gender relations in which male relatives' sovereign claims over women's bodies are abolished.

At the same time, interventions into violence inflicted on women do more than shape gender relations. In Afghanistan as elsewhere, rulers have used—or sought to use—the institutionalized regulation of family and kinship as a means of centralizing power. For instance, by prohibiting forced marriage or curtailing bride price, the state might seek to curb the autonomy of kinship groups and to enter into a direct relationship with individuals. Likewise, by claiming the right to adjudicate in rape cases, previously settled among the families of the parties or a council of community elders, the government might expand its sovereign domain vis-a-vis those of kinship or local elites. Literature on state formation and gender in the Middle East and beyond have demonstrated historical variation in the exact ways in which the state comes to intervene in family domains and showed such variation to be contingent on rulers' power bases and ideological orientation, as well as the political strength of local women's rights movements (Kandiyoti 1991; Noelle-Karimi 2002; Joseph 2000; Hajjar 2004; Al-Ali 2007; Charrad 2001). Yet, this literature has tended to leave unexamined the exact forms of sovereign power that operate as "the state" seeks (or is called on) to intervene into erstwhile "private" domains. As is now well accepted in scholarly debates about statehood, claims to act on behalf of the state should not lead us to assume the actual existence of a monolithic, unitary state (Mitchell 1999). Moreover, as in the case of Bosnia-Herzegovina discussed in another chapter of this book, in sites of intervention such as Afghanistan, there are starkly transnational aspects to statehood, to the extent that international actors have explicitly tasked themselves with the wholesale building of the state. This transnationalization of statehood makes it problematic to assume that the sovereign power we see operating, for instance, when an Afghan man is punished for rape or wife-beating in a national court, is that of an unitary Afghan state. As in the Bosnian case, we see here the ways in which actors claim forms of sovereign agency in the context of a state that is both transnationally administered and "unsovereign." In what follows, I use three recent attempts to construct or shape state interventions into gender violence to demonstrate how sovereign agency operating through the Afghan state apparatus cannot be reduced to that apparatus. Instead, I show how such agency can be—simultaneously—globally, nationally, and locally constituted, and take different and even contradictory forms.

The Law on Elimination of Violence against Women

For much of the post-2001 period, local activists and Western donors made the adoption of a new law on violence against women central to their considerable efforts of promoting gender equality in Afghanistan. Signed by President Karzai in the summer of 2009 (Wimpelmann 2017) the Law on Elimination of Violence Against Women (hereafter, the EVAW law) was unprecedented in Afghan history. It listed twenty-two acts as violence against women and mandated punishments for them. It also obliged the government to take specific actions to prevent violence and to support its victims. The EVAW law was regarded as important because, unlike the existing 1976 Penal Code, it designated rape (*tajavoz-e jinsi*) as a crime distinct from consensual adultery, provided considerably stricter punishments for forced and underage marriage, and criminalized a number of violations of women's civil rights, such as the deprivation of inheritance or preventing a woman from attending work or education. In general, the law was regarded by many as an important tool of advocacy, signaling that women were independent holders of rights, whom the Afghan state had an obligation to protect from abuses at the hands of families. Although the existing Penal Code covered crimes such as beating and murder, those who supported the new law argued that there was a tendency in legal practice and more broadly in Afghan society to view such acts as problematic only when they were carried out by nonfamily members. For them, the law was important because it explicitly stated that these actions were also punishable crimes when they took place inside the family.

Yet the particular manner in which this law came into force, and the subsequent push for its implementation, indicates that the sovereign claim it embodied was partial and ambiguous. First, the law was never ratified by the Afghan parliament, but was instead signed as a presidential decree. Some of the backdrop to this was another law, the Shia Personal Status law, which came into force at the same time. This latter law, which was to be the family code for the country's Shia minority, had created considerable controversy both in Afghanistan and in NATO capitals. It contained articles highly problematic from a women's rights perspective, such as the sanctioning of underage marriage and of husbands' right of regular sexual access to wives. When women activists and Western embassies were unable to prevent the Shia law (as it was often referred to) from coming into force, the EVAW law, by then in its final stages of drafting, increasingly featured as a potential counterweight to the Shia law. This line of reasoning was made possible by the fact that the EVAW law, like many Afghan laws promulgated in this period, contained an article stating that "the provisions of this law, if contradicted with provisions of other laws, shall prevail." The US embassy, in particular, started actively lobbying the president's office regarding the passing of the law (Embassy of the United States Kabul 2009a; Embassy of the United States Kabul 2009b). For President Karzai, who was keen to placate the constituencies who had been upset by the Shia law without sacrificing the latter, the idea that the EVAW law could be presented as a neutralizer of the Shia law was evidently a convenient one. Thus, whereas the Shia law had been ratified by parliament and subsequently presented to the president for final signature (Oates 2009), the activists and embassy supporting the EVAW pushed for it to be entered into force as a decree. This was apparently based on article 79 of the Constitution, which allowed room for the president to adopt legislation during parliamentary recess in "emergency situations." Decrees signed by the president in this vein became laws on signing but were to be submitted to parliament within thirty days of the first session of the National Assembly, who had the power to reject the laws decreed.

However, many activists opposed the idea of introducing the EVAW law to the Parliament, where conservative former mujahedin, reinstated to power after the 2001 invasion, dominated much of the landscape. When one female MP, Fauzia Koofi, took the lead in seeking parliamentary ratification of the law, others argued that she was merely motivated by the prospect of personal fame (Wimpelmann 2017). And indeed, in preliminary discussions of the law, conservative MPs denounced the EVAW law as a foreign, anti-Islamic invention—in effect, a Western assault on Afghan sovereignty and the country's Islamic foundations. As one of the law's key adversaries said to me: "This law is just a copy of foreign laws. Seeking to undermine our Islamic values and create disorder in our society, the foreigners have given us this law as a gift." Predicting that the law was likely to suffer diluting revisions, and even risked being rejected altogether, many women activists, including other female MPs, argued that the EVAW should be left in peace as a presidential decree. In effect, this was what happened (ibid.).

Its tenuous status notwithstanding, after the EVAW law was signed into decree on July 2009 it quickly became the focus of those parts of the international aid apparatus that were oriented toward women and legal reform. Donors funded the establishment of special prosecution units across the country, specifically tasked to investigate and prosecute cases of violence against women (Wimpelmann 2017). In addition, training sessions on the law for judges, prosecutors, and other government officials were organized; booklets were produced and disseminated; and various conferences and meetings were arranged where the law was discussed and promoted.

Despite this, the law was unevenly enforced. Many judges continued to apply the existing penal code, either out of personal preference or because they were unsure of the status of the EVAW law. Afghan activists and aid donors did their best to track prosecution and convictions and to push the government to implement the EVAW law. The law was repeatedly on the agenda in meetings between the Afghan government and aid donors, with the latter eventually demanding that the Afghan government produce a report about the status of all cases registered with the authorities nationwide, or face aid cuts. The report, published in early 2014 after much delay, showed that the EVAW law's reach remained incomplete. The data suggested that around 8 percent of the 4,505 registered cases had resulted in a criminal conviction, whereas 40 percent of the cases had been "solved" through mediation. The rest of the total caseload, 2,129 cases, was still being processed.

In the years that followed, the EVAW law would lose some of its international backing. A new administration, headed by the reformist Ashraf Ghani, came to power in late 2014, and women's rights moved to the center of Afghan government priorities. Rather than remain a standalone law, the provisions of the EVAW law were to be mainstreamed into a new comprehensive penal code that would incorporate all the various pieces of legislation with criminal provisions that had been produced in the post-2001 period. Afghan legal scholars, UN staff, and Western embassies generally supported this initiative. As opposed to a partial and alternative legal framework, which was regarded as the only achievable option during the leadership of conservative President Karzai, the protections in the EVAW law could now be incorporated into the country's main criminal law. At this point, however, many Afghan women activists had become invested in the law, arguing that a separate law for women's protection represented a valuable accomplishment and that to incorporate it into another law would represent a setback for women. Despite skepticism from across the board, including from the new president, they succeeded in preserving the law as the only standalone piece of legislation outside of the comprehensive new penal code enacted in 2018. Arguably, this maintained, and possibly even reinforced—the law's position as a partial sovereign claim over gender violence.

While the EVAW law represented a clear attempt to challenge the sovereignty exercised by household heads over female family members, it was less clear to where and to whom such sovereignty was (potentially) transferred. Although the law was to be enforced through Afghan state institutions, it was certainly not a product of a modernizing ruler's intent to increase the state's power by wresting autonomy away from kinship groups. Instead, the law—conceived and promoted by an alliance of women's rights activists, justice officials, foreign aid workers, and diplomats—was enacted by the president as an offering to one group of allies, in a bid to neutralize their concerns over the conservative Shia law. Effectively, by offering his different constituencies different (and contradictory) laws, President Karzai extended invitations of partial sovereignty to the supporters of both the EVAW law and the Shia law. Thus, rather than a bid to emancipate women, or to centralize power, the politics driving the enactment of the EVAW law was a balancing act of patronage politics. At the same time, this patronage logic, and the landscape of fragmented sovereignty it reinforced, was not merely the creation of the Afghan president. Both Afghan and international supporters of the EVAW law reinforced the law's partialness as a sovereign claim, and the kind of politics underpinning this partialness: as these groups chose to directly approach the executive for favors, rather than to follow legislative procedure, they strengthened the president's personal power at the expense of institutionally anchored reform. And by settling for a law with an ambiguous legal status and thus a partial claim to sovereignty, they endorsed a fragmented and contradictory legal landscape. At the level of enforcement, too, the supporters of the EVAW law carved out a partial domain of Afghanistan's legal sector. Specialized prosecution offices and courts, financed and monitored by Western countries, were set up to accelerate the law's implementation. To an extent, the EVAW law brought Afghan women into an international protection order, where sovereignty was exercised by global actors. At the same time, this sovereignty worked through national institutions, making clear-cut distinctions between the national and global unsustainable. Even "the global" was not a monolithic force in Afghanistan, because as it turned out, the EVAW law, or at least the formal legal apparatus through which it was to be implemented, was challenged by other sections of the international "community" in a brief but intense fascination with "tribal" Afghanistan.

Turning Tribal

Since the initial colonial encounters during the nineteenth century, Western discourse about Afghanistan and Pashtun society often casts these as uniquely stateless places, built around community consensus and an egalitarian ethos. Even if this discourse has had scholarly and empirical foundations, the image of Afghanistan as a country of "free" tribesmen locked in constant conflict with an alien, encroaching state has found particular resonance at certain geopolitical moments. In the late nineteenth century, British colonizers seeking to wrest the area away from the Afghan king questioned Afghan statehood and sovereignty, asserting that the people inhabiting the area known until recently as the Federally Administered Tribal Areas (FATA) were independent tribes with no history of living under a higher political authority (Haroon 2007). And during the 1980s, Western support for the mujahedin fighting the Soviet army and the socialist Afghan government was often accompanied by celebratory accounts of brave mountain people resisting not only the Soviet invaders but also an inherently alien central state.

By contrast, the initial focus of the rapidly expanding Western agenda after the 2001 invasion was on building Afghan formal state institutions. This was also the case in the justice sector, where aid organizations and embassies set out to reform the legal framework, train judges and prosecutors, and set up legal aid organizations and a host of other "justice sector reform" activities. There was, however, an alternative vision, promoted by actors such as the United Nations Development Program (UNDP), and the United States Institute of Peace (USIP). These organizations suggested that Afghanistan's informal justice system, so-called jirgas and shuras, should be given formal support and recognition. This idea was vehemently opposed by urban human rights activists and women's rights advocates, who argued that these customary processes were part and parcel of patriarchal power relations, that they discriminated against women and the poor, and that they were inherently problematic since they did not refer to codified law. Yet organizations such as USIP and UNDP backed up their claims in the language of academic expertise. Their research, they suggested, showed the informal institutions' widespread use and popularity and that this in turn demonstrated that they had more resonance with Afghan culture than did the formal courts. These organizations admitted that informal justice mechanisms had problematic aspects but suggested that these could be mitigated through expert interventions based on contextual understanding and "intimate local knowledge" (USIP 2010).

As I have argued in some detail elsewhere (Wimpelmann 2013), the way in which informal justice mechanisms were sought, promoted, and supported amounted to an alternative government constellation, based not on Afghan statehood and formal courts, but on the country's "traditional" nonstate mechanisms of governance, mediated through expert knowledge of the "real" Afghanistan. I have also argued that despite references to authenticity and the nonimposition of "Western ideas," the interest in informal justice was in fact deeply connected to Western foreign policy (ibid.). For when, around the end of the last decade, informal justice eventually moved from a special interest field to mainstream policy among aid donors such as the United Kingdom and the United States, it was not necessarily due to a newfound understanding of Afghan reality. Instead, this interest in everything "tribal" coincided with the apex of NATO military operations and was linked to the military doctrine at the time, in which victory was predicated on "good governance," the provision of which would encourage the population to turn away from the insurgents. Finding little such good governance within the Karzai administration, many in the military argued that they had no choice but to avoid the state apparatus and instead turn to tribal leaders and community elders (Ledwidge 2009). The United States subsequently awarded large contracts for the training and support of community elders, particularly in areas that had been "cleared" by US military operations. The hope was that bolstering justice provision through "elders" would provide the governance needed to stall the Taliban (Wimpelmann 2013).

In the Afghan capital, USIP and others who had wanted not only these ad hoc aid programs but also a comprehensive hybrid legal system where customary justice was given formal recognition by the Afghan state, met determined resistance, both from human rights activists and from state officials. And as the NATO military operations drew down, so did the aid programs supporting informal justice. Yet, for a brief period it was possible to discern an alternative governance constellation in the country—a configuration of expert knowledge, NGOs, traditional elites, and military actors. Although I have analyzed this in more depth elsewhere (Wimpelmann 2013), I mention this constellation here because it clearly shows that the post-2001 international project in Afghanistan embodied multiple, and contradictory, claims of sovereignty. As Heathershaw and Lambach formulate it, sites of international "peacebuilding" interventions have to be understood as "fields of power where sovereignty is constantly contested and negotiated among global, elite and local actors" (Heathershaw and Lambach 2008). In this vein, challenges to and negations of the single sovereign (the nation-state) in sites of intervention and elsewhere are best conceived not as from "below" (local) or "above" (global) but as parallel or alternative alignments that often are transnationally woven. There were at least two parallel transnational alignments in Afghanistan. On the one hand, Western "experts" and specific NGOs sought to confer power on "traditional" rulers in a bid to construct an alternative form of rule and authority grounded in what they celebrated as "local traditions and reality." On the other hand, parts of the progressive judiciary joined forces with gender activists, aid workers, and supporters in foreign embassies to implement the EVAW law.

The forms of rule, protection, and rights created through such constellations are often ambiguous and indeterminate, characterized by compromise or contradictions. For instance, the establishment of transnational alliances around Afghan women's rights, while effective in securing funds, new frameworks of protection, and mobilizing a certain amount of political pressure, only held a partial sovereign claim over the domain of gender violence. But even the processes that appeared more clearly rooted within the Afghan state structure, and with less obvious transnational dimensions, might challenge the notion of a sovereign agency exercised by a unitary state. To illustrate, I revisit the rape cases in Sarepul, where my first impressions of a momentous renegotiation of state and societal domains proved quite mistaken.

Returning to Sarepul

As I mention in the introduction, the way the families from Sarepul launched public campaigns following the rapes of their daughters and nieces appeared to be an unusual pursuit of justice through the government courts for something of a very private nature. The man at the heart of these efforts, Sayed Noorullah, made increasingly indignant calls on the government to see that justice would be served:

> I am the father of a thirteen-year-old girl who was kidnapped and then raped by the son of Haji Payenda, a member of parliament.[2] . . . Several times through Aryana Television and other media the issue has been made known to all the government officials and even president Karzai . . . all the ministers, all the parliament members are aware of the incident and know everything. . . .
>
> I have just one question for Mr. Karzai: For the sake of God, if this had happened to your daughter, what would you have done? Then would you have felt my feelings? Only two days ago, you sacked the attorney general, and since then all the offices that I approach reject me by saying that even your attorney general has been fired.[3] Today in the public health office, even the prosecutor that is dealing with my case tells me to go away and that now that the attorney general is no more in office no one is going to listen to your stories anymore. Was justice there only in the attorney general? By sacking him, did his office, his laws and everything also vanish? Is there no system anymore? Should we just abandon our case and mind our own business? Once again, I am repeating it; if this would have happened to your daughter Mr. Karzai, Qanooni, Chief Justice and Attorney General, would you have tolerated it? Would you have just watched?
>
> If we are deceivers, if our case is unfair, and if our accusations are false, Mr. Karzai if you have any *gheirat* [manly honor] then please kill us and finish us. If you do not have any *gheirat* then may God's curse be upon you and your whole clan, whoever you are.[4]

This, it seemed, was a demand that the Afghan state carry out its formal duty of punishing rapists—a brave leap of faith in the government by entrusting it with a matter conventionally considered deeply private—and a call for the government to rein in powerful people and uphold the rights of the weak. In short, it appeared as an attempt, from below, to redraw the boundaries of state and society domains; to expand the scope of state responsibility and to make the government accountable to ordinary people.

However, closer attention to the language used by the uncle Sayed Noorullah shows that the case was not framed exclusively as an offense against Bashira, who had suffered the rape, but also, if indeed not primarily, as an offense against Noorullah himself. For instance, when later recounting to me how he had been offered money in order to withdraw his complaint, he indignantly said: "We are

Afghans. And in our custom, taking money in such cases is like selling your *namus* [honor, female dependents, that which should be inviolable]." The government and the president were denounced as allies of the usurpers of people's honor. They had allied with warlords and oppressors and as a result, they were selling the namus of ordinary people. Noorullah recounted, with some embarrassment, how he had in anger hurled a great insult at the president even when called in for a personal audience, a meeting which had taken place following his denunciation of the country's leaders on national TV. After this rather strongly worded speech on TV ("Mr. President . . . if you don't have *gheirat* then may God's curse be upon you and your whole clan, whoever you are"), the president's office had demanded that Noorullah be immediately brought in to speak to Hamid Karzai. There, according to his own account, he had continued to use strong language. The Taliban government might have been brutal and unpopular, he had said, but they were not *be-namus* (without possession of honor). They had not been selling people's honor.

Yet even if the state obligations invoked in Norullah's phrasings were primarily about upholding citizen (i.e., male) honor, as opposed to women's rights to legal protection, Noorullah's campaign nonetheless appeared as part of an attempted expansion of the state domain. Most people I spoke to saw his public call for government action as unprecedented, and a significant break with notions that a man's status is measured by his ability to independently protect his dependents (Abu-Lughod 1986). In other words, Noorullah was relinquishing his own sovereignty over family members, instead placing the responsibility for policing transgressions against his female family members onto the state. Initially, these efforts seemed successful—both in this case and in the case of Anisa, several perpetrators were sentenced to long-term prison sentences.

However, when I met him a year and half later in Sarepul, Noorullah told a tale of disappointment and defeat. Having pursued the rape of his niece through the courts, Noorullah said he had eventually settled for a reconciliation agreement with the rapists' families, brokered by political leaders and allies of the president. Although three people, including the son of the influential MP Payenda had been sentenced to life imprisonment for the rape of his niece in Kabul's primary court, the verdicts were appealed, and the threats against Noorullah continued. At this point, Noorullah said, he had lost his resolve, fearing for the safety of his family. When senior parliamentarians and presidential advisors initiated a settlement between the two families, he reluctantly agreed. As part of the deal, Noorullah would stop pursuing the case and declare himself reconciled with the MP's family. He would be compensated with a *baad*—a girl from the MP Payenda family given to his son as a bride and a guarantee of his life signed by the elderly statesman Mujadidi. Meanwhile, his niece's rapists had their sentenced reduced on appeal, and the son of MP Payenda was rumored to be out of prison most of the time. Noorullah, who had wanted "to be symbol for people fighting against cruelty," had lost.

But there were certain cracks in this narrative, and as time passed they were becoming increasingly difficult to ignore. I wondered why, if the case was as sensitive as Noorullah claimed, and his position in the province so precarious, he had insisted on meeting us at a government office, where his contact with a foreigner would no doubt be detected and raise suspicions that he was breaking his vow not to pursue the case. Noorullah had contended that despite the promise, he had wanted to talk to me. I was a researcher and it was important that what had happened to his family should be documented. His fight against injustice and oppression had to be recorded so that future generations could learn from history. But his acceptance of the baad from MP Payenda's family also sat uneasily with his story of fighting injustice. Even if he had felt too threatened to continue pursuing the case in government courts, and wished to have guarantees for his safety, what was the need for accepting the baad, something that discredited him among his liberal supporters in Kabul? Could he not have settled for just the guarantee?

When I returned to Kabul, other fractures appeared. The judge who had presided over the rape case in the primary court in Kabul contradicted Noorullah's assertion that the sentence of the MP's son had been lowered in the appeals process of the court system. On the contrary, the sentence of twenty years' imprisonment for the MP's son, his bodyguard, and their female abettor had been confirmed in the appeal court and finally in the Supreme Court. Details of this had been published in an edition of the *Mizan Gazette*, a Supreme Court newsletter of which I obtained a copy. If the government courts had applied the full force of the law, the local reconciliation and the baad made even less sense, as the justice the uncle was calling for already appeared to have been served.

Eventually, through a series of conversations, an alternative version of the events following the rape of Bashira emerged. On important points, this version diverged from the way the case had become known to me through the media and the accounts of Noorullah and his backers. Firstly, Bashira's family background was not quite as powerless and poor as had been implied. They hailed from a lineage claiming holy descent. Moreover, members of Bashira's family held important government positions in the province, including in the national intelligence agency. It was partly through these positions that the family was able to get access to the media, and doubtless, to mobilize some of their support among politicians and officials. Another dimension of the story, which had not featured in the national media coverage, in the calls for justice by human rights officials and activists, or in the depictions of the uncle, was the ethnicized politics that quickly became part of the aftermath of the case.

In order to understand how the aftermath of Bashira's rape appears to have become enmeshed in Sarepul politics it is necessary to relate some of the local historical background. Sarepul Province, like most of Afghanistan has a recent history of oft-changing and contested control over territory, state institutions, and resources. Pashtun migrants had arrived in Sarepul from the late nineteenth century onward (Tapper 1991) as part of a larger, government-supported Pashtun migration to northern Afghanistan. Backed by the central state, the mainly nomadic Pashtuns seized land and lucrative government posts, establishing themselves as a dominant minority group in much of the province, where groups of Hazaras, Uzbeks, Aymaqs, and Arabs were also living (ibid.).

The advent of war altered the ethnic balance in the area. As armed resistance formed against the communist government that seized power in Kabul in 1978, mujahedin and progovernment militia groups emerged, and in the North they often proved a vehicle for non-Pashtun groups to assert themselves. Arabs, claiming descent from Arab tribes from the time of the original Islamic conquest and previously a marginal group of pastoralists, gained a new position in the province through this route. Four brothers, among them Haji Payenda, the MP whose son was to be sentenced for the rape of Bashira, rose to prominence as members of a local self-defense unit mobilized by the Najibullah government. The brothers served under Abdul Rashid Dostum, the Uzbek military strongman who was to emerge as a key regional powerbroker in the decades that followed.[5] With Dostum, the Uzbeks in the northern region also strengthened their position. Initially working with Najibullah, by 1992 Dostum had, increasingly in defiance to the Pashtun-dominated central government (Giustozzi 2009), established a regional network consisting of both progovernment militias and mujahedin commanders until he spectacularly defected from the government in 1992 (ibid.). This network became the Junbesh Party, an important political actor in post-2001 Afghanistan and in Sarepul.

In the mountainous south of Sarepul, mainly Hazara groups formed armed resistance factions against the communists, and in yet other districts, Tajik-dominated mujahedin emerged. These groups generally aligned with national-level mujahedin parties. In a pattern seen elsewhere in Afghanistan, local rivalries were fed by support from national party formations, which in turn led to a fragmentation of the local political landscape along party and ethnic lines. The importance of these fault lines lessened during the Taliban government, although many areas in Sarepul remained completely controlled by the mujahedin. With the overthrow of the Taliban government in 2001, factions rooted in the mujahedin and militia groups of the pre-Taliban period again became dominant actors in Sarepul politics. In sum, the upheavals of the decades of conflict had created a fluid situation where previously enduring political and ethnic hierarchies were constantly up for renegotiation. The post-2001 period saw the new elites of the jihad era, and their broader, mostly ethnically defined constituencies, vying for control over government posts, land, and influence.

It was this factional competition, some of my informants argued, that had been the driving force in the dynamics of the aftermath of Bashira's rape. In a bid to weaken Haji Payenda, and by extension, Arab domination, two key groups involved themselves in the case and threw their support behind Bashira's family. One of these groups consisted of local Uzbek power holders belonging to the Junbesh Party. Sometime earlier, Payenda had switched his allegiance from Junbesh, the Uzbek-dominated party headed by Dostum, who in turn were supporting President Karzai. Instead, Payenda and a number of other Arabs had established their own political group, which eventually supported the opposition candidate, Dr. Abdullah, in the 2009 presidential election. The case against Payenda's son was also supported by Hazara groups who wanted to strengthen their position in the province. Bashira was Hazara, and according to one of my informants, the case became overstated as a way of unifying them: "When the case first came to the media, the Shia people got angry and they united on how their honor had been insulted. They made it a big and very complicated case, in order to unite the Shias, make them one power."[6] In these accounts, Bashira's young uncle Noorullah appeared less a self-driven campaigner for justice, and more of a figurehead for these discontented groups, having been handpicked as a suitable front person when Bashira's father, in ill health, could not play that role. The pressure for Payenda to give a baad was not imposed from above, as an attempt by powerful actors to make the case go away. Instead the giving of baad had formed an integral demand of the uncle's campaign all along, a demand which, if successful, would have placed Payenda on par with his adversaries. Giving a daughter in these circumstances would have signaled that Payenda was not above other groups in the province, that he was a social equal to Bashira's family; a daughter taken had to be compensated with a daughter given. On this account, there was in the end only a partial victory. While the demand had been that Payenda give his own daughter, he successfully refused this. Instead, a daughter of a poor man from Payenda's tribe, reportedly paid by Payenda, was given as a baad to Bashira's family. In the opinion of one of my informants, this showed how Payenda remained able to defy obvious attempts to weaken him.[7]

Nonetheless, in versions that emphasize how the aftermath of Bashira's rape became a vehicle for local politics, it was MP Payenda who appeared as the compromised party. Despite spending considerable money to influence the courts, he had been unable to prevent his son from feeling the full force of the law. Having been exposed as less than all-powerful in the province, he also lost his parliamentary seat in the next election, in 2010. As Noorullah stated, acknowledging that his campaigns had yielded some results even if meagre; "Before this case, everyone in Sarepul thought this family to be all-powerful and beyond the law. If Kamal Khan [the brother of Payenda] had killed someone it would be as if God had killed someone. Now, their power has been reduced. The government is more cautious."

In the subsequent chapters of Sarepul politics, the groups that had supported Bashira's family came to dominate the local government. And in a further reversal of positions, episodes of rape and kidnapping of women now served as focal points of mobilization by factions linked to Haji Payenda and his brothers—against the now Hazara-dominated provincial administration (Ruttig 2012). It seemed that public protestations against sexual infractions had become a standard part of the political repertoire in Sarepul. In a sense, protests were directed against the impunity afforded by government connections, impunity which was facilitated by access to government office and in the next round of local politics, became the privilege of the new power holders.

If the unusual persistence of Bashira's family in pursuing the rape case in public could be explained, partly or fully, by the interest of local groups in using the case to challenge the political position of Payenda and his allies, this in turn serves as a reminder that "the state," as many scholars have argued, is a claim, a construct, not a thing or a fact. Bashira's uncle might have called for government action in a sense that suggested that there existed a unitary, independent Afghan "state" capable of sovereign agency in one direction or the other. Likewise, other actors invoked similar images when calling for the state's responsibility to protect women against family abuses, or alternatively, to uphold kinship control over them. But these contending notions of state responsibility and justice are disputes over internal boundaries and personhood, the outcome of which has consequences for authority over domains and persons. They should not lead us to believe that there is such thing as a unitary, coherent state—"a person writ large" (Mitchell 1999, 83), a judgelike character insulated from society as a whole. As Mitchell argues, the appearance of the state as a discreet and relatively autonomous social institution is itself a reification that is constituted through everyday social practices. In reality, claims to statehood, the emergence of government apparatuses, armies, and bureaucracies are always intertwined with struggles over resources and power.

This means that demands and counterdemands for state action, and claims to act on behalf of "the state," must be situated in the local political economy—in other words, in conflicts between groups and classes over resources and influence. Absent this perspective, the Afghan "state" is reduced to an ahistorical project, and struggles over control of the state to a fight between "good" state builders and corrupt saboteurs, obfuscating the material, ethnic, and class interests at stake as people seek to consolidate, resist or co-opt "state" sovereignty (see also Coburn 2011). As the history of Sarepul clearly illustrates, access to government positions—and the associated ability to call on bureaucratic and military enforcement mechanisms—have served as a tool for appropriation and accumulation. The primary fault line, then, is not necessarily between kinship (or families) and the government (i.e., between "society" and the "state"). The fault line can also be between competing factions, whose success in controlling and accessing state power has waxed and waned. Sarepul—and Afghanistan more broadly—appears to be a striking confirmation of Lombard's observation (chapter 2, this volume) that in contested state spaces the categories of "us" and "ours" do not have stable, broadly agreed-on content. As she suggests, in settings where the state is less consolidated, who is on the outside and inside is much more up for constant renegotiation. In turn, this unsettledness makes the processual nature of state sovereignty as a project more visible. Applying this perspective, it looks as if the Sarepul case, instead of being one man's thwarted campaign to secure a government reaction against the abuses visited on his family, was locally understood, or at least seized on, as an infraction against a larger collective by a rival group. This violation had to be reacted against in a manner that asserted the position of Payenda's rivals—a reaction that showed that Payenda and his group were not above, but of equal standing, to other groups, who simultaneously could undermine his grip on power. The "state" here features as a vehicle for intergroup competition, in which authority over women serves as a marker of position and status.

In other words, the ongoing renegotiation of power hierarchies in Sarepul—in which official positions constitute an important resource, and which in the last decades had become increasingly open-ended as war offered novel paths of assertion to previously marginal groups—took place, in part, through public contestations over claims over women. Government courts and the media provided novel and additional arenas for such claims, which should be understood as assertions of position and status, expressed through idioms of honor. But in these latter arenas, claims were framed somewhat differently. When Bashira's uncle appeared on national TV, he did not ask President Karzai to arrange for a baad from Payenda's family (such a demand could not have been expressed nor granted openly) but for the government to see that the rapists would feel the full force of the law. The rape was still spoken of as a violation of family honor, but demands for government action were framed in the language of justice and punishment.

It was this kind of language that led many outsiders and national actors to believe that something novel was happening: that people were now bravely speaking out against the violations visited on their daughters by government allies, breaking a taboo in a desperate bid for some kind of reparation. Admittedly,

the Bashira case and other episodes from Sarepul were novel in the way the victims' families were willing to openly mobilize national public opinion for their
case. Still, the exceptional intensity with which public redress was sought must
be understood as an extension of factional political conflict, played out in part in
the public arenas of the media and the courts, rather than an attempt by families
to rearticulate government obligations to its (male) citizens.

I believe that the Sarepul case also illustrates the pitfalls of regarding the
language of honor as somehow integral to a nonstate logic of "kinship" society.
According to the evolutionary perspectives often applied to Afghanistan, honor
(namus) is a "tribal" value, consonant with a prestate social system based on
kinship, egalitarianism, autonomy, and the strict seclusion of women. If such
idioms make an appearance in state arenas, they are typically considered spill-
overs from the tribal system, where they properly belong, and are assumed to be
eventually eradicated by the modernizing touch of the state. The Sarepul case
unsettles such binaries particularly well. First of all, as this case shows, intensified state regulation of gender violence and relations do not necessarily lead to
a more equal status for women. On the contrary, government regulation might
instead affirm family control over female bodies and validate notions of honor
by framing rape as an offense against male standing.[8] But moreover, honor, as a
vocabulary of power and boundary marking, as a way of articulating violations
and entitlements, can equally be employed in struggles over state power. It is
often those with a degree of influence and access to the state who can utilize
official positions and public arenas to pursue gender violations—whether as
a standalone issue or as a component of larger political projects—as was the
case in Sarepul.

Contestations over gender violence—over its definition, regulation, or avenging—
constitute entry points to fields of sovereign power. Applying this analytical lens,
it becomes clear that, as in the case of Bosnia-Herzegovina discussed in chapter 3, the very notion of "the Afghan state" as a nationally contained, unitary, sovereign body makes little sense. I have shown, for instance, how in the
case of the EVAW law globally constituted sovereign claims worked through
the nation-state apparatus. National institutions—courts, prosecutors, and
legislators—became part of a globalized sovereign regime in which Afghan
women's security was made a global concern and ultimately guaranteed by
external funds and pressure. In other words, the Afghan state was denationalized
(Sassen 2008) in the sense of being reassembled as a vehicle for the operation of
global sovereign claims.

At the same time, these efforts were mediated by more local dynamics. But
these local dynamics were certainly not driven by the centralizing impulses of an

Afghan ruler seeking to expand government power by drawing women into the circle of government justice, thereby wresting away the autonomy or sovereignty of their male relatives. In fact, President Karzai's strategy on violence against women was much more opportunistic and appeared primarily informed by his efforts to create and maintain personalistic alliances. One activist went as far as to suggest to me that, unlike the former socialist government, "Karzai is not personally committed to women's rights, he is just committed to the international funding that comes with it." Neither were there any signs that the Afghan president attempted to use government courts to achieve tighter state regulation of family and kinship in order to centralize power. As the Sarepul case had shown, government response to issues such as rape was reactive and entangled in patrimonial politics. Whether by effect or intent, the EVAW law instead constructed a globalized zone of protection for Afghan women, much dependent on external funds and political pressure.

However, this was never a complete process, nor was the EVAW law the only transnationally constituted sovereign claim. Global relations of governance were multifarious. This was illustrated by the temporary emergence of an alternative configuration of justice and sovereignty centered on informal justice processes and demonstrating that global, and in particular Western, interventions in Afghanistan were heterogeneous and even contradictory. My research into this process was in fact prompted by the incredulous complaints of an Afghan human rights official, who protested what she saw as a problematic Western othering of Afghans, denying them access to formal justice and rights. In contrast to the universalizing templates of the EVAW law, the starting point for the interventions of this informal justice constellation was to be "Afghan reality." Yet, this reality still needed to be modified and validated by foreign-educated experts. The vision of justice presented by these experts was one in which shuras and jirgas would function as a kind of enlightened tradition, devoid of power relations and hierarchies and cleansed of their excesses by the training and monitoring programs carried out by NGOs. State structures were made marginal in this alternative sovereign configuration. In fact, it can be argued that in the imagery of this informal justice constellation, there no longer featured an Afghan state. Instead the local was directly connected to the international, but, as has been suggested, in ways that were deeply asymmetrical. Despite assertions to the contrary, rather than local actors it was expatriate expertise and Western militaries that reigned supreme through this sovereign claim.

Finally, in this chapter I have examined state interventions into cases of gender violence such as rape, from an alternative angle. Rather than being an expression of increased state regulation, such interventions (or their specter) might also serve as vehicle for factional conflicts. This perspective further adds to the problematization of state sovereignty in Afghanistan, showing that calls for it to be exercised might be less about increasing state power and more about diminishing rivals' access to it.

Notes

1. Parts of this text first appeared in *The Pitfalls of Protection* (Berkeley: University of California Press, 2017). It is reprinted here with permission.

2. Although he was in fact the girl's uncle, he often referred to himself as the father, since Bashira's actual father was ill and could not represent her.

3. In an unrelated event, President Karzai had dismissed Attorney General Abdul Jabar Sabet on July 17, 2008.

4. 6 Tolo TV, July 19, 2008.

5. At the time of writing Dostum is the first vice president of Afghanistan.

6. Author's interview with human rights workers, Mazar-e Sharif, 2010.

7. Ibid.

8. Dicle Koğacıoğlu (2004) makes a similar argument for Turkey, where she points out that the legal and institutional accommodation of "honor killings" makes questionable these same institutions' presentation of them as acts of tradition.

References

Abu-Lughod, Lila. 1986. *Veiled Sentiments: Honor and Poetry in a Bedouin Society.* Berkeley: University of California Press.

Al-Ali, Nadje. 2007. *Iraqi Women: Untold Stories From 1948 to the Present.* London: Zed Books.

Charrad, Mounira M. 2001. *States and Women's Rights: The Making of Postcolonial Tunisia, Algeria, and Morocco.* Berkeley: University of California Press.

Coburn, Noah. 2011. *Bazaar Politics: Power and Pottery in an Afghan Market Town.* Stanford, CA. Stanford University Press

Comaroff, Jean, and John L. Comaroff. 2006. "Law and Disorder in the Postcolony: An Introduction." In *Law and Disorder in the Postcolony*, edited by Jean and John L. Comaroff, 1–56. Chicago: University of Chicago Press.

Embassy of the United States in Kabul. 2009a. "Elimination of Violence Against Women Law: MOJ Draft Complete." Cable, May 6.

Embassy of the United States Kabul. 2009b. "Justice Minister Danesh, Slow Movement on Shia Law Amendments, Faster on Eliminating Violence against Women Draft Bill," May 27.

Embassy of the United States Kabul. 2009c. "With Deep Pockets, Governor Atta Leads Charge for Abdullah." Cable, 09KABUL1838.

Giustozzi, Antonio. 2009. *Empires of Mud: Wars and Warlords in Afghanistan.* London: Hurst.

Hajjar, Lisa. 2004. "Religion, State Power, and Domestic Violence in Muslim Societies: A Framework for Comparative Analysis." *Law and Social Inquiry* 29: 1–38.

Haroon, Sana. 2007. *Frontier of Faith: Islam in the Indo-Afghan Borderland.* New York: Columbia University Press.

Heathershaw, John, and Daniel Lambach. 2008. "Introduction: Post-Conflict Spaces and Approaches to Statebuilding." *Journal of Intervention and Statebuilding* 2: 269–289.

Humphrey, Caroline. 2004. "Sovereignty." In *A Companion to the Anthropology of Politics*, edited by Daniel Nugent and Joan L. Vincent, 418–436. Oxford: Blackwell.

Joseph, Suad. 2000. "Civic Myths, Citizenship, and Gender in Lebanon." In *Gender and Citizenship in the Middle East*, edited by Suad Joseph, 107–136. Syracuse, NY: Syracuse University Press.

Kandiyoti, Deniz, ed. 1991. *Women, Islam, and the State*. Basingstoke, UK: Macmillan.

Kargar, Zarghuna. 2008. "Facing Up to Rape in Afghanistan." *Washington Post*, September 11.

Koğacıoğlu, Dicle. 2004. "The Tradition Effect: Framing Honor Crimes in Turkey." *Differences* 15: 118–151.

Ledwidge, Frank. 2009. "Justice and Counterinsurgency in Afghanistan: A Missing Link." *Rusi Journal* 154: 6–9.

Mitchell, Timothy. 1999. "Society, Economy, and the State Effect." In *State/Culture: State-Formation After the Cultural Turn*, edited by George Steinmetz, 76–97. Ithaca, NY: Cornell University Press.

Noelle-Karimi, C. 2002. "History Lessons." *Women's Review of Books* 19(7): 1–3.

Oates, Lauryn. 2009. *A Closer Look. The Policy and Law-Making Process Behind the Shiite Personal Status Law*. Kabul Afghan Research and Evaluation Unit.

Ruttig, Thomas. 2012. "Protests and Factional Conflict in Sarepul." http://www.aanaf ghanistan.org/index.asp?id=2499. Accessed February 14, 2012.

Sassen, Saskia. 2008. *Territory, Authority, Rights: From Medieval to Global Assemblages*. Princeton, NJ: Princeton University Press.

Schneider, Elizabeth M. 1991. "The Violence of Privacy." *Connecticut Law Review* 23: 973.

Tapper, Nancy. 1991. *Bartered Brides: Politics, Gender, and Marriage in an Afghan Tribal Society*. Cambridge: Cambridge University Press.

UNAMA. 2012. "Still a Long Way to Go: Implementation of the Elimination of Violence against Women Law in Afghanistan." December. Kabul, Afghanistan: United Nations Assistance Mission to Afghanistan.

USIP. 2010. "Informal Dispute Resolution in Afghanistan." USIP Special Report, United States Institute of Peace.

Wimpelmann, Torunn. 2013. "Nexuses of Knowledge and Power in Afghanistan: The Rise and Fall of the Informal Justice Assemblage." *Central Asian Survey* 32: 406–422.

Wimpelmann, Torunn. 2017. *The Pitfalls of Protection: Gender, Violence, and Power in Afghanistan*. Berkeley: University of California Press.

EVERYDAY SOVEREIGNTY IN EXILE

People, Territory, and Resources among
Sahrawi Refugees

Alice Wilson

In refugee camps in the southwest corner of Algeria's Sahara Desert, many flags combining red, green, white, and black adorn administrative buildings, schools, homes, and in recent years, cell phone screens. Despite their combining a familiar set of colors, these flags are not those of Algeria, the nation-state within the territory of which the refugee camps are technically located. Rather, the flags represent the Sahrawi Arab Democratic Republic (SADR). This partially recognized state authority claims the disputed territory of Western Sahara. SADR was founded in 1976 by Western Sahara's national liberation movement, the Polisario Front. As well as hosting a civilian refugee population, the refugee camps are the home of the government in which a partially recognized state authority (SADR) and a liberation movement (Polisario Front) intertwine. This governing authority operates ministries, law courts, a Parliament, a police force, prisons, and more. Sahrawi, rather than Algerian, laws and constitution hold here.

Situations such as that of the Sahrawi government—operating in exile on borrowed territory—challenge dominant ideas about the sovereignty of nation-states. In the commonplace understanding of sovereignty, prevalent in international relations and in many popular accounts, the state wields supreme power over a territory, and by extension over the people living within this territory.

Yet empirical work has challenged such idealized accounts. The territorial nation-state has a history of only a few hundred years. Even in the postimperial age of the nation-state, which in the twentieth century has seen several waves of the creation of new nation-states due to decolonization and the breakup of

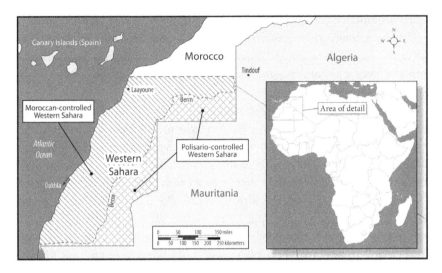

FIGURE 8.   Map of Western Sahara. The refugee camps for Sahrawis are located near Tindouf.

the Soviet Union, there are divergent practices and experiences of sovereignty. Geographical and political anomalies, such as annexed territories and partially unrecognized states, persist and proliferate. Even where such formal anomalies are absent, globalized flows of goods, persons, and commodities, as well as globalized regimes of governance, call into question the force of borders and sovereignty.

Such observations have led to important qualifications about the nature of sovereignty, and in particular the sovereignty of states. An idealized account of sovereignty as supreme authority over territory emerges as historically specific to a particular understanding of the nation-state; where such a model is relevant, the notion of the sovereign power of states is not self-evident but is a social construct (Biersteker and Weber 1996) produced through specific material and social practices (e.g. Navaro-Yashin 2002; Reeves 2014). Given the variety of political and territorial forms, it may be helpful to think of sovereignty less in terms of authority over territory but rather as relations between people (Sneath 2007, 10).

In the light of such revisionist accounts of sovereignty, should a case such as the Sahrawi refugees' government be apprehended merely in terms of a lack of "true" sovereignty? It must be stressed that for Sahrawis (in the refugee camps and beyond) who support self-determination for Western Sahara, the refugee camps indeed fail to provide the sovereignty over territory that they desire. Any analysis of the refugee camps must recognize the extent to which refugees' everyday acts, ranging from the chanting of political slogans to the daily struggle of survival, bespeak a persistent desire for Sahrawis' right to vote (and, potentially, fight) for a Sahrawi sovereign nation-state. But a fuller examination of the refugee camps should also explore the extent to which this setting presents an opportunity to probe some of the assumptions that underlie accounts of sovereignty as supreme authority over territory.

The Polisario Front operates from exile: the front only controls about a quarter of its claimed territory of Western Sahara while Morocco has annexed the remaining, westerly portion. Yet many routine activities of state power operate in the refugee camps. Some of these activities, as noted above, take the familiar forms of ministries, Parliament, law courts, and policing. The SADR bureaucracy produces passports and national identity cards valid in countries that recognize SADR, license plates for cars, and keeps records for workers' future pension rights. As a result of the constraints of exile, however, other activities of state power in this context are less familiar. Instead of a ministry responsible for collecting taxes such as a Treasury one finds a ministry responsible for distributing rations, the Sahrawi Red Crescent. There is not an absence of state power here, but a presence and even arguably a surfeit of state power. For refugees readily invoke the existence of the Sahrawi state through material symbols, such as flags, and in conversations about what "the state" (al-dawla) has given them. In the words of one woman who was a child and adolescent in the early years of exile, "the state was my father."

Clearly, a traditional approach to sovereignty as supreme authority over territory captures what the refugees desire for their future, but it fails to capture their daily experience living as citizens of an active state power. By drawing on critical approaches to sovereignty, it is possible to take up the refugee camps as a means for further rethinking sovereignty beyond the constraints of normative assumptions narrowly based on the territorial nation-state. In what follows, I pursue two analytical tacks.

First, taking a cue from anthropological studies that have understood the state as a social relation (e.g. Verdery 2003), I examine sovereignty as a set of social relations explored here through the case of the Sahrawi refugee camps. Full territorial sovereignty as desired by the refugees is absent in this setting; nevertheless, the various governance activities suggest that the *social relations* of sovereignty are very much present in the Sahrawi refugee camps.

Secondly, I address what kinds of ethnographic forms these social relations of sovereignty take in exile. I suggest an approach that skirts the seeming disjuncture between, on the one hand, the commonplace notion of sovereignty understood as dominion over territory, and, on the other hand, an alternative approach to sovereignty understood as relations between people. The claimed territory of Western Sahara is an essential feature of Sahrawis' aspirations for full sovereignty in the future; the Polisario Front currently controls part of this claimed territory.

But in the context of Sahrawis' exile, the claimed territory either is not readily accessible for refugees on a daily basis due to distance (the closest of the camps being located some fifty kilometers from the border with Western Sahara), or is under Moroccan annexation. As a result, I explore how, in exile, the social relations of sovereignty take the form of relations between people—governing authorities and governed constituencies—with these relations playing out with regard to resources that, due to displacement, take nonterritorial, mobile forms such as rations and refugees' labor. Thus, whether in "ordinary" (e.g., territorial) or extraordinary (e.g., exilic) forms, sovereignty is understood here as relationships between people playing out in relation to resources, whether or not these resources take territorial form.

Elsewhere I have examined in greater detail both the approach taken here, and further implications of analyzing the social relations of sovereignty in exile (Wilson 2016). I have examined how efforts on the part of the Polisario Front and the refugees to make the social relations of state power as a particular "project of sovereignty" entail a recycling of the social relations of what I consider to be a previous "project of sovereignty" familiar to Sahrawis, namely tribes (in some of the specific historical forms that tribes have taken in the northwest Sahara). I have also traced how Sahrawi refugees' improvisations in exile on the social relations of sovereignty rework and at times contest both Euro-American and North African models of sovereign power. These wider findings further underscore the need to revise narrow definitions of sovereignty based on the (Euro-American) model of the nation-state. In this chapter, my focus is on rethinking the relationships between people, territory, and resources that may play out in the social relations of sovereignty.

In making these arguments I draw on two years of ethnographic fieldwork with Sahrawi refugees from January 2007 to January 2009.[1] My geographical focus was on the refugee camps in Algeria where I lived with refugee families. In addition, I made short research trips between 2006 and 2014, including one trip to the Moroccan-controlled areas of Western Sahara in 2012. I conducted most of my work in the local Hassaniya dialect of Arabic. As I observed and participated in both mundane and extraordinary events in refugees' lives, interlocutors shared insights, aspirations, and frustrations relating both to their desire for a different kind of territorial sovereignty in the future, and to their experience of what here I explore as the everyday social relations of sovereignty in exile.

Rethinking Sovereignties

Most Sahrawi refugees would probably endorse the Westphalian notion of sovereignty as the supreme authority that a state wields over territory, and by extension the people and resources within it. It is this notion of sovereignty that Sahrawis who support self-determination in Western Sahara ardently desire. They voice this aspiration in Sahrawi political slogans such as "A full struggle to impose sovereignty and independence."[2] Max Weber's (1958) notion that states should hold a monopoly on the use of legitimate violence within their territory, and Carl Schmitt's (1985) proposition that sovereign power is defined by the unique authority to decide on the state of exception, have provided powerful theorizations of such an idealized sovereignty of states.

Yet, in light of the messiness of actual practice, such a notion of sovereignty needs supplementing—and has even been called a "fiction" (Brown 2010). As discussed in the introduction to this collection, exceptions to this model abound in the form of annexed territories (a recent addition to this category being Crimea), unrecognized or partially recognized states (such as Somaliland and Transnistria), disputed territories (e.g., Kashmir), and states that enjoy formal recognition but little authority in practice (e.g., Somalia). Even when the hegemonic model of state sovereignty is not overtly contested, in both relations with other states and in the internal affairs over which an idealized sovereign state is supposed to enjoy full control, states regularly violate the alleged principle of their independence—which has led to claims that the idealized account of sovereignty is a routinized "hypocrisy" (Krasner 1999). Historians and anthropologists have shown how the meaning of sovereignty has altered across different historical and geographical contexts (e.g. Benton 2009; Hansen and Stepputat 2005; Ong 2006). The meaning and definition of sovereignty may thus have to be sought in the plural rather than the singular.

If a meaning of sovereignty that could span divergent historical contexts is arguably elusive, there might nevertheless be merit in suggesting a framework through which to approach sovereignty—or rather sovereignties. Both the anthropological impulse to understand the state as a set of social relations (e.g., Chalfin 2010; Navaro-Yashin 2002; Reeves 2014; Verdery 2003), as well as the move to see sovereignty as a social construct (Biersteker and Weber 1996), are suggestive of how sovereignty may also be understood as a set of social relations. As regards the idea of the state as a social relation, David Sneath's (2007) reworking of Neera Chandhoke's notion of a "state relation" between governing authorities and governed persons, offers one such interpretation of state power. Sneath uses the idea of a state relation to interpret premodern, aristocrat-ruled polities in the steppe lands of Inner Asia as nonterritorially based manifestations of a state relation. As regards the extension of insights about state power as a social relation to sovereignty, Brenda Chalfin (2010, 42) has observed that in accounts of the state as a social relation it is often the case that sovereignty may just as much be understood as a social relation.

By drawing on these insights I approach sovereignty as a set of social relations, understanding these social relations to converge on specific "projects of sovereignty." To conceptualize sovereignty as social relations provides a lens through which to acknowledge that state power, the context in which influential theories of sovereignty have been developed (e.g. Schmitt 1985; Weber 1958), is a particular kind of project of sovereignty—though, as the editors of this volume note and other chapters show, it is not necessarily the only ethnographic form that a project of sovereignty might take. Likewise, such an approach offers a framework through which to trace how the social relations of a particular kind of project of sovereignty may be reconfigured to constitute an alternative project of sovereignty. As concerns Sahrawis, I have argued that the social relations of tribes as a project of sovereignty relevant in previous historical contexts have been recycled as refugees have sought to forge revolutionary state power as a new project of sovereignty (Wilson 2016). In addition, and of particular concern here, to approach sovereignty as a set of social relations helps in reassessing the role of territory in projects of sovereignty.

Even though dominion over territory is constitutive of classic understandings of sovereignty, contrasting analyses of sovereignty have questioned the alleged foundational importance of territory. In certain contexts, sovereignty over people has been of greater importance than, or equally as important as, sovereignty over territory (e.g., Comaroff and Comaroff 2009; Hansen and Stepputat 2005; Sneath 2007). Even nation-states that do not fall into the category of anomalies operate nonterritorial forms of sovereignty, such as taxing citizens located abroad (e.g., the United States, Eritrea) or extending political representation in national institutions to citizens living abroad (e.g., France). For Latvians in the early twenty-first century, the participation of the diaspora in claiming "existential sovereignty"—"a claim to coherence and continuity of a collective self"—is crucial, with these claims and diasporic participation therein having become potentially more important than claims for other kinds of sovereignty (chapter 7, this volume). A situation of long-term exile, such as Western Sahara, might appear to offer further support for a nonterritorially focused conceptualization of sovereignty. Just as Lisa Malkki (1995) has observed that nationalism can thrive in an exile that uproots nationalists from territory, so a study of sovereignty in the setting of exile might seem to reinforce a deterritorialized notion of sovereignty as a relation between people (rather than a claim to authority over territory).

An ethnographic reading of life in the refugee camps nevertheless suggests that even if the desired territory of Western Sahara is not accessible to most refugees on a daily basis, other nonterritorial, mobile resources emerge as crucial in the relationship between the refugees as governed constituencies and the governance of the Polisario Front. These resources, we shall see, include the rations that the Sahrawi government distributes to refugees, as well as the labor which refugees have historically given, and in certain circumstances have continued to give to the Polisario Front.

By exploring how the circulation of resources between people helps constitute the social relations of state power in the Sahrawi refugee camps, we can rethink how sovereignty over people and sovereignty over resources (whether in territorial or other forms) may be connected. In her study of the legally ambiguous Turkish Republic of Northern Cyprus, Yael Navaro-Yashin (2012, 43) has already shown how sovereignty is "an enactment of agency (back and forth) between people and things in and on a given territory." In the case of exiled Sahrawis, their displacement from their claimed territory necessarily means that social and material processes take different forms from the Cypriot case. To develop a broader framework for understanding the connections between sovereignty, people, things, and territory that can encompass both apparently conventional cases and anomalous cases such as Northern Cyprus and Western Sahara, anthropological approaches to property offer helpful insight.

For anthropologists, property is understood not as a relation between persons and things, but as a social relation between persons with regard to things (e.g., Pottage and Mundy 2004). When we conceive of sovereignty in terms of social reactions, we can think in terms comparable to the anthropological approach to property: sovereignty would constitute social relations between persons— governing authorities and governed constituencies—in relation to "things," that is, resources but not necessarily in territorial form. In other words, territory would be a common, but not necessarily essential, form of resource in reference to which the social relations of sovereignty play out.

It is such an approach that I explore here: in sum, that sovereignty can be understood as social relations between governing authorities and governed constituencies played out in relation to resources, not necessarily in territorial form. To examine this ethnographically, I turn to the Sahrawi refugee camps and the circulation of mobile resources therein.

The Creation of the Sahrawi Refugee Camps

Spread over five main sites by the twenty-first century, the Sahrawi refugee camps host Sahrawi exiles numbering some 173,600 as of December 2017 (UNHCR 2018). The camps were formed in the wake of Morocco's partial annexation, beginning in 1976, of the former Spanish colony of Spanish Sahara. (Mauritania also partially annexed the territory between 1976 and 1979 before renouncing its claims on the territory and later recognizing SADR.) As Morocco encroached on major population settlements, the coast with its rich fishing waters, and the phosphate mines at Bou Craa, many Sahrawis fled the incoming military forces. The liberation movement for Western Sahara, the Polisario Front, founded in 1973 originally to fight for independence from Spain, oversaw the gathering of these refugees in camps over the border in the territory of the Polisario Front's ally, Algeria. Other Sahrawis remained in the territory and have become the Sahrawi population living under Moroccan control. The population figures for all Sahrawi populations, and indeed for Moroccans who have moved to live in Western Sahara since Morocco's partial annexation, are disputed. Annexed Sahrawis may number more than the refugee population, according to the UN list of voters for a potential referendum on self-determination.[3] There are also significant communities of Sahrawis living outside the refugee camps and Western Sahara, in southern Morocco, northern Mauritania, and in European countries such as France, Spain, and Italy.

Those in the refugee camps and their peers living elsewhere habitually refer to themselves as "Sahrawis," usually meaning both an ethnic group as well as a perceived national identity. The use of the term to describe indigenous inhabitants of what was then a Spanish colony can be found in colonial writing dating back to at least the 1940s (e.g., Flores Morales 1946). Nevertheless, prior to Spanish colonialism, those who now identify as Sahrawis did not use this or an equivalent term to describe themselves as one group. For outsiders, the inhabitants of the northwest Sahara were known as "the Moors," Bedouin who spoke the distinctive dialect of Arabic known as Hassaniya and that today is used in Western Sahara, Mauritania, and some adjoining areas. Until their adoption of national identities in the context of colonialism, anticolonial struggles, and in the case of Western Sahara, failed decolonization, speakers of Hassaniya referred in their own terminology to social groupings centered on patrilineal "tribes" (*qabīla* pl. *qabā'il*), and stratified status groups (elite warrior and religious groups, tribute payers, blacksmiths, slaves, and freed slaves).[4] The Polisario Front, like many anticolonial liberation movements of the 1970s (e.g., Lackner 1985; Lewis 1979; Takriti 2013), officially sought to break with hierarchical tribal identities. This rejection of tribes has been a key tenet of the Polisario Front's program of revolution (*al-thawra*). In parallel though, as we shall see, at times the Polisario Front has drawn on the social relations of tribes in constituting forms of state power in the refugee camps.

Both Morocco and the Polisario Front claim the full territory of Western Sahara, and currently each controls a portion of the territory—Morocco the larger, westerly portion that is richer in resources, and the Polisario Front the smaller, easterly portion. The two sections are divided by a Moroccan-built military wall. Having brokered a ceasefire between the two parties in 1991, the UN has run the United Nations Mission for the Referendum in Western Sahara (Minurso), ostensibly to achieve an act of self-determination through a referendum. Although the UN produced a potential list of some 86,000 voters in 2000, Morocco appealed the decisions regarding more than 120,000 applicants (Zunes and Mundy 2010, 214), and has since refused to cooperate in a referendum that includes the option of independence. With the Polisario Front insisting on the inclusion of independence as an option, diplomatic initiatives toward conflict resolution have so far proved ineffectual. Face-to-face talks resumed in December 2018. With each party enjoying strong support from respective allies (the United States and France for Morocco, Algeria for the Polisario Front), the current status quo, and the refugee camps, look set to remain in place for the foreseeable future.

From its safe haven in Algeria, the Polisario Front has been able to get on with the business of governing a civilian population within the constraints of exile. Beyond the refugee camps, SADR engages in bilateral relations, including running embassies in states that recognize SADR and membership (as of 2017 alongside the recently readmitted Morocco) in the African Union.[5] As has been the case for governing authorities in exile such as Tibetans in India (McConnell 2016) and the Palestine Liberation Organization in Lebanon in the 1970s (Peteet 2005), for the Polisario Front the governance of a civilian population in exile provides many opportunities to practice state power. It is to refugees' daily experiences of state power in exile that I now turn.

Material Boundaries of Sovereignty

The circulation of resources, and who has the power and/or opportunity to influence that circulation, is key to understanding not only economic but also political life. If the Westphalian model sovereignty is understood as dominion over territory, this is envisaged as translating into dominion over the resources within that territory. For those states lacking the capacity to exploit a territory's resources, a variant of sovereign power may entail the power to oversee the rights of others to exploit those resources (Ferguson 2005). In such scenarios, territory offers a geographical definition of the limits of sovereignty and political community. Such territorial bounding is shadowed, however, by a further materialization of boundaries. The state's right to claim resources from persons, often in the form of taxes, marks an additional material boundary of sovereignty and political community. Conversely, the range of persons who can make material claims on a state marks another boundary of the social relations of a project of sovereignty.

For Sahrawis, whether refugees, annexed, or living elsewhere, the territory of Western Sahara as defined by the borders as at 1975 is one powerful means of marking the limits of the future form of territorial sovereignty that proindependence Sahrawis desire. Those Sahrawi refugees who can muster the necessary resources can go physically to visit or live within these geographical bounds in Polisario-controlled Western Sahara; those with the political will to do so can go to live in Moroccan-controlled Western Sahara; refugees also make a variety of informal temporary visits to Moroccan-controlled Western Sahara (Wilson 2014, 2017). But for most Sahrawi refugees whose main place of abode is the refugee camps, the opportunity to spend time in Western Sahara proper is constrained by a lack of resources to sustain oneself there. Since any families who live permanently in Polisario-controlled Western Sahara would no longer have crossed an international border, and thus would no longer be classed as a refugee under international humanitarian law, they could no longer receive rations.

For most refugees in the camps, then, a more quotidian means of experiencing one's relationship to the Sahrawi state authority comes not from being *in* Sahrawi territory, but falling within one of the other material boundaries of the current Sahrawi project of sovereignty. Refugees make claims on the Sahrawi state power for rations. Meanwhile, the Sahrawi state power has very few opportunities to take taxes from the refugees (although in the 2000s traders bringing goods for resale into the camps from Mauritania or Algeria were charged a proportion of the value of the goods as a tariff). Rather, this state power has a history of claiming labor from refugees. It is especially in relation to these mobile resources of rations and refugees' labor that the social relations of sovereignty here play out.

In the early years, rations were crucial to the survival of the refugees. The area of desert in which the refugees gathered is known as the ḥamāda, infamous for the harshness of its arid summers as well as the severity of its winters. Some Sahrawi tribes had a long history of frequenting this area as part of their mobile herding patterns (Caratini 1989). A historical presence of some members of the refugee community that predates mass exile is not an uncommon backdrop for refugee camps: similarly, the sites of refugee camps in Kenya for Somali refugees (Horst 2006), and in Senegal for Mauritanian refugees (Frésia 2009), fall within territories that members of the refugee community had frequented before displacement. For Sahrawis, the harsh ḥamāda did not offer the resources to host a large, long-term population. Thus, an inflow of resources, such as rations, was crucial for the survival of the refugees.

In the early years of exile, aid was funded primarily by the Algerian government. Algeria has continued to provide various forms of direct support, but from the mid-1980s the center of gravity in the provision of aid shifted to international aid organizations such as the World Food Program, the UNHCR, and eventually, the European Civil Protection and Humanitarian Aid Operations (ECHO). Since the 1991 ceasefire and the post–Cold War boom of international development NGOs, nonstate-funded philanthropical initiatives have also flourished in the camps, especially from NGOs based in Spain and Italy.[6] In the 2000s, a wide range of items were provided through rations from different sources: flour, pulses, sugar, tea, some fruit and vegetables, canned tuna, gas bottles, a hob for cooking, soap, sanitary towels, secondhand clothes, tents, and sometimes even luxury foods such as dates and meat for special occasions such as Eid (Wilson 2016, 122–123). Refugees take a lively interest in discussing which particular organization has provided specific rations. During the divvying up of secondhand clothes, a woman addressed both her fellow workers and me as she said, "The people of Sweden are good people. May God increase their wealth." On another occasion, one host family was delighted when the fruit delivery that Oxfam Belgium oversaw included bananas rather than apples, making it much easier for the family's elderly, toothless father to enjoy.

FIGURE 9. Gas distribution. Photo by Alice Wilson.

FIGURE 10.   Homemade license plate. Photo by Alice Wilson.

By the 2000s there were other avenues through which refugees could access resources: pensions from the Spanish government for those who had been employees of the colonial administration, revenue from local trading or animal husbandry and, for those families with a relative or relatives abroad, migrants' remittances. Thus, the acute dependence of refugees on rations had attenuated. But there is a point of continuity in access to rations both from the mid-1970s to the mid-1990s, when rations were the main means of survival (and refugees recalled meal after meal of lentils), and from the late 1990s to the present, when some richer families might not even bother to drag their heavy rations from the distribution point to home.

Throughout refugees' time in exile, by whatever means rations are funded (and duly noted as such by refugees), refugees' immediate, practical experience is of being able to access these rations through the Polisario Front. The Sahrawi Red Crescent, which has the status of a SADR ministry, and the related Ministry for Equipment (which deals with items such as tents and cooking equipment), organizes all ration distributions. Local state structures—until 1995 Popular Committees, and thereafter Councils—run the physical ration distributions. Local women staffed both the Committees and these Councils. These women know the families in their local area by face and by name. As women and girls collect rations, and families enjoy better meals in the ensuing days, rations become a crucial means through which Sahrawi refugees experience their relationship with the state authority.

Rations are not merely important as a means for refugees to experience that the Sahrawi state is providing for them. Indeed, refugees also experience that their state authority provides for them in other ways, such as when using free schooling and free healthcare (the latter including referrals to Algeria and Spain when necessary). Crucially, rations can be received but also, at least in theory, lost. At times, the Polisario Front reportedly deploys the capacity to withhold rations as a tool of governance.

From 2007 to 2009, only one residential camp, then known as 27 February School (named after the day of the founding of SADR, and renamed Boudjour in 2012) had access to the electrical grid.[7] To benefit from access to electricity and nearby job opportunities, some families from the larger residential camps such as Smara camp or Ausserd camp might decide to relocate to 27 February School. However, refugees explained to me that those who moved from one refugee camp to another without the permission of the Polisario Front would no longer receive rations at their new location until the move was approved—a process that might involve a wait of several months. In 2008, when the Polisario Front was trying to discourage refugees from spending what the front (and many refugees) perceived to be excessive amounts of money on wedding celebrations, refugees believed that any couple who disregarded the new restrictions on festivities would lose their rations for two years (Wilson 2016, 174)—although I never met any family who claimed to know of the sanction being imposed. Both scenarios speak, at least in theory, to the circulation of rations as an instrument through which the state authority seeks to discipline refugees.

Here we see clearly how the relationship between the Polisario Front as governing authorities and the refugees as governed constituencies plays out around the mobile resources of rations. The giving of rations marks one boundary of inclusion of living as a citizen of the Sahrawi state power. At the same time, the possibility of the withholding of rations is one of the forms of legitimate violence that the Sahrawi state power can potentially wield, or threaten to wield, over refugees.

In addition to rations, refugees' labor has also proved significant in constituting the social relations of everyday sovereignty in the refugee camps. During the early, extremely austere years of exile, the refugees' physical labor—supplemented at times with the labor of Moroccan prisoners of war, the last of whom were released in 2005—physically built the refugee camps and staffed the ministries and sites of welfare provision. A common refrain among older refugees was the idea that in the early years "you could only see children and old people in the tents," since everyone else was undertaking labor for the state authority. Consequently, the capacity to recruit and retain refugees' labor was of vital importance. Over the course of exile, the Polisario Front has operated various mechanisms to mobilize refugees' labor.

From the early years until the mid-1990s, a system of national conscription operated. For men, this conscription focused on the army. The Sahrawi People's Liberation Army (SPLA) engaged in active warfare with Morocco from 1975 into the late 1980s in the lead-up to the ceasefire in 1991. The SPLA is still mobilized at the time of writing, with troops stationed across the military zones of Polisario-controlled Western Sahara. In the first decade of the 2000s, many men served for only part of the year, and still others might only be mobilized in a perceived national emergency. For instance, in 2001, when the organizers of the Paris-Dakar rally initially omitted to seek permission from the Polisario Front to cross Western Sahara, Sahrawis reportedly returned from abroad to mobilize as part of the army (Bhatia 2001).

Since the ceasefire, conscription to the army has declined. Men who serve regularly expect remuneration, however modest. At the same time, the SPLA retains a very high social prestige among male and female refugees. At the mere mention of the army, women within earshot usually ululate (an expression of celebration). Many refugees, male and female, continue to place a high value on the legitimacy of potential recruitment to the army in case of perceived national need.

For women, labor conscription initially focused on recruitment to staff the various activities of welfare service provision. (Note, though, that women's official roles for the Polisario Front are not constrained to the welfare sector, and that women increasingly hold leadership positions such as at the ministerial or ambassadorial level.)[8] In the early years all adult women were recruited to Popular Committees (Lippert 1985). These committees mobilized women's labor. Women sewed clothes for the refugee community, tended (alongside male colleagues) to garden crops, and staffed schools and health centers.

During the years of the Popular Committees, all this work was not formally waged. Following the ceasefire, the refugee camps opened up to greater freedom of movement of people and things into and out of the camps, and the Polisario Front relaxed its earlier authoritarian tendencies in what has been called the Sahrawi "perestroika" (Shelley 2004, 179); in 1995 the Polisario Front disbanded the Popular Committees. Smaller groups of women staffed the replacement Councils. Thus, in parallel to the diminution of recruitment to the army for men, there has also been a decrease in the conscription of female labor.

From the late 1990s on, women and (demobilized) men working in public services expected remuneration. Wages, however, could be modest indeed. For instance, in 2007 an elementary school teacher might earn some thirty euros a month, paid irregularly, at a time when I heard the Polisario president suggest in a press conference that a family needed a hundred euros a month to survive. With wages in the public sector so low or symbolic, the Polisario Front has struggled to retain workers in key sectors such as education and health care. Refugees looked for more lucrative opportunities for commoditized labor either in the refugee camps or in international markets. (International migration to destinations such as Spain or France is only an option for those who can acquire non-SADR travel documentation that will be recognized in these countries.)

The vicissitudes of the conscription and deployment of refugees' labor over the course of exile mark another material boundary of the social relations of sovereignty in the Sahrawi refugee camps. In parallel to the task of distributing rations to refugees, the state authority operating in the refugee camps has had the task of claiming refugees' labor. In the giving/conscripting of labor, just as in the distribution of rations, the governing authorities and the refugees have engaged with one another. In addition, just as rations were believed by refugees to play a potential role in the wielding of legitimate coercion, so has labor played an equivalent role at times. In their memories of the late 1970s and 1980s, refugees recalled that for a refugee who transgressed a rule, such as by using the nomenclature of tribes, the Polisario Front might punish the offender by imposing a fine of extra physical labor, such as to make mud bricks. In a context in which the refugees construed themselves, and in which the Polisario Front construed the refugees as dispossessed, another historical form of legitimate coercion has been the imposition not of fines but of labor penalties.

Such labor penalties are not currently practiced in the refugee camps and have not been practiced for some years. But the widespread decline of conscription in the period following the ceasefire, both as regards the army and the Councils that have replaced Committees, is not necessarily a sign that the claiming of labor is no longer a resource through which refugees and the Polisario Front as a state authority engage with one another. As we have seen, potential mobilization in the army in case of national need remains legitimate in the eyes of many refugees. Furthermore, although the government's distribution of rations is no longer matched by such a ubiquitous conscription of labor, one unwaged form of the Polisario Front's claiming of refugee labor has survived. This system is known as *ḥamla*, meaning campaign. It takes a specific ethnographic form: there are different ḥamla activities for men and women, such as cleaning a school at the beginning of the school year for women or trash collection for men. Moreover, ḥamla activities are always accompanied by some food and drink (funded by the Polisario Front), which encourages relaxed joking and socializing in breaks or when work is completed. Ḥamla is unwaged, and voluntary. There are no penalties imposed on persons called to take part and who choose not to do so.

This socially specific form of labor recruitment is significant, for ḥamla can be read as a reworking of the labor-pooling mechanisms that previously existed within tribal networks, known among Sahrawis (and among other North Africans) as *twīza* (Wilson 2016, 137–140). Not only is ḥamla, then, an instance of the recycling of the social relations of one project of sovereignty (tribes at specific historical moments) in order to constitute the social relations of another project of sovereignty (here: state power). Also, ḥamla as a punctual form of labor recruitment indicates how, despite the decline of labor conscription, the social relations of sovereignty in the Sahrawi refugee camps still entail a relation between the Polisario Front and the refugees with regard to a mobile resource, namely refugees' labor. In certain contexts, refugees continue to voluntarily give a key resource, their labor, without the Polisario Front needing to resort to coercive conscription. Actual and potential giving of labor thus marks another material boundary of inclusion in the social relations of everyday sovereignty in exile.

Everyday Sovereignty in Exile

Exceptions have often provided the means through which to reflect on the wider category from which exceptions are apparently excluded (Agamben 1998; Schmitt 1985). Anomalous and exceptional manifestations of state power—whether on the margins of territory (Reeves 2014; chapter 10, this volume), of international recognition (Feldman 2008), of the operation of state power (Das and Poole 2004), or of a globalizing form of governance (Chalfin 2010)—have illuminated contexts from which to probe the workings and meanings of state power. In such a fashion, the anomalous case of the Sahrawi refugee camps, and the broader anomaly of Western Sahara as a case combining unfinished decolonization, exile, partial annexation, and partial international recognition, opens up fresh perspectives on how sovereignty relates to people, territory, and resources.

Where classic interpretations of sovereignty have stressed authority over territory, and critical reinterpretations have emphasized state power and sovereignty as social relations, the unusual circumstances of Sahrawi refugees prompt reconsideration. As refugee camps located outside the claimed homeland territory, the Sahrawi refugee camps present an exception to idealized forms of territorial sovereignty. The intensity of the activities of state power in the Sahrawi refugee camps underscores how sovereignty as relations between people play out in this setting. But a close analysis of the role of mobile, nonterritorial resources in the relations between the governing authorities and the governed constituencies provides the impetus for questioning any temptation to draw a contrast between understanding sovereignty in terms *either* of power over territory *or* of relations between people. Rather, anthropological approaches to property, whereby property relations are understood as relations between people playing out with regard to things/resources about which property claims are made, suggest an alternative approach to sovereignty. Sovereignty too may be understood in terms of a relationship between people playing out in relation to resources, which may (or may not) take territorial form. From this perspective, in the familiar scenario of sovereignty as alleged supreme authority over territory the social relations of sovereignty play out as a relation between people (governing authorities and governed constituencies) in relation to resources in the form of territory. In the Sahrawi refugee camps, where claimed territory is inaccessible on a daily basis, the social relations of sovereignty are nevertheless by no means absent. In this setting the social relations of sovereignty play out as relations between the governing authorities (a combination of the Polisario Front and the SADR) and governed constituencies (the refugees) in relation to resources other than territory: a range of mobile resources including rations and the refugees' labor. People and resources—the latter potentially but not necessarily in territorial form—help constitute the social relations of sovereignty in exceptional as well as unexceptional forms.

In paying close attention to the circulation of mobile resources in the Sahrawi refugee camps, we observe how classic interpretations of the sovereignty of states take on specific forms in the Sahrawi refugee camps. Weber (1958) claims that the sovereignty of states entails a monopoly on the use of legitimate violence within a given territory; such a monopoly can itself be understood as an instance of Schmitt's (1985) definition of sovereignty as the power to decide on the state of exception. In the Sahrawi refugee camps, one of a number of ways in which claims to such forms of power manifest themselves concerns the circulation of mobile resources. Rations can be threatened to be withheld, and labor has historically been imposed, as legitimate forms of violence. Yet the exceptional space of the Sahrawi refugee camps where a liberation movement leads a revolution also illustrates the need to go beyond these classic interpretations of sovereignty—for Sahrawi refugees continue in certain circumstances to "volunteer" (e.g., in ḥamla activities) the very resource, labor, that the governing authorities have historically mobilized at times through coercion. Legitimate coercion can only ever be part of a much wider range of the social relations of sovereignty, which, like power relations more broadly (Foucault 1978, 1979), also work through the production of subjectivities to govern and to be subjects.

Tracing the convergences of people and resources in Sahrawi refugees' constitution of the social relations of sovereignty illuminates how the social relations of past projects of sovereignty, such as tribes in this context, can be recycled in the constitution of the social relations of alternative projects of sovereignty, such as state power in the setting of the refugee camps. The desires for the future of many Sahrawis are firmly fixed on the dream of territorial sovereignty in the claimed homeland of Western Sahara. The fervor of this desire for the future fuels refugees' experiments with an everyday sovereignty in exile.

Notes

1. I am grateful to my Sahrawi hosts for their generosity, and to the Polisario Front for facilitating research access. The main fieldwork was funded by the UK's Economic and Social Research Council. For a fuller analysis of some ideas discussed here, see Wilson 2016.

2. The Sahrawi refugee case contrasts with the Israeli case (chapter 9, this volume) where, despite the achievement of territorial sovereignty, citizens' diverse political and religious orientations mean that the practice of popular sovereignty is compromised by the fact that some of the "the people" experience the state as a threat to their potential emancipation. Sahrawi refugees lack a fully recognized nation-state but look on its achievement as the potential source of, rather than threat to, their emancipation.

3. The UN's list of voters referred to the Sahrawi population as identified in 2000. This list found 41,150 Sahrawi voters in Moroccan-controlled Western Sahara and 33,998 in the refugee camps in Algeria (Zunes and Munday 2010, 214).

4. "Tribe" is a problematic term in anthropology (see Sneath 2007). On the *qabīla* and status groups among speakers of Hassaniya, see Caro Baroja 1955.

5. For a list of eighty recognitions of SADR by other states to 2006 (including twenty-two withdrawn or cancelled recognitions), see Pazzanita 2006, 376–378.

6. This overview of the kinds of organizations providing aid is not exhaustive.

7. The main residential camps (*wilayāt*) and their component districts (*dawair*) are named after cities in Western Sahara.

8. The activism of a Sahrawi women's movement demanding greater rights and opportunities for participation in activities beyond reproductive labor predates the Polisario Front (see Allan 2019). Polisario Front from its early days endorsed a women's movement, which voices demands for gender equality. The leadership of the Sahrawi refugee women's movement has nevertheless been criticized to the extent that their claims about the existing levels of emancipation among Sahrawi women rest on problematic and orientalizing depictions of perceived Western and Arab others (Allan 2010; Fiddian-Qasmiyeh 2014).

References

Agamben, Giorgio. 1998. *Homo Sacer: Sovereign Power and Bare Life*. Stanford, CA: Stanford University Press.

Allan, Joanna. 2010. "Imagining Saharawi Women: The Question of Gender in POLISARIO Discourse." *Journal of North African Studies* 15(2): 189–202.

Allan, Joanna. 2019. *Silenced Resistance: Women, Dictatorships, and Genderwashing in Western Sahara and Equatorial Guinea*. Madison: University of Wisconsin Press.

Benton, Lauren A. 2009. *A Search for Sovereignty: Law and Geography in European Empires, 1400–1900.* Cambridge: Cambridge University Press.

Bhatia, Michael. 2001. "Western Sahara under Polisario Control: Summary Report of Field Mission to the Saharawi Refugee." *Review of African Political Economy* 88: 291–298.

Biersteker, Thomas J., and Cynthia Weber, eds. 1996. *State Sovereignty as Social Construct.* Cambridge: Cambridge University Press.

Brown, Wendy. 2010. *Walled States, Waning Sovereignty.* New York: Zone.

Caratini, Sophie. 1989. *Les Rgaybāt (1610–1934): Des chameliers à la conquête d'un territoire.* Vol. 1. Paris: Harmattan.

Caro Baroja, Julio. 2009. *Estudios Saharianos.* Madrid: Consejo Superior de Investigaciones Científicas, Instituto de Estudios Africanos.

Chalfin, Brenda. 2010. *Neoliberal Frontiers: An Ethnography of Sovereignty in West Africa.* Chicago: University of Chicago Press.

Comaroff, John L., and Jean Comaroff. 2009. "Reflections on the Anthropology of Law, Governance, and Sovereignty." In *Rules of Law and Laws of Ruling: On the Governance of Law,* edited by F. Von Benda-Beckmann, K. von Benda-Beckmann, and J. Eckert, 31–59. Farnham: Ashgate.

Das, Veena, and Deborah Poole, eds. 2004. *Anthropology in the Margins of the State.* Oxford: School of American Research Press.

Feldman, Ilana. 2008. *Governing Gaza: Bureaucracy, Authority, and the Work of Rule, 1917–1967.* Durham, NC: Duke University Press.

Ferguson, James. 2005. "Seeing Like an Oil Company: Space, Security, and Global Capital in Neoliberal Africa." *American Anthropologist* 107(3): 377–38.

Fiddian-Qasmiyeh, Elena. 2014. *The Ideal Refugees: Gender, Islam, and the Sahrawi Politics of Survival.* Syracuse: Syracuse University Press.

Flores Morales, Ángel 1946. *El Sahara español: ensayo de geografía física y económica.* Madrid: Alta Comisaría de España en Marruecos.

Foucault, Michel. 1978. *The History of Sexuality.* Vol. 1. *Introduction.* Translated by Robert Hurley. New York: Pantheon Books.

Foucault, Michel. 1979. *Discipline and Punish.* New York: Vintage.

Frésia, Marion. 2009. *Les Mauritaniens réfugiés au Sénégal: une anthropologie critique de l'asile et de l'aide humanitaire.* Paris: Harmattan.

Hansen, Thomas Blom, and Finn Stepputat, eds. 2005. *Sovereign Bodies: Citizens, Migrants, and States in the Postcolonial World.* Princeton, NJ: Princeton University Press.

Horst, Cindy. 2006. *Transnational Nomads: How Somalis Cope with Refugee Life in the Dadaab Camps of Kenya.* Oxford: Berghahn.

Krasner, Stephen D. 1999. *Sovereignty: Organized Hypocrisy.* Princeton, NJ: Princeton University Press.

Lackner, Helen. 1985. *P. D. R. Yemen: Outpost of Socialist Development in Arabia.* London: Ithaca Press.

Lewis, Ioan M. 1979. "Kim Il-Sung in Somalia: the End of Tribalism?" In *Politics in Leadership: A Comparative Perspective,* edited by William A. Schak and Percy S. Cohen, 13–44. Oxford: Clarendon Press.

Lippert, Anne. 1985. *The Saharawi Refugees: Origins and Organization, 1975–1985.* Ada, Ohio: SPSC Letter.

Malkki, Liisa H. 1995. *Purity and Exile: Violence, Memory, and National Cosmology among Hutu Refugees in Tanzania.* Chicago: University of Chicago Press.

McConnell, Fiona. 2016. *Rehearsing the State: The Governance Practices of the Exile Tibetan Government.* Oxford: John Wiley.

Navaro-Yashin, Yael. 2002. *Faces of the State: Secularism and Public Life in Turkey*. Princeton, NJ: Princeton University Press.

Navaro-Yashin, Yael. 2012. *The Make-Believe Space: Affective Geography in a Postwar Polity*. Durham, NC: Duke University Press.

Ong, Aihwa. 2006. *Neoliberalism as Exception: Mutations in Citizenship and Sovereignty*. Durham, NC: Duke University Press.

Pazzanita, Anthony. 2006. *The Historical Dictionary of Western Sahara*. Lanham, MD: Scarecrow Press.

Peteet, Julie Marie. 2005. *Landscape of Hope and Despair: Palestinian Refugee Camps*. Philadelphia: University of Pennsylvania Press.

Pottage, Alain, and Martha Mundy, eds. 2004. *Law, Anthropology, and the Constitution of the Social: Making Persons and Things*. Cambridge: Cambridge University Press.

Reeves, Madeleine. 2014. *Border Work: Spatial Lives of the State in Rural Central Asia*. Ithaca, NY: Cornell University Press.

Schmitt, Carl. 1985. *Political Theology: Four Chapters on the Concept of Sovereignty*. Cambridge, MA: MIT Press.

Shelley, Toby. 2004. *Endgame in the Western Sahara: What Future for Africa's Last Colony?* London: Zed Books.

Sneath, David. 2007. *The Headless State: Aristocratic Orders, Kinship Society, and Misrepresentations of Nomadic Inner Asia*. New York: Columbia University Press.

Takriti, Abdel Razzaq. 2013. *Monsoon Revolution. Republicans, Sultans, and Empires in Oman, 1965–1976*. Oxford: Oxford University Press.

UNHCR. 2018. *Sahrawi Refugees in Tindouf, Algeria: Total In-Camp Population*. UNHCR. http://www.usc.es/export9/sites/webinstitucional/gl/institutos/ceso/descargas/UNHCR_Tindouf-Total-In-Camp-Population_March-2018.pdf. Accessed April 25, 2019.

Verdery, Katherine. 2003. *Vanishing Hectare: Property and Value in Post-Socialist Transylvania*. Ithaca, NY: Cornell University Press.

Weber, Max. 1958. "Politics as Vocation." In *Max Weber: Essays in Sociology*, ed. by H. H. Gerth and C. Wright Mills, 77–128. New York: Oxford University Press.

Wilson, Alice. 2014. "Cycles of Crisis, Migration, and the Formation of New Political Identities in Western Sahara." In *Crises et migrations dans les pays du sud*, edited by Marc-Antoine Pérouse de Montclos, Véronique Petit, and Nelly Robin, 79–105. Paris: Harmattan.

Wilson, Alice. 2016. *Sovereignty in Exile: A Saharan Liberation Movement Governs*. Philadelphia, PA: University of Pennsylvania Press.

Wilson, Alice. 2017. "Ambivalences of Mobility: Rival State Authorities and Mobile Strategies in a Saharan Conflict." *American Ethnologist* 44(1): 77–90.

Zunes, Stephen, and Jacob Mundy. 2010. *Western Sahara: War, Nationalism, and Conflict Irresolution*. Syracuse, NY: Syracuse University Press.

EXISTENTIAL SOVEREIGNTY

Latvian People, Their State, and the
Problem of Mobility

Dace Dzenovska

In the story that Latvians tell themselves about themselves, the Latvian cultural nation and national state are embattled. In the long aftermath of what the Latvian public refers to as Soviet occupation, the sense of embattlement derives from the proximity to Russia as a potential aggressor and the presence of a large Russian-speaking minority in the territory of Latvia (Laitin 1998; Dzenovska 2018a). The sense of national embattlement translates into compensatory politics. For example, one of the factors legitimating the post-Soviet Latvian state's restrictive citizenship and punitive language policies that aim to Latvianize the polity and public space is the dramatic shift in the ethnic composition of Latvia's population over the course of the twentieth century.[1] If before Soviet rule in 1935 Latvians made up 77 percent of the population of 1.9 million, then just before the collapse of the Soviet Union in 1989 Latvians made up 52 percent of the 2.6 million population (following the collapse of the Soviet Union in 1991 and the accession to the European Union in 2004, Latvia's population fell to 1.9 million by 2015).[2]

Despite—or perhaps precisely because of—the aggressive post-Soviet policies of compensatory Latvianization, the Latvian public continuously doubts the loyalty of the Soviet majority-cum-Russian minority toward the Latvian state as a national state, that is, as a state established for the purpose of ensuring the continuity and flourishing of the cultural nation of Latvians. In the 2000s, this distrust was exacerbated by Vladimir Putin's pronounced support of compatriots abroad (*sootechestvenniki*), whereby Russian speakers in the "near abroad" were depicted as subjects who could avail themselves of the protection of the Russian state. While the compatriot discourse was short-lived and fairly quickly replaced by the more expansive and arguably less controversial support for *Russkyi Mir*, that is, a transnational Russian cultural space, post-Soviet states with significant Russian-speaking populations took Putin's statements seriously.[3] With regard to Ukraine, for example, Catherine Wanner writes that, given the geographic concentration of Russian speakers in Ukraine, Russia's *sootechestvenniki* politics introduced the possibility of converting some regions of Ukraine into "zones of diminished sovereignty" (2014, 430). Russia itself continues to be perceived as a military threat by the bordering post-Soviet states, including Latvia. For the Latvian public and government, recent events in Crimea and Eastern Ukraine have confirmed the validity of this fear, resulting in significant increase in NATO troops in the Baltics (Dzenovska 2018c).

The threat of Russia and the Russian-speaking minority is widely considered to be the legacy of Soviet occupation, that is, of a period of unfreedom. However, in conditions of post-Soviet freedom, there has emerged another unexpected threat: expelled from the global circuits of capital in their places of residence, Latvia's residents, ethnic Latvians and Russian speakers alike, are leaving to live and work in Western European states. Outmigration began as a trickle in the 2000s but intensified after Latvia's accession to the European Union in 2004 and even more so during and after the financial crisis of 2008. When I began my research on the emptying of the Latvian countryside in 2010, it was referred to as "the Great Departure" (Dzenovska 2012, 2013, 2018b). Not much statistical or other information was available, but researchers estimated that about 10 percent of Latvia's residents had left (Hazans 2011, 2016). While scholars and policymakers mobilized to produce data, the contours of the Great Departure were most tangible in the accounts of those who stayed behind. People across Latvia's cities, towns, and villages reported that there were fewer children in schools, that the streets were notably emptier than they used to be, that it was difficult to find someone to fix your roof, and that social life had broken down, because so many people had left. Alongside this everyday sense of emptiness, demographers, economists, and psychologists identified a number of impending social, economic, and political threats: demographic crisis, deterioration of the infrastructure, unraveling of the social fabric, and last, but not least, a threat to the existence of Latvians as an ethnos, a cultural nation, and a polity, and a threat to the existence of the Latvian state as a state primarily legitimated by Latvian aspirations for self-determination (e.g., Zvidriņš 2005). A popular saying reflected the existential fear—at once physical and political—conjured up by outmigration: "What the Russians did not do to us, we will do to ourselves." Resonating with Joyce Dalsheim's (chapter 9, this volume) discussion of the Jewish threat to the Jewish state, Latvians were pondering whether perhaps freedom was a form of self-elimination rather than self-determination. However, if in Dalsheim's chapter the Jewish threat to Jews lies in the struggle between legal and divine authorities for defining Jewishness and a Jewish way of life, the Latvian threat to Latvians lies in the inability of the Latvian state to care for the physical bodies of Latvians in conditions of capitalist freedom.

In this chapter, I ask what it means when a significant number of individuals who constitute the "state-bearing nation" that is thought to legitimate the existence and legal identity of the Latvian state move to live and work in territories of other states (Konstitucionālo tiesību komisija 2012). Put another way, what does freedom of movement mean for an embattled nation? To be sure, constitutive threats are a truism in studies of nationalism and nation-building. However, I use "embattled" here to denote a much deeper existential fear about the viable existence of both a people and a state. There is a difference, for example, between France or Denmark, where various political forces posit different threats to the fabric of the nation, however defined, in different historical moments, and Israel, a state that is constituted vis-à-vis foundational existential threats, such as that of the Holocaust and the present-day consequences of settler colonialism, that are said to threaten the physical and political existence of the people and the state. With regard to public and political life, Latvia, I suggest, is more like Israel than France. While some in France may be worried about the Frenchness of France (even if understood as a "community of value" (Anderson 2013) rather than ethno-cultural community), many in Latvia are worried about the political existence of the Latvian state as a guarantor of the physical and cultural existence of the people.

"Embattled nationhood," then, refers to a situation whereby a culturally distinct people claim a state, while at the same time exhibiting deep existential fear about a potential breakdown of the articulation of the people with the state, and the loss of the state. In addition to perceiving the existence of a national state as a guarantor for the existence of the people, Latvian politicians and members of the public also perceive the existence of the state as an indication of political maturity and civilizational status. As a member of a conservative political force said in a public demonstration against corruption in July 2017: "Not every people have their own state. We have our own state, and we have to protect it!" This is to say that Latvian existential fears emerge within a modernist developmental frame, whereby only a people that has a state has become a mature and democratic people insofar as it has evolved from an ethnic group to a mature nation with consciousness, political will, and the ability to establish, uphold, and protect its own state.

This developmental frame cuts across various political regimes, from liberal to socialist to postcolonial. If the Soviet party-state sorted peoples into ethnic

groups (*narodnost'*), nationalities (*natsional'nost'*), and nations (*natsiia*), depending on whether they exhibited national consciousness and had political institutions (Hirsch 2005, 10), postcolonial nations, too, strove to become "sovereign
moderns" with "the right to a passport, a flag, a stamp, a coin, and the formation
of a native state" (Bonilla 2015, 13). Having one's own state—or what Rebecca
Bryant and Madeleine Reeves (Introduction) call "state desire"—is important for
Latvians who wish to be recognized as historical and political agents who shape
their own lives, that is, as a people with sovereign agency (Bryant and Reeves,
Introduction). While state desire among Latvians may be relatively recent, dating back to late nineteenth and early twentieth centuries (Dzenovska 2018a; Ījabs
2009; Ijabs 2012), it is no less efficacious in shaping the self-understanding of
Latvians as not only legible historical and political agents, but also as emplaced
human beings.

This is to say that in the case of Latvians the sense of embattlement and
aspirations for sovereign agency, while most visible in the political realm and
on the collective register, are intricately linked—often inseparable—from individual selfhood, or what Anthony Cohen (1996) calls "personal nationalism." In
Cohen's interpretation, personal nationalism may diverge from political nationalism, thus political nationalists face the challenge of unifying a diverse group of
people, all of whom recognize themselves as members of a cultural nation, but
who may politically diverge to the point of unrecognizability (1996, 809). In the
case of Latvia, this may be so if one looks at party politics, but there is a strong
overlap of personal and political with regard to people's understanding of themselves as human beings with particular life trajectories and as legible political
agents. Vieda Skultāns's (2007) work on life narratives supports this observation.
Skultāns points out that many of her Latvian interlocutors narrated their personal
lives through the life of the nation. Skultāns could not access personal experiences
that were separate from the history of the nation, even though she had initially
assumed that there would be personal experiences underneath the collective layer.
If there were any, they were not accessible through life narratives. The nation
was deeply constitutive of how her interlocutors knew themselves and narrated
themselves. The existentialist question of the meaning of being was answered
here in the collective register. To be was to be a member of the nation; personal
life trajectories were inseparable from the fate of the nation. Fears about personal
existence were fears about the existence of the nation and vice versa.

Most of the literature on nationalism, especially on nationalism in the region,
does not get to the exact combination of elements that I am discussing here.
By way of one example, in their analysis of nationalism in Romania, Rogers
Brubaker and his team (Brubaker et al. 2007) separate nationalism as a political
ideology from everyday ethnicity. The latter may entail in-group and out-group

distinctions and even prejudice, but in the authors' view, nationalism occurs in the political realm. This and similar takes on nationalism cannot capture the existential sense of embattlement and associated political claims that I trace in this chapter through analysis of how mobility is perceived and accommodated by the embattled nation of Latvians. In this chapter, then, I propose to speak of these practices in the rubric of "existential sovereignty."

Articulations of sovereignty in critical theory and anthropology tend to be primarily influenced by or be in conversation with Carl Schmitt's (1985) notion of the sovereign as he who decides on exception (e.g., Brown 2010) and Giorgio Agamben's (1998) articulation of sovereignty as power over life (e.g., Hansen and Stepputat 2005; Dunn and Cons 2013). Some also draw on international relations understandings of sovereignty as territorial self-determination in a community of nation-states (Krasner 1999). The notion of self-determination also informs concepts of cultural sovereignty (Winegar 2006), food sovereignty (Campbell and Veteto 2015), or resource sovereignty (Folch 2016).

The concept of existential sovereignty, as I use it in this chapter, pertains to the ability to bring into existence a people and their state and to ensure the continued physical and political existence of both.[4] Rather than—or in addition to—ensuring control over territory or fighting for the right to self-determination, existential sovereignty pertains to practices that coconstitute the subject that can aspire for sovereign agency and the political institutions that make this subject "politically recognizable and capable of agentive action" (Bryant and Reeves, Introduction). The concept combines existentialist concerns with the meaning of human existence with concerns about political existence, one becoming inseparable from the other. It also adds an additional layer to theories of sovereignty, one brilliantly elaborated by Anya Bernstein (2012) in her analysis of the Buryat Buddhist notion of the "ideal sovereign body," where Bernstein argues that individual bodies are not only sites on which sovereign power can be and is exercised, but can also become embodiments of sovereignty, as in the case of reincarnate lamas that move across borders. However, it is not just leaders, such as kings or lamas, who have two bodies—one natural and the other political (Kantorowicz 1998), but also ordinary people who have both physical bodies and political bodies that lend legitimacy to political authority, especially in modern nation-states where sovereignty is thought to inhere in the people (Santner 2011; Yurchak 2015). Just as biopower works at the intersection of the individual and the population insofar as individual conduct is crucial for the life of the population at large (Foucault 2003), sovereign power, too, works at the intersection of the individual and the body politic. Rather than an abstraction fixed in territory, the body politic is an aggregation of living individuals who are engaged in crafting lives. It is precisely for that reason that migration, often thought of as an individual rather than a collective act, becomes a collective problem both for the polities that people leave and for the polities in which people arrive.

In the rest of the chapter, I elaborate the phenomenon of existential sovereignty on the basis of analysis of how government and nongovernment actors handle the problem that post-Soviet freedom of movement introduces for the embattled Latvian nation and the state. In particular, I focus on the Latvian state's diaspora politics, as well as two political events—a referendum on whether to make the Russian language the second state language that took place in 2012 and the 2014 constitutional reform that reaffirmed the national nature of the Latvian state. On the basis of this analysis, I argue that existential sovereignty is not a state of being, but a claim to the coherence and continuity of a collective self, pursued with the tools of statecraft. It is not primarily a matter of control over territory, but rather of the existence of self in space and time. Within the modernist frame of national self-determination, claims of existential sovereignty remain articulated with a territorial state, that is, the physical and political existence of the sovereign subject requires the existence of a national territory, even if many of the individuals who constitute the sovereign subject do not live in it. At the same time, existential sovereignty allows for the distribution of collective selfhood across territories of several historically existing states. In that sense, existential sovereignty entails a transfer of political sovereignty from a territorially defined state to a reterritorialized collective self that operates transnationally alongside corporations, international organizations, God, and other actors that compete for the status of the sovereign.

Migration and Diaspora Politics

The current wave of emigration is not the first migration-related threat to the embattled Latvian nation. The self-narrative of the embattled nation includes two other stories of threatening migration—one of forced emigration and the other of organized immigration. The forced emigration story pertains to the pre–World War II elites—e.g., intellectuals, politicians, civil servants, military officers—fleeing Latvia on the cusp of the reestablishment of Soviet power in 1944, as well as to the mass deportations that took place during the first decades of Soviet power in Latvia. The organized immigration story, in turn, refers to the movement of Russian-speaking Soviet citizens from other parts of the Soviet Union to live and work in Soviet Latvia (Riekstiņš 2005; Dzenovska 2018a). Both the deportations and the organized immigration are commonly attributed to deliberate Soviet policies of mixing populations in order to create generic Soviet citizens out of unruly national subjects. Both are also widely recognized as threatening to the nation, as well as to the existence of the Latvian state as a national state.

The loss of independence at the end of World War II and the dispersal of the nation to Siberia and the West shaped the twentieth-century self-narrative of Latvians as a nation that has been physically violated, politically alienated from its territory, as well as forcefully kept apart insofar as exit from and entry into the Soviet Union were restricted.[5] Consequently, independence struggles of the late 1980s that culminated with the restoration of the pre–World War II (1918–40) Latvian state in 1991 simultaneously drew on national and liberal imaginaries: on the one hand, they drew on the imaginary of a cultural nation reunited as a political community in its rightful territory, and on the other hand, they drew on the imaginary of liberal freedoms, including the freedom of movement.

With the restoration of independence, exit and entry restrictions were lifted. Latvians living abroad were encouraged to return. Some did, but many did not, as they had established lives elsewhere. Certain forms of emigration were also encouraged—for example, the return of retired Soviet military personnel to Russia and other former Soviet republics or the emigration of Soviet-era Russian-speaking residents who did not wish to live in the independent state of Latvia (Dzenovska 2018a). But nobody could have predicted that the newly found freedom of movement in conjunction with the neoliberalization of the economy would result in such significant westward migration.[6]

People left for multiple reasons. In surveys launched by Latvia's social scientists and in my own ethnographic encounters, aspirations for social mobility and professional advancement were mentioned alongside unemployment, low wages, debt, and social and political discontent (Hazans 2011, 2015; Dzenovska 2012, 2018b). The 2008 financial crisis exacerbated job loss and pressure on indebted segments of the population, thus pushing more people to leave. While some of those who left struggled with balancing patriotic feelings with professional advancement opportunities (Lulle and Bužinska 2017), many labor migrants and debt refugees were angry and resentful toward the Latvian state for having let them down, that is, for not having created the kind of conditions within which they could lead livable lives at home—earn enough money, repay debt, educate their children, support family, or get heating in the winter. Most, including students and professionals, criticized political elites and public institutions for corruption, excessive bureaucracy, incompetence, or more generally, lack of care. "The state does not care about us," I heard over and over again from those who had left, but also from those who had stayed behind (Kaprans 2015; Ķešāne 2011; Dzenovska 2012, 2018b). In response, political and intellectual elites claimed that those who left angry with the state only wanted things from the state but did not contribute to making Latvia a better place to live. However, there were also politicians, civil servants, and activists, both within and outside Latvia, who thought that the mutual sense of betrayal must be overcome for the sake of ensuring the continuity of the Latvian nation and the state. This was the main impetus for attempting to institutionalize relations with the dispersed nation in the form of diaspora politics.

State-based diaspora politics is nothing new in the global arena (though states attempt to govern or influence their citizens abroad by other means as well, see Bozzini 2015). Many states have diaspora policies and even specific institutions dealing with diaspora affairs (Gamlen 2014). Émigrés, previously barely noticed or considered to be traitors, have suddenly become sought-after contributors to national development and ambassadors of their nations abroad. The proliferation of diaspora politics and policies on a global scale since the late 1980s has gone hand in hand with new inflections in diaspora scholarship. Contrary to the cultural studies–based and identity-focused perspectives on diaspora as a site of hybridity where rigid categories of identification are or can be subverted (e.g., Gilroy 1995; Brah 1996), the policy and political turn to diaspora is analyzed, even promoted, within the rubric of development (e.g., de Haas 2010). Here the focus is on remittances—economic, political, and social (de Haas 2007; Levitt 1998; Tabar 2014; Darieva 2011)—on forms of diaspora engagement in the affairs of the home country (e.g., Bernal 2014; Van Hear and Cohen 2017; Kaprans 2015; Anderson 1992), as well as on forms of citizenship and belonging (e.g., Soysal 2000; Lulle et al. 2015). Debates focus on whether remittances help or hinder development, whether diaspora engagement is politically progressive or regressive, as well as on what forms of membership and political participation are appropriate for diaspora.

In Latvia the term *diaspora* appeared when the Latvian government launched a diaspora program in 2004.[7] At first, the term *diaspora* largely pertained to cultivating and institutionalizing relations with "Latvians in exile" (*trimdas latvieši*) or "Latvians abroad" (*ārzemju latvieši*), that is, post–World War II refugees and their descendants who left or were forced to leave as part of the two constitutive stories of migration. However, whatever mechanisms there may have been for tending relations with the "old exile," these were not sufficient for governing people who had left in conditions of freedom. Thus diplomats, policymakers, and civil servants had to rethink their approach. The "new emigration" (*jaunā emigrācija*) presented a problem of government for the state. The "new emigration" seemed to lack the willingness and capacity to organize or to engage with the cultural and social institutions established by the trimda (old exiles), which was highly organized and self-sufficient. I often heard civil servants and members of trimda say that the "new emigration" was too preoccupied with economic concerns to understand the value of the Latvian language and culture and of political organization in exile. As many of the "new émigrés" initially did not seek out Latvian organizations and institutions abroad, they were difficult to find and therefore to govern. The first task for the state, thus, was to find and get to know its diaspora.[8]

During our first meeting, Kārlis, a civil servant at a line ministry who worked on a document that would serve as the basis for the state's diaspora strategy, showed me a big pile of printouts of Irish, Lithuanian, Israeli, and other diaspora policy documents. These documents were produced by the respective states' institutions charged with the task of cultivating relations with diaspora. Many of them were produced with the assistance of academics involved in research on the development potential of diasporas. Kārlis had selected diaspora strategies of those states that were not commonly thought of as "developing," and whose diaspora policies aimed to cultivate national identity as much as benefit from diaspora economically. Kārlis told me that he could easily copy any of the diaspora strategy documents in front of him for the purposes of producing a document, because they were good and, moreover, the "best practices" approach was quite common in governance. However, he wanted to know what was going on with the Latvians and that is why he sought out people who knew things about Latvians abroad, as well as engaged in generating this knowledge himself.

Kārlis's initial activities seemed quite chaotic. He sought out people who seemed to be engaged in activities relevant for diaspora politics, yet most of these conversations did not translate into institutionalized collaboration. Kārlis explained that it did not matter, because one important aspect of his work was to motivate people and to put them in touch with each other, that is, to generate civic—and at the same time national—activity. Similarly, Kārlis picked up on some initiatives only to drop some later. He was always on the road to yet another meeting or conference and continuously sought out people who were doing something because they were either concerned that Latvians abroad were losing themselves—that is, losing the sense of who they were in relation to others—or because they were proud of being Latvian and wanted to invest their skills or knowledge at home.

In these initial stages, Kārlis often spoke of "a general lack of understanding" in the government about the need to transform governance to include Latvians abroad, as well as complained about a myriad of bureaucratic obstacles that often drove him to despair. Yet, he was well suited for the task. Born to Latvian parents in exile, he had at some point in his youth turned away from the Latvian language and society—that is, he had lost himself, as he put it—only to rediscover their significance later in life. He was convinced of the value of self-knowledge and considered that losing oneself—like he had for a moment—introduces great psychological stress for individuals. Life among others—other selves and other states—could become a source of vulnerability for both the selfhood of the migrants and the nation at large. He thought that diaspora work could prevent further self-loss and alienation from the nation. Kārlis's work revealed a philosophy of what it means to be human.[9] For Kārlis, being human was to be embedded in a historical and cultural community. It also meant being connected to a territorial state that ultimately served as the guarantor of the existence of the nation, but that allowed for the possibility that the nation was territorially dispersed and adapted its practices of governance accordingly.

The months went on and what at first looked like an ad hoc initiative of a small network of affiliated individuals began to look like a state project, though it still largely depended on individual commitment rather than institutionalized practices. About a year and a half after we first met, Kārlis and I both sat on the same panel at a high-level political meeting on the new Latvian diaspora in the United Kingdom. Kārlis's central message was: "Know your diaspora!" For the still fledgling project of diaspora work that was ongoing in the corridors of ministries, embassies, church halls, informal meetings in cafes, newspaper articles, cheap airline flights, and elsewhere, knowing diaspora was crucial: what they did, who they were, what they thought, and how they felt. This form of knowing exceeded knowing oneself as a historically and socially embedded being insofar as by inviting his audience to "know your diaspora" Kārlis appealed to the state's capacity to govern and thus to the state's ability to demonstrate to the sovereign, that is, to the people, that the state was indeed the guarantor of their collective existence.

In the following months and years, several institutionalized knowledge-production projects were launched. In addition to the formalization of the diaspora strategy, the Ministry of Foreign Affairs funded the establishment of a Diaspora Research Center within the University of Latvia with a research agenda closely linked to the political objective of institutionalizing state-diaspora relations. One of its first outputs was an extensive research report on political representation, which also entailed thorough theoretical reflections on transnational political communities (Lulle et al. 2015). Alongside research, the Ministry of Foreign Affairs, together with diaspora organizations, established an annual diaspora conference held in Riga every summer, as well as a business forum for Latvians abroad. Local governments were approached, and several came aboard with their own diaspora initiatives targeting their former residents abroad. The Ministry of Economy launched a remigration plan, and the local administering body of the European Social Fund sponsored a large-scale quantitative survey, which enumerated the diaspora and surveyed respondents on questions of identity, political participation, quality of life, and return possibilities (Mieriņa 2015).[10]

All the while, "knowing diaspora" as a project of government remained closely linked with "knowing oneself" as a project of existential sovereignty, that is, making sure that a people existed and knew itself as a people. On the one hand, it was necessary for the state to generate data about Latvians abroad in order to govern.

On the other hand, it was necessary for Latvians abroad to know themselves so that they could inhabit the nation and thus contribute to its continuity and thus also legitimate the Latvian state. The dual nature of the quest for knowledge present in diaspora politics—that is, as ontological knowledge of oneself and as sociological knowledge about ourselves—blurred boundaries between subjects and objects of knowledge and produced a novel knowledge apparatus that along with more conventional social sciences methods entailed a quest for knowing oneself shared by state officials, researchers, and the public alike. Modes of producing knowledge were mixed: informal knowledge generated by encounters between people was combined with formal knowledge generated by surveys. For example, at the already mentioned high-level meeting, Kārlis presented some basic statistical data generated by Latvian economists and geographers. This created a sense that the state knew or was working toward knowing its diaspora. However, Kārlis also provided anecdotal evidence from his own encounters with Latvia's mobile citizens on planes, at dinner tables, and in meetings.

Despite the fact that the state intensified its diaspora activities and Kārlis produced more and more stories of Latvians—and even some Russians—who realized that, despite being abroad, they were, after all, Latvian, not all of Latvia's citizens took up the call of the state. Many, especially Russian speakers, remained distant, even hostile, engaging with the Latvian state only when they needed to take care of paperwork (for example, to renew the passport). At the same time, more and more people did turn up for various communal events, such as the midsummer celebrations at the Latvian property Straumēni (Catthorpe Manor) acquired in 1975 by the Latvian organization Daugavas Vanagi, which was established in a post–World War II war prisoners' camp by former Latvian legionaries. Latvians turned up for these events regardless of their political orientations. Many of those who attended the celebrations continued to be critical of the Latvian state, its politicians, and public life in Latvia (Kaprans 2015; Ķešāne 2011).

And yet, despite critical attitudes toward the state, many of Latvia's citizens abroad, both Latvians and Russian speakers, turned up not only for celebrations, but also for the 2012 referendum on the status of Russian language in Latvia. The referendum, as I show in the following section, was perceived to be crucial for the continued existence of Latvia as a national state. Thus, Latvians abroad readily mobilized to assert their and the Latvian state's existential sovereignty, while at the same time criticizing the Latvian state for its failure to care for the well-being of the population.

Reterritorialized Nation and Sovereign Agency

In 2011, a group of Russian-speaking activists initiated a referendum on the introduction of Russian as the second state language in Latvia (Druviete and

Ozoliņš 2016; Ijabs 2016). This initiative came in response to the post-Soviet state's language politics, which aim to counter the effects of the Soviet nationalities policy by designating Latvian as the state language and regulating language use in the public sphere (Dzenovska 2018a). The activist group, led by Vladimir Linderman and Yevgeny Osipov, both referred to as radicals due to their involvement with Russia's National Bolshevik Party in the case of Linderman and a small left-wing extremist group in the case of Osipov (Ijabs 2016, 298), gathered the ten thousand signatures necessary for the state to initiate the process of organizing a national referendum. The organizational process involved another stage of signature gathering, during which one-tenth of Latvia's citizens signed in support of the referendum. The referendum was set for February 18, 2012.

Despite expert calculations that the referendum did not pose a serious threat to the Latvian language and thus the national foundation of the state, the fact that a significant portion of Latvia's Russian-speaking citizenry supported it created a palpable public sense of embattlement among Latvians, including among those residing abroad. As a result, the language referendum turned out to be the most widely attended referendum after the restoration of independence, with 71.3 percent of Latvian citizens coming to the polls and 74.8 percent voting against the motion, that is, against making Russian the second state language. Among Latvians abroad, attendance was also high, with 79.2 percent voting against the motion and 20.5 percent for.[11] Most important, however, the referendum produced not only a high voter turnout, but also what Iván Arenas and I have previously described as "barricade sociality," namely an affective and visceral togetherness that conjured up a sovereign people with constituent power (2012, 646).

In January 1991, Latvia's residents mobilized to defend the newly reestablished Latvian state from Soviet military units that wished to prevent the dissolution of the Soviet Union. In expectation of the arrival of the Soviet military units, known as OMON, Latvia's residents built barricades around strategic points in the city, such as the parliament building and the radio, and television headquarters. People came from all over Latvia to build and guard the barricades. On the barricades, the differences between Latvians and Russian speakers were momentarily dissolved, though never forgotten (Dzenovska and Arenas 2012, 652–653). Nevertheless, the barricade moment conjured up the people as a revolutionary and constituent power, a subject with a will and ability to refound, defend, and legitimate the independent Latvian state. In the barricade moment, the people were more like a "cosmic force" than a body of citizenry (Dzenovska and Arenas 2012, 652), united in diversity against a hostile military force. It was the liminality of the revolutionary moment and the ephemeral nature of the people as a sovereign that allowed for embracing the presence of Russian speakers without a sense of embattlement. This barricade moment has remained in collective memory as a moment of unity and possibility, even as political frontiers between variously defined majorities and minorities began to emerge as soon as the restored state began to govern (Dzenovska and Arenas 2012).

The 2012 language referendum produced resonant affective togetherness, especially abroad, where Latvia's citizens, both Latvians and Russians, felt that they needed to go the extra mile to assert—or contest—the existential sovereignty of Latvians as the state-bearing people of the Latvian state. For example, one London-based acquaintance produced a video of people standing in a line that curved around the block, waiting in rain to cast their votes. Some of those standing in the line could be heard singing.[12] Another acquaintance posted a Latvian News UK video on her Facebook page, accompanied by a commentary that she, too, voted, and that this entailed some sacrifice insofar as she had put on clothing inappropriate for the rainy weather.[13]

In the news video that lasts about eight minutes, an elderly man points out that the referendum is an unprecedented event, when a people wish to defend their rights to language, while living in another country and standing in a very long line in rain. Another man, who refused to speak in Latvian, stated in English that he voted for making Russian the second state language in Latvia. The tension—and therefore the sense of embattlement—was palpable. Another man, originally from an eastern region of Latvia, but residing in London for three years, explained, in Latvian, that he had come to vote for a different Latvia, for a Latvia that can find a compromise, for a Latvia that is willing to accommodate people who speak Russian, and thus prevent them from leaving the country. A young woman, born and raised in London within a trimda family, but holding Latvian citizenship, said she had come to vote, because language is the "flag of our state." Another woman, also born in an "old exile" family and living in London, stated that she is voting against the motion to make Russian the second state language, because she does not wish to visit "her state" and not be able to participate in public life, because it takes place in Russian.

Subsequently, in interviews conducted by Latvia's social scientists as part of a large-scale project on migration and diaspora, UK-based citizens described their experiences in terms similar to those used in the early 1990s, when describing the barricades.[14] Only the frontier had shifted (Laclau 2007). The frontier no longer stood between an all-inclusive, if ethnically diverse people and hostile foreign forces as in 1991 (Dzenovska and Arenas 2012), but between citizen groups, one defending the existential sovereignty of the Latvian nation, and the other contesting the national identity of the state and the status of Latvians as the state-bearing nation. However, the sense of embattlement was similar. For example, a woman interviewed by Mārtiņš Kaprans said: "The line to vote in London was really very, very long, and so Dainis and I considered leaving. But then we heard some of Latvia's Russian-speaking citizens call out: 'Down with the dog's language! Down with the dog's language!' And then we are standing in that line and I say to

Dainis: 'You know, even though it's cold and the line is long, I am not going any-where, I will stand in this line, I will go and vote. . . . If the guy had not said it . . .'" (Kaprans 2015, 122). Another interviewee noted his desire to decide for himself: "Had to do something, could not afford not to participate and have someone else decide for us. In London, you had to stand in a very long line for several hours, it was very cold. . . . But it was, in a way, touching to see such a large crowd of Latvians and Russians. There were some emotions. . . . But, largely, people were cozy, friendly, and talkative" (Kaprans 2015, 122).

Civil servants and activists involved with diaspora politics were very pleased with the political activity of Latvia's citizens abroad. They thought that their political activity was a surprise for Latvia's politicians, and that it demonstrated how diaspora matters for the nation and the state. Kārlis, especially, repeatedly invoked the referendum in subsequent events to point out that: "We see motiva-tion . . . when people realize that they can be useful to the state, when they realize that their vote counts, they go and vote."

Despite the result of the referendum, and the warm feelings produced by the sense of embattlement and the resulting ethnonational solidarity in voting lines, the Latvian public, legal experts, and politicians found it worrisome that the foundational aspects of the state could be subjected to a popular vote, thus opening the possibility that a demographically reconfigured people might undo the national foundations of the state through democratic process. The presi-dent's Constitutional Rights Commission argued that popular sovereignty was misused here, that the "actually existing people" did not have the authority to change the foundations of the state once they had been established by the con-stitutive power of the "original people" (Konstitucionālo tiesību komisija 2012). And the original constitutive power, they argued, most certainly belonged to Latvians as a cultural nation with a political will to establish their own state (Konstitucionālo tiesību komisija 2012, 71).[15] Even though the pre-2014 Lat-vian constitution did not explicitly state this, the commission argued that the document should not be viewed in the spirit of positivism (that is, as a position that there is nothing outside the text) and that therefore the state-bearing status of Latvians could be inferred from historical analysis (Konstitucionalo tiesību komisija 2012, 94).

The 2012 opinion of the Constitutional Rights Commission served as jus-tification for the constitutional reform that followed in 2014.[16] As part of this reform, the parliament approved a preamble to the Latvian constitution for the purpose of rendering the implicit constitutional core explicit, that is, for the pur-pose of stating that the Latvian state is a national state established by Latvians and for the purpose of ensuring the continuity and flourishing of the cultural nation of Latvians.[17] The opinion posits two immutable features of the Latvian constitu-tion: the legal identity of the state—that is, the Latvian nature of the state, and the political order of the state, namely democracy. These two features, the commission argues, cannot be changed by a demographically defined people (i.e., the majority of the current body of citizenry), because then the actually existing people would be violating the legal order established by the constitutive people (Konstitucionālo tiesību komisija 2012, 20). The only way to change the legal identity and the political order is through revolution, which the commission, not surprisingly, does not recommend. In that sense, the language referendum could be considered anticonstitutional even though, as the commission notes, the actually existing people did manage to act as a "qualified constitutional legislator," namely a legislator that reaffirmed—rather than contested—the national identity of the state (Konstitucionālo tiesību komisija 2012, 45–46).

The opinion also states that a politically mature people requires its own state, if it is to operate in the international community of sovereign states, thus providing a legal argument for what exists in the public sphere as an existential state desire and civilizational aspiration (Konstitucionālo tiesību komisija 2012, 12). Moreover, the commission explicitly addresses the question of mobility insofar as the opinion states that "everyone who considers himself or herself as belonging to the Latvian nation [*latviešu nācija*] has a relationship with the Latvian state—between every Latvian, regardless of where he is located, and the Latvian state, there is a real, sociologically identifiable nationally cultural tie" (Konstitucionālo tiesību komisija 2012, 76). "Every Latvian," the opinion continues, "can say that Latvia is their state." The political nation can be more expansive, the commission concludes, and include minorities, but this does not in any way affect the state-bearing function of the Latvian cultural nation (Konstitucionālo tiesību komisija 2012, 77).

Taken together, diaspora politics, the language referendum, and the constitutional reform that followed reiterate the constitutive and ontological link between the self, the cultural nation, and the Latvian state. Importantly, the claims to existential sovereignty that these events and practices entail allow for a reterritorialization of the nation, while at the same time affirming the importance of a territorial state. In such conditions, when existential sovereignty seems to be the primary form of sovereignty of concern to the Latvian polity, other functions of the state—for example, care for the population as a social body—become less important and can be more easily "delegated" to other territorial states. For example, if the Latvian state is widely recognized to be crucial for the continued existence of the nation, the British state might be recognized as better able to care for the physical bodies of the members of the nation. As a result, Latvia's residents living in the United Kingdom happily paid taxes, which they tried to avoid when they lived in Latvia. Thus, statecraft and sovereignty came to be disarticulated from each other and differently distributed across territories of several historically existing states. Put another way, existential sovereignty—as practices constituting the physical, cultural, and political people and the institutions that make them legible as such—is clearly distinct from statecraft as "social relations between the governing authority and people in relation to resources" (chapter 6, this volume).

For at least the last two decades, there has been a significant proliferation of scholarship on shifts in statehood and sovereignty. Much of it has attributed these shifts to economic globalization, and thus has viewed sovereignty and the state in relation to economic governance. For example, Aihwa Ong (2000) has written on graduated sovereignty in Southeast Asia as a mode of governance that differentiates between segments of population according to how they relate to the global market, as well as a mode of governance that is subordinated to the needs of special production zones. Saskia Sassen (1996) has argued that sovereignty and territory remain constitutive elements of the international system, but that they are reconstituted and displaced onto institutional arenas outside the state, such as new emergent legal regimes or supranational institutions, and outside the framework of national territory (see also Brenner 1998). More recently, Wendy Brown has argued that as "nation-state sovereignty wanes, states and sovereignty do not simply decline in power or significance, but instead come apart from one another. States persist as non-sovereign actors, and the characteristics of sovereignty appear today in two domains of power that are, not coincidentally, the very domain of powers that the Peace of Westphalia emerged to contain within or subordinate to nation-states: political economy and religiously legitimated violence" (2010, 23). Brown argues that "key characteristics of sovereignty," which she, building on classical political theory, depicts as a composite figure consisting of supremacy, perpetuity, absoluteness, decisionism, nontransferability, and specific jurisdiction (2010, 22), "are migrating from the nation-state to the unrelieved domination of capital and God-sanctioned violence" (2010, 23).

This scholarship juxtaposes political sovereignty of the nation-state to transnational flows of capital, forms of economic governance, or belonging, such as religion, that reconfigure sovereignty and territory. In analyses that attribute reconfigurations of sovereignty to transnational—or, more accurately, transstatal (Verdery 1994)—flows of capital and forms of economic governance and belonging, the nation as a political community is undermined.[18] This does not mean that states do not try to defend their territories, as Wendy Brown (2010) points out. However, these are no longer sovereign acts, but rather desperate attempts to keep out a variety of illegitimate and undesirable disturbances, mostly in the form of other human beings.

I suggest here that analysis of outmigration and diaspora politics, at least within the political space of Europe, brings a new dimension to rethinking sovereignty, statecraft, and territory. Namely, it shows that reterritorialized nations are emerging as sovereign actors alongside markets and religion, alongside private legal regimes and supranational organizations. While diasporas and diaspora politics are not entirely new phenomena, the extent to which political communities are cultivated across territorial borders of states suggests that the center of gravity, as it were, of political communities may be shifting. As analysis of Latvian outmigration and diaspora politics shows, the center of the nation is no longer fixed within the territory of a state, but rather reterritorialized across multiple state territories. It could be said that the political community has become trans-statal (Verdery 1994). In contrast to the widely discussed diaspora engagement in homeland politics or what Benedict Anderson has termed "long-distance nationalism," the phenomenon of reterritorialized existential sovereignty is not about embattled ethnics in global metropolises channeling unaccountable political agency to homelands (Anderson 1992, 12; see also Kaprans 2015), but about the spatial reconfiguration of historically constituted concerns with the physical and political existence of the self. The framework of long-distance nationalism does not get to the problem of existential sovereignty and its reterritorialization, though it does enable discussion of the constitution of diasporic subjects as political agents via imagined homelands rather than actual places of residence. In the case of long-distance nationalism, diasporic subjects' political agency is reterritorialized toward the nation-state. In contrast, in the case of reterritorialized existential sovereignty, sovereign agency is being distributed across territories of multiple nation-states in order to ensure the continuity of the self in time and space, even as the existence of "our own state" as a territorial unit remains important. The shift may be subtle, but noteworthy. The reterritorialized political community claims sovereign agency—in the case of Latvia, existential sovereign agency—alongside other sovereigns—for example, markets and religion—in a global space still ordered along the lines of territorial states. In other words, it is not that the market and religion—or legal regimes and supranational organizations—are replacing the nation-state. Rather, sovereign aspirations are exhibited by multiple and reterritorialized agents that are not all of the same type and that do not share the same desires.

Notes

1. The first post-Soviet citizenship law defined the body of citizenry as all those who had held citizenship during the first period of independent statehood (1918–40) and their descendants. This effectively excluded Soviet-era incomers and their children who were

granted the right to naturalize through a series of amendments and on meeting Latvian language requirements. The language law, in turn, stipulates that all those occupying public positions, from bus drivers to parliamentary deputies, must demonstrate a set level of proficiency in the Latvian language. See Dzenovska 2018 for a more elaborate discussion.

2. See http://www.mfa.gov.lv/arpolitika/sabiedribas-integracija-latvija/integracijas-politika-latvija-daudzpusiga-pieeja/etniskais-sastavs-un-mazakumtautibu-kulturas-iden titates-veicinasana.

3. See activities of Russkyi Mir here: http://russkiymir.ru/en/.

4. See Houston 2009 on Kurdish efforts to prove continuous existence via Western colonial and orientalizing texts.

5. There were some exceptions—for example, Jewish emigration from the Soviet Union to Israel starting in the 1970s.

6. It should be noted that this freedom of movement was partly restricted, insofar as only three European Union members states—the United Kingdom, Ireland, and Sweden—opened their labor markets to citizens of the new European Union member states in 2004. All others instituted a grace period during which capital could flow freely, but people could not.

7. https://likumi.lv/ta/id/94728-par-latviesu-diasporas-atbalsta-programmu-2004-2009-gadam.

8. Some parts of this section were previously published as a brief essay in *Diasporas Reimagined: Spaces, Practices and Belonging* (see Dzenovska 2015).

9. See Ījabs 2009 for an elaboration of the liberal thought of Paul Schiemann who held that being human means being cultured.

10. See migracija.lv.

11. The precise number of those voting abroad was 39,703, which is three times more than during the last parliamentary elections. It is impossible, however, to tell what percentage this is of citizens living abroad, as the total number of citizens residing abroad is not known. See http://www.delfi.lv/news/national/politics/valodas-referenduma-rekordliela-latvijas-pilsonu-aktivitate-arzemes.d?id=42143006.

12. https://www.youtube.com/watch?v=QzLA5GiPLK4&feature=youtu.be.

13. https://www.youtube.com/watch?v=gKgkp_yNyzU.

14. See more on the project and its publications here: http://migracija.lv/.

15. Throughout the opinion, the state-bearing nation, that is, Latvians, exists as an a priori subject with a political will and ability to legitimate the founding of a state. The opinion cannot allow for the coconstitution of the subject and the state, as is common in studies of nationalism (e.g., Anderson 1983), because that would undermine the logic of the argument.

16. https://likumi.lv/doc.php?id=267428.

17. Ivars Ijabs (2016) has referred to this as militant democracy.

18. Verdery suggests that the concept of "transnational" betrays the hegemony of the "nation-cum-state" thinking in Western political theory and assumes that the nation and the state are coterminous (1994, 3). Drawing on the case of Eastern Europe, Verdery suggests that it would be more appropriate to distinguish between trans-statal, trans-ethnonational, and transnational processes.

References

Agamben, Giorgio. 1998. *Homo Sacer: Sovereign Power and Bare Life.* Translated by Daniel Heller-Roazen. Stanford, CA: Stanford University Press.

Anderson, Bridget. 2013. *Us and Them? The Dangerous Politics of Immigration Controls.* Oxford: Oxford University Press.

Anderson, Benedict. 1983. *Imagined Communities: Reflections on the Origin and Spread of Nationalism*. London: Verso.

Anderson, Benedict. 1992. *Long-Distance Nationalism: World Capitalism and the Rise of Identity Politics*. Wertheim Lecture. Amsterdam: Center for Asian Studies.

Bernal, Victoria. 2014. *Nation as Network: Diaspora, Cyberspace, and Citizenship*. Chicago: University of Chicago Press.

Bernstein, Anya. 2012. "More Alive Than All the Living: Sovereign Bodies and Cosmic Politics in Buddhist Siberia." *Cultural Anthropology* 27(2): 261–285.

Bonilla, Yarimar. 2015. *Non-Sovereign Futures: French Caribbean Politics in the Wake of Disenchantment*. Chicago: University of Chicago Press.

Bozzini, David. 2015. "The Fines and the Spies: Fears of State Surveillance in Eritrea and in the Diaspora." *Social Analysis* 59(4): 32–49.

Brah, Avtar. 1996. *Cartographies of Diaspora: Contesting Identities*. London: Routledge.

Brenner, Neil. 1998. "Between Fixity and Motion: Accumulation, Territorial Organization and the Historical Geography of Spatial Scales." *Environment and Planning D: Society and Space* 16(4): 459–481.

Brown, Wendy. 2010. *Walled States, Waning Sovereignty*. New York: Zone Books.

Brubaker, Rogers, Margit Feischmidt, Jon Fox, and Liana Grancea. 2006. *Nationalist Politics and Everyday Ethnicity in a Transylvanian Town*. Princeton, NJ: Princeton University Press.

Campbell, Brian C., and James R. Veteto. 2015. "Free Seeds and Food Sovereignty: Anthropology and Grassroots Agrobiodiversity Conservation Strategies in the US South." *Journal of Political Ecology* 22: 444–465.

Cohen, Anthony. 1996. "Personal Nationalism: A Scottish View of Some Rites, Rights, and Wrongs." *American Ethnologist* 23(4): 802–815.

Darieva, Tsypylma. 2011. "Rethinking Homecoming: Diasporic Cosmopolitanism in Post-Socialist Armenia." *Ethnic and Racial Studies* 34(3): 490–508.

De Haas, Hein. 2007. "Remittances, Migration and Social Development: A Conceptual Review of the Literature, Technical Report." United Nations Research Institute for Social Development.

De Haas, Hein. 2010. "Migration and Development: A Theoretical Perspective." *International Migration Review* 44: 227–264.

Druviete, Ina, and Uldis Ozolins. 2016. "The Latvian Referendum on Russian as a Second State Language, February 2012." *Language Problems and Language Planning* 40(2): 121–145.

Dunn, Elizabeth Cullen, and Jason Cons. 2013. "Aleatory Sovereignty and the Rule of Sensitive Spaces." *Antipode* 46(1): 92–109.

Dzenovska, Dace. 2012. *Aizbraukšana un tukšums Latvijas laukos: Starp zudušām un iespējamām nākotnēm*. Rīga, Latvia: Turība.

Dzenovska, Dace. 2013. "The Great Departure: Rethinking National(ist) Common Sense." *Journal of Ethnic and Migration Studies* 39(2): 201–218.

Dzenovska, Dace. 2015. "'Know Your Diaspora!': Knowledge Production and Governing Capacity in the Context of Latvian Diaspora Politics." In *Diasporas Reimagined: Spaces, Practices, and Belonging*, edited by N. Sigona, A. Gamlen, G. Liberatore, and H.N. Kringelback. Oxford: Oxford Diasporas Programme.

Dzenovska, Dace. 2018a. *School of Europeanness: Tolerance and Other Lessons in Political Liberalism in Latvia*. Ithaca, NY: Cornell University Press.

Dzenovska, Dace. 2018b. "Emptiness and Its Futures: Staying and Leaving as Tactics of Life in Latvia." *Focaal—Journal of Global and Historical Anthropology* 80(1): 16–29.

Dzenovska, Dace. 2018c. "The (In)significance of Latvia in the Battle Between Good and Evil." Hot Spots, *Fieldsights*, April 25. https://culanth.org/fieldsights/the-insignificance-of-latvia-in-the-battle-between-good-and-evil.

Dzenovska, Dace, and Iván Arenas. 2012. "Don't Fence Me In: Barricade Sociality and Political Struggles in Mexico and Latvia." *Comparative Studies in Society and History* 54: 644–78.

Folch, Christine. 2016. "The Nature of Sovereignty in the Anthropocene: Hydroelectric Lessons of Struggle, Otherness, and Economics from Paraguay." *Current Anthropology* 57(5): 565–585.

Foucault, Michel. 2003. *Society Must Be Defended*. Translated by David Macey. New York: Picador.

Gamlen, Alan. 2014. "Diaspora Institutions and Diaspora Governance." *International Migration Review* 48(1): 180–217.

Gilroy, Paul. 1995. *The Black Atlantic: Modernity and Double-Consciousness*. Cambridge, MA: Harvard University Press.

Hansen, Thomas Blom, and Finn Stepputat, eds. 2005. *Sovereign Bodies: Citizens, Migrants, and States in the Postcolonial World*. Princeton, NJ: Princeton University Press.

Hazans, Mihails. 2011. "Latvijas emigrācijas mainīgā seja 2000–2010. Latvija," in Pārskats par tautas attīstību. 2010/2011. *Nacionālā identitāte, mobilitāte, rīcībspēja*. Rīga, Latvia: Latvijas Universitātes, Sociālo un politisko pētījumu institūts, 70–91.

Hazans, Mihails. 2015. "Emigrācija no Latvijas 21: Gadsimtā reģionu, pilsētu un novadu griezumā." In *Latvijas emigrantu kopienas: Cerību diasporas*, edited by Inta Mieriņa. Riga: Latvijas Universitātes Filozofi jas un socioloģijas institūts, 11–26.

Hirsch, Francine. 2015. *Empire of Nations: Ethnographic Knowledge and the Making of the Soviet Union*. Ithaca, NY: Cornell University Press.

Houston, Christopher. 2009. "An Anti-History of Non-People: Kurds, Colonialism, and Nationalism in the History of Anthropology." *Journal of Royal Anthropological Institute* 15(1): 19–35.

Ījabs, Ivars. 2009. "Republikas vārdā." *Politika.lv*, November 17. Accessed January 15, 2015. http://politika.lv/article/republikas-varda.

Ijabs, Ivars. 2012. "Break Out of Russia: Miķelis Valters and the National Issue in Early Latvian Socialism." *Journal of Baltic Studies* 43(4): 437–458. http://dx.doi.org/10.1080/01629778.2012.687901. Accessed January 15, 2015.

Ijabs, Ivars. 2016. "After the Referendum: Militant Democracy and Nation-Building in Latvia." *East European Politics and Societies* 30(2): 288–314.

Kantorowicz, Ernst. 1998 (1957). *The King's Two Bodies: A Study in Mediaeval Political Theology*. Princeton, NJ: Princeton University Press.

Kaprans, Mārtiņš. 2015. "Lielbritānijaā dzīvojošo Latvijas emigrantu attaālinātā nacionālisma izpausmes: Kulturālā un politiskā dimensija." In *AkadēmiskāDzīve*. Rīga: LU Akadēmiskais apgāds, 77–88.

Ķešāne, Iveta. 2011. "Emigration as a Strategy of Everyday Politics: The Case of Latvian Labour Emigrants in Ireland." In *(Post)transformational Migration: Inequalities, Welfare State, and Horizontal Mobility*, edited by M. Nowak and M. Nowosielski, 121–149. Peter Lang GmbH.

Konstitucionālo tiesību komisija. 2012. *Par Latvijas valsts konstitucionālajiem pamatiem un neaizskaramo Satversmes kodolu*. Rīga, Latvia.

Krasner, Stephen D. 1999. *Sovereignty: Organized Hypocrisy*. Princeton, NJ: Princeton University Press.

Laclau, Ernesto. 2007. "Bare Life or Social Indeterminacy?" In *Giorgio Agamben: Sovereignty and Life*, edited by Matthew Calarco and Steven DeCaroli, 11–22. Stanford, CA: Stanford University Press.

Laitin, David. 1998. *Identity in Formation: The Russian-Speaking Populations in the Near Abroad*. Ithaca, NY: Cornell University Press.

Levitt, Peggy. 1998. "Social Remittances: Migration Driven Local-Level Forms of Cultural Diffusion." *International Migration Review* 32(4): 926–948.

Lulle, Aija, and Laura Buzinska. 2017. "Between a 'Student Abroad' and 'Being from Latvia': Inequalities of Access, Prestige, and Foreign-Earned Cultural Capital." *Journal of Ethnic and Migration Studies* 43(8): 1362–1378.

Lulle, Aija, Evija Kļave, Gunda Reire, Ieva Birka, and Elza Ungure. 2015. *Diasporas politiskā pārstāvniecība Latvijā un Eiropas Savienībā: Parlamentārā Dimensija* [Political representation of diaspora in Latvia and the European Union: Parliamentary perspectives]. Rīga: Latvijas universitātes Diasporas un migrācijas pētījumu centrs.

Mieriņa, Inta, ed. 2015. *Latvijas emigrantu kopienas: Ceribu diaspora* [The Emigrant Communities of Latvia: Diasporas of Hope]. Riga, Latvia.

Ong, Aihwa. 2000. "Graduated Sovereignty in South-East Asia." *Theory, Culture, and Society* 17(4): 55–75.

Riekstiņš, Janis. 2005. "Colonization and Russification of Latvia 1944–1953." In *The Hidden and Forbidden History of Latvia under Soviet and Nazi Occupations 1940–1991*, edited by Valters Nollendorfs and Erwin Oberländer, Symposium of the Commission of the Historians of Latvia 14, 228–241. Riga: Institute of the History of Latvia.

Santner, Eric L. 2011. *The Royal Remains: The People's Two Bodies and the Endgames of Sovereignty*. Chicago: University of Chicago Press.

Sassen, Saskia. 1996. *Losing Control? Sovereignty in the Age of Globalization*. New York: Columbia University Press

Schmitt, Carl. 1985. *Political Theology: Four Chapters on the Concept of Sovereignty*. Translated by George Schwab. Chicago: University of Chicago Press.

Skultāns, Vieda. 2007. *Empathy and Healing: Essays in Medical and Narrative Anthropology*. Oxford: Berghahn Books.

Soysal, Yasemin Nuhoğlu. 2000. *Limits of Citizenship: Migrants and Postnational Membership in Europe*. Chicago: University of Chicago Press.

Tabar, Paul. 2014. "'Political Remittances': The Case of Lebanese Expatriates Voting in National Elections." *Journal of Intercultural Studies* 35(4): 442–460.

Van Hear, Nicholas, and Robin Cohen. 2017. "Diasporas and Conflict: Distance, Contiguity and Spheres of Engagement." *Oxford Development Studies* 45(2): 171–184.

Verdery, Katherine. 1994. "Beyond the Nation in Eastern Europe." *Social Text* 38: 1–19.

Wanner, Catherine. 2014. "'Fraternal' Nations and Challenges to Sovereignty in Ukraine: The Politics of Linguistic and Religious Ties." *American Ethnologist* 41(3): 427–439.

Winegar, Jessica. 2006. "Cultural Sovereignty in a Global Art Economy: Egyptian Cultural Policy and the New Western Interest in Art from the Middle East." *Cultural Anthropology* 21(2): 173–204.

Yurchak, Alexei. 2015. "Bodies of Lenin: The Hidden Science of Communist Sovereignty." *Representations* 129(1): 116–157.

SOVEREIGN DAYS

Imagining and Making the Catalan Republic from Below

Panos Achniotis

On October 1, 2018, the streets of the Gavó district of Barcelona have an air of celebration. "It's been a year and a ballot box," reads a large banner strung in front of the Buenaventura primary school. Now a commemorative item, a ballot box used in the referendum exactly a year earlier sits on a table in the middle of the street as people linger around it, drinking vermouth and sharing snacks. My friends Manel and Aima lead me on a tour of schools in Gavó, which act as centers of referendum anniversary celebrations. Cork boards have been hung outside the schools, and people are pinning photos of themselves from the time of the referendum, or they are writing words that they associate with the referendum on poster boards: *rain, self-organization, goosebumps, tension, emotion.*

Right in front of the Buenaventura school, some celebrants have spread a custom-made board game across the street. Naming it "Pictionary of the Republic," the squares that contestants might land on bear appropriately political names, such as *poder popular* (people power). When a team lands on that square, the master of ceremonies tells the team that the police are about to arrive at the voting center. The team members need to gather others to make a human wall against another team, assigned the role of police. As the police push unsuccessfully against the human chain, the master of ceremonies gives a running commentary, as in a football match: "The people are resisting, the violence is hard, but people keep resisting, they still resist, and yes! Yes! The power of the people has defeated the forces of the state!" Everyone laughs intensely at the scene that played out in this game, but it is a laughter born of mutual recognition among those who had experienced the real force of the police the year before. My friend Aleix had earlier described to me the combination of fear and defiance that had bonded neighbors together in 2017. A year later, their laughter reproduced that moment of solidarity, a laughter that only those who had experienced that solidarity the first time round could share.

In this chapter I argue that in the wake of the 2017 referendum on Catalan sovereignty, the imagined community of the nation (Anderson 2006; Clua I Fainé 2014) became concretely manifest in neighborhood communities of solidarity. The referendum, known by its numeronym 1-O (for 1 October), produced a continuing grassroot mobilization that was rooted in the experience of solidarity that so many people went through on that day. Indeed, for the neighborhood that I call Gavó, where I conducted four months of fieldwork, many residents claim that the intimacy that they felt on that day and continue to share with their fellow neighbors has no parallel in any previous electoral process. Moreover, that experience of continuing solidarity rooted in the 1-O informs the way they perceive self-determination and imagine the Catalan Republic.

What the neighbors of Gavó experienced those autumn days went far beyond a mere "yes" or a "no" to a proposed dilemma. My own research focused primarily on the local Committee for the Defense of the Republic (CDR), a grassroots pro-independence initiative like so many that sprung up during the critical autumn of 2017. Based on direct democracy in the form of assemblies, such neighborhood-centered initiatives played a crucial role in the self-determination referendum organized by the local Catalan authorities. Indeed, many people say that it was the CDRs that made the staging of the vote possible, and since then they have become a critical and radical mobilizing agent in favor of independence.

The 2017 referendum was the culmination of a five-year campaign for independence, known as the *procés*, that had been put forward by the Catalan regional government and civil society associations. With a 43 percent turnout (over two million votes) and a 92 percent Yes vote in favor of independence, the referendum is not remembered so much for its electoral result but rather for the peculiar sociopolitical context in which it took place. Prior to the referendum date, the Spanish Constitutional Court had ruled the vote illegal, and the Spanish state engaged in an unprecedented police operation to dismantle it. The response was an equally unprecedented wave of civil disobedience seeking to defend the polling stations and enable the vote to proceed.

Many people credit "self-organization" practices at polling stations for the fact that several thousand residents of Gavó were able to cast their vote despite the various obstacles caused by the ban. Through open assemblies, social media, and messaging apps, the neighbors coordinated themselves and took over the logistics of the vote: informing the residents where to vote; setting up computers and internet access to enable voter registration; volunteering as election officials to collect and count the votes; organizing the defense to a possible police raid. The minimal presence of the Catalan authorities due to the judicial and police siege of the Spanish state created a power vacuum that was filled with the collective practices of the voters. Sleeping at schools during the weekend with persons previously unknown, sharing meagre meals and blankets or even suffering violence together, introduced a social meaning to the event beyond its mere electoral purpose. Analyzing and comprehending this experience is crucial in order to grasp how the ideal of national sovereignty that drives the procés intersects with notions of communal neighborhood living and solidarity, emotional resilience as well as grassroots noninstitutional organization.

Most of the literature regarding the 1-O, as well as the procés in general, focuses on state institutions and constitutional law (Beltrán de Felipe 2019; Cámara Villar 2019; Lecours 2018); on political parties and the clash of interests (Rubner Hansen 2017); or even the role that the media have played during the so-called Catalan conflict (Coromina 2018; Cartes Barroso 2018; Almiron 2018; Carrasco Polaino, Villar Cirujano, and Tejedor Fuentes 2018). Contrary to these analyses, Letamendia (2017) as a participant-observer and Poblet (2018), by analyzing civic engagement through technology, have discussed the subjective experience of the people during the 1-O and have highlighted the participatory nature of the event. As an activist-scholar, Milian Nebot (2019) traced the development of the CDR phenomenon as a process of popular empowerment following the referendum. It has become evident that throughout the 1-O, a nexus has emerged between grassroots participation and the quest for national sovereignty, giving way to a particular political praxis at the neighborhood level. Drawing on anthropological critiques of sovereignty and understandings of the state, and building on what Bryant and Reeves call, in the Introduction to this volume, sovereign agency, I aim to examine the ways in which the political praxis of the Gavó neighbors who took part in the 1-O and who participate in the local CDR interpellate the "state," producing specific practices and imaginaries of emancipation.

The political line of the CDRs in Catalunya, as observed in their public discourse, reproduces a sovereign-asserting (soberanista) imaginary that seeks emancipation through the establishment of a people-created and people-owned state. However, certain practices and discourses that I stumbled on in Gavó have made me question what is ultimately meant by sovereignty, independence, and self-determination when these are articulated at the everyday neighborhood level. While taking part in the broader CDR network of Barcelona and adhering to mass mobilizations, the CDR of Gavó maintains the neighborhood as the geographical focal point on which it seeks to unfold its repertoire of action.

By collaborating with the numerous social entities and associations of Gavó, the CDR aspires to set in motion a "popular constituent process" that will eventually lay the foundations of the so-called Catalan Republic. Thus, the question is not so much whether the Catalan Republic will replace the Kingdom of Spain as the new sovereign of Catalunya, but what kind of political imagination and practice emerges out of 1-O, something that one might formulate as "sovereignty otherwise" (Magnusson 2011). Based on empirical data that I have gathered through my participant-observation in the CDR and interviews with the relevant actors, I explore what sense is made of notions such as republic and sovereignty through processes of self-organization during the 1-O and subsequently through the CDR in Gavó. In so doing, I demonstrate how the CDR's understanding of sovereignty and independence seeks to transcend the mere formation of a new state.

Thinking with Sovereignty

The question of sovereignty within the Spanish state is as old as the state itself. The so-called territorial question, that is, territorial cleavages dating back to medieval times, and the emergence of "peripheral nationalisms" like the Basque and the Catalan, undermined the attempt to build an integrated and homogenized nation-state (Muro and Quiroga 2005). Twentieth-century Spanish politics were characterized to a great degree by the question of governance of the distinct territories. After forty years of harsh dictatorship and homogenizing centralism (1939–75), territorial governance became yet again a major political preoccupation during the democratic years (Guibernau 2004; Keating 2008), despite the fact that the 1978 Constitution was tailored to resolve the issue by establishing a quasi-federal system of power devolution. Keating and Wilson (2009, 537) assert that "questions about territorial distribution of power are not resolved in a definitive constitutional moment, but are part of everyday politics."

For more than a century, there have been various parties and other political forces in Catalunya, mainly on the Left, that campaigned for Catalan independence. However, when the Catalan regional government proposed a new Statute of Catalunya that would increase the region's autonomy and gained approval for it in a 2006 referendum, the statute was then struck down by the Spanish Constitutional Court in 2010. As a result of the court's decision, the idea of planning a political process that would ultimately lead to independence began to take shape and support. A mass social movement formed during those years in favor of the so-called right to decide and promoting the organization of a binding referendum for Catalunya's future. Two massive but formal civil society organizations, the preexisting Omnium Cultural and the newly formed Catalan National Assembly (ANC), became the mobilizing vehicles of the movement (Crameri 2015). Support for such a right to decide gradually grew across the Catalan political spectrum (López 2017; Milian Nebot 2019). Traditional proindependence parties of the Left gained increased significance, while the big Catalan right-wing party, which governed Catalunya for many years, took a turn to independence. Since 2012, all regional elections in Catalunya have hung on candidates' and parties' stances regarding the question of independence and the implementation of a referendum. This led to successive proindependence governments up to this day.

Sovereignty has been understood conventionally in political theory as the attribute that enables the state to be the sole actor of legitimate authority over a specific territory and a population (Bierkester and Weber 1996; Wilmer 2008). Contrary to such nominal definitions, sovereignty has also been understood as a socially and historically constituted relation under constant negotiation, that is, a "historical practice" (Howland and White 2009) and "a particular way of knowing, representing and ordering the social and political world" (Walker 2008, 23). Jens Bartelson (2014, 2) contends that both of these stances lead to the same end and describes sovereignty as a symbolic form "by means of which Westerners have perceived and organized the political world since the early-modern period." Moreover, scholars have distinguished between de jure sovereignty, that is as a legal principle, and de facto sovereignty, that is actually exercised power in a "world where state sovereignty is challenged from above and below, in relation both to its functional capacity and to its normative claims" (Keating 2006). Drawing on such problematizations and building on anthropological approaches to the state that see it as a structural effect rather than a reified object (Mitchell 2006), ethnographic studies of sovereignty have tended to highlight its performative dimension and have sought to deconstruct the idea of the all-powerful state from which authority should emanate (Bonilla 2012, 2017; Bryant 2018). Reeves (2014, 9) noted that the state can be "done and undone, invoked or ignored" by social actors, while Painter (2006) has drawn attention to the everyday practices through which the state is constructed, essentially as an effect rather than a reification.

Other chapters in this volume question sovereignty as mere authority over territory and instead explore how it circulates as a claim and social fact in everyday life (see chapters 6 and 7, this volume). In such a way, it is possible to begin making sense of how sovereignty is reclaimed, imagined, and practiced in a grassroots proindependence movement as a form of agency rather than as an a priori attribute of the nation-state. The ethnographic analysis that follows is thus located in this nexus of mutual interpellation between subjects and institutions. I argue that desires for sovereignty are the founding principle and catalyst of that movement's organization, and I explore both the potentialities for and limitations of political action that emerge from that desire.[1]

Sovereignty Attacked: Feeling Besieged

Everyone with whom I spoke about the referendum in the Gavó neighborhood of Barcelona described in excited terms their own participation that made the 1-O a radically different experience from other electoral occasions. As I shall show below through the reconstruction of events, the main factor of differentiation was a sense of solidarity that emerged in each polling center, produced by the special conditions under which the vote took place. Moreover, that solidarity fostered an intensified sense of belonging in the neighborhood, as the logistical staging of the referendum ultimately depended on the practices of self-organization within each center. That is to say, the incapacity of the Catalan authorities to centrally organize the vote because of the judicial siege, and the will of the people to see the vote through, produced a unique sense of sociality that was geographically bound to the polling stations at each neighborhood. If we are to understand how a sense of sovereign agency may have emerged within the CDR of Gavó, it is crucial to understand the concrete practices of self-organization that occurred in the voting centers over the referendum weekend and turned them into sites of intimate agency (Bryant 2020, 86), at least for those who thought that such a referendum was legitimate and who felt compelled to participate. While referendums are thought to be divisive to the extent that people are asked to choose a side in a binary formulation, the Catalan referendum divided people over the question of its legitimacy to happen or not. Thus, it was the people who found the referendum to be legitimate who were on the streets and in the polling stations on October 1. Indeed, the harsh police violence during the first hours of the referendum day convinced many people who were not initially planning to vote, to go to the polling stations as a form of protest. Beyond the images of police violence seen around of the world, the referendum is remembered by the participants in Gavó for these very intimate interactions, both physical and emotional, between those who mostly encountered one another as strangers.

Listening to people talking about the referendum, it seems that September 20, 2017 was the first crucial date in understanding the political climate that prepared people for the referendum. This was the date on which the Spanish police intervened in the economic and political structure of the Generalitat (Catalan regional government) and arrested several senior officials in an attempt to paralyze the referendum and dismantle its logistics. For many of the people with whom I spoke, this date represented a definitive conceptual rupture with the central state. The police operation was met with massive spontaneous protests outside the affected government departments and ultimately led the attorney general to accuse civil society leaders Jordi Cuixart and Jordi Sanchez of rebellion and sedition and to order their provisional imprisonment. The experience of this unprecedented intervention that affected Catalan institutions and of participating in the protests led many of the current members of the Gavó CDR to see the procés from that day onward as something "real" and not as a mere "political game."

In contrast, I heard many people ironically characterizing as *mere performance* the mass mobilizations organized by proindependence civil society groups that had been staged during the previous few years (Crameri 2015). Raquel, one of the first persons I met in Gavó, told me once that the Catalans are the people with the most absurd demonstrations in the world. She characterized them as purely symbolic without real outcomes, and retrospective assessments such as hers have gained substantial ground since October 2017. The annual celebration of the Catalan national day, *La Diada,* is an excellent example of something that many people characterize as a *performance*. Each year it has a theme that people are expected to enact, for instance through constructing a human chain across the entire Catalan territory in 2013 or creating a human sound wave in 2018. In contrast to these generally ceremonial events, in which people participate with less than full commitment or emotion, September 20, 2017, was experienced and interpreted as one of the most important events in the procés. The spontaneity of the mobilizations, the fact that they lasted all day, and the general mood of determination and gaiety demonstrated people's will to actively disobey the ban imposed by the Constitutional Court. It ultimately laid the groundwork for the self-organization practices that would be necessary for the referendum's success.

For instance, Atína was at work on September 20, but as soon as she heard from the radio what was going on, she left her work and went immediately to the city center to participate in the protests. She confessed to me, "When I was a kid at school, I was the strange one because I used to draw *Esteladas* (the independentist flag). But on the twentieth I realized that we were not few but many." It is striking that previously she had felt like an outsider because of her political views, despite the fact that in previous years the number of people participating in Diadas was quite large, on one occasion reportedly reaching 2 million. It is also striking that she came to the realization that they were many on a day when there were in fact fewer people protesting than had participated in Diadas. Similarly, Atína's friend Sofía described September 20 as a day that changed her life.

Olga, a woman originally from Chile, was not in favor of Catalan independence before that day. In fact, for many years her Catalan husband and her elder daughter wanted to hang the Estelada from the balcony. She and the younger daughter were insisting that they should hang the *Senyera* instead, the official flag of the region of Catalunya. However, on that day in the afternoon, she went down to the protest outside the Department of Economy where about 50,000 people had spontaneously gathered. "I used to live anaesthetized for many years [and suddenly] there was a click inside me, and it was then that we took the decision that on the first of October we are going to participate." In the words of Sergio, a forty-five-year-old teacher, September 20 was "our moment" to the extent that the crowds behaved peacefully. In fact, as he later reflected, the whole procés was about many "key moments" or "our moments" that shaped the course of the campaign.

Wagner-Pacifici (2017) explains how political semiosis, that is, the process through which certain incidents are deemed eventful and are imbued with social and political meaning, is key in shaping the course and outcome of history. She describes such events as "bright lights in the stream of time" (Wagner-Pacifici 2017, 3). These lights illuminate the present and enable new imaginations of the future. This suggests that an event is not only defined by what it does but also by the possibilities it opens up, whether they are fulfilled or not in the end (Garcés 2018, 153). In this sense, the police raids of September 20 were indeed significant in preparing people for the siege and violence under which the referendum would take place. The proindependence movement quickly portrayed the referendum violence as an attack on the sovereignty of the Catalan people, even as that people was expressing its sovereign agency through the will to defend the voting stations. It was in this moment that it seems a sovereignty effect emerged, in which institutions that appear to belong to "us" become vehicles for subjects' agency (see chapter 1, this volume). The perceived state of siege converted the referendum into an open question that interpellated people in a new sense of "stateness" even as it compelled them to answer.

In the weeks following the referendum, grassroots mobilization emerged around the voting centers, and the number of CDRs multiplied exponentially to reach almost two hundred across the Catalan territory. For the first time in the course of the procés, the campaign of staking a claim to one's own sovereignty was not fully or exclusively in the hands of institutional political actors, such as the proindependence political parties or the more formal organizations Omnium Cultural and ANC. Milian Nebot (2019) notes that practices of self-organization and the leading role of the citizens were in direct contrast to the silence and lack of response to the situation on behalf of the proindependence political leaders. Resonating with what Dzenovska and Arenas (2012) call "barricade sociality," the self-organization practices in voting centers produced a togetherness rooted in the neighborhood and set the ground for a very particular imagination of the *poble* (the people) and of the desired republic to surface. Paraphrasing Dzenovska and Arenas, I use the term *voting-center sociality* to account for the practices and perceptions of sovereignty that emerged in Gavó during the referendum and that are still reproduced within the local CDR today.

Voting-Center Sociality: Feeling Sovereign

As the day of the referendum approached, there was growing doubt among the neighbors of Gavó as to whether a referendum would actually take place. They had received very scant information from the Generalitat, the Catalan political representatives who were organizing the vote. Aima checked her mailbox every day, waiting for the vote notification that never arrived, as all referendum-related post was intercepted by the Spanish state. She and her partner, Manel, remember the moment when they discovered their voting station through a clandestine website set up for that purpose. However, they still did not know if the vote would actually happen. Manel says: "I would laugh at the police for searching and not being able to find the ballot boxes but then I was thinking 'so, where are they?' They tell me that on the 1-O I will be able to vote but there isn't any ballot box, it's so strange that the police couldn't find anything."

Despite this, at 5:00 a.m. on October 1 they were in front of their voting station, "Doing our part at least." Aima told me, "I was hyper-nervous. . . . I had the sensation that I was sitting for the most important exam in my life and everything was at stake. . . . I was never before so conscious of how the sky turns from black to blue." At 8:00 a.m. a silence fell over the crowd when two people carrying trash bags arrived, and the crowd parted to make way for them. Manel admits that "the most emotional moment that I have experienced, not of 1-O but of all my fifty-five years, was to see that there were ballot boxes." He qualifies that "you couldn't see anything," meaning that although they couldn't see what was in the trash bags, they could tell that it was the ballots and the boxes arriving. Aima interrupts him with tears in her eyes, "No, no!" she insists. "I actually saw the ballot box when a gust of wind opened the trash bag for a moment!" It was at that moment that they realized that the vote would actually take place.

Jonathan Spencer (2007, 72) comments that "the imaginary potency of democracy rests in its promise to bring alien machines like the state under the control of human will, to enable a community of political equals . . . to make their own history." If elections are the critical events of democratic control that the people have over shaping the structures of governance, the 1-O referendum created a superlative manifestation of this feeling, enhanced by the ban. Although those participating knew that their vote was unlikely to alter the structures of governance and enable independence—as was suspected before the ballot and subsequently confirmed—the fact that two million persons consciously disobeyed the ban already meant a political and symbolic victory of the(ir) democratic imaginary. Although the ballots and boxes were distributed by a small and secretive group of individuals (Vicens and Tedó 2017), the organization in the voting centers over the weekend was carried out through open assemblies where hundreds of persons got involved. This is an important shift when it comes to analyzing social movements and sovereignty, that is, how people envision taking control over their lives from and through institutional practices that have become increasingly alienating and disenchanting, such as electoral processes (Newton 2014). Marina Garcés, Barcelonese philosopher and activist, has recently written with respect to the 1-O:

> Voting, which for so long has been the image of an insufficient democracy that limits our participation as citizens in choosing between political parties every four years, ... was converted in this case into a sovereign act. We had said so many times that "our dreams do not fit in your ballot boxes," and now at that moment it was our ballot boxes that couldn't fit in their democracy. (Garcés 2018, 227)

For instance, three days before the referendum, even as the Catalan police were holding a meeting with the political leadership to disagree with the leadership's refusal to cancel the referendum even in the face of possible violence, the recently formed CDR of Gavó gathered neighbors in an open assembly in the central square of the neighborhood to coordinate the local vote. Persons voting at the same center were able to meet each other, form WhatsApp groups, and start organizing themselves around their respective locations. The idea was to set up various seemingly unrelated activities during the weekend, in this way disguising the voting stations so that they would not be shut down by the police. Using humor and imagination, the CDR organized a neighborhood carnival, the anniversary of a school, an international music day called "We Sing Together," and an autumn fiesta as some of the activities that disguised the act of voting in Gavó. Employing metaphors from popular culture, some people made pins with the logo of the Alliance to Restore the Republic from Star Wars.[2]

What comes through in these accounts is the "carnivalesque chaos" of this act of disobedience, a characteristic of contemporary social movements of dissent according to Çelikkol (2014). The carnivalesque, according to Mikhail Bakhtin, are those activities that escape daily realities and restrictions, a laughing at authority (as Manel was saying) and a polyphony of voices (Sener 2013, 41). Most carnivals are annual rituals, something that the referendum obviously was not. However, the day of the referendum certainly represented for most people a departure from everyday normality: figuring out how the logistics of a vote work; sleeping on the floor with thirty other persons; or preparing a *xocolatada* (hot chocolate event) at 5:00 a.m. under the rain. While the carnivalesque and other rituals of reversal or rebellion have been understood as functionally useful for "letting steam off" before a return to normality and order (Gluckman 2017), James Scott (1992) has also argued that such instances create space for a dissident culture to be formulated and reproduced.

Indeed, the carnivalesque chaos of the 1-O enabled a constant reformulation and resignification of the political situation. One humorous example came in the form of a large cruise ship that the Spanish government had hired to house riot police in the Barcelona port. The government apparently had not noticed that the cruise ship came with a large Looney Tunes advertisement on its side. In quick order, Tweety Bird came visually to represent police repression in memes and jokes on social media. After the authorities used large pieces of cloth to try to cover up Tweety Bird, attempting both to protect themselves from ridicule and from legal troubles with the Looney Tunes company, the cartoon bird was unexpectedly converted into an ally of the referendum. On a poster depicting Tweety enclosed in a cage and waving an Estelada, it read *"El 1-O volarem"* ("On the 1-O we will fly," making a pun with the word vote). A year later, Atína would show me a drawing she made during those days that depicted how she imagined the Catalan Republic would be. In it, many Tweetys flew around the canvas. The carnivalesque chaos, then, was not only about letting off steam, and certainly not about returning to order. Rather, the humor and inventiveness of the carnival infused voting-center sociality, enabling participants to engage in a sort of artistic *détournement* (Debord and Wolman 2006, 14–21), appropriating and reversing representations of power and spectacle.

For many, the horizontal practices and carnival of voting-center sociality represented a new way of viewing power. In that sociality, a new political space began to emerge that for some had been unthinkable before and that shapes the way that people currently envision what sovereignty might be and feel like. All of the people with whom I talked who participated in the referendum activities or even slept over at the voting stations pointed out the feeling of solidarity as well as fear that was shared among the participants—something that Marina Garcés, in the account cited above, described as the emergence of the "us" (*nosaltres*). I was impressed to observe that groups of people who currently share solid friendships and political trajectories were at first united only by the act of voting in the same place. Ramón, a sixty-year-old core member of the CDR, told me: "Look, if all this doesn't pull forward and we end up more screwed than ever, I will still be grateful for all the people I met during that time." The people of Gavó, then, remember the referendum as an event of self-organized democratic practice that has produced a more lasting sense of belonging within the neighborhood and a sense of becoming a collective subject named el poble comprised by the *veins* (neighbors). More important, and given the sensation of having organized a vote on their own, the referendum weekend endowed the participants in Gavó with the feeling of empowerment and control over their own future. It is therefore no surprise that currently the 1-O stands as a symbol of what sovereignty is and how it can be achieved: the self-organized people taking control over the political developments, and they themselves determining the outcome.

Intimate Voting: Becoming the Referendum in Gavó

As early as 9:00 a.m. on October 1, videos of police violence began spreading on social media, and people watched them on their phones in the intense morning rain. Impatience and frustration reigned, particularly because of problems with the digital network. At Buenaventura school, where Aleix and Ramón were, the vote could not begin, because volunteers were unable to connect virtually to the electoral roll.[3] Finally, at around noon, they were able to connect to the internet and begin voting with the help of computer engineers like Miguel, who volunteered on the spot, and a neighbor who extended a LAN cable from his balcony. In the meantime, some people had gone to other polling stations in Gavó in order to ensure that they would be able to vote.

As midday approached, rumors circulated that police would raid Gavó in the afternoon. Aleix, experienced in tense situations with the police, tells me that he spent most of the day trying to calm people and persuade them not to circulate images of violence, which they literally had at their fingertips. At their polling station, volunteers and persons waiting to vote paid special attention to the *curas* (healing practices), that is the practice of caring for each other and treating the emotional breakdown that many people were suffering. Olga tried to explain to me what the word *curas* means, as it is a word that often comes up in the CDR assemblies even today: "All my neighbors are there and they are also scared, they have their demons as well. To take care of each other is to continue being there, take your fear and move ten meters away. Maybe you cannot overcome your fear but at least you try not to infect others with it." This element of mutual care came to inform CDR practice even after the referendum and to an extent reflects the conscious turn to feminist practices of care within the social movements in Spain and Catalunya (Garcés 2018).

Atína calls the referendum a victory to the extent that it brought together a heterogeneous group of people who for the most part did not know each other beforehand but who acted together without leaders and with respect for each person's contribution. She vividly recalls how everyone shared items like sleeping bags, blankets, or sweaters as an unspoken norm, without this being explicitly agreed on. She tells me, "I woke up on the second of October wearing clothes that were not mine, not knowing where all my stuff was and having things that I had no idea to whom they belonged." Olga tells me of later encountering in the neighborhood people who were with her that weekend: "There are some invisible threads that unite us. Their life has nothing to do with mine, we don't share anything, we wouldn't be friends. But if that person needs anything, I will be there for them. It was a moment of nudity. It's like we saw each other stark naked." It was through visible and corporeal practices, such as linking arms to create a human wall against the police or sharing clothes, food and hugs, that these invisible threads were created and rendered politically meaningful through defending what people considered to be "theirs."

Key in analyzing how sovereign agency is performed on the neighborhood level, is to realize that participating in the referendum—a decentralized act of mass civil disobedience—was tied to each neighborhood's peculiar characteristics and contingent circumstances. Normal electoral processes are significant for their overall outcome, for the totality of the votes over a given sovereign territory are made up of many electoral districts. In contrast, due to the circumstances and conditions described above, the experience of casting one's vote on the 1-O was confined within the neighborhood and to the incidents at each polling station. Obviously, people were worried about what happened in other places and especially to know if their friends and relatives voting elsewhere were safe. Ultimately, though, the experience of the event was confined within each polling station and the relations that developed there among the participants. This enabled the idea of sovereignty, otherwise diluted in the abstractness of the imagined community and of alien institutions, to find a concrete manifestation and performance among more or less defined groups of neighbors and familiar spaces. One of the important outcomes of the referendum, then, was the relocation of sovereignty from the national level to the neighborhood, as the spatial confinement of each polling station enabled people to create intimate bonds of solidarity and a strong sense of neighborhood.

The absence of the Catalan authorities on the one hand, and the unparalleled presence of the Spanish state in the form of crude violence on the other, created an unusual political landscape over which practices of self-organization at the neighborhood level could unfold and place the exercise of popular sovereignty, often located on the abstract macroinstitutional level, in each and every one of the polling booths. It is precisely this element that allows us to speak of sovereign agency, that is, the moment in which the individuality of the subjects became woven in recognizable collective practices, which interpellated the Catalan and Spanish political institutions before being interpellated back by them. As we shall see in the following section, the perceived failure of the political leaders of the procés to continue with the independence project and "do their part" further enhanced the idea of placing the neighborhood at the center of the political imagination and made the project of the CDRs meaningful.

I Ara Que? Envisioning Sovereignty in the Neighborhood

During the weeks that followed the 1-O, Aima remembers encountering people in the elevator or in the street whom she had seen at the polling station. After exchanging a wink of complicity, they would ask each other "i ara que?" (and now what?). The general feeling of hope and empowerment after the 1-O was quickly supplanted by one of uncertainty and confusion in face of the strange political developments that took place during that October. On the one hand, this was provoked by the apparent lack of strategy on behalf of the leaders of the procés manifested by the two (!) quasi-declarations of independence that were quickly suspended by the declarants themselves.[4] It became evident that the political leaders did not have a clear plan and that they were taken off guard by the way that the events of the referendum unfolded. On the other hand, the application of direct rule over Catalunya by the Spanish State, the dismantling of the Generalitat, and the imprisonment of various Catalan politicians further contributed to this feeling of uncertainty and even fear.

Through exploring the workings of the CDR in Gavó I will attempt to analyze how the project of "Making Republic"—that is, a desire for being sovereign that has been produced, performed, and imagined out of the referendum—is currently rerouted as a neighborhood project. Within a context of uncertainty, the CDRs attempted to gain a leading role by strengthening neighborhood institutions and working toward implementation of the republic from below (Milian Nebot 2019). As the chant *votarem* (we will vote) changed to *hem votat* (we have voted) by the evening of the 1-O, hundreds of such initiatives were forming across the Catalan territory employing the franchise name Committees for the Defense of the Republic. For the first time in the course of the procés, a body of social actors was conceptualizing the construction of a new state, the Catalan Republic, as a task to be carried out by grassroots initiatives within the neighborhoods. This was to be accomplished through the so-called *procés constituent popular* (popular constituent process) and a campaign of generalized civil disobedience that would revoke the direct rule imposed by the Spanish government. The idea is that citizens, the poble, should not solely act as supporters of a proindependence government but instead become active agents in shaping and implementing the republic in their neighborhoods. The feeling of being betrayed by a government who has failed its republican promises became an increasingly present ingredient of the CDR discourse, making these groups into vocal critics of the Catalan government.

Reflecting on her participation in the CDR, Raquel sees the group as a vehicle for maintaining social links "post-uno" (after the referendum) and getting to know each other "a foc lent" ("over slow heat"), that is, in a relaxed manner in contrast to the frantic rhythms of the referendum weekend. What really inspired her, though, was that the group provides the space "to imagine what we want." In an informative manner, she stated that the CDR, in her opinion, is about "actively constructing the desired reality." She then went on to explain to me each word of the sentence she had just pronounced. "Actively" signifies participation and implication, while "constructing" refers to the idea of making something out of scratch. According to her, there is not just one "reality," that is, "the reality of the system," but many other possible realities that emanate from "the will and the desire of the people." On various occasions, I was impressed to see people engaging in conversations of what the "new republic" would look like, what policies it should pursue and what principles it must adopt, as if they were trying to give a name and a shape to a world that they imagine "carrying in their hearts."

While the making of a Catalan Republic seemed utopian even to many of those planning it, and even though "the way might be long," as Ramón and Sergio often say, it is experienced by people as a real possibility to the extent that it allows them (at least for the time being) to politically mobilize in a *recognizable* collective project. In this sense, the emergence of a Catalan Republic becomes increasingly imaginable not so much as a Westphalian territorial entity but as the coming together of a people articulated through practices of collective sense-making that change their own political reality (see also chapter 6, this volume).

"Filling the republic with content" is thus a project that consists primarily in imagining and "designing" how the new society might be by weaving a network with other groups within the neighborhood to address a variety of pertinent social issues. Interestingly, this project began to materialize during the autumn of 2018 at the very time when disillusion began to take hold within the pro-independence campaign. Examples of issues on which the CDR and other civil society initiatives sought to collaborate included labor relations, housing, education, migration, religion, and gender inequality. In doing so, they aspired to incorporate the knowledge and practice of these entities into the design of the new republic at the level of the neighborhood so as to create "a more socially just country." Confused about this shift, I asked Sergio, whom I considered to be one of the most passionate persons in this project: "The objective is that Gavó disconnects from the Spanish state. If every CDR disconnects their neighborhood

or village from the Spanish state there will be a moment that we will be more . . .
I mean, it will be more and more easy for us to create the Republic." The aim on
the one hand is obviously to design the foundations of the new state with respect
to each social realm and, on the other hand, to offer credit and visibility to the
work carried out by diverse existing groups, making use of the large social media
network that the CDR has built since the referendum. Ideally, neighbors would be
empowered to participate in a popular constituent process, which would enable
them to envision what they want their neighborhood and country to look like.
For this purpose, their linking up with other sovereignty projects that have been
abundant in Catalunya over the last years, like energy sovereignty, technological
sovereignty and food sovereignty, comes in handy.

Active involvement in CDRs also leads certain people to identify the neighborhood as the foundational layer where the republican project might develop.
Counter to much of classical political theory that takes the foundational unit of
the state to be the family (Daub 2011; Foucault 2006; Held 2008), the centrality
of the neighborhood is a result of the spatiality of the referendum as a political
act, but is also rooted in the tradition of municipalism and neighborhood asso-
ciationism, which has been on the rise across Catalunya and Spain (García Espín
2012; Ubasart Gonzàlez 2016).[5]

Nevertheless, the relation between the idea of national sovereignty and the
realm of the neighborhood is bound to be complicated, and it remains to be seen
as to how it might develop. I was particularly intrigued to observe discourses and
elements that complicate what the republic or independence might mean for the
CDR participants. When I first contacted Atína, I was struck by her status on the
messaging app: "I wouldn't wish a state on anyone." I had previously seen that
slogan on a publication. When we got together one evening, I asked her what she
meant by this and whether that statement was not in direct contradiction with
"making a republic."

> [The republic] is not about making a State. It is about doing many 1-Os.
> It's about the practices [*las practicas*]. . . . For me, the 1-O it's not just an
> independence movement but also a movement for basic human rights.
> This is what made many people take to the streets, and I don't know if it
> could happen in a normal referendum. . . . I could support it etymologi-
> cally as republic means many times public [a pun in Spanish]. . . . For
> me, republic is not what it says in the dictionary but what is achieved
> during the process of thinking of making a republic. For me, it is stron-
> ger than the fact of having a state.

In a similar manner, Manel told me in our very first conversation that he
supported independence as a means of challenging the status quo, "the regime

of 1978." On another occasion, Aima told me that she is independentist because "that's how they call it nowadays." In a heated discussion during yet another beer session, I heard Sergio half-jokingly saying that once independence is achieved, he will fold away his Estelada, as it will no longer have any meaning, and he will become an anarchist. Hearing this, I remembered a graffiti of an Estelada with the Circle-A painted over the star and next to it saying, "Independence without limits: we decide for everything."

What might all these examples tell us then? Perhaps what emerges is a conceptualization of independence and the republic as a process rather than an end goal, more as "aspiration than realization" (see Introduction, this volume). Arousing unresolved histories of the past (Garcés 2018, 233), the word *republic* becomes an effective vehicle and a historically meaningful node around which transgressive projects materialize. Apart from a set of institutional practices, the republic becomes a reason for a specific politicization and socialization within Gavó as well as across Catalunya. A political community emerges, which seems to be less sustained by imaginations of "the Catalan people" in its totality or by an imagination of the nation (in my interviews I received confusing answers as to who the Catalan people are), and more by the feeling of belonging to the neighborhood. The question that arises is how a campaign for national sovereignty, the latter always bound to an imagined community (population) and to a motherland (territory), is translated in terms of neighborhoodness in which the community is not just imagined but is sustained through the everyday materialities of coexistence, or "a network between people and materialities" (Navaro-Yashin 2012).

Notwithstanding the pronounced focus on the neighbor, and despite the fact that each local CDR is supposedly "sovereign," in the sense that it is independent from the rest, it seems that politics in Gavó are still bound to the current political conjuncture in Catalunya. Although the goal is to unfold a repertoire of action tailored to the neighborhood by engaging in local struggles and building sovereignty in the everyday, the CDR's capacity to mobilize and create continuity seems handicapped by the wider climate of the proindependence campaign, which at the time of writing is going through a new period of challenges. While police and judicial repression against the proindependence movement has been on the rise after the referendum, with hundreds of people facing trials and many of the political leaders imprisoned or in self-exile, the unity between the proindependence parties has also been fractured. The CDRs for their part accuse the Catalan government of betraying the people and not materializing the expected independence. This reality points to the limitations of sovereign agency and the language of sovereignty in efforts to mobilize: at the same time that the language facilitates political organization among the neighbors of Gavó and enables them to imagine their collective being as sovereign, it traps them and their desires in the sovereign space of the state, Catalan or Spanish, which is necessarily far away from Gavó. What marks the procés at the current stage, then, is the dialectic between the centrifugal interpellation that the grassroots initiatives aspire to exert and the centripetal processes of institutionalization and party politics.

The question that looms large, therefore, is what traps might the appropriation of the language of sovereignty pose—unavoidably linked to the national realm—in the face of a political context in flux? This language was in the first instance effective in translating the campaign of national independence into people's empowerment within the neighborhoods. But what happens when sovereignty is "lost" to the institutions again? What happens when the magic of sovereign agency withers away? It might be in its essence that sovereign agency, as a moment of madness when everything seems possible, will ultimately cede space to normality, where everything seems predictable. As the desire for sovereignty is materialized less and less in agentive action and resides more and more within the collective imaginary and memory, the question is to trace what legacies it leaves behind. How is the memory of having been and having felt sovereign informing the future worlds that are imagined in Gavó and in Catalunya?

The referendum of the 1-O gave rise to situated practices of sovereign agency, which found spatialized manifestation at each polling station and produced a very particular form of sociality among the participants. The collective practices of self-organization filled up a space that under normal circumstances is occupied and run by the state institutions. This development came about as the product of the mutual interpellation between the institutions and the citizens' initiative, producing a particular understanding of the "people" as comprised by the mobilized *veïns* (neighbors). In this sense, the major impact of the 1-O and of the subsequent experience of organizing locally in the CDRs is the feeling of empowerment through practices that for a moment in time creates the feeling of controlling one's fate. The CDR puts forward a civic model of inclusive citizenship and democratic enhancement codified in the mantra "the people give the orders and the government obeys," seeing the proindependence campaign as a challenge to the low-capacity democratic regime of Spain rather than an identitarian movement. Indeed, the proindependence sovereigntist campaign has been increasingly reclaimed by the CDRs as a project of total social emancipation and thus has little to do—ideologically, politically, and historically—with other political projects cast as sovereigntist such as Brexit in the United Kingdom, PEGIDA in Germany, or Viktor Orbán in Hungary. However, it remains to be seen over time to what extent the imagined political community can effectively transcend ethnic articulations around identity and culture, which are inescapably exclusive.

The concept of sovereign agency has been useful in accounting for the agentive action that produced a feeling of collective and personal empowerment among the neighbors of Gavó. However, and precisely because such agency interpellates subjectivities that are bound to notions of national identity and "oneness," we should be aware that other social realities, such as class composition, immigration, or mass touristification, also inform and condition the Catalan society (and subsequently the proindependence campaign). As sovereign agency withers away, ceding ground to everyday disenchanted party politics, such social dimensions resurface, and the limitations of agentive action become palpable. While the enactment of sovereign agency can unleash historical processes that for a moment seem to transcend institutional politics, the necessary constituent practices that would canalize its emancipatory promise are not self-guaranteed as the Catalan experience tells us. While "grassrootsness" and "noninstitutionality" are the magic attributes and the reason why sovereign agency is effective in interpellating emancipatory dreams, at the same time the desires that give birth to such agency perhaps cannot be realized if they are not institutionalized themselves—and thus disenchanted from their "madness."

Notes

1. The chapter is based on four months of fieldwork in the neighborhood of Gavó during the course of my research at Utrecht University. During fieldwork, I directly participated in the assemblies and events of the local CDR and engaged in extensive discussions and interviews with many of the participants and neighbors.

2. In Star Wars, the Alliance to Restore the Republic, also known as the Rebellion or the Rebel Alliance, is a resistance movement against the Galactic empire, which is formed by various resistance cells who disagree with the imperial order and fight for the restoration of the old Galactic Republic. The metaphor could allude to the Second Spanish Republic (1931–39) and to the fact that post-Francoist Spain is officially a constitutional monarchy and not a republic as such.

3. In the early hours of the referendum day, the Generalitat announced that the referendum would be carried out using a universal electoral roll. This meant that any person could vote at any polling station through a digital database. It is considered one of the bright moves of the Generalitat that outsmarted the Spanish government and the police operations. Throughout the day however, hackers working against the referendum were attacking the platform, causing it to crash, while hackers working in favor of the referendum were working to restore it. Within Gavó, Whatsapp groups were used to communicate different needs that were emerging at the various centers, including the need for computer engineers in cases where the system crashed. The 1-O involved a deep intertwinement of online and offline strategies of participatory practices (Poblet 2018) in what has been framed as the first cyberwarfare between the Spanish State and civil society (Milian Nebot 2019).

4. On October 10, following the result of the referendum, the Catalan president Carles Puigdemont declared independence only to suspend it eight seconds later, supposedly as a

demonstration of willingness to negotiate with the Spanish state and EU. After two weeks of backstage talks, threats, and an apparent flight of capital from Catalunya, on October 27 the Catalan parliament voted for a motion declaring the independence of Catalunya. The bill, however, was never published in the government gazette, and independence never materialized de facto.

5. In Gavó, some informants, especially those of older age, attributed their participation in politics and their Catalan identity to their engagement in cultural neighborhood associations when they were young, such as scouting, choruses, the human castles (*castellers*), and social centers. It seems that such entities functioned as disguised carriers of political and social agency during the dictatorship (Kammerer 2014; Giori 2014). More recently, the 15-M movement in 2011, which took over the squares of the big cities all over Spain, has been subsequently diffused in neighborhood-based initiatives, especially in antieviction initiatives (Calle Collado 2016). The municipalist turn has also been accompanied by the rise of analogous political formations, such as Podemos in Spain and CUP in Catalunya, that came to power in various municipalities and produced significant electoral results.

References

Almiron, Núria. 2018. "'Go and Get' Em !': Authoritarianism, Elitism, and Media in the Catalan Crisis." *Political Economy of Communication* 6(2): 39–73.

Anderson, Benedict. 2006. *Imagined Communities: Reflections on the Origin and Spread of Nationalism*. London: Verso.

Bartelson, Jens. 2014. *Sovereignty as Symbolic Form*. London: Routledge.

Beltrán de Felipe, Miguel. 2019. *Myths and Realities of Secessionisms: A Constitutional Approach to the Catalonian Crisis*. London: Palgrave MacMillan.

Biersteker, Thomas J., and Cynthia Weber, eds. 1996. *State Sovereignty as Social Construct*. Cambridge: Cambridge University Press.

Bonilla, Yarimar. 2012. "Non-Sovereign Futures? French Carribean Politics in the Wake of Disenchantment." In *Caribbean Sovereignty, Democracy, and Development in an Age of Globalization*, edited by Linden Lewis, 208–227. New York: Routledge.

Bonilla, Yarimar. 2017. "Unsettling Sovereignty." *Cultural Anthropology* 32(3): 330–339.

Bryant, Rebecca. 2018. "Sovereignty." In *The International Encyclopedia of Anthropology*, edited by Hillary Callan. Hoboken, NJ: Wiley-Blackwell.

Calle Collado, Ángel. 2016. "Ciclos Políticos Y Ciclos De Movilización. Entre El 15M, Podemos Y Nuevos Municipalismos." *Historia Actual Online* 40(2): 79–94.

Cámara Villar, Gregorio. 2019. "Federal Reform of Spain vs Secession in Catalonia: Could Constitutional Reform Provide a Response to the Demands Upon Which the Justification for Secession Are Based?" In *Claims for Secession and Federalism: A Comparative Study with Focus on Spain*, edited by Alberto Lopez-Basaguren and Leire Escajedo San-Epifanio, 443–459. New York: Springer.

Carrasco Polaino, Rafael, Ernesto Villar Cirujano, and Laura Tejedor Fuentes. 2018. "Twitter Como Herramienta de Comunicación Política En El Contexto Del Referéndum Independentista Catalán: Asociaciones Ciudadanas Frente a Instituciones Públicas." *Revista ICONO14 Revista Científica de Comunicación y Tecnologías Emergentes* 16(1): 64.

Cartes Barroso, Manuel Jesus. 2018. "El Uso de Instagram Por Los Partidos Políticos Catalanes Durante El Referéndum Del 1-O." *Revista de Comunicación de La SEECI* 47: 17–36.

Çelikkol, Aşkın. 2014. "Saturnalia Revisited: Gezi Park Protests and Carnival Today." *Cultura, Lenguaje y Representacion* 12: 9–25.

Clua I Fainé, Montserrat. 2014. "Identidad y Política En Cataluña: El Auge Del Independentismo En El Nacionalismo Catalán Actual." *Quaderns de l'Institut Catala d'Antropologia* 19(2): 79–99.

Coromina, Oscar. 2018. "Análisis de Las Desinformaciones Del Referéndum Del 1 de Octubre Detectadas Por Maldito Bulo." *Quaderns Del Cac* 21(44): 17–26.

Crameri, Kathryn. 2015. "Political Power and Civil Counterpower: The Complex Dynamics of the Catalan Independence Movement." *Nationalism and Ethnic Politics* 21(1): 104–120.

Daub, Adrian. 2011. "The State as a Family: The Fate of Familial Sovereignty in German Romanticism." *Republic of Letters: A Journal for the Study of Knowledge, Politics, and the Arts* 2(2): 127–157.

Debord, Guy, and Gil Wolman. 2006. *Situationist International Anthology*. Revised and expanded ed. Edited by Ken Knabb. Berkeley, CA: Bureau of Public Secrets.

Dzenovska, Dace, and Iván Arenas. 2012. "Don't Fence Me In: Barricade Sociality and Political Struggles in Mexico and Latvia." *Comparative Studies in Society and History* 54(3): 644–678.

Foucault, Michel. 2006. "Governmentality." In *The Anthropology of the State: A Reader*, edited by Akhil Gupta and Aradhana Sharma, 131–143. Malden, MA: Blackwell.

Garcés, Marina. 2018. *Ciudad Princesa*. Barcelona: Galaxia Gutenberg.

García Espín, Patricia. 2012. "El 15M, de Vuelta Al Barrio Como the 15M Movement : Back To the Neighborhood As the Space for Politics." *Revista Internacional de Pensamiento Político* 7: 291–310.

Giori, Pablo. 2014. "Les Etapes Del Món Casteller." *Revista d'Etnologia de Catalunya* 39: 160–167.

Gluckman, Max. 2017. "Rituals of Rebellion in South-East Africa." In *Readings for a History of Anthropological Theory*, edited by Paul A. Erickson and Liam D. Murphy, 218–236. Toronto: University of Toronto Press.

Guibernau, Montserrat. 2004. *Catalan Nationalism: Francoism, Transition, and Democracy*. London: Routledge.

Held, David. 2008. *Models of Democracy*. Edited by Polity Press. Malden, MA: Polity.

Howland, Douglas, and Luise White. 2009. *The State of Sovereignty: Territories, Laws, Populations*. Bloomington: Indiana University Press.

Kammerer, Nina. 2014. "Catalan Festival Culture, Identities, and Independentism." *Quaderns de l'Institut Catala d'Antropologia* 19(2): 58–78.

Keating, Michael. 2006. "Sovereignty and Plurinational Democracy: Problems in Political Science." In *Sovereignty in Transition*, edited by Neil Walker, 191–208. Oxford: Hart.

Keating, Michael. 2008. "Thirty Years of Territorial Politics." *West European Politics* 31(1–2): 60–81.

Keating, Michael, and Alex Wilson. 2009. "Renegotiating the State of Autonomies: Statute Reform and Multi-Level Politics in Spain." *West European Politics* 32(3): 536–558.

Lecours, André. 2018. "The Political Consequences of Independence Referenda in Liberal Democracies: Quebec, Scotland, and Catalonia." *Polity* 50(2): 243–274.

Letamendia, Atalunya Arkaitz. 2017. "Movilización, Represión Y Voto : Rastreando Las Claves Del Referéndum de Autodeterminación Del 1 de Octubre de 2017 En Catalunya." *Anuari de Conflicte Social* 7: 1–32.

López, Jaume. 2017. *El Derecho a Decidir: La Via Catalana*. Tafalla: Txalaparta.

Magnusson, Warren. 2011. *Politics of Urbanism: Seeing Like a City*. Oxford: Routledge.

Milian Nebot, Xavier. 2019. *El Poder Del Poble: L'autorganització Veïnal Dels CDR*. Valencia: Sembra.

Mitchell, Timothy. 2006. "Society, Economy, and the State Effect." In *The Anthropology of the State: A Reader*, edited by Aradhana Sharma and Akhil Gupta, 169–186. Malden, MA: Blackwell.

Muro, Diego, and Alejandro Quiroga. 2005. "Spanish Nationalism: Ethnic or Civic." *Ethnicities* 5(1): 9–29.

Navaro-Yashin, Yael. 2012. *The Make-Believe Space: Affective Geography in a Postwar Polity*. Durham, NC: Duke University Press.

Newton, Ken. 2014. "Trust and Political Disenchantment: An Overview." In *Political Trust and Disenchantment with Politics: International Perspectives*, edited by Christina Eder, Ingvill C. Mochmann, and Markus Quandt, 19–30. Leiden: Brill.

Painter, Joe. 2006. "Prosaic Geographies of Stateness." *Political Geography* 25(7): 752–774.

Poblet, Marta. 2018. "Distributed, Privacy-Enhancing Technologies in the 2017 Catalan Referendum on Independence: New Tactics and Models of Participatory Democracy." *First Monday* 23(12): 1–17.

Reeves, Madeleine. 2014. *Border Work: Spatial Lives of the State in Rural Central Asia*. Ithaca, NY: Cornell University Press.

Rubner Hansen, Bue. 2017. "Winter in Catalonia." *Viewpoint*. https://www.viewpoint mag.com/2017/12/19/winter-in-catalonia.

Scott, James. 1992. *Domination and the Arts of Resistance: Hidden Trnascripts*. New Haven: Yale University Press.

Şener, Ömer. 2013. "The Gezi Protests, Polyphony, and 'Carnivalesque Chaos.'" *Journal of Global Faultlines* 1: 40–42.

Spencer, Jonathan. 2007. *Anthropology, Politics, and the State: Democracy and Violence in South Asia*. Cambridge: Cambridge University Press.

Ubasart Gonzàlez, Gemma. 2016. "L'aposta Municipalista: El Potencial Transformador Del Món Local." *Kult-Ur Revista Interdisciplinària Sobre La Cultura De La Ciutat* 2(3): 125–139.

Vicens, Laia, and Xavi Tedó. 2017. *Operació Urnes*. Barcelona: Columna Edicions.

Wagner-Pacifici, Robin. 2017. *What Is an Event?* Chicago: University of Chicago Press.

Wilmer, Franke. 2008. "Sovereignty." In *International Encyclopedia of the Social Sciences*, edited by William A. Darity, 2nd ed. Vol. 7. Course Technology.

THE FALSE PROMISES OF SOVEREIGNTY

Enclaves, Exclaves, and Impossible Politics in the Jewish State

Joyce Dalsheim

This chapter considers some of the processes by which sovereign citizens are produced and maintained as "the people" who have popular sovereignty. It looks at how Jewish Israelis are engaged in multiple layers of struggle. They struggle with and against each other and the government to determine the character of "the people" who are sovereign. The Kafkaesque nature of such struggles illustrates how modern democratic nation-states, meant to liberate citizens through rule by "the people" and for "the people," instead create and maintain "a people" *for* the state and its projects. In the case of the modern state of Israel, achieving sovereignty has been understood as a form of liberation. It freed "the people" from being ruled by foreign powers, claimed to ensure their continuity, and provide a space in which they could flourish. As Dzenovska (chapter 7, this volume) suggests for the case of Latvians in Latvia, Jews in Israel have demonstrated "the ability to will into existence a people and a state," although often by force. Considering what this means for those at the center of popular sovereignty, this chapter questions the existential nature of what she terms "existential sovereignty," suggesting that self-determination also involves self-elimination.

Israel is the self-described Jewish state, a place where Jews should be free to be Jewish. Indeed, the national identity of sovereign citizens of Israel is not "Israeli," it is "Jewish." But this means that what will count as Jewishness must be formally defined and regulated. Because the modern categories of "nation" and "religion" are at once disarticulated and conflated in the figure of the Jew, all sorts of conundrums ensue. This, in turn, threatens to undermine the liberating forces often presumed to accompany political self-determination. Indeed, self-determination in the nation-state, as I argue in greater detail elsewhere, also involves forms of self-elimination (Dalsheim 2019). According to Eugen Weber (1976), national sovereignty is at once liberating and colonizing—colonizing precisely those whom it presumes to liberate. In this case it limits the possible ways of being Jewish in the Jewish state. Thus, if existential sovereignty attests to the ability to produce collective selves as a "people" and the political power to establish a state for that people, it *also* involves all manner of struggle among those people over their defining features. Those struggles thereby demonstrate the contingency and partiality of claims to enact "sovereign agency." The examples explored in this chapter demonstrate some of the ways that the capacity to speak "for the people" is contested, and how certain claims to enact sovereign agency come to stand for the nation-state as a whole—even if only temporarily—while others are marginalized.

The moral foundation of the nation-state is its promise of sovereignty, of liberation through the rights granted by citizenship. As Hannah Arendt explained, the rights of man, *human* rights, were from the outset inextricably entangled with "national emancipation," such that only "emancipated sovereignty of the people" seemed capable of achieving or ensuring such rights (Arendt 2003[1948]). And yet, in the modern state of Israel, which is supposed to be a place of national emancipation and flourishing for the Jews, the people can only grow and prosper at the expense of another people. They can only gain self-determination by exclusion and oppression of another people. It seems paradoxical that they can only attain sovereign citizenship by reproducing for others the exclusionary conditions visited upon them in Europe.

This problem is well known and documented in the scholarly critique of nationalism. Arendt herself was critical of the ethnonational state for precisely these reasons. But there is a deeper level of paradox we have yet to fully explore. As Yarimar Bonilla reminds us, concepts such as sovereignty, democracy, and freedom are not neutral categories. "These are native categories of the West as a *project* not a place," and we are called upon to interrogate "the consequences of their normative dominance" (Bonilla 2017, 334). If we have primarily been concerned with those consequences for excluded or marginalized populations, here I shift the focus to those at the center of sovereign citizenship to consider the consequences of inclusion.

This chapter is part of a larger project that looks into such consequences by considering the deeper paradoxes of the concept of popular sovereignty.[1] In order to attain political self-determination in their own state, a people must have the capacity and endurance to produce themselves as a national group, which results in certain kinds of limitations. That entails the quality and character of peoplehood, the extent to which people must be "the people" in order to attain sovereignty, and the intricate, intimate details of being made and maintained as such. A particular collective must be able to imagine itself as a people, but the details of that collective identity can become the subject of debate, struggle, and conflict. The processes involved in producing and maintaining a national majority, I suggest, call into question the very idea of what popular sovereignty might mean. In the case of the modern state of Israel, the myth of liberation through self-determination finds itself challenged in two apparently distinct yet connected ways.

First, if the people who supposedly exercise authority over a territory and its population must constantly be produced, clearly they must be fashioned as such in very specific ways. The means through which this is accomplished in the context of a nation-state may contradict with at least some of the ideas and practices of identity, norms, ethics, and traditions that have historically defined "the people" as a living and internally differentiated collective or as an aggregation of internally differentiated collectives. If this is the case, then what does "emancipation" mean when it takes the form of political self-determination that will require a unified, purified, or homogenized "people"? To what extent is the achievement of sovereignty liberating for those it aims to set free? Producing a national majority requires processes of cultural homogenization, at least in certain respects, that allow for particular kinds of differences to appear as cultural diversity while other differences must be contained or erased.

Second, this chapter focuses on two cases of observant Jewish Israelis who come into conflict with state policies over what it means to be Jewish. The conflicts each of these groups—religious Zionists (*dati leumi*) and ultra-Orthodox (*Haredim*)—has with the state are nearly mirror opposites: one challenging the state to increase its sovereign power over contested territory and religious sites, the other rejecting such sovereignty.[2] Both cases raise questions about the possibility of emancipation and the meaning of self-determination, which in turn suggests that the "who" of sovereign agency is never obvious, and always contested. At the same time, both groups are concerned with enacting God's Sovereignty, sometimes in opposition to state policy and sometimes in opposition to the existence of the modern state in its current form. "The state" in democracy is presumed to represent the will of the people—that is popular sovereignty—but these two groups undermine that ideal. The ultranationalists (religiously motivated Jewish settlers and their compatriots in the national-religious camp) endanger the state's stable borders as they also endanger everyone's children through the violence, actual and potential, provoked by their ever-increasing colonization. The antinationalists (ultra-Orthodox/Haredim) endanger a set of ideals often associated with modernity itself—democracy, gender equality, rational distribution of material resources, individual autonomy, and rule of secular law. As one member of the *Haredi* community explained to me, "Haredim don't think the law is above all. God is above all."

These challenges lead me to ask whether, in the case of the modern state of Israel, human liberation through popular sovereignty has been rendered impossible through the creation of the state itself. In other words, does the capacity to will into existence a national collective and attain political sovereignty in a nation-state also undermine particular forms of human liberation? We know of the outcomes for Palestinians, those excluded and marginalized by the Zionist project. But here I am asking whether popular sovereignty also precludes human liberation for those presumed to be at the center of an ethnonational state, "the people" themselves. And if, at the same time, "the people" threaten the possibility of modern sovereignty.

Enclaves

In February 2014 the spiritual leader of a group of strictly observant Haredi Jews, the Belzer Rebbe, called on his followers to prepare to leave Israel and seek political asylum as refugees in the United States.[3] The headline in the Belz newspaper read: "Initial preparation for mass emigration from Israel." It was reported that American senators had already "promised assistance in obtaining refugee status for every Haredi family that wishes to leave Israel."[4] The Belzer Hasids are one of many strictly observant Jewish groups who together make up a small but growing percentage of the total population of Jews in Israel.[5] The Rebbe was worried about the future for Jews in Israel. He was worried that life in Israel was becoming too dangerous. But perhaps not exactly in the ways one might expect. The Rebbe was not talking about problems of violence or the threat of war. He was worried about the possibility of living *as* Jews in the state of Israel and leading life according to the Torah. He was concerned that the conditions for living the Torah life were worsening in Israel and that such conditions might be better in New York. This might seem strange or even contradictory. How could Jews be worried about their freedom to be Jewish in the Jewish state?

In this case, the Belzer Rebbe was reacting to a proposed law that would make conscription into the Israeli armed forces mandatory for members of his community, which would interfere with their responsibility to study the Torah. It should be noted, however, that this is only one of the recent and most visible problems for Torah Jews. Thousands of members of the Haredi community have come out on numerous occasions to protest the draft, sometimes literally shutting down the city of Jerusalem. However, over the years, the Israeli state has also tried to dismantle their informal economy, change their education system, and incorporate them into the national labor force. Strictly observant Jews (the ultra-Orthodox) have historically been opposed to Zionism and the human intervention in what should be God's work. They worried about whether or not they could live their lives according to their beliefs before the state was established, and worried that the secular state would have dire outcomes for the Jewish people. Now, the issue of a citizen's responsibility to serve in the armed forces might interfere with a Jew's responsibility to live according to the Torah, which requires studying the text and its interpretations.

If studying the sacred texts is an integral part of being Jewish, a commandment, a requirement, a duty, if it is more than a way of life, but the means for protecting life itself, then clearly such study should take priority. And surely state policies in one's own state should not impede such study. Indeed, for many years strictly observant Jews who studied the Torah, yeshiva students, were exempt from compulsory military service in Israel.[6] But that protection was beginning to erode, and members of the Haredi community found themselves struggling against state policy in the Jewish state in order to protect their right to *be* Jewish. What does it mean to be part of a sovereign people if basic group norms, traditions, and values are violated by the "self-determination" promised by the state?

Scholars have often noted the breach of the promises of sovereignty to subaltern groups, minorities, those excluded, or other marginalized populations. But we have yet to adequately examine what such self-determination means for national majorities. If the possibility of freedom in one's own country is insecure even for members of the national majority group, and even when that group constitutes a formal ethnocracy (Yiftachel 2006), then what might we learn by shifting the focus of critical theories of subjectification from subaltern groups to those who appear to be at the center of the sovereign nation?

The Belz community of Haredi Jews are part of a larger subset of strictly observant Jews who struggle to hold on to their traditions wherever they live (Goldshmidt 2006; Fader 2009). They often reside in segregated neighborhoods and towns, enclaves that bear some resemblance to the *shtetls*, or ghettos, of Europe from which many fled. One summer I visited such a neighborhood in the Jerusalem area. I was doing fieldwork and had come to interview a member of the Haredi community. But I was not exactly sure how to find the precise address. Understanding that very religious men should not look at women other than their own wives, I waited for some women to approach so that I might ask their help in finding the apartment.

Finally, two women pushing baby carriages approached. I called out to them, "excuse me." But there was no response. I tried again, "excuse me." And then, "may I ask . . ." But the women walked right past me. They kept their gaze focused straight ahead and did not even look in my direction. Although I had dressed modestly, following the precepts of Halakha (Jewish law) and had done my best not to offend, the women avoided me entirely, as though I was not there.

Later, when I asked about this near-encounter I was given a number of explanations. "They might have been in shock," one person told me. "After all, they were not used to seeing outsiders." Another member of the community proposed that this behavior might be explained as a form of bodily habit memory; a result of life-long training to avoid looking at that which offends their way of life. I was told by members of the Haredi community that they often harbor "stereotypes" of people who lead more secular lives. The secular are often represented as criminals, *avariyanim* in Hebrew. An *avariyan* is one who "crosses" the law. In this case, the term might primarily refer to those who do not keep the commandments as written in the Torah, but the word also means "criminal" and conjures up all sorts of negative connotations. Secular women, in particular, are often considered "open," I was told, sexually permissive; another way of crossing or breaking the laws specified in the Torah. For secular Israeli Jews, such openness can mean dancing in nightclubs, and wearing whatever one wants, such as bikinis on the beach. It might connote precisely the kinds of freedom they seek to attain through collective self-determination. Zionism, based on Enlightenment values, was supposed to free Jews from the constraints of the European ghetto and also from the conservative norms of religion. But for observant Jews, these kinds of behaviors are to be avoided. Such behaviors are dangerous to one's moral integrity, dangerous to one's Jewishness.

Like the broader Western moral narrative of modernity, Zionist ideology is embedded in ideas about progress toward greater human freedom, which has often meant leaving tradition behind. Dipesh Chakrabarty (2000) reminds us that such "progressivist" thinking, with its origins in the European Enlightenment, had no room for the traditional norms, organization, or forms of exchange found among people in places where Europeans colonized. In particular, there was no room for the gods and spirits who functioned in people's everyday lives. Scholars of postcolonial studies have thus been concerned with the outcomes of European Enlightenment ideals for traditional communities that have been colonized, and about the danger to and destruction of particular ways of life that European colonization and nationalism brought (Chatterjee 1986; Nandy 1995). While colonizing forms of disenfranchisement are not identical to forms of discrimination against disenfranchised groups inside European nations, colonization and the production of national majorities share in processes of Orientalizing and excluding Europe's Others (see Boyarin 1994, 428).

Zionism, self-consciously modeled after European nationalism, has rightly come under a great deal of criticism for dislocating, excluding, and disenfranchising local Palestinian Arabs. But Othering in Orientalizing fashion is not limited to non-Jewish Arabs (Said 1979), nor to Jewish Arabs, known as *Mizrahim* (Shohat 1988; Shenhav 2006). The processes involved in producing a national majority include disciplining all sorts of Jewish communities to produce particular kinds of subjectivities (Althusser 1971; Foucault 1988 [1982], 1991 [1978]; Ong 1996) aligned with the projects of the Jewish state.

If being Jewish means upholding the precepts of the Torah, then open defiance of those principles—especially by people who are supposed to be Jewish—is dangerous to Jewishness itself. Thus members of the Haredi community are often taught to avert their eyes because the modern, secularist dreams of the founders of the state of Israel can also be offensive to some of those who seek refuge in the state. More than offensive, for these observant Jews, the self-proclaimed secular state threatens Judaism and by extension, is a threat to Jews.

Exclaves

"It wasn't supposed to be this way," he lamented. "All these young people becoming newly observant Jews—it's a nightmare for Zionism!"

—Gideon (secular Israeli Jew)

Modern political Zionism narrates its rise as a response to antisemitism in Europe. It was foundationally a secular political movement with the goal of allowing the Jews to become "a nation like all others." According to sociologists Gershon Shafir and Ilan Peled, "Zionism . . . has always proclaimed itself a secular national movement in the tradition of the Enlightenment, intending, in [Theodor] Herzl's famous words, to keep the rabbis in their synagogues and the soldiers in their barracks" (2002, 137). Like other modern projects inspired by Enlightenment values, Zionism held the hope of a better future; the hope of liberation, inlcuding liberation from the contraints of religion.

The Israeli man quoted above was referring to a recent trend among young Jewish Israelis, more and more of whom seemed to be seeking answers to life's big questions by turning to religion (*chozrim b'tshuva*), specifically to Judaism, and often to the form of Judaism that is known in Hebrew as "national-religious" (*dati leumi*).[7] Gideon, like most of his friends, is a proud secular Zionist Jew. He is very knowledgable on issues of Jewish history, tradition, and religion. But he raised his children to be secular citizens of the modern state because he values independence and individual freedoms, open debate, and what he sees as rational decision making. So, when one of his own children became observant, like other parents in similar situations, he and his wife were horrified. They tried to be open and accepting, but under his breath, Gideon muttered and complained. It seemed to him that his daughter, now in her early twenties, was behaving quite irrationally. He told me about some of her newly aquired behaviors, like the seemingly endless preparations for the Sabbath each week. According to Gideon and his wife these preparations could be so onerous they seemed to completely negate the point of observing the Sabbath, which, they thought, was all about taking a day to rest.

To prepare for the Sabbath one has to make sure all the food for Friday night and Saturday is ready in advance. The house should be cleaned and all meals ready before sunset on Friday. Cooking is not permitted on the Sabbath. Gideon understood how that made sense. Cooking is work, he thought, and the Sabbath should be a time of rest. But in addition to all the cleaning and cooking and baking and setting up a hot water heater in advance so as not to turn on electricity during the Sabbath, his daughter, Aliza, had also been tearing toilet paper. Tearing toilet paper into neat little squares so that this most ordinary private labor of self-care might not have to be performed on the day of rest.

This, her father thought, is bordering on insanity. Why on earth would anyone think that tearing toilet paper was work? Wasn't this just creating *more* work? Didn't it just make the Sabbath more difficult, to say nothing of more annoying? Aliza never explained to her father that avoiding tearing paper on the Sabbath had a deeper symbolic meaning. On the Sabbath, she knew, the world is complete. One recognizes the wholeness of God's creation and does not take something that exists in one form and make it into something new. Thus, if paper must be put into a new form, that tearing should be done prior to the Sabbath.

Beyond their scorn at the rites and rituals practiced by Orthodox Jews, Gideon and his wife were especially concerned because they thought their daughter might take on what they saw as "extremist" positions. Joining the community of nationalist-religious Jews meant being part of the religiously motivated settler movement. And that was dangerous. Their daughter might move to a dangerous place, like one of the settlements in the West Bank. She might drive along roads, like route 60, where Jews had been ambushed by Palestinians, shot dead on that road (Harel 2011). Or, she might take part in confrontational demonstrations or be among the "hilltop youth" who establish illegal settlements in the Occupied Territories. Or, she might even become involved with those religiously motivated settlers who have been carrying out "price tag" acts of violence against Palestinians in the West Bank.[8] These parents, and many others like them, worried that becoming an observant Jew meant their daughter could become part of a politics they oppose; a political movement they see as undermining the state itself. In other words, this Judaism was dangerous to the Jewish state.

What, then, does it mean to be sovereign citizens in a Jewish state? What does "existential sovereignty" do in the case of Jewish self-determination? What can it mean if particular forms of Judaism are dangerous to Jewish sovereignty and, at the same time, if Jewish sovereignty is dangerous to particular forms of Judaism? Are there parallel situations in other nation-states? Can particular ways of being French endanger the French state? Can the existence of a Muslim state endanger Islam? Can particular ways of being Christian endanger a Christian nation?

These parents were partially relieved, thinking that at least the nationalist-religious did not segregate themselves from secular Israel; they took full part. While the Haredim generally expressed opposition to much of what might be termed secular modernity and avoided interactions with secular Jews, which included avoiding conscription in the Israeli armed forces, the nationalist-religious had become prominent soldiers and officers. They often studied and worked among the secular. They were not only fully integrated into Israeli society, they had become leading figures. These parents were relieved, at least, that their daughter had not become Haredi, because that might mean their relationship would suffer even more. If she became Haredi it might be more difficult for her to visit her parents' home. Maybe she would shelter herself, and one day her children, from the vices of secular life. In spite of their fears for their daughter as a newly observant nationalist-religious Jew, they were also sometimes thankful that she had not—or not yet—become Haredi. And yet, they remained concerned that she would become part of a dangerous politics.

Nationalist-religious Israeli Jews do not necessarily live in segregated enclaves like the ultra-Orthodox (Sivan 1995). But, one might argue, they often live in "exclaves" beyond the internationally recognized boundaries of the state. Seeking to fulfill their belief that God promised the Land of Israel to His people, the nationalist-religious establish settlements beyond the Green Line, in post-1967 Israeli Occupied Territories.[9] Sometimes they come into conflict with the state over the illegal outposts they establish there, or for praying at holy sites both inside and outside the nation's borders in ways that defy the law (Inbari 2009).

The Lawmaker and the Law

In September 2016, a relatively new member of the Israeli parliament (Knesset) posted an emotional video on his Facebook page. Yehouda Glick, like many other nationalist-religious Jews, promotes Jewish prayer at the Temple Mount in Jerusalem. On numerous occasions he has made his way to the area above the Western

Wall plaza in the ancient walled city to pray. Jewish prayer at the Temple Mount is currently prohibited by Israeli law.[10] But this lawmaker considers such prohibition an infringement of his freedom to worship. To pray on the Temple Mount, he explains, to pray at the very site of the ancient Temple built in Jerusalem with the direction of God, is a deeply spiritual experience. But Jewish prayer in this location has become quite contentious. Glick posts videos of himself attempting to make his way to the Temple Mount and being stopped by Israeli police. One video shows him standing in a corner, near some steps blocked by policemen, as he engages in deep, heartfelt prayer. When he was elected to the Knesset, Israeli newspapers printed a photograph of him shaking hands with the prime minister. In his other hand, Glick held a large, framed photo of the Temple Mount.

Jewish prayer on the Temple Mount is controversial for both religious and political reasons. Some Jewish religious leaders forbid prayer there because the site is so holy that only the high priests of Judaism (*Kohanim*) should ever be allowed to approach it, and then only after ritual purification. Others forbid it to avoid creating a situation in which state law rather than rabbinic interpretation of Jewish law (*halakha*) will determine norms for prayer. Other religious leaders believe Jews should be permitted to pray on the Temple Mount. But the place known as the Temple Mount to Jews is also known as al-Haram al-Sharif (the holy sanctuary) by Muslims. It is the location of two of the world's most important mosques, one of which marks the place from which the Prophet Mohammed is said to have ascended to Heaven. The Dome of the Rock and Al Aqsa Mosque are more than a thousand years old, and al-Haram al-Sharif/the Temple Mount has become a site of intense political contention.

In September 2000, then-Israeli Prime Minister Ariel Sharon made a highly publicized and controversial visit to the Temple Mount. This visit was seen as a direct provocation by many Palestinians, and it is often considered the spark that began the Second Intifada (uprising), also known as the Al-Aqsa Intifada. But Glick, representing the Likud Party and also a founding member of the Temple Mount Institute, does not think that Jews should be prevented from praying at this holy site. In fact, he sees no reason why Jews and Muslims should not share the spiritual experience of prayer there. Such prayer, he thinks, could lay the foundations for peaceful coexistence. The Temple Mount Institute is an organization dedicated to rebuilding the ancient Jewish Temple on the site of its ruins. The organization runs a museum and visitor's center where they tell the story of the First and Second Temples in Jerusalem and raise funds to rebuild and restore its glory to Jerusalem.

Haredim might see the state and its secular foundations as threatening to Jewish ways of life, even threatening to Judaism itself. Historically, Haredim have seen the very existence of the current state that calls itself Jewish as contradictory

to what being Jewish means. The establishment of the state violates Jewish theology. A Jewish state will only—should only—arrive with the coming of the
Messiah. Human beings should not intervene in divine processes. National-
religious Jews, on the other hand, view the secular foundations of the state as
temporary. Their theology reverses Enlightenment inspired ideas of progress.
For the nationalist-religious, secular Zionism is the metaphorical shell that will
disintegrate and nourish the religious seed that is its true core, its destiny. Based
on the teachings of Rabbi Abraham Isaac Kook, nationalist-religious Jews have
a vision of a messianic future that includes the reestablishment of the Temple
in the place "that the Lord has chosen for all eternity" (Rabbi Kook quoted in
Inbari 2009, 33). Thus, when nationalist-religious beliefs and practices come
into conflict with the state policies, this is all part of a process leading toward
redemption. While many left-wing and secular Israeli Jews see the nationalist-
religious as threatening to peace and therefore to the very existence of the state
of Israel, religious nationalists may view state policy as interfering with the fulfillment of God's promise to His people to live on all the Land of Israel and
to rebuild the Temple in Jerusalem (Dalsheim 2011). But they are certain that
His promise will ultimately be fulfilled. And, their perspective has been steadily
moving from the margins to the center of Israeli politics.

God's Sovereignty

In either case, human political sovereignty—the sovereignty of "the people"—
cannot take precedence over the true sovereign of the universe. On this point,
both these groups of observant Jews seem to agree: God is the true sovereign, and
His law is to be obeyed first and foremost.

Ironically, the conflicts each of these groups has with the state are nearly mirror opposites. Some analysts have argued that what appear as conflicts between
members of the nationalist-religious community and the state are not really conflicts at all. Instead, the state actually tolerates and even encourages religiously
motivated settlers to break the law (Mendelsohn 2014). Religiously motivated
settlers set up illegal outposts in post-1967 Israeli occupied territories, which are
sometimes dismantled, but also often become permanent, state-sanctioned communities (Zertal and Eldar 2007). Thus, one might argue that this sector of the
Israeli population is currently sovereign in Schmitt's (1985) sense—they make
the law and its exception. Some of the ultra-Orthodox, on the other hand, have
control over decisions regarding who is a Jew, and who will be granted citizenship
under Israel's right of return. They have control over marriage and family law for
Jewish citizens and its exceptions. In Agamben's (1998, 2005) terms, we might

say that they have control over determining whose lives will count as "political life." Perhaps, then, the ultra-Orthodox should be considered sovereign, that is, as those who bear sovereign agency. But what about the secular Zionists, the founders of the state and their descendants?

Impossibilities

Aliza, the newly observant Jewish woman, had a cousin who was planning his wedding. Ari and his fiancé never cared much for religious observance, but they are proud, patriotic Israeli Jews. Ari and Anna were born in Israel and grew up there. They both served in elite combat units in the army and continue to have their regular lives interrupted by calls to serve in the army reserves. Now, the two are ready to get married, and they have been trying to plan their wedding. But secular Jews in Israel, those who make up the majority, can be made to feel like strangers in their own country when they want to marry.

The state-sponsored Orthodox Rabbinate has control over Jewish marriage and family law, and only Orthodox wedding ceremonies are recognized by the state. So, any Jewish couple that marries must follow Orthodox rules and procedures. This young couple was more interested in the food they would serve at their wedding than anything else. They found a caterer and booked a venue. But the caterer apparently was not officially certified as kosher. This meant that the Rabbinate would not perform the wedding because they will not perform ceremonies in a place where nonkosher food is being served. They cannot defy Jewish law in order to perform a Jewish wedding. The happy couple was not so happy anymore. They began to seek alternatives. Maybe they could get married at the offices of the Rabbinate and have their party another day. But they really were hoping their family and friends could be there with them and that the marriage and the party could coincide. "Is that too much to ask?" Anna wondered. And Ari found the whole situation completely absurd. "I'm not inviting the Rabbi for dinner," he said. "I'm just asking that he perform the ceremony. Why should he care if the food is kosher?"

Ari and Anna were annoyed, but not surprised. Many of their friends ran into complications with the Rabbinate for all sorts of reasons. Women are required to undergo ritual purification prior to the ceremony. They must visit a *mikve*, a ritual bath, and be inspected in the nude for cleanliness by an Orthodox woman whose job it is to oversee the bath. Many women refuse to partake in this ritual, and some try to find ways around it. Sometimes a woman will send her sister or friend in her place to avoid the unpleasantness and circumvent the rules, which some women consider highly offensive.

The Rabbinate also determines who is considered Jewish based on family genealogy, and only Jews are permitted to marry other Jews. Sometimes people have difficulty demonstrating their family history. Some people might have converted to Judaism or be descendants of converts, or they might have had only one Jewish parent. Others might have names that do not sound Jewish or fail to be able to produce Jewish marriage documents for their parents or grandparents. These are only some of the obstacles secular Israelis encounter when they try to get married. Secular Israeli Jews sometimes find the rules and processes of getting married in Israel so troublesome that they choose to travel abroad. A growing number of Jewish citizens elect to leave the country—the Jewish state—so they can more easily get married. Nearby Cyprus has developed a vibrant wedding-tourism industry catering to them. These obstacles seem to undermine the possibility of enacting sovereign agency, or in the very least make such agency conditional.

Free to Be Jewish?

> "Who are these people? Who are these people?" He shouted in Yiddish . . . "Goyim! [Gentiles!] Ben Gurion and his goyim will build Eretz Yisroel? They will build for us a Jewish land? They will bring Torah into this land? Goyishkeit they will bring into the land, not Torah! God will build the land, not Ben Gurion and his goyim! When the Messiah comes, we will have Eretz Yisroel, a Holy Land, not a land contaminated by Jewish goyim!"
>
> —Rebbe Isaac Saunders in Chaim Potok's *The Chosen*

While members of the strictly observant Haredim Orthodox community have control over marriage and family law, they also often feel their way of life may be threatened because they live in a state they see as far from Jewish. Indeed, some orthodox Jews would suggest that secular Zionists are more gentile than gentiles themselves and dangerous to Jews and Judaism.[11] For these Jews, sovereignty might be tantamount to collective suicide (Rabkin 2016, 2006). "The Jewish State" under such conditions might be seen as a threat to Jews as severe as that posed by settler-colonial regimes to the indigenous populations whose culture, traditional ways of living, and local communal norms they destroy.

Patrick Wolfe has written about the ways in which assimilation to settler society can be understood as another form of elimination—genocide—for native peoples. It is not the same as mass murder, Wolfe explains, but when a people are reeducated to the norms, culture, and language of those in charge, the outcome is very much the same. The continuity of that people is at stake (Wolfe 2006). Haredim in Israel are generally considered part of the sovereign ethnos who make up this ethnonational state. Yet, their norms, culture, and language are threatened by forces aimed at assimilating them through mandatory conscription in the armed forces, nonrecognition of Yiddish as a national language, and through attempts to change their school curriculum to include "secular" subjects so that they can be made more productive to the Israeli economy.

While Haredim struggle to hold on to their traditional way of life, the nationalist-religious have been gaining power in successive Israeli governments. Nonetheless, they must sometimes break the law to pray at their most holy sites. Haredim have felt their traditional way of life and life itself for Jews threatened in Europe and must continue to struggle for their way of life in the modern state of Israel, facing European Enlightenment values that consider their ways of life a thing of the past. But the nationalist-religious movement, which is also challenged by government regulations and policy, ironically only exists *because* of the state and because of the modern idea of liberation through popular sovereignty over territory. And secular Israeli Jews, descendants of the founders of the modern state, must struggle against state authorities to have a Jewish wedding in their own country. While these are a just a few of the countless examples of the struggle to be Jewish in the self-proclaimed Jewish state, they seem to indicate that the establishment of Israel has precluded some of the kinds of liberation that self-determination promises, and in some sense actually endangers the continuity of the Jewish people.[12]

The establishment of the state creates an illusion that there can be a "Jewish" citizen; a particular kind of unity or uniformity that is also somehow different from traditional understandings of what being Jewish means. Sovereignty relies on there being "a people" over whom the sovereign rules. Popular sovereignty suggests that "people" are sovereign, having achieved political self-rule. And yet, such freedom for those "people" also produces them—"the people"—in ways that call into question what precisely popular sovereignty connotes. Thus "sovereign agency," too, is revealed as illusive, always partial and necessarily exclusionary.

The story of why these seemingly bizzarre situations occur in Israel is often told as part of a narrative of an ongoing religious-secular struggle over the character of the modern Jewish state that can trace its history to what is known as the "status quo" agreement (Ben-Porat 2013).[13] This was a compromise arrangement that the secular state made with Orthodox Jewry, giving certain rights and powers to the Orthodox community. According to many of the secular Jews who make up the majority of the population, this agreement was a mistake and should be rectified. If religion and state are separated, they argue, life would be much improved because secular Jewish Israelis would no longer suffer from what they see as religious coercion by the Orthodox. But this interpretion misses a more fundamental set of issues relating to identity, history, political power, and legibility.

The early Zionist aspirations for self-determination of the founders of the state were based in Enlightenment ideals: aspirations for liberation and equal rights based on post–French Revolution modern, secular notions. But what kinds of "liberation" could these ideals promise? Secularism is generally understood as the modern project of separating religion and politics, or religion from the state. In modern states this separation should protect freedom of religion by protecting religion from state interventions and by protecting citizens against religious impositions. But more recent theorizations of the secular have shown how secularism can also *prevent* such freedoms; that, in fact, the secular is a space in which the state determines what counts as legitimate religion in the first place. The secular modern has produced understandings of religion that emerge from a primarily Protestant idea (Asad 1993, 2011; Keane 2007) in which "belief" is privileged over practice and religion is conceived as a private or individual matter. In the case of Israel the inherent contradictions embedded in secular modern ideals come into dramatic relief. Zionism was, at its inception, a marginal movement. As Yacov Rabkin reminds us, there has always been Jewish social, political, and religious opposition to the Zionist project. "Most practicing Jews," he writes, referring to nineteenth-century Europe, "both Orthodox and Reform, rejected Zionism . . . as a project . . . that conflicted with the values of Judaism" (Rabkin 2016, 122).

In "secular states" the supposed separation of religion and state does not end religious conflict. Instead, it exacerbates it (Mahmood 2016). But, I would argue, Israel is also a special case because Jewishness is at once conceived of as a "religion" (Batnitzky 2011) within the framework of the secular imaginary, and a nationality. Because the state of Israel was established as a "Jewish" state, being Jewish is an integral part of citizenship. Through its official rabbinate, the state determines who is a Jew and intervenes in what Jewishness means in countless ways. In contemporary Israel we find a broad range of ways in which Jews struggle over the definition of Jewishness, and with and against each other and the state over being Jewish. This includes control over practices (Lahav 2013) and over bodies (Weiss 2002). There are all sorts of laws and regulations aimed at *keeping* people Jewish, such as prohibiting Jews from working on the Sabbath, which can interfere with some people's ability to make a living. Some struggles to be Jewish are marginalized or ignored, others are primarily conceived as details to be worked out as part of a narrative of progressive freedom, and yet others are seen as crucial to determining the character of the state. Approaching these issues by gauging who is winning or losing the presumed religious/secular struggle emphasizes the partiality of any claim to speak on behalf of "the people." In addition, it also misses a far more fundamental set of issues: racialization, the separation of "Jew" from "Arab," what counts as "religion" and freedom of conscience, and what it means to be an ethical community (Goodman and Fischer 2004; Raz-Krakotzkin 1996; Shenhav 2003; Dalsheim 2011; Anidjar 2006; Derrida 2008; Land and Boyarin 2012).

In the modern state of Israel being Jewish has come to mean, first and foremost, not being Arab because "Arab" designates the enemy (Anidjar 2003; Derrida 2008; Shohat 1988). Thus for Jews from the Middle East and North Africa, including Jews who lived in Palestine before the establishment of the current state, being Jewish has entailed enduring the force of assimilation to a form of Israeliness that denigrates Arabness and equates it with being the enemy.[14] For Haredim, it has meant struggling against the forces of assimilation that denigrate their way of life as backward and belonging to the past. For secular Jews it has meant struggling to become "European" by leaving Europe, in the sense of emulating the European nation-state. And, for the nationalist-religious it has meant waiting for the secular shell of the Zionist state to disappear so that people can finally be Jewish.

Hannah Arendt wrote that emancipation for European Jews should have meant acceptance into society "as Jews." Instead, they were asked to assimilate, to be citizens in public and Jews at home. Or they were asked to convert to Christianity. But neither option would ensure their survival in Europe. Israel claims that its existence makes it possible for the Jews to flourish, in Arendt's terms, "as Jews," and yet the forces of assimilation seem to have followed the Jews to Israel. Such forces of assimilation have been equated with cultural elimination, which, according to Patrick Wolfe, should be considered tantamount to genocide by other means. After all, what does survival and continuity of a people mean when language, culture, norms, systems of law, and economy must be transformed for such "survival"? If assimilation is best understood as another form of the elimination of a people, then Zionism is inherently self-destructive. It destroys the people for whom it was established by conflating sacred practice with national identity, reproducing the political structures of exclusion that led to the near destruction of the Jewish people in Europe and the conditions in which that people could claim the need for sovereign self-determination as a means for survival. All of which raises questions about the *existential* nature of existential sovereignty. Political sovereignty may physically protect people while at the same time endangering particular aspects of their culture. Does a people continue to exist without its norms, traditions, social and economic system, and general way of life? We know that no national group is ever coterminous with humanity, but as this chapter illustrates, gaining national sovereignty does not mean that all "the people" will have equal access to sovereign agency. Indeed, sovereign agency will always be partial, contested, and necessarily exclusionary.

Notes

1. This chapter is part of a larger project that includes my book, *Israel Has a Jewish Problem: Self-Determination as Self-Elimination* (2019).

2. For the purpose of clarity, I maintain a sharp distinction between these groups in this chapter. But it should be clear that, as with all cultural groups, neither of these is completely internally homogenous nor is either one culturally static. Indeed, some of the distinctions between these groups are shifting as nationalist-orthodox Jews come to reject state sovereignty in some cases and Haredi Jews become more accepting of the state in others. See Dalsheim 2011 and 2019, and Harel 2015 for additional details.

3. These strictly observant Jews, often referred to as the "ultra-Orthodox," include a range of theologically strict adherents to the Torah. While the term *ultra* Orthodox seems strange, it has been used to distinguish among a variety of observant Jews. The ultra-Orthodox themselves, generally see themselves as "Jews" and use the term *Haredi* to refer to their community when communicating with outsiders. One Haredi woman told me, "Haredi is a counter-culture." It arose as something definable in resistance to tendencies toward assimilation in post-Enlightenment Europe.

4. This was reported in the Israeli daily newspaper *Haaretz* on February 28, 2014. Israeli daily papers reported other members of the ultra-Orthodox community would organize to protest because of the importance of Torah study. One rabbi reportedly commented that the purpose of the state of Israel is to support Torah study.

5. The Belzer Hasidim follow the descendants of a spiritual leader from the town of Belz in the Ukraine. The majority of Israeli Jews are secular and, according to most estimates, strictly Orthodox Jews make up only about 10 percent of the entire population of Israel. The Belz Jewish community in Ukraine was nearly completely destroyed when the Nazis invaded. They reestablished themselves in Israel and in New York.

6. Strictly observant Jews had been exempt from military conscription since the establishment of the state of Israel in 1948. This was part of an agreement, known as the "Status Quo Agreement," reached with the first prime minister of the new state, David Ben Gurion.

7. National-religious might be more accurately called "nationalist-religious" because even national holidays have been integrated into the religious practices of this group, including special prayers for Israeli Independence Day. Thus "dati leumi" is often translated as religious Zionist. From here forward, I will use the term nationalist-religious.

8. A new wave of violence against Palestinians, called "price tag" retaliations, began following the 2005 disengagement from Gaza. Being angered by the actions of their government, particularly about removing settlers from their communities in the Gaza Strip and destroying their homes, some settlers had begun exacting punishment on Palestinians every time the Israeli government made a decision they opposed.

9. For more detail on religiously motivated settlers see Lustick 1988; Dalsheim 2011; Zertal and Eldar 2007; Feige 2009; and Aran 1991.

10. Visiting the site is closely monitored by Israeli authorities. Non-Muslims are permitted to visit at designated times. Jews may visit but are prohibited from prayer. Jewish

sacred items, like prayer books, are also prohibited as are any outwardly religious displays. Since 2015, Israeli parliament members have been prohibited from visiting the site, although the current government may reverse that decision.

11. Rebbe Saunders is a fictional character in Chaim Potok's well-known novel, *The Chosen*. His words, spoken in the novel's chronology in the mid-1940s, here represent early reactions to Zionism among Hasidic Jews.

12. This issue is explored in greater detail in Dalsheim 2019.

13. The Status Quo agreement was a set of arrangements made in the form of a letter sent by the man who would become Israel's first prime minister, David Ben Gurion, to the leaders of the ultra-Orthodox party, Agudat Israel. Ben Gurion was about to meet with the UN Special Committee on Palestine and was negotiating with religious factions for political support just prior to the establishment of the state. The letter promised that ultra-Orthodox yeshiva students would be exempt from military service. It included statements about the character of the future state, which would observe Saturday (Shabbat) as its official day of rest, and would maintain Jewish dietary laws in all public establishments. This meant mandatory closing of stores and public services on Shabbat. It also gave authority over matters of family law, marriage, divorce, and burial to the Orthodox.

14. For more on the question of Mizrahim, or Arab Jews, see Anidjar 2006; Chetrit 1997; Dalsheim 2008; Khazzoom 2005; Motzafi-Haller 2001; Raz-Krakotzkin 2005; Shenhav 2006; Shohat 1988; Yiftachel 1998.

References

Agamben, Giorgio. 1998. *Homo Sacer: Sovereign Power and Bare Life.* Translated by Daniel Heller-Roazen. Stanford, CA: Stanford University Press.

Agamben, Giorgio. 2005. *State of Exception.* Translated by Kevin Attell. Chicago: University of Chicago Press.

Althusser, Louis. 1971. "Ideology and Ideological State Apparatuses (Notes towards an Investigation)." In *Lenin and Philosophy and Other Essays*, 127–186. New York: Monthly Review Press.

Anidjar, Gil. 2003. *The Jew, The Arab: A History of the Enemy.* Stanford, CA: Stanford University Press.

Anidjar, Gil. 2006. "Secularism." *Critical Inquiry* 33: 52–77.

Aran, Gideon. 1991. "Jewish Zionist Fundamentalism: The Bloc of the Faithful in Israel (Gush Emunim)." In *Fundamentalisms Observed*, edited by Martin E. Marty and R. Scott Appleby, 265–344. Chicago: University of Chicago Press.

Arendt, Hannah. 2003 (1948). "The Perplexities of the Rights of Man." In *The Origins of Totalitarianism*, in *The Portable Hannah Arendt*, edited by Peter Baehr, 31–45. New York: Penguin.

Asad, Talal. 1993. *Genealogies of Religion: Discipline and Reasons of Power in Christianity and Islam.* Baltimore: Johns Hopkins University Press.

Asad, Talal. 2011. "Thinking about Religious Beliefs and Politics." In *The Cambridge Companion to Religious Studies*, edited by Robert Orsi, 36–57. New York: Cambridge University Press.

Batnitzky, Liora. 2011. *How Judaism Became a Religion.* Princeton, NJ: Princeton University Press.

Ben-Porat, Guy. 2013. *Between State and Synagogue: The Secularization of Contemporary Israel.* Cambridge: Cambridge University Press.

Bonilla, Yarimar. 2017. "Unsettling Sovereignty." *Cultural Anthropology* 32(3): 330–339.

Boyarin, Jonathan. 1994. "The Other Within and the Other Without." In *The Other in Jewish Thought and History: Constructions of Jewish Culture and Identity*, edited by J. Silberman and R. L. Cohen. New York: New York University Press.

Chakrabarty, Dipesh. 2000. *Provincializing Europe: Postcolonial Thought and Historical Difference*. Princeton, NJ: Princeton University Press.

Chatterjee, Partha. 1986. *Nationalist Thought in the Colonial World: A Derivative Discourse?* Minneapolis: University of Minnesota Press.

Chetrit, Sami Shalom. 1997. "The Dream and the Nightmare: Some Remarks on the New Discourse in Mizrahi Politics in Israel—1980–1996." *News From Within* 13: 49–59.

Dalsheim, Joyce. 2008. "Twice Removed: Mizrahim in Gush Katif." *Social Identities* 14(5): 535–551.

Dalsheim, Joyce. 2011. *Unsettling Gaza: Secular Liberalism, Radical Religion, and the Israeli Settlement Project*. New York: Oxford University Press.

Dalsheim, Joyce. 2019. *Israel Has a Jewish Problem: Self-Determination as Self-Elimination*. New York: Oxford University Press.

Derrida, Jacques. 2008. "Abraham, the Other." In *Religion: Beyond a Concept*, edited by Hent de Vries, 311–338. New York: Fordham University Press.

Fader, Ayala. 2009. *Mitzvah Girls: Bringing up the Next Generation of Hasidic Jews in Brooklyn*. Princeton, NJ: Princeton University Press.

Feige, Michael. 2009. *Settling in the Hearts: Jewish Fundamentalism in the Occupied Territories*. Detroit: Wayne State University Press.

Foucault, Michel. 1988 (1982). "Technologies of the Self." In *Technologies of the Self: A Seminar with Michel Foucault*, edited by Luther H. Martin, Huck Gutman, and Patrick H. Hutton. Amherst: University of Massachusetts Press.

Foucault, Michel. 1991 (1978). "Governmentality." In *The Foucault Effect: Studies in Governmentality*, edited by Graham Burchell, Collin Gordon, and Peter Miller. Chicago: University of Chicago Press.

Goldshmidt, Henry. 2006. *Race and Religion among the Chosen Peoples of Crown Heights*. Piscataway, NJ: Rutgers University Press.

Goodman, Yehuda, and Shlomo Fischer. 2004. "Towards Understanding Religiosity and Secularism: The Secularism Thesis and Alternative Conceptualizations." In *Maelstrom of Identities*, edited by Yossi Yonah and Yehuda Goodman, 346–390. Jerusalem: Kibbutz HaMeuchad and Van Leer.

Harel, Assaf. 2011. "Highway 60 Visited: Part 1." *Anthropology Now* (March 4). http://anthronow.com/online-articles/highway-60-visited.

Harel, Assaf. 2015. "The Eternal Nation Does Not Fear a Long Road: Time among Jewish Settlers." Ph.D. diss., Department of Anthropology, Rutgers University.

Inbari, Motti. 2009. *Jewish Fundamentalism and the Temple Mount: Who Will Build the Third Temple?* Albany, NY: SUNY Press.

Keane, Webb. 2007. *Christian Moderns: Freedom and Fetish in the Mission Encounter*. Berkeley: University of California Press.

Khazzoom, Aziza. 2005. "Did the Israeli State Engineer Segregation? On the Placement of Jewish Immigrants in Development Towns in the 1950s." *Social Forces* 84(1): 115–134.

Lahav, Pnina. 2013. "Israel's Rosit the Riveter: Between Secular Law and Jewish Law." *Boston University Law Review* 93: 1063–1083.

Land, Martin, and Jonathan Boyarin. 2012. "The State between Race and Religion: A Conversation." In *Race and Political Theology*, edited by Vincent W. Lloyd, 213–233. Stanford, CA: Stanford University Press.

Lustick, Ian. 1988. *For the Land and the Lord: Jewish Fundamentalism in Israel*. New York: Council on Foreign Relations.

Mahmood, Saba. 2016. *Religious Difference in a Secular Age: A Minority Report*. Princeton, NJ: Princeton University Press.

Mendelsohn, Barak. 2014. "State Authority in the Balance: The Israeli State and the Messianic Settler Movement." *International Studies Review* 16: 499–521.

Motzafi-Haller, Pnina. 2001. "Scholarship, Identity, and Power: Mizrahi Women in Israel." *Signs: Journal of Women in Culture and Society* 26(3): 697–734.

Nandy, Ashis. 1995. "History's Forgotten Doubles." *History and Theory* 34(2): 44–66.

Ong, Aihwa. 1996. "Cultural Citizenship as Subject-Making." *Current Anthropology* 37(5): 737–750.

Potok, Chaim. 1967. *The Chosen*. New York: Fawcett Crest Books.

Rabkin, Yakov. 2006. *A Threat from Within: A Century of Jewish Opposition to Zionism*. Translated by Fred A. Reed. London: Zed.

Rabkin, Yacov. 2016. *What Is Modern Israel?* Translated by Fred A. Reed. London: Pluto Press.

Raz-Krakotzkin, Amnon. 1996. "A Religious-Colonial Nationalism: A Review of Ya'akov Barnai's Historiography and Nationalism: Directions in Research on the Land of Israel and its Jewish Settlement, 634–1881." Magnes Press, Jerusalem.

Raz-Krakotzkin, Amnon. 2005. "The Zionist Return to the West and the Mizrahi Jewish Perspective." In *Orientalism and the Jews*, edited by Ivan Davidson Kalmar and Derek J. Penslar, 162–181. Waltham, MA: Brandeis University Press.

Said, Edward. 1979. "Zionism from the Standpoint of its Victims." *Social Text* 1: 7–58.

Schmitt, Carl. 1985 (1922). *Political Theology: Four Chapters on the Concept of Sovereignty*. Chicago: University of Chicago Press.

Shafir, Gershon, and Yoav Peled. 2002. *Being Israeli: The Dynamics of Multiple Citizenship*. London: Cambridge.

Shenhav, Yehouda. 2003. "The Cloak, the Cage and Fog of Sanctity: The Zionist Mission and the Role of Religion among Arab Jews." *Nations and Nationalism* 9(4): 511–531.

Shenhav, Yehouda. 2006. *The Arab Jews: A Post-Colonial Reading of Nationalism, Religion, and Ethnicity*. Stanford, CA: Stanford University Press.

Shohat, Ella. 1988. "Sepharadim in Israel: Zionism from the Standpoint of its Jewish Victims." *Social Text* 19(20): 1–35.

Sivan, Emmanuel. 1995. "The Enclave Culture." In *Fundamentalisms Comprehended*, edited by Martin E. Marty and R. Scott Appleby, 11–68. Chicago: University of Chicago Press.

Weber, Eugen. 1976. *Peasants into Frenchmen: The Modernization of Rural France 1870–1914*. Stanford, CA: Stanford University Press.

Weiss, Meira. 2002. *The Chosen Body: The Politics of the Body in Israeli Society*. Stanford, CA: Stanford Univesity Press.

Wolfe, Patrick. 2006. "Settler Colonialism and the Elimination of the Native." *Journal of Genocide Research* 8(4): 487–409.

Yiftachel, Oren. 1998. "Nation-Building and the Social Division of Space: Ashkenazi Control over Israeli Periphery." *Nationalism and Ethnic Politics* 4(3): 33–58.

Yiftachel, Oren. 2006. *Ethnocracy: Land and Identity Politics in Israel/Palestine*. Philadelphia: University of Pennsylvania Press.

Zertal, Idit, and Akiva Eldar. 2007. *Lords of the Land: The War for Israel's Settlement in the Occupied Territories 1967–2007*. New York: Nation Books.

SIGNS OF SOVEREIGNTY

Mapping and Countermapping
at an "Unwritten" Border

Madeleine Reeves

In November 2004, I moved into the home of Parviz and Sharofat, a couple in their early thirties, to undertake research in Uzbekistan's Sokh *tuman* (district). Sokh is a Tajik-majority district and, with a population of more than fifty-five thousand in twenty-three village (*mahalla*) communities, it is Central Asia's largest territorial exclave.[1] Sitting in the adobe guest room that they had recently added to their home, Parviz, Sharofat, and I spent an evening shortly after my arrival looking over the books that I had acquired over the preceding months of ethnographic fieldwork on the other side of the exclave's border, in Kyrgyzstan's Batken *oblast'*.

It was an incongruous assortment, and most of the books left the couple underwhelmed. When I showed them a small book on yellowing paper that I had bought from a street-seller in Khujand, Tajikistan, however, Parviz suddenly became animated. Rahim Masov's *Istoriia topornogo razdeleniia* (The History of a Blunderous Delimitation), published in Tajikistan in 1991 and translated into English in 1996 as *The History of a National Catastrophe*, is an explicitly revisionist and ethnonational (indeed, nationalist) historiography of the national-territorial delimitation of Central Asia. The front cover of Masov's original 1991 text shows a map with the borders of the Tajik Soviet Socialist Republic (Tajik SSR) superimposed on an older map depicting the Bukharan emirate and Samarqand *oblast'* in Turkestan *krai*: the administrative divisions that predated the creation of national republics in Soviet Central Asia.

Masov's text is a classic of late-perestroika revisionism and a particularly poignant text for Tajik-identifying citizens of Uzbekistan such as Parviz. It describes the local politics of the early Soviet delimitation that occurred between 1924 and 1936, a process that left the newly established Tajik SSR deprived of the historically Persian cultural and spiritual centers of Samarqand and Bukhara, as well as from Tajik-majority agricultural districts, such as Sokh.[2] The cover of Masov's book renders this historical injustice in stark primary colors: a small mountainous republic all that remains of a vast Persianate space. The unequal outcomes of the delimitation are cast in Masov's text as the result of a conspiracy by pan-Turkic elites that continued a long-standing civilizational drama of Tajik/Uzbek and Persian/Turkic animosity. The text is at once revelatory and polemical, drawing on previously censored archival materials and drafted in a context of vocal perestroika-era commentary on the "national question" in Tajikistan (Epkenhans 2016, 62–64; Suyarkulova 2011; Scarborough 2018, 136).[3]

Masov's book appeared when Parviz himself was resident in the Tajikistan capital during the heady—and ultimately violent—days of late perestroika. Like many Tajik-speaking young men from Sokh who had finished school in the 1980s in what was then a provincial district at the eastern fringes of the Uzbek SSR, he had moved to the capital of the Tajik SSR to gain a higher education in his native language, training, as linguistic minorities often did in Soviet Central Asia, as a teacher of Tajik language and literature. He had been present in the Tajikistan capital for the first—and still relatively muted—demonstration of perestroika outside the Tajik Supreme Soviet in February 1988, when calls had been made for Tajik to become the official language of the Tajik SSR. Parviz had come across Masov's book during his years in Dushanbe, but it was inaccessible now in Uzbekistan, and its searing political critique of pan-Turkic "chauvinism" would make it politically unpalatable there. Tajikistan's civil war (1992–97) and the authoritarian peace that followed the war had led to a cooling of relations between Uzbekistan and Tajikistan, leading Parviz and other bilingual, Dushanbe- educated young men of his generation with a profound sense of loss and cultural isolation from a wider Tajik-speaking space. On another occasion, Parviz commented how on a rare visit to Tajikistan (for which, as a citizen of Uzbekistan, he now required a visa), he discovered that the "language had progressed without us": the Tajik of Tajikistan, formalized in newspaper text and replete with newly coined vocabulary, was now increasingly distant from the Uzbek-inflected version spoken in Sokh.

These contexts made Masov's book a "sensitive object" (Frykman and Przanović Frykman 2016, 20) in Sokh. Parviz held my copy for a long time before opening it. He seemed to be both excited by this reencounter with Masov's work and perturbed by it, evoking as it did a moment of impassioned commentary on previously censored themes and the increasingly tense prelude to civil war in newly independent Tajikistan. It was also an illicit object of sorts. To be seen reading such an explicitly critical and anti-Uzbek text in Sokh might invite curiosity, commentary, a visit from the security services. Parviz first asked me whether he could borrow Masov's book to read. Then, after a few moments leafing through the text, he thought better of it and returned the book to me. He instructed me to keep it out of sight at the bottom of my rucksack.

A vignette about a perestroika-era book and the ambivalent response that it elicited fifteen years later might seem an unusual place from which to approach the question of sovereignty and its social lives. Discussions of sovereignty, after all, tend to lead us quickly to considerations of statehood and its attributes: to control, to the marking of populations beyond the protection of law; to taxation and subordination; to territory and its integrity; and—perhaps especially in a post-Soviet context—to "verticals of power." It invites, in other words, a particular kind of scalar thinking in which sovereignty "stretches" (with more or less success, more or less reach) from the center of a polity to its multiple peripheries. This is sovereignty approached, we might say, from the sovereign: from the question of how the founding order of a polity—and ultimately, the capacity to "decide on the exception" (Schmitt 1985)—is asserted, sanctified, and sustained.

My focus in this chapter, by contrast, is on sovereignty as it appears and disappears from view in everyday life in sites where that stretch and reach is contested or problematic. It is concerned with the social circulation of sovereignty claims that are understood to be contingent, arbitrary, and ultimately fragile, and it is an exploration of one particular material form, the map, through which such assertions are both articulated and contested. In this respect, my approach is both indebted to, and distinct from, recent studies of sovereignty that have sought to account for, interpret, and explain the capacity of the (singular) sovereign in a given social field to decide on the exception, to articulate and enforce the boundary between "bare" and "political" life. New political configurations in the wake of 9/11 drew scholars' attention to the question of sovereign violence as the durable "hard kernel of modern states" (Hansen and Stepputat 2005, 296) and led them to think about power beyond governmentality and biopolitics. As we discuss in the introduction, much of this recent engagement with sovereignty has taken inspiration from the Italian political philosopher, Giorgio Agamben, and his Schmittian political theology of sovereignty as the capacity to "decide on the exception": that is, to determine which beings within a polity are to be included within the protection of law, and which are excluded, denied a fully political existence (Agamben 1998). Agamben's provocative argument, and the descriptive categories with which he has become associated—bare life, homo sacer, the state of exception—have proven immensely generative within social anthropology, even as his own work was abstract and emphatically nonempirical. It also spoke to a particular intellectual moment when making sense of the performative violence of the sovereign (the sovereign of "shock and awe," of "flushing out terrorists") felt politically urgent. Like other chapters in this collection, however, my ethnography attempts to approach sovereignty from another direction: less concerned with what "the" sovereign, as presumed singularity, does than with how sovereignty appears and disappears from view from the perspective of the thinking, feeling, desiring, mobilizing subject—or the prospective future subject—of a politically sovereign space. Drawing on several periods of fieldwork over the course of a decade (2004–14) in Central Asia's Ferghana Valley, and focusing here on fieldwork around two geographical exclaves, Sokh (Uzbekistan) and Vorukh (Tajikistan), I explore how sovereignty might appear differently if we track its movement through claims, names, and objects as they circulate and reverberate in the region of a historically contentious and still, in parts, officially "unwritten" (*neopisany*) and internationally disputed border.

The Sokh and Isfara valleys, side valleys of the larger Ferghana basin, provide a generative site for such an enquiry. These are regions of multiple, and often competing, modes of regulatory authority and sovereign claims on space. Here, alongside the border forces and security services of three newly independent states, one encounters the interventions of parity commissions and drug control agencies; development initiatives and large-scale infrastructure projects aimed at "securing" the border; a variety of local big-man patrons who sponsor local infrastructure projects in return for political loyalty; and now, increasingly, Chinese mining companies prospecting for gold and other metals.

Sometimes these agencies and agents work in tandem with each other; sometimes they are violently opposed. Along the borders between the states that meet here—Kyrgyzstan and Uzbekistan in the Sokh Valley, Kyrgyzstan and Tajikistan in the Isfara Valley—authority is rarely transparent and uncontested. In Batken town, the district capital of Kyrgyzstan, forty kilometers from Parviz and Sharofat's home in Sokh, for instance, stories often circulated about the indignity suffered by a high state official who was stopped by a "mere" border guard and asked for his documents, or about fights between the customs officers of neighboring states who had claimed primacy in control over the spoils from a lucrative customs post (compare chapter 2, this volume). Claims of territorial primacy were also often signaled and contested in the fabric of daily life: in flags mounted and torn down, in fences mounted or destroyed; or more mundanely, in the language used to name a given village or landmark. In the Sokh and Isfara valleys, for instance, many settlements have colloquial "Kyrgyz" and "Tajik" variants, and their use in daily life can be read as a way of gesturing toward claims of histori-cal primacy: Batken or Botkand? Tangy or Kapchygai? Kök-Tash or Govsuvar? Machai or Khojai-A'lo?

In a situation of contested histories, moreover, the challenge for local residents was often not so much that of "obeying the law" as knowing "whose rules rule" (Kuehnast and Dudwick 2008) in any given encounter. Local residents became adept at reading the signs of sovereignty—or, we might say, of *sensing* sovereignty as it figured in particular institutions, objects, and people: in flags, in uniforms, in white jeeps, in gifts of infrastructure or "humanitarian aid" at election time, or in the "cool" license plates of wealthy and well-connected individuals. Claims to represent or authorize state power were also often contested. A local taxi driver, for instance, might assert a (fictional) relation to the district procurator when stopped for speeding by a traffic policeman as a way to avoid a fine; an elderly woman might shout out indignantly that she is "from here" when stopped by a young uniformed man asking her for her passport. Though this was a zone of contested sovereignty, it was not, I want to suggest, therefore, a site of state "weakness" or "failure": indeed, the "state" in the person of the border guard, the customs officer, or the national security agent was often experienced as viscerally and excessively present here. Rather, my aim in this chapter is to attend to the intrinsic partiality and indeterminacy of sovereignty: the fact that sovereignty is a claim that needs to be both articulated and recognized for it to work, and that such claims may be multiple and contested (Rutherford 2012).

I focus on maps, and stories of past mappings and countermappings, as a vehicle for exploring these local signs of sovereignty and their (non-)recognition in everyday life. There is a simple empirical reason for this focus. Throughout this volume, chapters have charted the totemic power of airlines to represent sov-ereign agency, the ways in which exiled administrative infrastructures may rep-resent a sovereign will, and how diasporic peoples may constitute an existential sovereignty. Maps have a particularly critical role to play in producing an affect of sovereignty at the juncture between people and territory. Maps define the nation's "geo-body" (Winichakul 1997), and when the maps represent contested terri-tories, they produce "cartographic anxieties" (Kabachnik 2012; Krishna 1994) about the nation's integrity. Moreover, because territory is inextricably linked to property, contests over mapping often play out at the local level through tales of belonging told in the sale of property (Bryant 2010).

Maps have a particular resonance in border villages of the Ferghana Valley as objects that are seen to formalize "illegitimate" exchanges of land, past and present. By codifying and normalizing de facto changes in the border and accord-ing the stamp of state authority, past territorial configurations are erased and the (often murky) politics that went into their production are concealed. The cover of Masov's book is one such example: the overlaid maps through which the graphic is composed visualizing a story of territorial loss and conspiratorial deceit. Through their circulation across borders and through their articulation with other objects, maps may elicit desire, hope, betrayal, or a more diffuse sense of historical injustice. They are also "sensitive" objects in the sense that they gesture toward a feeling, often articulated but rarely diagnosed, that state territory itself is liable to shift and that the line between de facto and de jure is often vanishingly small: a new map, or a new road, or even an illicit orchard plot or rejigged fence might just bring about a change in the very contours of the state. As such, maps render visible and material the paradox of law-making violence at the heart of all sovereign claims.

Foregrounding the map in this way, as an affectively charged material artifact and a circulating sign of sovereignty, moves my analysis in a slightly different direction from much of the illuminating critique of cartography that has emerged in recent anthropology and critical geography, focused on the map as representational mode and tool of knowledge production. This literature has highlighted how, in their two-dimensional simplifications of spatial relations, maps can reify ethnic and linguistic complexity, erase subaltern histories of place, discipline national subjects, and freeze dynamic and changing geographies into static geometrical space (e.g. Jansen 2005; Neocleous 2003). This literature has illuminated how mapping is linked with power, and with the differential capacity to "see" and identify in graphic form which differences (ethnonational, religious, economic, and so on) matter.

Maps are powerful technologies of rule, to be sure. But for all their power to represent, to distort, and to discipline national subjects, maps are not merely two-dimensional abstractions. Nor, in regions of contested territoriality, is their truth value necessarily taken for granted. For maps are also material objects that get hung on walls, hidden in safes, copied, passed around, written on and written over, discarded, or reprinted on the cover of national histories such as Masov's *History of a National Catastrophe*. In their presence and absence, their marks and their gaps, in what they represent and what, because of their scale, their size, their age, or the time-lag in their production, they fail accurately to represent, in their papery (in)substantiality and their links to an authoritative state gaze, they elicit intensely powerful responses from those who handle them. As Franck Billé has shown in an insightful exploration of what he calls territorial "phantom pains" on the Russia-China border, maps "come to act as an organizing principle of nation-bound affect"; that is to say, they elicit strong emotive attachments that "frequently exceed or run counter to the state's explicit aims" (2014, 167). Their materiality matters, just as much as their form or their representation of sovereign reach.

Moreover, as objects that necessarily gain traction as meaningful social forms only in relation to other objects and infrastructures, maps exceed their own rational and representational logics. This is not just because their particular aesthetic and representational form serves to render some information and some causal relations visible, while obscuring others. It is also because their political efficacy depends on the capacity of maps to reembed, and in so doing to articulate with other persons or things, becoming, for those who navigate or negotiate with them, a habitual reminder of materialized inequalities or histories of violence. My approach, then, considers maps to be not simply technologies of rule, or expressions of a state's "will to legibility" (Scott 1998) but performative and affectively charged material objects that, in appearing, disappearing, and circulating in a given social field, open up and foreclose particular political possibilities.

Like documents that obfuscate even as they claim to reveal (Kelly 2006; Pinker 2015), maps are both material and referential; they both reveal (an identity, a spatial relation, a claim about what exists) *and* they conceal (the conditions of their own manufacture; the decisions that underlie a given representation of the truth). In their visible forms and their invisible movements, maps can obfuscate as much as they can illuminate; they can foster uncertainty as well as transparency; they can quietly recast issues of justice into questions of technical expertise or a natural geographical order of things. It is this that makes them sensitive things. Indeed, the very materiality of such objects, I would suggest, is critical for understanding their capacity to move between settings, to appear banal one moment and saturated with political significance the next.

Signs of Sovereignty

It is in this sense, I want to suggest, that we can consider maps in the Ferghana Valley as signs of sovereignty through which a particular awareness of violence and arbitrariness at the heart of state-making erupts into daily life. Sovereignty, in this reading, is not an a priori correlate of state rule so much as a distributed set of capacities that may be institutionally and personally dispersed. Drawing on research in the Central African Republic, in a region where state presence is fleeting and contingent at best, Louisa Lombard (2012) focuses attention on what she calls, following political theorist, Hugo Grotius, "marks," or capabilities of sovereignty. In this region of multiple and competing sources of authority, Lombard examines the different modes or forms that authority takes and the capacities that different agents have to extract tribute, provide security, guarantee claims, undertake diplomatic relations, and so forth.

For Lombard, a mark, or capability, of sovereignty, is "a mode of authority exercised in relation to others bearing perhaps overlapping, or perhaps more-or-less separate, modes of authority" (2012, 5). Whereas Lombard focuses on how such capabilities are manifest in this region of experiential abandonment by the state, however, my interest is primarily on how certain materialized signs of sovereignty come to be locally registered, interpreted, and contested. For those modes of authority, disparate and contested as they are, depend on a host of accompanying signs for their recognition: for a border guard to be recognized as a bearer of state authority, for instance—rather than simply a "goat in uniform" as they are often described in Batken—depends on particular signs (a uniform, a gun, a state insignia on the shoulder) being accorded legitimacy and recognized as something other than a fake. Sovereignty, in other words, is a relational claim, and as such it is fragile: it depends on the repeated performance of assertion and recognition for its efficacy.

Of the multiplicity of state insignia that one can find here, maps have a particular salience as signs of sovereignty: more specifically, an artifact bearing traces of *past* sovereign claims, and of the opaque relations that came to sanctify a claim of ownership or a mark of sovereign reach. Maps—or state-issued maps, at least—articulate a singular relationship between place and national territory, and in so doing they erase history and modes of belonging to places that do not fit into a nation-state frame: modes of belonging defined, for instance, by seasonal migrations, by the sacred geographies of martyrs' graves, and by memories of ancestral lands that today transect state boundaries.

Moreover, in a region of repeated attempts at redelimiting republican borders to keep up with changing land use and settlement patterns, maps also reveal the instability and arbitrariness of particular territorial claims. They can never quite keep up with reality: they are always merely partial representations of an actually existing geography. The Ferghana Valley is a region that has been progressively delimited and redelimited during the twentieth century, eliciting contested histories of autochthony and belonging, competing memories of entitlement and ownership, swathes of officially contested borderland (*spornaia territoriia*), and a great deal of speculation concerning the deliberate or unintended consequences of particular practices of demarcation. Border negotiations between Kyrgyzstan and Tajikistan, for instance, have stalled since the two countries' independence because the two states refer to different maps from different eras as the basis for negotiation: a 1958 map that is recognized as "official" in Kyrgyzstan, because the territorial exchanges that it reflects were ratified by the Supreme Soviet of the Kyrgyz Soviet Socialist Republic, does not have the same authority in Tajikistan, where the Supreme Soviet of the Tajik SSR never ratified the prior exchanges of land and where a 1927 map is taken as authoritative.

If maps are recognized here to be "sensitive objects" because of their capacity to erase and manipulate history (that is—because of a particular capacity to represent and to represent differently) their material work as signs of sovereignty here also derives from the fact that they are themselves, in their materiality and their elusiveness, the focus of intense affective claims: of hope, of desire, but also of suspicion and intrigue. A certain kind of map has a ubiquitous presence in the Ferghana Valley, to be sure—the outline map of a state, usually monochrome, often portrayed as floating in a sea of surrounding nonspace—typically revealing little detail of topography or geography. This is the map as icon rather than as tool for navigation: its symbolic function is analogous to that of the image of the flag, the visage of the president, or the coat of arms. It is usually found nailed high on a wall: it is to be viewed and committed to memory rather than carried or used.

But maps for navigation are rare and may be regarded with suspicion (Who gave you that? What are you doing with it? What does it portray?). When I showed the late Soviet regional maps that I had bought in the Kyrgyzstan capital, Bishkek (at a ratio of 1:100,000, hardly the scale that would be useful to a spy), friends and interlocutors in the Ferghana Valley often responded with surprise, and sometimes with indignation and suspicion, as they sought to map their lived geography, and in particular, their own learned, experiential geography of territorial limit points, within the precise orange limit lines provided by the map. On more than one occasion my interlocutor told me outright that the map that I had was "wrong": that Kara-Bak village did not end there; that the border did not run like that. Maps, then, are not just "artefacts of modern knowledge" (Riles 2006); they are constitutive of contemporary forms of subjectivity through the uncertainty and suspicion they foster—and thus, I would add, are intrinsic to the way that contemporary geopolitical formations are encountered and mediated.

Moving Borders, Making Maps

To unpack this idea a little I want to turn to the distinctive spatial history of the Ferghana Valley borderlands. My ethnographic examples come from fieldwork in the Sokh and Isfara valleys, at the southern rim of the Ferghana basin. Like the densely populated Sokh Valley, where Parviz and Sharofat live, the Isfara Valley is a region historically characterized by a pattern of overlapping Kyrgyz and Tajik settlement, a fact reflected in the density of Turkic and Persianate toponyms and the multiplicity of settlements and sacred sites that have both Kyrgyz and Tajik names (Bushkov 1990). For much of the pre-Soviet and Soviet period, the residential formation was characterized by a pattern found throughout southern Ferghana, with predominantly agricultural Tajiks found in the irrigated valley basin, and predominantly pastoral Kyrgyz moving seasonally between low-lying winter settlements and higher summer pastures. Postwar Soviet resettlement policies aimed at sedentarizing pastoral populations, together with population increases and the conversion of small collective farms into larger, industrially managed state farms (*sovkhozy*), led to a radical reconfiguration of this landscape in the last few decades of Soviet rule (Bushkov 1995). New areas were made available for cultivation due to the expansion of irrigation infrastructure, and the dispersed populations of high mountain settlements were consolidated into so-called planned villages in the valley basin. Previous patterns of Kyrgyz and Tajik settlement were transformed into a so-called chessboard formation, with Kyrgyz and Tajik villages, subordinate to Kyrgyz and Tajik republics respectively, organized into contiguous mono-ethnic villages in the valley basin. The villages in the Isfara Valley are characterized by some of the highest population densities anywhere in Central Asia.

The Isfara River and the irrigated lands surrounding it was crisscrossed multiple times by interrepublican borders between the Kyrgyz and Tajik soviet republics. There was little in the way of boundary markers here, however: road and irrigation infrastructures crossed back and forth between the two neighboring republics; markets and land plots often de facto transected the interrepublican boundary, and residents on either side crossed with little awareness of the administrative boundaries. Moreover, as Kyrgyz and Tajik collective farms and village settlements expanded to accommodate new agricultural lands, so, de facto, did the respective republican boundaries.

In the postwar years a variety of parity commissions sought to regularize the borders between the two republics, recognizing, as the 1949 parity commission put it, that previously published maps no longer reflected the actual distribution of land between the Kyrgyz and Tajik SSRs:

> In order to prevent future potential land conflicts and misunderstandings in the use of unallocated (*neraspredelennykh*) lands, [we] . . . consider it imperative in the near future to clarify the interrepublican boundaries between the Tajik SSR and the Kirgiz SSR, considering that the borders shown on the maps . . . published in 1938–40 do not reflect the actual location of both republics [*fakiticheskogo raspolozheniia obeikh respublik*], as a result of which fourteen collective farms belonging to Batken district of the Kirgiz SSR have found themselves [having lands] within the borders of the Tajik SSR, including settlements belonging to eight of these collectives. (Alamanov 2010, 39–40)

Repeated parity commissions between the 1950s and 1980s sought to "clarify" these apparently indeterminate borders. That process of clarification, however, typically consisted of readjusting the current republican boundaries according to existing land use and residential configuration, rather than reaffirming the sanctity and inviolability of the original national-territorial delimitation. This was everyday sovereignty in an informal key: the precedent, established through the visits of repeated parity commissions in the postwar era was that the existing de facto boundaries of Kyrgyz and Tajik collective farms should be used to determine the future de jure boundaries of the respective Kyrgyz and Tajik republics.

Although appeals were made not to cultivate "indeterminate" land, economic pressures to meet five-year plans and expand the areas brought under irrigated agriculture led to constant pressures to readjust the interrepublican borders. The principle of notional "sovereignty" as enshrined in the USSR constitution thus ran up against the very different logic of late Soviet developmentalism: of expanding production and cultivation; of "consolidating" dispersed villages and sedentarizing nomadic populations; of expanding irrigated agriculture as a means to boost economic growth. Neither parity commissions nor their cartographers could keep up with an ever-shifting reality of residential settlement. The map was always a claim toward a reality that no longer existed.

Public discussion of such land exchanges was relatively muted during the postwar decades of "developed socialism," when internal Soviet borders represented few obstacles to regional mobility or trade and "brotherly friendship" muted public criticism of unjust border readjustments. With perestroika, however, rising commentary throughout Central Asia on the "national question" gave new momentum to critiques of past border policies, and in particular, to the ongoing indeterminacy over where the interrepublican boundaries lay. This was the era, after all, of Masov's revisionist history of the national-territorial delimitation of Central Asia; and it was a moment of growing grievance in Uzbekistan especially about the deleterious impact of land and water shortages, overgrazing, and the cotton monoculture on rural livelihoods (Poliakov 1992). As Epkenhans (2016, 61) has argued in his analysis of perestroika-era Tajikistan, "through the lens of Tajik intellectuals, the border delimitation of Soviet Central Asia in 1924/1929 was the last chapter of the continuous marginalization and humiliation of the Tajiks by the Uzbeks," one that summarily disconnected Tajiks from their historical cultural and religious centers of Samarqand and Bukhara. Perestroika allowed such local grievances to be catalyzed by experiences of growing insecurity into public articulations of discontent and, when other contingent conditions materialized, to morph into overt displays of intercommunal violence.

In the Isfara Valley, the most significant such dispute occurred in the spring and summer of 1989 when members of the 100 Years of Lenin collective farm (a "Kyrgyz" farm at the edge of the Kyrgyz SSR) began constructing individual residential plots on land that was disputed between the two republics. Local tensions over land and water use had flared up periodically over the preceding decades. What was new by the late 1980s was the possibility to report on them (comparatively) openly and to appeal to politicians to give voice to local grievances. Writing in the heady perestroika days of 1989 in the regional Tajik newspaper, *Leninabadska Pravda*, the journalists Kriuchkov and Morozov launched a searing attack on the failures of previous parity committees, which had created the conditions for current conflicts to escalate. Drawing on a metaphor from Russian literature that likened the work of boundary drawing to cutting out a piece of cloth from a roll of fabric, these commissions, they argued, had acted "on the principle of Trishkin's coat," when in order to fix the torn elbows of the coat "you cut out a part of the sleeve, and to mend the shortened sleeves you cut away at the coat-tails." Repeated commissions had sought to remedy past failures in determining the location of interrepublican boundaries but in doing so, they "hastily [*v pozharnom poriadke*] tried to put out the hot-spots without solving the problem in any global way." Today, the authors concluded,

> we urgently need the borders of land use to be determined in a completely clear and legally rigorous way. We are not just talking about the redrawing [*perekroika*] of the borders between the two republics, but also about a clear determination of the right to appropriate empty lands. These need to be resolved at the very highest levels. All the preceding republican commissions didn't resolve anything. (Kriuchkov and Morozov 1989)

In September 1989, in the wake of a spring and summer of unprecedented violence that had left many people injured, crops devastated, and a curfew in place, one more parity commission arrived in the Isfara Valley on the order of the Supreme Soviet to try to establish the "definitive" interrepublican border. According to the protocol of the meeting between the respective First Secretaries of the Kyrgyz and Tajik SSRs, published simultaneously in the Kyrgyz and Tajik press, the parity committee would be charged with "specifying the line of the border between the republics . . . proceeding from the de facto existing land use between the republics" (*iskhodia iz fakticheski slozhivshegosia zemlepol'zovaniia mezhdu respublikami*). The committee was charged with studying all of the relevant documents since the establishment of the two republics in the 1920s and 1930s and redefining the current location of the border based on current land use (*S uchetom vzaimnykh interessov 1989*).

The commission was given two months in which to conduct its work (Isliamov 1989)—a remarkably short amount of time to resolve disputes that had been simmering for years. The results of the 1989 committee appear never to have been published, nor to have been ratified by the respective Supreme Soviets of the Kyrgyz and Tajik SSRs, creating the conditions for ongoing disputes over the rightful location of the border to independence and into the post- Soviet period. Indeed, it is a bitter irony of history that in May 1991 the new presidents of the Tajik and Kyrgyz SSRs were due to meet to discuss the intractable disagreement over maps, the Tajik side having decided that the only authoritative map that could be used as a reference document dated from 1927 rather than 1955 (Shozimov, Beshimov, and Yunusova 2011, 194). The newly appointed president of the Kyrgyz SSR, Askar Akaev, failed to attend the meeting, however, and the issue remained unresolved, even as the very institutions of the Soviet state came tumbling down over subsequent months.

"Straight Away They Put it on the Map"

Fifteen years later, when I began conducting fieldwork in the Isfara Valley, the indeterminacy that these authors had lamented in the final years of the Soviet Union was heightened by the fact that Kyrgyzstan and Tajikistan were now negotiating their borders as independent states without the pressure or the mediating hand of the Soviet center. In the Isfara Valley, multiple tracts of land, some of them just a few hectares in size, others hundreds of hectares large and now densely built up with homes, schools, and garden plots, remained officially "undescribed" (*neopisany*) and disputed between the two states. While daily life was mostly peaceable, according to informal understandings of where "Tajikistan" and "Kyrgyzstan" began and ended based on the residential distribution of "Kyrgyz" and "Tajik" homes, the *map* was an object that was seen with a great deal of suspicion.

At stake in the post-Soviet negotiation of the now interstate border was not just the line of the border itself, but the normative acts and accompanying maps—ratified in one Soviet republic but not the other—that would act as the basis for future negotiation. As I was later told, when the availability of internet connections in border villages allowed people to engage with Google Maps' bird's-eye view of their region, "even America can't agree where the border is": the orange, pixelated boundary line cutting through a satellite image of Isfara Valley homes strikingly out of synch with lived geographies of the border.[4] In this context, maps seemed to figure less as indices of truth ("this is where the border *really* is") than as material manifestations of historical injustices and shady illicit exchanges.

A small vignette from one of my periods of fieldwork, when maps burst into the weave of conversation, can help to illuminate. In March 2010, a lengthy conversation at the home of Anvar-aka, who lived in Ak-Sai village in the Isfara Valley, became animated when we were joined by a relative who was visiting from further down the valley from the village of Kök-Tash. Anvar had been telling me about the history of his own resettlement to Ak-Sai village, from a so-called futureless (*besperspektivnoe*) village high in the mountains above the Isfara Valley in the 1970s. As Mansur joined us, however, our conversation switched from the frustrations of territorial indeterminacy to the historical "gifting" of land for money and favors and the violent inscription of such exchanges "into the map":

> ANVAR: It turned out like that—Kyrgyz, Tajik, Kyrgyz, Tajik—because our leaders back then didn't divide up the land properly. The Tajiks used to have a place up there that they needed to reach. . . .

Mansur, intervening, corrected his relative, and the conversation continued in a vigorous exchange between the two men about the "gift" of a 270 meter stretch of road:

> MANSUR, INTERRUPTING: No! I'll tell you. In those days the Kyrgyz had lots of land and the leaders sold it.
> MADELEINE: Sold it?
> MANSUR: To the Tajiks. For money.
> MADELEINE, QUERYING: This was in Soviet times?
> MANSUR: Yes.
> ANVAR: This was at the time of the Union, at the very time when socialism was on the way.
> MADELEINE: And did it happen with some permission from above?
> MANSUR: Without any permission. You would never get permission if you were to ask for it!
> ANVAR: [It was] in 1956. I can tell you. Look, at that time there was just one [Kyrgyz] collective farm. It was a time when they were just beginning to divide it. Until that time, Samarkandek, Ak-Sai, Kök-Tash, Ravat—all of these were just one collective farm. And then they divided it into two—Ak-Sai and Kök-Tash were separated. . . .
>   It used to be the Lenin Sovkhoz at that time. The 100 Years of Lenin Sovkhoz—it was divided into two. There was a [collective farm] director who came at that time, Kondakov, who was responsible for telling people where to graze their cows. And he would say to people, "Look, the Tajiks want a route to drive their animals. They have become an enclave, the Tajiks have requested a route. You should give them permission to pass their animals through."

MANSUR, IMITATING KONDAKOV: "You should give them a road"

ANVAR, IMITATING KONDAKOV: "They need a road to Chychyrkana—to the pastures on the side of the river." *But* [Kondakov] *turned those into Tajik land!*

MANSUR: You see, they are like that! They asked for a route to a bit of land, and from a bit of land they just asked for a route to cross over. But straight away they put it into the map [*srazu kartaga kirip koet*]. Later, later, little by little [*kiiin, kiiin, postepenno, postepenno*] they wrote it all in.

The agent of this illicit action here remains ambiguous (Kondakov himself? Soviet elites? Tajik elites? The leaders of the collective farm?), just as the detail of the exchange of land for money remained murky and unspecific in this account. Later in the conversation, in response to my question of how the transfer of money allegedly occurred, Anvar elaborated:

There are lots of pieces of land like that near Kök-Tash. There was the Jumabai brothers' land, Sapyr's brothers' land, Belek's brother's land. All that land along the river, that was Kyrgyz land. And Kondakov would say to them, "Eh, Jumabai aka can you free up that land so the Tajiks can cross over with their animals as they are asking. We'll give you some other land." And then he sold it to the Tajiks.

MADELEINE: Sold it in the direct meaning?

ANVAR: How do you give money to a Sovkhoz? They didn't show us the money, of course! You find an intermediary and leave it with them. But then people said to the director, "Hey, I gave you permission for a temporary crossing [through my land]." But then they found that their land had been sold! *The map had been changed.*"

What is significant here, I would suggest, is the way in which an action that is recalled as illegal and immoral—treating as alienable land that had been merely loaned temporarily, and "selling" it to the neighboring republic—is legitimized through the act of insertion into the map: it is the inscription and codification that gives official weight to an unofficial act of exchange; that formalizes a moment of sovereign violence into a moment of "normal" politics and eventually into the routine "taken for granted" of regional geography. For once the map is there, the border reinscribed to erase past ownership of land, how can one contest it, even though—as Anvar was eager to prove to me—he knew exactly who the land along the river used to belong to. He could show it to me, he said.

On the Tajik side of the border in the Isfara Valley, such grievances concerning past illicit exchanges of land are, if anything, even more intense. As Olimova and Olimov (2017, 28) have argued, if the Kyrgyz have tended to understand claims on land through narratives of repeated seasonal mobility, codified through practice and custom, for ethnic Tajiks cultivating land along the valley floor, local understandings of rightful ownership are largely traced back to nineteenth-century *waqf* documents endowing land to be used by a given mahalla community in perpetuity (25). While such characterizations of so-called ethnic territoriality may overstate contrasting ways of apprehending territorial claims by historically nomadic and historically sedentary populations, it is unambiguously the case that for many of those descended from the sedentary population of the valley basin, the fact of land being "given away" by Soviet authorities to the newly resettled Kyrgyz in the late Soviet period was remembered as an affront to pre-Soviet modes of reckoning ownership through waqf.

The enforced sedentarization of formally nomadic populations in the valley basin, together with dramatic increases in population during the twentieth century, meant that multiple new villages were created on what were remembered as "Tajik" lands.[5] In the case of the larger settlements in the Isfara Valley, Chorkuh and Vorukh, such "giving away" was apparently compounded by concerns on the part of the Soviet authorities to undermine these settlements' status as centers of religious learning and pilgrimage.[6] Whatever the intention, the effect in practice was to create a situation in which villages on both sides of the border, including Chorkuh in Tajikistan and Ak-Sai in Kyrgyzstan, found themselves as de facto enclaves upon independence, surrounded on three sides by the borders of the neighboring state, and on the fourth by sheer mountains that are both impassable and impossible to irrigate.

In 2011, the head of the village community immediately bordering Kök-Tash on the Tajik side of the border, Chorkuh, gave an interview to a Dushanbe journalist about his own perception of where the "illicit" land exchanges lay. Recalling the last Soviet-era parity commission of 1989, the village head, Abdukhalil Sharipov, gave a strikingly similar account of illicit land exchanges to the one that I had recorded with Anvar and Mansur the previous summer in which the moment of cartographic inscription was also critical. Instead of the Tajiks being favored in the exchange, however, it was the agricultural residents of the valley basin who suffered through the shady actions of the leadership of what was then the Tajik Pravda kolkhoz:

> The last time that land was divided between Tajikistan and Kyrgyzstan was in 1989. At that time the head of the commission from among the

rayon and oblast' leaders, who was representing our republic, didn't act fairly. They put together a map, according to which all of the lands beyond the last house [in Khoji-A'lo village, in the Tajik SSR] would be counted as Kyrgyz. As a result of which, all four mountains that surround our village have remained the property of our neighbors.

Here, too, the map making serves as the final illegitimate act: the writing that sealed an opaque and questionable exchange. Sharipov, in turn, referenced an older set of documents in order to dispute the authenticity of the 1989 map:

> I've got a load of historical manuscripts demonstrating the fact that this land belonged to our ancestors. As late as the start of the twentieth century, the khan of Kokand, Khudayarkhan confirmed, with his stamp and his signature, that a vast area of land belonged to Mullo Khakimbai Chorkuhi, who came from Chorkuh. [On that basis] we could make claims on land going twenty kilometers deep inside Kyrgyzstan. (Rasul-Zade 2011)

What we see in both of these vignettes is a recollection of past territorial injustice in which a leader or leaders acted "unfairly" or in their own mercenary interests to bring about an illicit exchange of land. In both cases, moreover, what seals the injustice is not so much a decree or ratification by a Soviet body as the fact of "putting together a map" that is powerful as much for its scarcity and local invisibility as through its capacity to circulate.

On Mapping and/as Violence

I turn now to a second ethnographic example, in which the map and its attendant sovereignty claims became an object of considerable political contention. In January 2014, just a few hundred meters from Anvar's home, Kyrgyz and Tajik border forces exchanged fire at one of several stretches of disputed interstate border. This was an unusual incident in its scale and its repercussions: while confrontations between border troops and civilians are frequent and rarely make national headlines, the conflict in January 2014 involved heavy weapons that left several border troops on both sides of the border hospitalized.

The immediate context for the conflict was the resumption, in early January 2014, of construction of a stretch of "bypass road" by Kyrgyzstani construction workers. The road would, for the first time, allow herders from Ak-Sai and downstream Kyrgyz villages to access their summer pastures above the Vorukh enclave without having to pass through Tajikistani territory. Attempts at road construction had been repeatedly initiated over the preceding months, and repeatedly stalled as Tajikistan claimed that the new road, rather than lying five hundred meters within Kyrgyzstani territory, in fact lay on land that was (still) officially "undescribed" and therefore subject to a moratorium on any new construction (Azattyk 2013; Dzhumasheva 2013; Reeves 2014a).

At stake in the dispute were two key issues: which map was to be taken as the authoritative basis for legitimizing (or prohibiting) construction, and what the consequences of the new road would be. According to the maps referenced by the Kyrgyzstani authorities, dating from 1989, Tajikistan had no right to dispute the route of the proposed road since it was more than five hundred meters inside the territory of Kyrgyzstan. But Tajikistani authorities insisted that the 1989 map carried no authority, since the interstate boundaries that it purported to show—while they had indeed been ratified by the Kyrgyz SSR—had never been ratified by the Supreme Soviet of the Soviet Union and thus carried no legal weight (Reeves 2014a, 251). According to my interlocutors in Vorukh, moreover, the new road was much more than a benign route of passage: it was effectively a way of de facto asserting the geographical limits of this enclave district, one that would "hem people in" through the presence of Kyrgyzstani border troops.

A more general, and politically sensitive, issue also appeared to lie behind the dispute. In the Isfara Valley, a fragile cross-border peace was maintained—or, perhaps, more accurately, an ongoing dispute was "frozen" and prevented from escalating—by the fact that Kyrgyz and Tajik villages alike relied on a shared water source (the Isfara River) and an intersecting road network. Periodic local border disputes were contained by the fact that pressure exerted on one side could be met with equal pressure on the other. If one community were to block the road access or to divert irrigation water from downstream users, their action would be mirrored by parallel water or road closure by lower-lying villages on the other side of the border. In this way, the incentives on both sides to resolve disputes were strong: neither side could survive long without access to irrigation water, or without road access to the local market. One of the key concerns for those in Vorukh was that the presence of the new road would reduce the incentives for their Kyrgyz neighbors to deescalate tensions, unsettling the delicate balance that kept an everyday peace more or less durable.

As the dispute escalated, with ambassadors recalled from the respective capital cities and mutual accusations of border troops illegally firing into the neighboring state's territory, a series of maps published in the respective national media themselves became objects of contention. On January 17, the head of the Tajik border forces, Major General Sharaf Faizulloev, accused Kyrgyz border troops of illegally crossing into Tajikistani territory, his claims accompanied by a map, indicating the line of the international border as it existed—in an official Tajik reading—at the time of the incident. Three days later, Kyrgyzstan's largest circulating newspaper, *Vechernii Bishkek*, responded with a very public map of its own, captioned as a "reply to the scheme presented by General Faizulloev." "On the map of the Border Forces of the Republic of Tajikistan," the headline read, "the territory of Kyrgyzstan has been reduced by 500 hectares" (*Na karte Pogranvoisk RT territoriia Kyrgyzstana umen'shilas' na 500 ga*) (Uraliev 2014). The map published in *Vechernii Bishkek* presented two sets of borders: the (putatively real) "Kyrgyz-Tajik border at the current moment" and the (putatively illegitimate) "Version of the Kyrgyz-Tajik border presented by the border forces of the Republic of Tajikistan." Highlighted in yellow on the map were several stretches of land—including village districts currently under Tajikistani administration—that Kyrgyzstan asserted to be part of Kyrgyzstani territory.

Here, again, the map that was published on the pages of the national press served both to assert a claim—this is where the border *really* lies—and to highlight the alleged sleight of hand that went into the making of Faizulloev's competing border claims. While the intention in publishing the map on the part of Kyrgyzstan's security and military authorities was perhaps one of clarification for a public who saw the Isfara Valley dispute as opaque and increasingly intractable, the effect, both for urban readers of *Vechernii Bishkek* and for those whose lives were lived across the competing lines of the two contrasting maps, was to magnify the space of suspicion: through which opaque deals did we arrive at this situation? Why can no one agree who fired first? And how did this disagreement come into being?

Rather than laying to rest domestic anxieties, then, the map served precisely to magnify the recognition that sovereign claims are fragile and contingent—its depiction of territorial limits less a representation of how the land *really* lies than a reminder of the intrinsically fragile and contested nature of all such sovereign assertions. This case is instructive, I suggest, for our broader attempt in this volume to think about how sovereignty figures in the everyday: as claim, as assertion, as aspiration, perhaps—but also, perhaps, as source of suspicion; the map a materialized reminder of the arbitrariness and fragility of sovereign claims, and of the violence that subtends them.

Recent literature has shown how accounts of sovereignty derived from political philosophy can be nuanced through ethnographic attention to the way that jural and social "spaces of exception" come into being, how they function, and how they persist; or as Humphrey (2004) puts it, how sovereignty becomes entangled with "ways of life." Approaching maps through their entanglements, I suggest, can give us a handle—ethnographically and analytically—on "sovereignty" not as an abstraction of political theory, but as an empirical claim, as a practice and a field of contestation, that is, to sovereignty as a properly ethnographic object of enquiry. For where Agamben (1998) and others drawing on his theoretical apparatus are concerned with developing a theoretical account of the "exception" as it appears and is normalized in contemporary political formations, ethnographic accounts of such empirical spaces of legal suspension, from refugee camps to curfew zones to favelas under the control of drug barons to unrecognized (quasi-)state administrations have illuminated how such spaces are not necessarily experienced as places of pure "bare life." As Humphrey notes of the mafia-run public transport in Ulan-Ude, "Micro-sovereignty has its own distinctive ways of instantiating symbolizing authority, which imposes a specific kind of relationality with its subjects. . . . 'Pure sovereignty' is qualified by the necessity of manifesting itself in life" (2004, 435). Moreover, ethnographic studies of plural legal orders and sites of state weakness show that the violence of such sites often results less from the will of a singular sovereign than from the intersections and conflicts between disparate sources of power and the difficulty, for those who have to navigate such domains, of knowing the local "rules of the game." Power in such sites is unpredictable because it is experienced as illegible: as Dunn and Cons note of the border zones and refugee camps that they subject to comparative analysis, such spaces are more helpfully thought of as "sensitive" than as "exceptional," where "more or less autonomous sovereignties compete, combine and overlap with one another to produce an often unstable footing of sovereign power" (2014, 96).

What I have sought to demonstrate here, through ethnographic attention to the claims and anxieties that circulate at an "unwritten" border, is the way that maps and other documents are felt to certify and normalize movements in the border that are both immoral and illegal. "Writing into the map" thus becomes a gesture of sovereign violence: one that signals and materially manifests the lawmaking violence at the heart of state practice. But there is something more, too. For people living at these repeatedly moving republican and now international borders, the claim that state territory is, in a certain sense, "artificial" and that that artificiality has real material consequences is no abstract claim of constructivist social science. It is recognized and remembered in stories about the flying visits of parity commissions and politicians during the second half of the twentieth century; in rumors of exchanges of land that were made hastily or in bad faith; in appeals to unseen but known maps hidden in safes in regional archives; in claims of manipulation to previously stable cartographic representations; and in widely shared hopes that, with a bit more political will and better technology, the problems of tense transboundary coexistence could be resolved. In this sense, we might consider such claims and critiques themselves as a form of "sovereignty work," one that highlights the indeterminacy and arbitrariness that is at the heart of state practice.

Notes

1. Sokh district (*tuman*) is an exclave of Uzbekistan and an enclave of Kyrgyzstan: administratively part of Uzbekistan's Fergana *viloyat*, the district is entirely surrounded by the territory of Kyrgyzstan, and there are border and customs checks on each of the roads entering and exiting the district. Tajik remains the dominant language of school instruction and, as of the mid-2000s, of local administration.

2. On the historical dynamics that led to this situation during the process of national-territorial delimitation, see Haugen 2003, 74–108; and Khalid 2015, 270–277; for specific local contestation around Sokh and neighboring valleys, see Bergne 2007, 52–3; Koichiev 2001, 29–31.

3. Indeed, Suyarkulova (2011, 112) notes that at some point Masov's text was banned in Uzbekistan.

4. The interested reader can get a measure of this by entering "Vorukh" into the search facility of Google Maps. Zoom in at the northwestern end of the Vorukh exclave, where Vorukh meets the Kyrgyzstani village Ak-Sai, and three settlements come into view. According to Google Maps, all three are inside Kyrgyzstan. In contemporary de facto administrative terms, two of the three are administratively subordinate to Vorukh in Tajikistan. Zoom in further, and at the extreme Western edge of the second of these, there is a Kyrgyz village (Bakai) nestled inside a Tajik village (Tojikon) that is an extraterritorial unit of Vorukh, itself an enclave within Kyrgyzstan.

5. Bushkov (1990, 4), drawing on pre-Soviet and Soviet census data, shows that the Isfara Valley increased in population 11.9 times between 1870 and 1990, in part due to natural population growth and in part due to the forcible relocation and sedentarization of formerly nomadic populations.

6. Chorkuh, for instance, is home to a mausoleum and mosque honoring the twelfth-century Khazrati-Bobo, just as it is to Kum Mazor and Langari Mokhien, a sacred lake that remains an important local pilgrimage destination. As Olimova and Olimov argue, this may explain why, in 1958 and again in 1989, the residents of Chorkuh were forced to concede lands that had historically been part of the *waqf* endowment to Kyrgyz households that had relocated to the valley basin (2017, 26).

References

Agamben, Giorgio. 1998. *Homo Sacer: Sovereign Power and Bare Life*. Chicago: University of Chicago Press.

Alamanov, Salamt. 2010. "Ob istorii, sovremennom sostoianii i perspektivakh iuridicheskogo oformleniia Kyrgyzsko-Tadzhikskoi gosudarstvennoi granitsy." In *Kyrgyzstan-Tadzhikistan: kurs na ukreplenie partnerstva v kontekste regional'nykh sviazei*, ed. Nur Kerim, 38–42. Bishkek: Friedrich Ebert Stiftung.

Azattyk. 2013. Batkende jangzhal kairadan chykty. April 27. https://www.azattyk.org/a/kyrgyzstan_tajikistan_border_conflict/24970456.html.

Bergne, Paul. 2007. *The Birth of Tajikistan: National Identity and the Origins of the Republic*. London: I. B. Tauris.

Billé, Franck. 2014. "Territorial Phantom Pains and Other Cartographic Anxieties." *Environment and Planning D: Society and Space* 32(1): 163–178.

Bryant, Rebecca. 2010. *The Past in Pieces: Belonging in the New Cyprus*. Philadelphia: University of Pennsylvania Press.

Bushkov, Valentin. 1990. "O nekotorykh aspektakh mezhnatsional'nykh otnoshenii v Tadzhikskoi SSR." *Issledovaniia po prikladnoi i neotlozhnoi etnologii Seriia A: Mezhnatsional'nye otnosheniia v SSSR*. No. 9. Moscow: Institute of Ethnography of the Academy of Sciences of the USSR.

Bushkov, Valentin. 1995. *Naselenie severnogo Tadzhikistana: formirovanie i rasselenie*. Moscow: Russian Academy of Sciences.

Dunn, Elizabeth, and Joseph Cons. 2014. "Aleatory Sovereignty and the Rule of Sensitive Spaces." *Antipode* 41(6): 92–109.

Dzhumasheva, Aida. 2013. "Prichinoi konflikta u anklava Vorukh nazvaly nevernyi marshrut ob"ezdnoi dorogi." *Vechernii Bishkek*. March 2. https://www.vb.kg/doc/226880_prichinoy_konflikta_y_anklava_voryh_nazvali_nevernyy_marshryt_obezdnoy_dorogi.html.

Epkenhans, Timothy. 2016. *The Origins of the Civil War in Tajikistan*. Lanham, MD: Lexington Books.

Frykman, Jona, and Maja Povrzanović Frykman. 2016. *Sensitive Objects: Affect and Material Culture*. Lund, Sweden: Nordic Academic Press.

Hansen, Thomas Blum, and Finn Stepputat. 2005. *Sovereign Bodies: Citizens, Migrants, and States in the Postcolonial World*. Princeton, NJ: Princeton University Press.

Haugen, Arne. 2003. *The Establishment of National Republics in Soviet Central Asia*. London: Palgrave MacMillan.

Hirsch, Francine. 2000. "Toward an Empire of Nations: Border-Making and the Formation of 'Soviet' National Identities." *Russian Review* 59(2): 201–226.

Hirsch, Francine. 2005. *Empire of Nations: Ethnographic Knowledge and the Making of the Soviet Union*. Princeton, NJ: Princeton University Press.

Humphrey, Caroline. 2004. "Sovereignty." In *A Companion to the Anthropology of Politics*, edited by David Nugent and Joan Vincent, 418–436. Oxford: Blackwell.

Isliamov, A. 1989. "Sokhranit' mir v svoem dome." *Leninabadskaia Pravda*, August 31, 4.

Jansen, Stef. 2005. "National Numbers in Context: Maps and Stats in the Representation of the Post-Yugoslav Wars." *Identities* 12(1): 45–68.

Kabachnik, Peter. 2012. "Wounds that Won't Heal: Cartographic Anxieties and the Quest for Territorial Integrity in Georgia." *Central Asian Survey* 31(1): 45–60.

Kelly, Tobias. 2006. "Documented Lives: Fear and the Uncertainties of Law during the Second Palestinian Intifada." *Journal of the Royal Anthropological Institute* 12(1): 89–127.

Khalid, Adeeb. 2015. *Making Uzbekistan: Nation, Empire, and Revolution in the Early USSR*. Ithaca, NY: Cornell University Press.

Koichiev, Arslan. 2001. *Nasional'no-territorial'noe razmezhevanie v ferganskoi doline (1924–1927 gg.)*. Bishkek: Kyrgyz State National University Press.

Krishna, Sankaran. 1994. "Cartographic Anxiety: Mapping the Body Politic in India." *Alternatives* 19(4): 507–521.

Kriuchkov, Iu., and V. Morozov. 1989. "Byt' liud'mi! Reportazh iz zony deistviia komendantskogo chasa." *Leninabadskaia Pravda*, July 21, 1, 3.

Kuehnast, Kathleen, and Nora Dudwick. 2008. *Whose Rules Rule? Everyday Border and Water Conflicts in Central Asia*. Washington, DC: Social Development Department, World Bank.

Lombard, Louisa. 2012. "Raiding Sovereignty in Central African Borderlands." Ph.D. diss., Duke University.

Masov, Rakhim. 1991. *Istoriia topornogo razdeleniia*. Dushanbe: Irfon.

Neocleous, Marc. 2003. "Off the Map: On Violence and Cartography." *European Journal of Social Theory* 6(4): 409–425.

Olimova, Saodat, and Muzaffar Olimov. 2017. "Konflikty na granitsakh v ferganskoi doline: Novye prichiny, novye uchastniki." *Rosiia i novye gosudarstva evrazii*. 2017(1): 21–40.

Pinker, Annabel. 2015. "Papering over the Gaps: Documents, Infrastructure, and Political Experimentation in Highland Peru." *Cambridge Journal of Anthropology* 33(1): 97–112.

Poliakov, Sergei. 1992. *Everyday Islam: Religion and Tradition in Rural Central Asia.* Armonk, NY: M. E. Sharpe.

Rasul-zade, Tilav. 2011. "Chorkukh, ostavshiisia bez gor." *Asia-Plus,* April 26. http:// old.news.tj/ru/newspaper/article/chorkukh-ostavshiisya-bez-gor.

Reeves, Madeleine. 2014a. "Roads of Hope and Dislocation: Infrastructure and the Remaking of Territory at a Central Asian Border." *Ab Imperio* 2(2014): 235–257.

Reeves, Madeleine. 2014b. *Border Work: Spatial Lives of the State in Rural Central Asia.* Ithaca, NY: Cornell University Press.

Rutherford, Danilyn. 2012. *Laughing at Leviathan.* Chicago: University of Chicago Press.

Scarborough, Isaac. 2018. "The Extremes It Takes to Survive: Tajikistan and the Collapse of the Soviet Union, 1985–1992." Ph.D. diss., London School of Economics.

Schmitt, Carl. 1985. *The Concept of the Political.* Chicago: University of Chicago Press.

Scott, James. 1998. *Seeing Like a State: How Certain Schemes to Improve the Human Condition Have Failed.* New Haven, CT: Yale University Press.

Shozimov, Pulat, Baktybek Beshimov, and Khurshida Yunusova. 2011. "The Ferghana Valley during Perestroika, 1985–1991." In *The Ferghana Valley: The Heart of Central Asia,* ed. Frederick Starr, 178–204. Armonk, NY: M. E. Sharpe.

Suyarkulova, Mohira. 2011. "Becoming Sovereign in Post-Soviet Central Asia: Discursive Encounters Between Uzbekistan and Tajikistan." Ph.D. diss., University of St. Andrews.

Uraliev, Marat. 2014. "Na karte Pogranvoisk RT territoriia Kyrgyzstana umen'shilas' na 500 ga." *Vechnernii Bishkek.* http://www.vb.kg/doc/258537_na_karte_pogran voysk_rt_territoriia_kyrgyzstana_ymenshilas_na_500_ga.html.

Winichakul, Thongchai. 1997. *Siam Mapped: A History of the Geo-Body of a Nation.* Honolulu: University of Hawaii Press.

Epilogue

THE IRONIES OF MISRECOGNITION

Jens Bartelson

For all their apparent rigor, definitions of sovereignty are fountains of ambiguity that fuel a desire to attain mastery over our own destiny and sometimes also that of others. To most people in my trade—academic international relations— sovereignty is taken to mean the presence of supreme authority within a given territory, to which is often added that for a state to be fully sovereign, it must also be recognized as such by a sufficient number of other sovereign states. Sovereignty is thereby taken to be a defining characteristic of states, and those political entities that do not conform to the above requirements have routinely been pushed to the margins of international order and excluded from serious consideration by most students of international relations.

It is therefore with great joy I have read this wonderful collection of essays, since they not only detach the meaningful experience of sovereign agency from the state form, but also demonstrate how these experiences might have a destabilizing impact on the conventional understanding of what sovereignty possibly can mean and what functions it can fulfill. In a world in which the state no longer can be assumed to remain the predominant locus of political authority and community, groups of people aspire to sovereignty only to find their claims to self-determination unrecognized by the international community, or more often than not, misrecognized by its more established and powerful members. By the same token, people within fragile communities often seek to claim sovereign agency for themselves, only to find their aspirations perpetually unrecognized by their own dysfunctional governments or misrecognized by the powers that be within their societies.

As the editors of this volume point out, the conventional antidote to the tendency to naturalize the sovereign state has been to argue that sovereignty is nothing more and nothing less than what we make of it through linguistic and other practices. But since many of those who have contested the essence of sovereignty still presuppose that it is accessible to inquiry, they cannot but perpetuate a certain fetishism of sovereignty so that which is contested is nevertheless uncontested at a more fundamental level. Hence the remarkable staying power of sovereignty in legal and political theory, because of, rather than despite, the sustained efforts to deconstruct this concept. Sovereignty becomes an offer you cannot refuse, an ontological commitment that you cannot shake off without a loss of theoretical coherence. But beyond these questions lurks the undeniable fact that sovereignty—however defined and understood—remains an object of desire and collective aspiration, especially in those places where it is weak or absent. As the contributions to the present volume make clear, sovereignty remains an aspiration precisely among those who have never tasted its fruits or borne the brunt of its brutal excesses. But what makes this desire for sovereign agency meaningful to agents? And what, more precisely, is being desired by those who want to obtain or reclaim sovereignty, and in whose name are such claims being raised? Finally, granted that the connection between sovereignty and statehood is contingent rather than necessary, how are the actual desires for sovereign agency connected empirically to the state form?

These are some of the questions that the contributions to this volume seek to answer. And although the answers provided diverge, they seek to identify voices expressive of the unfulfilled desires for belonging made elusive by a precarious blend of historical accidents and blind fate. Granted that the desire for sovereign agency emerges from the sense of loss that almost invariably accompanies its absence or erosion, what does this desire imply in more philosophical terms? As some of the contributions to this volume make plain, even in those cases where the desire for sovereignty does not translate into a wish for statehood proper— rather it sometimes seems to be a clever way of avoiding its burdens—the fulfillment of sovereign agency nevertheless depends on recognition by relevant audiences, whomever they comprise in the context at hand.

The Politics of Misrecognition

In what follows, I will provide a gloss on the contributions to this volume by situating them in a different theoretical context. As I will suggest, the desire for sovereign agency and recognition are by no means innocent aspirations, since the quest for sovereign agency often tends to circumscribe the autonomy of other actors thereby making it difficult to sustain equality among them. As Patchen Markell has argued, the ideal of sovereign agency and recognition is beset by a profound irony, since "the very desire that makes that ideal so compelling— the desire for sovereign agency, for an antidote to the riskiness and intermittent opacity of social life—may itself help to sustain some of the forms of injustice that many proponents of recognition rightly aim to overcome" (2003a, 5). This is so, since "the desire for sovereignty is impossible to fulfill, because it is itself rooted in a misrecognition of the basic conditions of human activity" (2003a, 22). As Markell elaborates on these conditions, the pursuit of sovereign agency and the corresponding quest for recognition risk being counterproductive because they are based on "a form of misrecognition, a failure to acknowledge the ways in which human agency is conditioned by such basic circumstances as plural- ity, which exposes action (and hence also identity) to an unpredictable future, at once limiting our control over what we do and who we shall become, and also making possible the distinctive pleasures of life and action among others" (Markell 2003a, 90). Thus, the desire for sovereign agency and corresponding quest for recognition are not only prone to backfire on their own terms but also run the risk of perpetuating the same practices of misrecognition and forms of domination that they were designated to escape in the first place.

This paradox has recently gained traction among students of international relations, who have argued that world politics is based on a desire for sover- eign agency that is bound to produce misrecognition precisely out of the many frustrated attempts to attain international recognition (Epstein et al. 2018). As Minda Holm and Ole Jacob Sending have argued, beneath the legal institutions of formal recognition and the corresponding norms of sovereign equality there is an omnipresent struggle for sovereign agency among states: "While the legalistic regime produces a mythical and non-social vision of 'like units' without an over- arching governing authority, the latter negates the ideal of sovereign agency and produces a system of super- and subordination, where some states define the criteria against which other states are compelled to seek recognition. The result . . . is a systemic misrecognition embedded in the very modern concept of state sub- jectivity" (2018, 830). As they go on to argue, "the ideal of sovereign agency that is embedded in it is based on a factual misrecognition of the interdependent char- acter of world politics, so that the phrase 'exclusive political authority within ter- ritorial limits' has more to do with the idea of the state as a person with rights in international law than with the actual conditions under which state sovereignty can ever be achieved" (2018, 845). Although this mechanism helps to explain why fragile states often so fervently pursue sovereign agency and recognition only to find their aspirations frustrated, it does not help us make sense of those instances in which agents raise claims to sovereign agency *outside* the protective shell offered by international law. Agents doing this are confronted with a peculiar dilemma. Either their sovereignty claims will be recognized as valid claims to statehood by significant parts of the international community, which will expose their desire for sovereign agency to misrecognition by dominant actors thereby condemning them to a position of lasting inferiority. Or, these claims will be left unrecognized by members of the international community, which will leave them unprotected from outside interference while remaining immune to the more or less automatic misrecognition that would ensue from membership in international society.

Although the way in which Patchen Markell has theorized misrecognition takes domestic politics as its starting point, recent attempts to transpose this notion to the realm of international relations have neglected the ways in which international and domestic practices of misrecognition are interconnected and reinforce each other. In this regard the contributions to this volume offer fresh opportunities to explore the connections between being internationally unrecognized or misrecognized as a sovereign state and being domestically unrecognized or misrecognized as citizens with legitimate claims to sovereign agency within that state. Many ills of the contemporary world seem to flow from situations in which citizens are misrecognized by their governments to the same extent as these governments in turn are misrecognized by international society.

Some efforts to make sense of nonrecognition presuppose an understanding of what statehood ought to be about, thereby perpetuating the foundational myth of academic international relations. The theory of *phantom states* is a case in point. Since substantial advantages might accrue from being left unrecognized, some statelike entities prefer to remain unrecognized to becoming misrecognized, even if this leaves those not complicit in the deal worse off (Byman and King 2012). Largely operating below the radar due to their lack of international legal recognition and formal sovereignty, phantom states might well display some of the internal characteristics of statehood, such as de facto control over a distinct territory and population, a claim to external independence as well as a modicum of popular legitimacy. Yet their very existence is often contested by the members of international society, and especially by the "base state" from which they might have broken away through a war of secession. Phantom states therefore often choose to remain in legal limbo rather than to aspire to formal recognition, or to accept the misrecognition of the base state in the form of a return to the status quo ante. As Byman and King argue, "It is preferable to a return to war, which would signal the complete failure of the good-offices or peacekeeping mission. It is preferable to full-fledged independence, which is by definition anathema to the base state and creates a precedent that many countries with restive minorities want to avoid" (Byman and King 2012, 49). But phantom states are also prone to leave the needs and desires of those that are not part of the bargain unrecognized. Built on shaky economic and political foundations, they often boost their legitimacy by means of nationalist ideologies while delivering very little in terms of public goods and formal accountability to their citizens. The burdens of nonrecognition thereby trickle down in society, producing a desire for sovereign agency and a desire for recognition that cannot be fulfilled within the institutional framework at hand, and with few options available to change that framework. Although phantom states are likely to be internally divided, they often enjoy a remarkable staying power on the fringes of the international system.

Other states seek and successfully obtain international legal recognition from the international community or at least from sufficiently important parts thereof to qualify as fully sovereign. These states are then exposed to the perils of misrecognition that ensue from their attempts to assert sovereign agency in an international society that is rigged to their disadvantage right from the start. As Chowdhury (2018) has pointed out, strong and well-consolidated states of the kind we are accustomed to find in the West constitute an exception in the international system. The majority of states have always been weak, often beset by inner discord, and unable to cater to the basic needs of their populations. Although European states were formed through costly wars against alternative political forms, that particular path to statehood has not been accessible to the latecomers in the international system. This being so since "*state formation itself* throws up the possibility of alternatives to the centralized state and reduces the need to emulate that institutional form, which counters the expectation that units in world politics should emulate the strongest units in order to survive" (Chowdhury 2018, 23). This implies that although weak newcomers to international society are equally unable to deliver public goods to their subjects, international norms nevertheless compel them to recognize them as citizens and conform to the most basic standards of democratic governance and human rights lest they should be exposed to humanitarian interventions or international ostracism. Yet their innate propensity to leave the desires and aspirations of their citizens unrecognized breeds discontent and sows the seeds of yet another phantom state.

Those actors who want to assert their sovereign agency are thus faced with the challenge of navigating the narrow space between nonrecognition and misrecognition in order to preserve a modicum of autonomy in the midst of rival claims to sovereign agency. This is not an easy game to play. Although unrecognized actors—whether in an international or a domestic context—do not have to play by the formal rules, they are vulnerable to the arbitrary exercise of power by other actors since they do not enjoy the thin protective shell that international and public law offer. And although actors who have successfully obtained recognition are protected by such a shell, they are thereby also exposed to the inequalities inherent in and sanctioned by these frameworks of international and public law. Let us now see how this dilemma plays itself out in the different international and domestic contexts described by the contributors to this volume.

Claims and Frames

To some of the contributors to this volume, sovereign agency finds its foremost expression in the *claims* to sovereignty raised by agents who find themselves in contexts in which the benefits supposed to accrue from sovereignty are in short supply. Yet even in those cases in which agents do not aspire to statehood proper, their claims will nevertheless be measured and judged against the framework of international law and the criteria of legal recognition contained therein by the dominant and established members of international society. These criteria tell us in rather uncertain terms what kind of entities should count as states, and bestow these with legal personality with little attention to their form of government, all while disqualifying those entities that fail to conform to these criteria from legal recognition and full membership in international society (Bartelson 2013). As Ayşe Zarakol has pointed out, however, although international society is premised on the sovereign equality of its members, this only serves to "mask relations of domination . . . and helps perpetuate the hierarchies of the international system" (2018, 862). And as Tanja Aalberts (2018) has emphasized in her analysis of the emergence of modern international law, what we label international law has always been shaped by the misrecognition of those forms of political subjectivity pushed outside its purview. Hence the aspiration to statehood is fraught with danger, since it increases the risks of subjugation at the hands of more powerful and predatory actors in international society.

But this also implies that those actors that seek some form of sovereign agency without first having obtained formal recognition and thus protection under international law can carve out pockets of resistance between "being unrecognized" and "being misrecognized" in ways that fully sovereign actors cannot. Judging from some of the contributions to this volume, sometimes it is better to remain unrecognized as a state than become a misrecognized state. For example, Sara Friedman describes how one of the most successful phantom states in modern times—Taiwan—has been able to harness a host of bureaucratic practices to perform sovereignty not despite but rather because of its lack of full international legal recognition, and by implication, how its strategic espousal of universal human rights has opened up a pathway to informal recognition unavailable to more established sovereigns. In a similar vein, Rebecca Bryant describes how a national airline carrier came to instantiate and materialize the desire for sovereignty among the inhabitants of Northern Cyprus who were struggling to maintain a sense of belonging and identity, and how the subsequent bankruptcy of that carrier came to symbolize the failure of their phantom state to channel this desire. Although the Central African Republic is an internationally recognized state, its lack of any real state capacity makes its population prey to misrecognition by their own government. Louisa Lombard shows in detail how people in the remote northeastern parts of the Central African Republic remain highly ambivalent about the prospects of sovereignty, on the one hand feeling abandoned by the state authorities and therefore desirous of law and order, while on the other fearing the possibilities of its excess and the infringements on their liberty that this would entail. Finally, Alice Wilson vividly narrates how claims to sovereignty have been reconciled with the brute fact of exile among Sahrawi refugees. Without any immediate access to the territory they claim as theirs, the Sahrawi desire for sovereignty finds a proxy expression in the social relations of people and property, as indicated by the capacity and willingness of their exile government to control the circulation of mobile resources in order to sustain its claims to sovereignty over their own people. This chapter well illustrates the extent to which even modern claims to sovereignty can be sustained without reference to any tangible or demarcated territory, thereby being decoupled from the standard definitions of statehood.

Stories about the elusiveness of sovereignty can tell us important things about the possibilities and limits of sovereign agency in world politics. Although the absence of international recognition leaves a people exposed to the arbitrary interference of other actors, it also creates spaces of positive freedom in which the desire for sovereign agency can find less constrained and more creative expressions. Yet such exercises of sovereign agency are fraught with danger as they are likely to provoke a reaction from other actors—whether domestic or foreign—who for different reasons have embarked on quests for sovereign agency outside the framework of international or public law. It is perhaps no coincidence that phantom states are often home to poachers, gunrunners, drug lords, and human traffickers whose ragtag coalitions compromise or overrule prima facie legitimate claims to democratic self-determination.

Apples of Discord

Ever since Eris threw the proverbial golden apple among the goddesses, it has been tempting to blame the tragic outcome of that episode on the vanity of the latter rather than on the cunning of the former. Yet what made the apple of discord into such was not the element out of which it was made but rather the inscription on it reading: "To the fairest." But irrespective of what they are made, while apples are divisible, the attribute of being the fairest is not. This implies that whenever something is believed to be indivisible, the seed of the dragon's teeth is sown in what thereby becomes fertile soil. The sowing of such teeth took place long ago in Western legal thought, and as long as people believe that sovereignty connotes indivisible authority, the misrecognition of other equally valid claims to sovereign agency will inevitably follow.

A claim to sovereignty is often also an implicit claim to *moral* authority—of fitness to rule—and whenever the credibility of that claim is in doubt, so is the mutual recognition between rulers and ruled on which any legitimate political authority ultimately must rest. As Axel Honneth has reminded us, "In order to be able to acquire an undistorted relation-to-self, human subjects always need— over and above the experience of affectionate care and legal recognition—a form of social esteem that allows them to relate positively to their concrete traits and abilities" (Honneth 1996, 121). Claims to sovereignty are legitimate only to the extent that they recognize the sovereign agency of those who are on the receiving end of such claims. If not, and as Anthony Simon Laden has pointed out, "A claim of misrecognition will serve as a reasonable deliberative move if it points out to the person with power that in failing to recognize me, he is depriving himself of the value of my recognition of him" (Laden 2007, 284–285). This implies that whenever mutual recognition between rulers and ruled is absent, claims to sovereignty by the former are bound to be contested by those who struggle to attain recognition: misrecognition and reciprocal alienation of rulers and ruled are two sides of the same coin and often the first steps toward a fracturing of the social and political order along the fault lines of communal belonging.

An example of this sad logic is evident in the case of Bosnia-Herzegovina, whose external sovereignty flows from an international grant but whose domestic institutions are too weak to effectively uphold the rule of law and maintain common norms across ethnic divides. As Azra Hromadžić notes in her chapter, this has led to a profound sense of disillusionment among the young, who respond to what they perceive to be a corrupt state by engaging—and taking considerable pride in—systematic cheating at school exams. But far from being a passive response to their dysfunctional and corrupt government, the practice of cheating can be understood as a kind of transformative critique and thus as a way of reasserting sovereign agency in order to get incorporated in, and eventually exercise some leverage over, a society devoid of basic trust and shared moral standards. Corrupt institutions are best beaten at their own game.

Social practices and political institutions are the bones of contention in Torunn Wimpelmann's penetrating account of gender violence in Afghanistan.

Those who happen to find themselves subjected to the Afghan government are caught in the midst of rival claims to sovereignty over a range of not readily commensurate practices and institutions. Whenever violence against women is considered permissible, women are considered to be subjected to the private authority of their husbands, which entails that any attempt to turn gender violence into a public issue will presuppose or imply a simultaneous transfer of sovereign authority to the public domain. As Wimpelmann shows, whenever such a transfer is brought about from the outside and with little domestic institutional support, concrete cases of gender violence can easily become weaponized by those struggling to regain local sovereignty, or in order to maintain precarious balances of power among ethnic factions, thereby unwittingly contributing to the corrosion of an already fragile state.

By the same token, since sovereignty perhaps more commonly connotes supreme authority over a territory, territory often becomes *the* bone of contention whenever sovereignty is contested, as much as territorial disputes are likely to issue in contestations of sovereignty proper (Branch 2013). Territorial contests will generate misrecognition whenever slices of space are believed to be indivisible by those involved. The standard method for settling such disputes is by the drawing of boundaries, with pens on maps and with swords on the ground (Goettlich 2019). But unless pen and sword are in perfect sync, all we will have is a temporary armistice that can be revoked at any moment and by means of the same sharp instruments. This finds perhaps no better illustration than in the essay by Madeleine Reeves, in which she describes in detail what happens when the territorial reach of sovereignty is disputed in the borderlands where the boundaries of Kyrgyzstan, Tajikistan, and Uzbekistan intersect. However precise, maps cannot offer any conclusive resolution to such disputes since they contain but partial representations shaped by equally arbitrary claims to sovereignty in the past. Their use in efforts at dispute settlement only add to the sense of arbitrariness and disorientation that already characterize the everyday experiences of sovereignty among people caught in those borderlands.

Dreams of Congruence

Modern nation-states are based on the idea that sovereign authority and political community ought to be congruent or at least sufficiently overlapping in order for political institutions to be democratically legitimate. Yet there is almost always a mismatch between these elements. While some states contain more than one community within their boundaries, most states contain people who are subjected to their sovereignty without being recognized as citizens or being self-identifying parts of the majority culture. Yet however fictitious, such congruence has long been regarded as a necessary condition of democratic governance, since without an already bounded people or nation, there is no *demos* there to warrant the legitimacy of sovereignty. And in the absence of such a bounded *demos*, only a multiplicity of discordant voices remains, making democratic legitimacy hard to attain and sovereignty thus contested to its very core.

But there is nothing particularly democratic about these requirements of modern democracy, something that makes democratic institutions prone to misrecognition. As Seyla Benhabib has recently argued, "The boundaries of the *demos*—of the self in democratic self-government—have not been formed democratically through the enfranchisement of the voice of all affected. The nation has been the privileged collective identity that has inserted itself into the gap between the ideal of democracy as the subjection to laws that come from *all who are affected*, and the reality of a closed demos founded on the privilege of *belonging* to the nation" (Benhabib 2018). Consequently, mature democracies have tried hard to redefine the *demos* and its boundaries whenever its composition has changed, either in response to transnational flows of people, or as a result of internal reconfigurations of identity and belonging. This has been done in the hope of overcoming the misrecognition that otherwise would ensue, and the subsequent weakening of social cohesion that threatens to fracture the legitimacy of the state in question.

But the need to maintain the illusion of a homogeneous people or nation as the ultimate source of sovereignty remains strong in many places, as indicated by the recent upsurge of populist and nationalist sentiment (Kaltwasser 2014). And although translating this illusion into practice must issue in the misrecognition of some people, it is perceived all the more necessary in newborn states that struggle to attain domestic legitimacy and international recognition all at once. Once again, international misrecognition easily spills over into its domestic counterpart. Dace Dzenovska provides a nice illustration of this dilemma when she describes how the Latvian government tries to handle the fact that so many individuals belonging to the Latvian nation have moved to other states, making the contours of nationality embattled and thereby challenging the ideal of congruence. The response has been to pursue claims to national cohesion and continuity by appealing to the diaspora in an attempt to reterritorialize the nation in the hope of restoring a modicum of congruence between nation and state, however dispersed the former happens to be. A similar dilemma, but with a reverse logic of identity at play, applies to the state of Israel. As Joyce Dalsheim points out, the Jewish quest for self-determination has been beset by inner contradictions from its inception right to the present day, thereby calling into question what popular sovereignty possibly might mean in the context of an already territorially bounded *demos*. Since the promises of popular sovereignty are often based on the possibility of sociocultural homogenization, the existence of irreconcilable cultural differences within a given people will pose a threat to the realization of those promises in time and thus allow for infinite postponement. Hence the possibility of a cohesive Israeli nation is undermined by rival and incommensurable claims to Jewish identity raised by secularists, religious ultranationalists, and orthodox antinationalists respectively, making dreams of a truly national democracy forever out of reach and instead a recipe for self-elimination. Although the Israeli case might seem extreme, a scratch on the surface of many democratic states will reveal similar underlying conflicts of identity between groups purporting to represent the people as whole. Yet aspirations to popular sovereignty are fully able to thrive without succumbing to the temptations of an institutionalized congruence of nation and state. As Panos Achniotis vividly describes the events that led up to the 2017 referendum on Catalan independence, dreams of self-determination for an imagined Catalan republic managed to galvanize an entire neighborhood in opposition to Spanish rule precisely by virtue of transcending conventional nationalist tropes and instead appealing to local senses of belonging and solidarity. Even after that fleeting exercise of sovereign agency had faded and aspirations to independence had been frustrated, the quest itself produced new and meaningful experiences of political life well beyond the stale confines of state institutions and established parties.

Be Careful What You Wish For

The desire for sovereignty comes in a misfortune cookie. Virtually all the actors in the above stories aspire to some kind of sovereign agency yet seem oblivious as to what such aspirations might imply. Those who aspire to sovereign agency are sleepwalking into the treacherous politics of misrecognition, precisely because quests for sovereign agency and recognition are likely to backfire on their own terms. As Patchen Markell (2003b) has pointed out, the quest for sovereignty and recognition can sometimes issue in tragedy. This happens because quests for sovereign agency are prompted by presuppositions about the makeup of the sociopolitical world whose looping effects constrain the positive freedom necessary for their attainment. Those in search of sovereign agency often take their search to be expressive of some authentic identity but fail to consider the extent to which the cherished identity is shaped by the search itself, as evident from the case of Catalunya described above. Those in search of sovereign agency often take the structures of the sociopolitical world to be cast in stone but fail to consider the extent to which their search for sovereignty actually can reproduce the same oppressive structures. Those in search of sovereign agency sometimes take the precious goods they wish to obtain to be indivisible or otherwise in short supply but fail to recognize the ease with which this becomes a self-fulfilling prophecy, yielding zero-sum conflicts out of thin air while making efforts at resolution but a recipe for their intractability.

References

Aalberts, Tanja. 2018. "Misrecognition in Legal Practice: The Aporia of the Family of Nations." *Review of International Studies* 44(5): 863–881.

Bartelson, Jens. 2013. "Three Concepts of Recognition." *International Theory* 5(1): 107–129.

Benhabib, Seyla. 2018. "Below the Asphalt Lies the Beach: Reflections on the Legacy of the Frankfurt School." *Boston Review* (October 9): http://bostonreview.net/philosophy-religion/seyla-benhabib-below-asphalt-lies-beach.

Branch, Jordan. 2013. *The Cartographic State: Maps, Territory, and the Origins of Sovereignty*. Cambridge: Cambridge University Press.

Byman, Daniel, and Charles King. 2012. "The Mystery of Phantom States." *Washington Quarterly* 35(3): 43–57.

Chowdhury, Arjun. 2018. *The Myth of International Order: Why Weak States Persist and Alternatives to the State Fade Away*. Oxford: Oxford University Press.

Epstein, Charlotte, Thomas Lindemann, and Ole Jacob Sending. 2018. "Frustrated Sovereigns: The Agency that Makes the World Go Around." *Review of International Studies* 44(5): 787–804.

Goettlich, Kerry. 2019. "The Rise of Linear Borders in World Politics." *European Journal of International Relations* 25(1): 203–228.

Holm, Minda, and Ole Jacob Sending. 2018. "States before Relations: On Misrecognition and the Bifurcated Regime of Sovereignty." *Review of International Studies* 44(5): 829–847.

Honneth, Axel. 1996. *The Struggle for Recognition: The Moral Grammar of Social Conflicts*. Cambridge, MA.: MIT Press.

Kaltwasser, Cristóbal Rovira. 2014. "The Responses of Populism to Dahl's Democratic Dilemmas." *Political Studies* 62(3): 470–487.

Laden, Anthony Simon. 2007. "Reasonable Deliberation, Constructive Power, and the Struggle for Recognition," in *Recognition and Power: Axel Honneth and the Tradition of Critical Social Theory*, edited by Bert van den Brink and David Owen, 270–289. Cambridge: Cambridge University Press.

Markell, Patchen. 2003a. *Bound by Recognition*. Princeton, NJ: Princeton University Press.

Markell, Patchen. 2003b. "Tragic Recognition: Action and Identity in Antigone and Aristotle." *Political Theory* 31(1): 6–38.

Zarakol, Ayşe. 2018. "Sovereign Equality as Misrecognition." *Review of International Studies* 44(5): 848–862.

Contributors

Panos Achniotis is a doctoral student in Social Anthropology at the University of Manchester. He completed his MSc in Cultural Anthropology in 2019 from Utrecht University.

Jens Bartelson is professor of political science at Lund University He is the author of *War in International Thought* (Cambridge University Press, 2017), *Visions of World Community* (Cambridge University Press, 2009), *The Critique of the State* (Cambridge University Press, 2001), and *A Genealogy of Sovereignty* (Cambridge University Press, 1995), among other works.

Rebecca Bryant is professor of anthropology at Utrecht University and a visiting professor at the European Institute of the London School of Economics. She is the author of *Imagining the Modern: The Cultures of Nationalism in Cyprus* (I.B. Tauris, 2004) and *The Past in Pieces: Belonging in the New Cyprus* (University of Pennsylvania, 2010). She is coauthor, with Mete Hatay, of *Sovereignty Suspended: Building the So-Called State* (University of Pennsylvania, 2020) and, with Daniel M. Knight, of *The Anthropology of the Future* (Cambridge University Press, 2019).

Joyce Dalsheim is associate professor in the Department of Global, International and Area Studies at the University of North Carolina at Charlotte. She is the author of *Unsettling Gaza: Secular Liberalism, Radical Religion, and the Israeli Settlement Project* (Oxford University Press, 2011), *Producing Spoilers: Peacemaking and Production of Enmity in a Secular Age* (Oxford University Press, 2014), and *Israel has a Jewish Problem: Self-Determination as Self-Elimination* (Oxford University Press, 2019).

Dace Dzenovska is associate professor in the anthropology of migration at Oxford University. She is the author of *School of Europeanness: Tolerance and Other Lessons in Political Liberalism* (Cornell University Press, 2018).

Sara L. Friedman is professor of anthropology and gender studies at Indiana University. She is the author of *Exceptional States: Chinese Immigrants and Taiwanese Sovereignty* (University of California Press, 2015) and *Intimate Politics: Marriage, the Market, and State Power in Southeastern China* (Harvard University

Press, 2006). She is coeditor (with Pardis Mahdavi) of *Migrant Encounters: Intimate Labor, the State, and Mobility across Asia* (University of Pennsylvania Press, 2015) and (with Deborah Davis) of *Wives, Husbands, and Lovers: Marriage and Sexuality in Hong Kong, Taiwan, and Urban China* (Stanford University Press, 2014).

Azra Hromadžić is associate professor of anthropology at Syracuse University. She is the author of *Citizens of an Empty Nation: Youth and State-making in Postwar Bosnia and Herzegovina* (University of Pennsylvania Press, 2015). The book was translated into Serbian in 2017 as *Samo Bosne nema: Mladi i građenje države u posleratnoj Bosni i Hercegovini* (Beograd: Biblioteka XX Vek). She is coeditor with Monika Palmberger of *Care Across Distance: Ethnographic Explorations of Aging and Migration* (Berghahn Books 2018).

Louisa Lombard is associate professor of anthropology at Yale University and author of *State of Rebellion: Violence and Intervention in the Central African Republic* (Zed Books, 2016) and *Hunting Game: Raiding Politics in the Central African Republic* (Cambridge University Press, 2020).

Madeleine Reeves is senior lecturer in social anthropology at the University of Manchester. She is author of *Border Work: Spatial Lives of the State in Rural Central Asia* (Cornell University Press, 2014). She is coeditor with Johan Rasanayagam and Judith Beyer of *Ethnographies of the State in Central Asia: Performing Politics* (Indiana University Press, 2014) and with Mateusz Laszczkowski of *Affective States: Entanglements, Suspensions, Suspicions* (Berghahn Books, 2017).

Alice Wilson is senior lecturer in social anthropology at the University of Sussex. She is the author of *Sovereignty in Exile: A Saharan Liberation Movement Governs* (University of Pennsylvania Press, 2016).

Torunn Wimpelmann is senior researcher at the Chr. Michelsen Institute in Bergen, Norway. She is the author of *The Pitfalls of Protection: Gender, Violence, and Power in Afghanistan* (University of California Press, 2017).

Index

CPSIA information can be obtained
at www.ICGtesting.com
Printed in the USA
LVHW051933110521
687117LV00010B/625

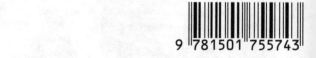